NĀGĀRJUNA'S TREATISE ON THE TEN GROUNDS

VOLUME II

BDK English Tripiṭaka Series

NĀGĀRJUNA'S TREATISE ON THE TEN GROUNDS

VOLUME II

(Taishō Volume 20, Number 1521)

Translated by

Bhikshu Dharmamitra

BDK America, Inc.
2025

First Printing, 2025
ISBN: 978-1-886439-94-8
Library of Congress Control Number: 2024944238

Published by
BDK America, Inc.
1675 School Street
Moraga, California 94556

Printed in the United States of America

A Message on the Publication of the English Tripiṭaka

The Buddhist canon is said to contain eighty-four thousand different teachings. I believe that this is because the Buddha's basic approach was to prescribe a different treatment for every spiritual ailment, much as a doctor prescribes a different medicine for every medical ailment. Thus his teachings were always appropriate for the particular suffering individual and for the time at which the teaching was given, and over the ages not one of his prescriptions has failed to relieve the suffering to which it was addressed.

Ever since the Buddha's Great Demise over twenty-five hundred years ago, his message of wisdom and compassion has spread throughout the world. Yet no one has ever attempted to translate the entire Buddhist canon into English throughout the history of Japan. It is my greatest wish to see this done and to make the translations available to the many English-speaking people who have never had the opportunity to learn about the Buddha's teachings.

Of course, it would be impossible to translate all of the Buddha's eighty-four thousand teachings in a few years. I have, therefore, had one hundred thirty-nine of the scriptural texts in the prodigious Taishō edition of the Chinese Buddhist canon selected for inclusion in the First Series of this translation project.

It is in the nature of this undertaking that the results are bound to be criticized. Nonetheless, I am convinced that unless someone takes it upon himself or herself to initiate this project, it will never be done. At the same time, I hope that an improved, revised edition will appear in the future.

It is most gratifying that, thanks to the efforts of more than a hundred Buddhist scholars from the East and the West, this monumental project has finally gotten off the ground. May the rays of the Wisdom of the Compassionate One reach each and every person in the world.

NUMATA Yehan
Founder of the English
Tripiṭaka Project

August 7, 1991

Editorial Foreword

In the long history of Buddhist transmission throughout East Asia, translations of Buddhist texts were often carried out as national projects supported and funded by emperors and political leaders. The BDK English Tripiṭaka project, on the other hand, began as a result of the dream and commitment of one man. In January 1982 Dr. NUMATA Yehan, founder of Bukkyō Dendō Kyōkai (Society for the Promotion of Buddhism), initiated the monumental task of translating the complete *Taishō shinshū daizōkyō* edition of the Chinese Tripiṭaka (Buddhist canon) into the English language. Under his leadership, a special preparatory committee was organized in April 1982. By July of the same year the Translation Committee of the English Tripiṭaka was officially convened.

The initial Committee included the following members: (late) HANAYAMA Shōyū (Chairperson), (late) BANDŌ Shōjun, (late) ISHIGAMI Zennō, (late) KAMATA Shigeo, (late) KANAOKA Shūyū, MAYEDA Sengaku, (late) NARA Yasuaki, (late) SAYEKI Shinkō, (late) SHIOIRI Ryōtatsu, (late) TAMARU Noriyoshi, (late) TAMURA Kwansei, (late) URYŪZU Ryūshin, and (late) YUYAMA Akira. Assistant members of the Committee were as follows: KANAZAWA Atsushi, WATANABE Shōgo, Rolf Giebel of New Zealand, and Rudy Smet of Belgium.

After holding planning meetings on a monthly basis, the Committee selected one hundred and thirty-nine texts for the First Series of the project, estimated to be one hundred printed volumes in all. The texts selected were not limited to those originally written in India but also included works composed in China and Japan. While the publication of the First Series proceeds, the texts for the Second Series will be selected from among the remaining works; this process will continue until all the texts, in Japanese as well as in Chinese, have been published. Given the huge scope of this project, accomplishing the English translations of all the Chinese and Japanese texts in the Taishō canon may take as long as one hundred years or more. Nevertheless, as Dr. Numata wished, it is the sincere hope of the Committee that this project will continue until completion, even after all the present members have passed away.

Dr. Numata passed away on May 5, 1994, at the age of ninety-seven. He entrusted his son, Mr. NUMATA Toshihide with the continuation and completion of the English Tripiṭaka project. Mr. Numata served for twenty-three years, leading the project forward with enormous progress before his sudden passing on February 16, 2017, at the age of eighty-four. The Committee previously lost its able and devoted first Chairperson, Professor HANAYAMA Shōyū, on June 16, 1995, at the age of sixty-three. In October 1995 the Committee elected Professor MAYEDA Sengaku (then Vice President of Musashino Women's College) as Chairperson, and upon the retirement of Professor Mayeda in July 2016, the torch was passed to me to serve as the third Chairperson. Despite these losses and changes we, the Editorial Committee members, have renewed our determination to carry out the noble ideals set by Dr. Numata. Present members of the Committee are Kenneth K. Tanaka (Chairperson), MAYEDA Sengaku, ICHISHIMA Shōshin, KATSURA Shōryū, MINOWA Kenryō, SAITŌ Akira, SHIMODA Masahiro, WATANABE Shōgo, and YONEZAWA Yoshiyasu.

The Numata Center for Buddhist Translation and Research was established in November 1984, in Berkeley, California, U.S.A., to assist in the publication of the translated texts. The Publication Committee was organized at the Numata Center in December 1991. In 2010, the Numata Center's operations were merged with Bukkyō Dendō Kyōkai America, Inc. (BDK America), and BDK America continues to oversee the publication side of the English Tripiṭaka project in close cooperation with the Editorial Committee in Tokyo.

To date, the project has completed about seventy-five percent of the seven thousand one hundred and eighty-five Taishō pages of texts selected for the First Series. Much work still lies ahead of us but we are committed to the completion of the remaining texts in order to realize the grand vision of Dr. Numata, shared by Mr. Numata and Professor Hanayama, to make the Buddhist canon more readily accessible to the English-speaking world.

Kenneth K. Tanaka
Chairperson
Editorial Committee of
the BDK English Tripiṭaka

Publisher's Foreword

On behalf of the members of the Publication Committee, I am happy to present this volume as the latest contribution to the BDK English Tripiṭaka Series. The Publication Committee members have worked to ensure that this volume, as all other volumes in the series, has gone through a rigorous process of editorial efforts.

The initial translation and editing of the Buddhist scriptures found in this and other BDK English Tripiṭaka volumes are performed under the direction of the Editorial Committee in Tokyo, Japan. Both the Editorial Committee in Tokyo and the Publication Committee, headquartered in Moraga, California, are dedicated to the production of accurate and readable English translations of the Buddhist canon. In doing so, the members of both committees and associated staff work to honor the deep faith, spirit, and concern of the late Reverend Dr. Yehan Numata, who founded the BDK English Tripiṭaka Series in order to disseminate the Buddhist teachings throughout the world.

The long-term goal of our project is the translation and publication of the texts in the one hundred–volume Taishō edition of the Chinese Buddhist canon, along with a number of influential extracanonical Japanese Buddhist texts. The list of texts selected for the First Series of this translation project may be found at the end of each volume in the series.

As Chair of the Publication Committee, I am deeply honored to serve as the fifth person in a post previously held by leading figures in the field of Buddhist studies, most recently by my predecessor, John R. McRae.

In conclusion, I wish to thank the members of the Publication Committee for their dedicated and expert work undertaken in the course of preparing this volume for publication: Managing Editor Marianne Dresser, Dr. Hudaya Kandahjaya, Dr. Carl Bielefeldt, Dr. Robert Sharf, and Rev. Brian Kensho Nagata, Director of the BDK English Tripiṭaka Project.

A. Charles Muller
Chairperson
Publication Committee

Contents

Translator's Introduction

Bhikshu Dharmamitra

As the latest in my series of translations of bodhisattva path texts important in the history of Classic Indian and Chinese Mahayana Buddhism, I present here my English translation of Tripiṭaka Master Kumārajīva's rendering from Sanskrit of Nāgārjuna's *Treatise on the Ten Grounds* (*Daśabhūmika-vibhāṣā*).[1] This is a text devoted to explaining in great detail the aspects of practice involved in ascending through the ten "grounds," "planes," or "levels" of bodhisattva path cultivation that are described in the *Ten Grounds Sutra* (*Daśabhūmika-sūtra*) and in the nearly identical "Ten Grounds" chapter of the *Flower Adornment Sutra* (*Avataṃsaka-sūtra*). In order to encourage and facilitate deeper study of this topic, I have translated both of these closely related texts which are available under separate cover from Kalavinka Press.

Although Dharmarakṣa was the first to translate this text into Chinese, his 265 C.E. translation of this treatise has been lost.[2] The edition of Nāgārjuna's *Treatise on the Ten Grounds* that I have translated here is the only one that exists in any language, namely the seventeen-fascicle *Shizhu piposha lun* 十住毘婆沙論 or *Daśabhūmika-vibhāṣā* that is preserved in the Taishō edition of the Buddhist canon (T. 1521). It was translated from Sanskrit into English by Tripiṭaka Master Kumārajīva as dictated to him from memory by Tripiṭaka Master Buddhayaśas sometime between the latter's arrival in Chang'an in 408 and his return to Kashmir four years later.

Although, having studied it closely, I find this thirty-five-chapter treatise to be beautifully and awesomely complete in itself as a close description of the principles and practices necessary for entering and mastering the first two of the ten bodhisattva grounds, it is probable that this text as translated by Kumārajīva was originally part of a much larger work. Fortunately, the edition that we have is, in and of itself, a wonderfully thorough training manual for moving from the life of a common unenlightened person to that of an irreversible bodhisattva well along on the path to buddhahood.

A Brief Description of the Treatise Contents

As noted above, this text consists of thirty-five chapters[3] in seventeen fascicles that describe in great detail the principles and practices involved in entering the bodhisattva path and in perfecting in correct sequence the practices of the first and second grounds, the "Ground of Joyfulness" and the "Ground of Stainlessness."

Chapter 1. "The Introduction" discusses the author's motivations and aims in composing this treatise. Chapters 2 through 27 explain the practices of the first ground. Chapters 28 through 35 explain the practices of the second ground.

Chapter 2. "Entering the First Ground" through Chapter 17. "On Entering the Temple" focus on the practice methods of the lay bodhisattva. Chapter 18. "The Jointly Shared Practices" through Chapter 27. "Summarizing the Practice [of the First Ground]" focus more on the bodhisattva practices that are common to both the lay bodhisattva and the monastic bodhisattva. Chapter 28. "Distinctions in Courses of Karmic Action on the Second Ground" through Chapter 35. "In Praise of Moral Precepts" focus somewhat more strongly on the practices of the monastic bodhisattva or very advanced lay practitioner.

Due to the length of this treatise, its contents are published in two volumes. Volume I (published previously) includes Chapters 1–18; this Volume II includes Chapters 19–35.

A Condensed Description of Each Chapter's Contents[4]

To give the reader a general idea of the content of each of the chapters, I present a brief description immediately below:

Chapter 1. The Introduction. This chapter consists of a general discussion of the whole treatise, a description of Nāgārjuna's motives in writing the treatise, and a close explanation of the "refuge" verse that opens the treatise.

Chapter 2. Entering the First Ground. This chapter lists the names and meanings each of the ten grounds, explains how one enters the first ground, and discusses why this ground is called the "Ground of Joyfulness."

Chapter 3. The Characteristics of the Ground. This chapter describes the character of the first-ground bodhisattva, focusing in particular on this bodhisattva's distinctive features. It also explains why his mind is for the most part joyful and explains the nature of his fearlessness.

Chapter 4. Purification of the Ground. This chapter describes twenty-seven dharmas involved in purifying the first ground.

Chapter 5. The Explanation of the Vows. This chapter describes the bodhisattva's ten great vows in great detail.

Chapter 6. On Producing the *Bodhi* Resolve. This chapter describes and explains the seven causes and conditions involved in generating the resolve to achieve the utmost, right, and perfect enlightenment.

Chapter 7. On Training the Mind. This chapter describes the many different sorts of causes and conditions that might cause the bodhisattva to lose his resolve to reach the enlightenment of a buddha.

Chapter 8. On the *Avaivartika*. This chapter describes the characteristics of the bodhisattva who has fallen into ruination and the characteristics of the bodhisattva who has become irreversible on the path to buddhahood.

Chapter 9. On the Easy Practice. This chapter describes using the path of "the easy practice," mindfulness of the buddhas, to succeed in reaching the ground of the *avaivartika* or "irreversible" bodhisattva.

Chapter 10. Getting Rid of Karma. This chapter describes the methods for purifying past bad karma, specifically referencing repentance, entreating, rejoicing in others' merit, and dedication of merit.

Chapter 11. Distinctions With Regard to Merit. This chapter discusses the merit and karmic rewards of repentance, entreating, rejoicing, and transference of merit and also explains how repentance results in less severe retribution from grave karmic offenses.

Chapter 12. Distinctions With Regard to Giving. This chapter discusses the karmic rewards of giving and also explains what constitutes pure giving and impure giving.

Chapter 13. Distinctions With Regard to the Giving of Dharma. This chapter explains the superiority of Dharma giving over material giving and discusses the qualifications of someone who teaches the Dharma.

Chapter 14. The Characteristics of the [Three] Refuges. This chapter discusses how one takes refuge in the Buddha, Dharma, and Sangha as well as how one practices mindfulness of the Buddha, mindfulness of the Dharma, and mindfulness of the Sangha.

Chapter 15. The Five Moral Precepts. This chapter explains the practices beneficial to self and beneficial to others while also explaining the dharma of the five lay precepts.

Chapter 16. On Realizing the Faults of the Householder's Life. This chapter details for the lay bodhisattva the faults of the household life, thereby encouraging the layperson to consider the advantages of becoming a monastic. It also describes the practice of the six perfections.

Chapter 17. On Entering the Temple. This chapter describes the practices adopted by the layperson on entering the grounds of stupas and temples, explains how to take and maintain the eight abstinence precepts, and compares lay practice with monastic practice.

Chapter 18. The Jointly Shared Practices. This chapter describes the practices common to both lay and monastic bodhisattvas while also describing a buddha's thirty-two major marks and the karmic causes that bring them about.

Chapter 19. The Fourfold Dharmas. This chapter explains how wisdom is the origin of the thirty-two marks while also setting forth many fourfold lists that explain how wisdom is acquired, how wisdom is lost, how one's roots of goodness are devoured, how one's roots of goodness increase, and so forth.

Chapter 20. Mindfulness of the Buddhas. This chapter describes the method for acquiring the *pratyutpanna samādhi* wherein one is allowed to see the buddhas. It explains that one should cultivate mindfulness and contemplation of the buddhas' form bodies in reliance upon their thirty-two major marks and eighty subsidiary characteristics.

Chapter 21. Forty Dharmas Exclusive to Buddhas (Part 1). This chapter lists forty dharmas exclusive to buddhas and discusses the first nine of those forty dharmas that serve as the basis for practicing mindfulness of all buddhas' Dharma body.

Chapter 22. Forty Dharmas Exclusive to Buddhas (Part 2)—Challenges to the Reality of Omniscience. This entire chapter is devoted to refuting the various challenges to the claim that buddhas are omniscient.

Chapter 23. Forty Dharmas Exclusive to Buddhas (Part 3)—Thorough Knowing of Unfixed Dharmas [and the Other Exclusive Dharmas]. This chapter begins by explaining the tenth of the exclusive dharmas, that of "thorough knowing of matters that are unfixed," continues by explaining the rest of the forty exclusive dharmas, and then ends by introducing an additional forty-four exclusive dharmas.

Chapter 24. Verses Offered in Praise. This chapter explains that one is to use the forty dharmas exclusive to the buddhas in one's practice of mindfulness of the Buddha and then presents praise verses to be used as a means for successfully entering the mindfulness of the Buddha *samādhi.*

Chapter 25. Teachings to Aid the Mindfulness of the Buddha *Samādhi.* This chapter sets forth the method for acquiring the *pratyutpanna samādhi* while also describing the karmic rewards derived from this *samādhi.*

Chapter 26.The Analogy Chapter. This chapter sets forth the analogy of the great guide leading fellow travelers across treacherous terrain to a great city while also describing in greater detail the knowledge essential to deeply understanding and practicing the bodhisattva path.

Chapter 27. A Summarizing Discussion of the Bodhisattva Practices. This chapter presents a general explanation of all the dharmas practiced by the bodhisattva along with a discussion of the differences between the practitioner who is a bodhisattva in name only and the practitioner who truly is a genuine bodhisattva.

Chapter 28. Distinctions in the Second Ground's Courses of Karmic Action. This chapter begins by introducing ten types of resolute intentions that should be adopted by the first-ground bodhisattva wishing to reach the second ground.

It continues then with a detailed explanation of each of the ten courses of good karmic action and the ten courses of bad karmic action.

Chapter 29. Distinctions Pertaining to *Śrāvaka*s and *Pratyekabuddha*s. This chapter begins by asserting that the ten courses of good karmic action enable the practitioner to access the ground of a *śrāvaka* disciple, the ground of a *pratyekabuddha,* and the ground of a buddha. It then describes which sorts of beings may reach the grounds of *śrāvaka* disciples and *pratyekabuddhas* by relying upon the practice of the ten courses of good karmic action.

Chapter 30. [Distinctions Pertaining to] the Great Vehicle. This chapter describes which sorts of beings may reach the ground of a buddha through cultivation of the ten courses of good karmic action. It also asserts that a bodhisattva's cultivation of the ten courses of good karmic action is superior to such cultivation as undertaken by adherents of the *śrāvaka* disciple and *pratyekabuddha* vehicles.

Chapter 31. Guarding the Moral Precepts. This chapter describes the general and specific karmic rewards resulting from cultivating the ten courses of good karmic action. It then presents sixty-five aspects of the perfection of moral virtue in accordance with the *Jeweled Summit Sutra.*

Chapter 32. An Explanation of the *Dhūta* Austerities. This chapter describes the correct practice of the twelve *dhūta* austerities, their benefits, and the conditions under which they may be set aside.

Chapter 33. Aids to Gaining the Fruits of *Śīla*. This chapter describes the dharmas that enable purification of one's practice of moral virtue. It also describes four types of monks, of which the first three are worthy of censure and the fourth is to be emulated.

Chapter 34. In Praise of the Moral Precepts. This chapter begins by asserting that "The bodhisattva who purifies his observance of the moral precepts in this manner is able to gather together all sorts of meritorious qualities and derive all manner of benefits." It then proceeds to quote Akṣayamati Bodhisattva's extensive praise of the moral precepts.

Chapter 35. The Karmic Rewards of the Moral Precepts. This chapter describes the second-ground bodhisattva's manifestation as a wheel-turning king who instructs beings in the practice of the ten course of good karmic action.

On the Completeness and Ultimacy of This Treatise

Although this treatise primarily focuses its discussions on how to understand the principles, how to develop the qualities, and how to master the skills required to reach the first two of the bodhisattva grounds, its utility is not limited to accomplishing that already very amazing, beautiful, and daunting feat. In fact, the broad and deep range of the discussions in this text apply to the entire path to buddhahood. Indeed, if one were to deeply study this text together with the *Ten Grounds Sutra,* one would then already possess a very complete map of how to proceed all the way to the perfect enlightenment of a buddha.

So many other additional aspects of knowledge, wisdom, powers, skills, and qualities are mastered on these first two grounds that I think it would be fair to say that most of us would need to cultivate the bodhisattva path for many hundreds of lifetimes before we could move beyond the teachings presented in this wonderful treatise by Nāgārjuna.

Finally, as noted in Chapter 29, this treatise does indeed provide all of the teachings a practitioner would need to reach all the way to buddhahood: "These ten courses of good karmic action enable the practitioner to reach the grounds of the *śrāvaka* disciples, also enable him to reach the ground of the *pratyekabuddhas,* and also enable him to reach the ground of the buddhas."

In the very next chapter, Chapter 30, Nāgārjuna answers the question, "Which sorts of beings can the ten courses of good karmic action also cause to reach the ground of buddhahood?", doing so by setting forth with the following verse distinguishing these bodhisattvas from practitioners attracted to the individual liberation paths idealizing arhats and *pratyekabuddha*s:

> The way they practice the ten courses of good karmic action
> is superior to that of the two other classes of practitioners,
> for they engage in measureless extraordinary cultivation
> superior to that of anyone else in the world.
>
> They bring forth vows that are both solid and good,
> perfect the great compassion that cannot be impeded,
> adeptly take on the practice of skillful means,
> and patiently endure every sort of pain and anguish.

They do not abandon any being,
deeply cherish the wisdom of the buddhas,
and delight in those who completely and thoroughly practice
the buddhas' powers and sovereign masteries.

They are able to refute all ideas involving wrong views
and accept and protect the buddhas' right Dharma.
They are valiant, able to endure, and vigorous,
and are possessed of solid resolve in teaching beings.

They do not covet or become attached to their own happiness
or to living a measurelessly long life.
They are supreme in all their endeavors
and free of fault in all the works they do.

They possess every kind of purity
and come forth through the practice of all the supreme bases.[5]
The courses of good karmic action enable these persons
to reach the ground of the bhagavats who possess the ten powers.

A close perusal of the above verses should put to rest any doubts any student of Dharma might entertain about the completeness and ultimacy of this treatise.

In Summation

I first happened on this text many years ago when searching the Buddhist canon for the most important bodhisattva path texts to translate into English. I immediately fell in love with it and started translating it back in 2004, but had to take a break from it for a few years due to health reasons and also because I was preoccupied with fourteen other bodhisattva path manuscripts I published as the first ten Kalavinka Press volumes in 2009.

I finally finished a first draft translation of this treatise in late spring of 2011, which I did not finish revising until early 2018, this because I was deeply involved in creating a translation of the *Ten Grounds Sutra* (now available) and the *Avataṃsaka Sutra* (which, though long since completed, is still being revised and edited).

I have always felt that Nāgārjuna's *Treatise on the Ten Grounds* is one of the most important and most inspiring bodhisattva path texts in the Buddhist canon and one that simply *must* be translated into English as soon as possible. Hence it gives me great pleasure to finally be able to bring forth this translation for the perusal of English-speaking Dharma students and practitioners devoted to the deep study of the bodhisattva path.

The accuracy and readability of this translation have been greatly improved by many corrections, preview comments, and editorial suggestions generously contributed by Bhikkhu Bodhi, Bhikshu Jianhu, Feng Ling, Nicholas Weeks, and Jon Babcock. Although I have given this translation my best effort and the greatest care to ensure accuracy, I am aware that there may still be room for refinements here and there. That said, I remain very confident that this translation will do much to advance the western reader's understanding of right practice of the bodhisattva path as taught by Ārya Nāgārjuna.

NĀGĀRJUNA'S TREATISE ON THE TEN GROUNDS

(Daśabhūmika-vibhāṣā)

(T.1521:20a2–122b13)

Composed by Ārya Nāgārjuna
Translated into Chinese in the Later Qin Era by
Tripiṭaka Master Kumārajīva from the State of Kuchā

Chapter 19

The Fourfold Dharmas

The bodhisattva should singlemindedly cultivate the above-discussed actions by which one acquires the thirty-two marks. Cultivating the actions that lead to acquisition of the thirty-two marks is an endeavor rooted in wisdom. Therefore:

> The bodhisattva should utterly abandon
> the four dharmas leading to lessening and loss of wisdom
> He should always cultivate and practice
> the four dharmas leading to the acquisition of wisdom.

There are four dharmas able to bring about the lessening and loss of wisdom that the bodhisattva should abandon. There are also four dharmas leading to the acquisition of wisdom that one should always cultivate. What are the four dharmas leading to loss of wisdom? They are:

The first is failing to revere the Dharma or one who speaks the Dharma. 66a

The second is being secretive and miserly in the teaching of essential dharmas.

The third is presenting an obstacle to someone fond of Dharma and thereby harming their motivation to listen to the speaking of Dharma.

The fourth is harboring an arrogant attitude and consequently elevating oneself while looking on others as inferiors.

What are the four dharmas leading to acquisition of wisdom? They are:

First, one reveres the Dharma as well as those who speak the Dharma.

Second, one explains Dharma for others as one has heard it and as one has studied and recited it, doing so with a pure mind and without seeking to receive offerings.

Third, knowing that the realization of wisdom occurs through extensive learning, one diligently and unremittingly applies oneself to one's study, doing so as urgently as if one were putting out a fire in his own turban.

Fourth, one accepts and upholds in practice, in a manner faithful to how it was taught, whatever Dharma one has learned, never forgetting it. In so doing, one esteems actions that are consistent with the words and does not esteem words alone.

These are the four. If one does not damage his roots of goodness, he will be able to abandon the four dharmas leading to loss of wisdom while being able to practice the four dharmas leading to acquiring wisdom. Consequently, one who strives to increase his wisdom acts in accord with the following verse:

As for the four dharmas that devour one's roots of goodness,
the bodhisattva should utterly abandon them.
As for the four dharmas that increase one's roots of goodness,
the bodhisattva should cultivate and practice them.

What then are those four dharmas that assail and devour one's roots of goodness? They are:

The first is the harboring of arrogance while coveting worldly matters.

The second is while being attached to offerings, coming and going from the households.

The third is giving rise to hatred and jealousy through which one slanders bodhisattvas.

The fourth is that on hearing scriptures one has not previously heard, one refuses to believe or accept them.

What then are the four dharmas conducing to the increase of one's roots of goodness? They are:

First, one strives insatiably to acquire any scriptures that one has not yet heard, in particular those that deal with the six *pāramitā*s and those that belong to the bodhisattva canon.

Second, one rids oneself of any arrogance toward other beings, adopting instead an attitude of humility and deferential regard for even to the lowest of the lowly.

Third, whatever wealth one gains is gained only in accordance with Dharma and is sought only to the degree that it satisfies one's needs. Thus one abandons all types of wrong livelihood while delighting in the practice of the four lineage bases of the *ārya*s.[6]

Fourth, one does not ridicule others' transgressions, whether real or not, and one does not focus on the shortcomings of others. Hence, if there happens to be something within the sphere of Dharma that one has not yet thoroughly understood, one must not harbor a mental opposition to it. Rather one should take the testimony of the Buddha as the basis for certifying its validity. [Thus, one should reflect,] "Given that the Buddha is possessed of all-knowledge, his dharmas are countless. He speaks of them in ways that are appropriate to any given circumstance. These are not matters about which I have direct knowledge."

And so it is that one increases one's roots of goodness.

In addition, there are four dharmas perfectible only by those without flattery or deviousness. Therefore:

The bodhisattva should utterly abandon
four dharmas characterized by flattery and deviousness.
He should always cultivate and practice
four dharmas characterized by a straightforward mind.

Both lay and monastic bodhisattvas should utterly abandon four dharmas involving flattery or deviousness. This is a matter analogous to the difficulty of extricating a crooked tree from a dense forest. In this same manner, there are disciples of the Buddha in the world who, although they have entered the Dharma of the Buddha, they are nonetheless unable to depart from the dense forest of samsara. What then are these four dharmas? They are:

First, one harbors doubts about, does not place faith in, and is unfixed in one's resolve regarding the Buddha's Dharma.

Second, one maintains an arrogant and hateful attitude toward other beings.

Third, one's mind is beset by covetousness and jealousy when witnessing benefits accruing to others.

Fourth, the defaming rumors emanating from one's slander of bodhi- 66b
sattvas spread about everywhere.

These are the four.

What then are the four dharmas characterized by a straightforward mind? They are:

First, if one commits some offense, one immediately reveals it, conceals none of it, extinguishes it through the confession of transgressions, and then proceeds along the path that is free of regrets.

Second, even if, by telling the truth, one would lose the royal throne as well all manner of valuable treasures, one still refuses to utter a falsehood. [What's more,] no words disparaging of others ever pass one's lips.

Third, if somebody assails one with harsh speech, curses, ridicule, disparagement, mocking, slanders, bondage, confinement, whipping, beating, torture, or other such offensive behavior, one only blames his own previous-life actions and does not fault others. Because one has faith in karmic retribution, one's mind remains free of anger or resentment.

Fourth, one peacefully abides in the meritorious quality of faith. It is very difficult to maintain resolute faith in the sublime Dharma of the buddhas. But because one's mind is pure, one is able to maintain faith in it and accept it all.

The bodhisattva fallen into ruin engages in the four sorts of flattery and deviousness. The well-trained bodhisattva has four straightforward practices to which he adheres. Consequently, if the bodhisattva wishes to refrain from engaging in actions characterized by flattery and deviousness and instead wishes to carry forth his practice with a straightforward mind, he should accord with the following lines:

One should abandon four kinds of dharmas
practiced by a bodhisattva fallen into ruin.
One should cultivate four kinds of dharmas
practiced by the well-trained bodhisattva.

What are the four dharmas practiced by a bodhisattva fallen into ruin? They are:

First, even though he may be learned, he nonetheless gives himself over to frivolous joking and thus fails to practice in compliance with the Dharma.

Second, he responds to transformative teaching with frivolous rationalizations and fails to respect or comply with instructions provided by monastic preceptors or monastic Dharma teachers.[7]

Third, he is unable to remain worthy of the offerings bestowed by the faithful. He does away with vigilant restraint of his behavior and yet still continues to accept offerings.

Fourth, he does not revere bodhisattvas who are gentle and good, but instead maintains an arrogant attitude toward them.

These are the four.

What then are the four dharmas practiced by the well-trained bodhisattva? They are:

First, he is always happy to hear Dharma that he has not heard before and, having heard it, he is able to practice in accordance with what is taught. He relies on Dharma, relies on its meaning, and relies on practicing in accord with how it was taught.

Second, he accords with the import [of the teachings], is not misled by words and expressions, and is agreeable and easy to instruct. In matters related to serving as a teacher, he carries on those responsibilities with conscientious purposefulness.

Third, he is unfailing in observance of the moral precepts and in cultivation of meditative concentration while also maintaining a pure livelihood.

Fourth, in his relations with well-trained bodhisattvas, he brings forth respectful thoughts, acts congenially, and treats them with high regard. Thus he does away with any tendencies toward arrogance and focuses on their meritorious qualities.

There are also four types of mistakes a bodhisattva may be vulnerable to committing, all the while seeking in these contexts to focus on the shortcomings of other bodhisattvas. These behaviors are the defining features of a bodhisattva fallen into ruin. If, on the other hand, he is able to draw close to four paths of goodness, these serve to define the bodhisattva who is well trained. This is as described in a verse:

The bodhisattva should utterly abandon
four types of bodhisattva mistakes.
The bodhisattva should cultivate
four paths of bodhisattva conduct.

What are the four kinds of bodhisattva mistakes? They are:

First, if one were to teach extremely profound Dharma to beings who are not adequate vessels to receive it, this would be a mistake.

Second, if one were to teach Small Vehicle doctrines to those who delight in profound and magnificent dharmas, this would be a mistake.

Third, if one were to act with condescending arrogance or disrespect toward someone engaged in right practice of the path who, with whole-
66c some mind, observes the moral precepts, this would be a mistake.

Fourth, if with regard to someone who is not yet adequately developed and cannot yet be trusted one were to nonetheless trust him, or if one were to attract a bad person [into the community] who is a breaker of precepts and take him to be a good person worthy of friendship, this would be a mistake.

What are the four paths of bodhisattva conduct? They are:

First, one treats all beings with a mind of equal regard.

Second, one uses the good Dharma to teach everyone.

Third, one teaches Dharma equally to all beings.

Fourth, one behaves with right conduct toward all beings.

If one always commits the four kinds of bodhisattva mistakes, fails to delight in judicious reflection on all dharmas, and fails to diligently cultivate good dharmas, then one is an imitation bodhisattva. Therefore:

> Among all of the bodhisattva dharmas,
> there are four that are indicative of imitation bodhisattvas.
> The Buddha said of such dharmas
> that one should utterly abandon each and every one of them.

What then are those four? They are:

First, one covets and esteems offerings and does not regard the Dharma as precious.

Second, one acts solely for the sake of fame and accolades and does not strive to acquire meritorious qualities.

Third, one seeks one's own happiness and is not mindful of other beings.

Fourth, one seeks to attract and delights in having a retinue of followers and does not delight in renunciation.

These are the four.

Question: How is one able to abandon the dharmas of an imitation bodhisattva?

Response: One who is a bodhisattva should cultivate the meritorious qualities associated with the initial bodhisattva practices. If one does this, he will then be able to abandon the dharmas of imitation bodhisattvas. Therefore, if a bodhisattva wishes to abandon the dharmas of imitation bodhisattvas, he should act in accordance with the following verse that states:

> With regard to the four meritorious qualities of the initial practices,
> one should be energetically diligent in causing them to arise.
> Once they have arisen, cause them to increase.
> Having caused them to increase, continue to guard them.

What then are these four? They are:

First, one develops a resolute belief in the dharma of emptiness and yet still believes in karmic retribution.

Second, one delights in the dharma of nonself and yet still brings forth the mind of great compassion for all beings.

Third, one's mind resides in nirvana and yet one's practice abides within samsara.

Fourth, one practices giving, wishing to facilitate beings' development [in the path] and not because one seeks any karmic reward in return.

If someone wishes to produce, increase, and guard the four meritorious qualities associated with the initial bodhisattva practices, he should draw near to a good spiritual guide.[8] This is as described in this verse:

> The bodhisattva should draw near
> to four kinds of good spiritual friends
> and he should also utterly abandon
> four kinds of bad spiritual friends.

The bodhisattva who delights in [the prospect of realizing] *anuttarāsamyaksaṃbodhi* should draw near to, pay reverence to, and make offerings to four kinds of good spiritual friends and should remain distant from four kinds of bad spiritual friends.

What then are the four kinds of good spiritual friends? They are:

First, one contemplates anyone who comes seeking something as a worthy friend, for he is thereby able to assist one in realizing the unsurpassable path.

67a Second, one contemplates anyone who speaks Dharma as a good spiritual guide, for he is able to assist one in achieving the wisdom that arises from extensive learning.

Third, one speaks in praise of monastics, contemplating them as good spiritual guides, for they are able to assist in the growth of all roots of goodness.

Fourth, one contemplates the buddhas, the bhagavats, as good spiritual guides, for they are able to assist one in successfully developing all of the dharmas of a buddha.

What then are the four types of bad spiritual friends? They are:

First, those who have resolved to seek success in the *pratyekabuddha* vehicle and delight in having but few desires and few tasks to attend to.

Second, *bhikṣus* seeking success in the *śrāvaka* disciple vehicle who [merely] delight in sitting in *dhyāna* meditation.

Third, those fond of studying the non-Buddhist Lokāyata scriptures,[9] decorous literature, poetry, and polemical sophistry.

Fourth, those who, if one draws close to them, esteem the acquisition of worldly benefits, not the acquisition of benefits associated with the Dharma.

Given the above, the bodhisattva should draw near to the four kinds of good spiritual friends while remaining distant from the four types of bad spiritual friends. If the bodhisattva can remain distant from the four kinds of bad spiritual friends while drawing near to the four kinds of good spiritual friends, then he will acquire four vast treasuries, will go entirely beyond all dharmas associated with the works of Māra, will produce measureless merit, and will exhaustively accumulate all good dharmas.

Questions:

What are the dharmas constituting the bodhisattva's vast[10] treasuries?
What is meant by being able to go entirely beyond all dharmas associated with the works of Māra?
What are the dharmas by which one is able to produce measureless merit?
And what all is meant by being able to accumulate all good dharmas?

Response:

All bodhisattvas are possessed of four
vast treasuries of the sublime Dharma.
Of the four that facilitate accumulation of all good dharmas,
the resolve to attain *bodhi* is foremost among them.

What then are the four? They are:

First, one is able to meet the Buddha.

Second, one is able to hear [teachings on] the six *pāramitā*s.

Third, one's mind remains free of the obstacle of hostility toward the teacher of Dharma.

Fourth, because one is not neglectful, one's mind delights in dwelling in a forest hermitage.

These are the four vast treasuries.

As for "being able to go beyond all [works of] Māra," there are four dharmas in this connection. What are the four? They are:

First, one never abandons one's resolve to attain *bodhi.*

Second, one's mind remains free of the obstacle of hostility toward any being.

Third, one becomes aware of and knows all views.

Fourth, one's mind remains free of arrogance toward any bodhisattva.

These are the four.

As for the dharmas by which one acquires measureless merit, there are four additional dharmas in this connection. What are the four? They are:

First, in one's giving of Dharma, one has nothing that he hopes for in return.

Second, one brings forth the mind of great compassion for bad people who break the moral precepts.

Third, in teaching other beings, one brings forth [the resolve to attain] the unsurpassable *bodhi.*

Fourth, in dealing with beings of base character, one practices patience.

These are the four.

As regards the accumulation of all good dharmas, this refers to four dharmas. And what are those four? They are:

First, when abiding in the solitary leisure of a recluse, one avoids adopting affected or eccentric practices.

Second, in the practice of the four means of attraction, one does not seek anything in return for one's kindness.

Third, in protecting and preserving right Dharma, one will not be sparing of even one's own body and life.

Fourth, when planting roots of goodness, one takes the resolve to attain *bodhi* as the foremost priority.

These are the four.

Ideally, one should take up an extensive explanation of each and every
67b one of these sets of four dharmas. However, because the text could become tediously complex, we do not present extensive discussions,[11] but now instead use verses to provide concise explanations that accord with what the Buddha has taught.

If a bodhisattva wishes to acquire the treasuries of the bodhisattvas, if he wishes to go beyond all the works of Māra, and if he wishes to accumulate all good dharmas, he should completely abandon all of the following things:

The two hollow attachments and the two types of bondage,
The two types of hindrances and the two defiling dharmas,
The two ulcerous sores as well as the two types of abysses,
The two causes of being burned and the two illness dharmas.

If the bodhisattva wishes to gain access to the bodhisattva treasuries and the other sorts of meritorious qualities, then he should utterly abandon all of these twofold dharmas.

What is meant by "the two hollow attachments"? The first is that of indulging a covetous attachment to ideas related to the Lokāyata scriptures. The second is adding decorative ornamentation to one's robe and bowl.

As for "the two types of bondage," the first is the bondage of being attached to views. The second is the bondage of coveting fame and profit.

Of the "the two hindrance dharmas," the first is that of forming close relationships with members of the laity and the second is that of remaining distant from good people.

As for "the two defiling dharmas," the first is that of simply enduring and accepting one's own afflictions. The second is that of delighting in carrying on friendships with benefactors.[12]

Of "the two ulcerous sores," the first is that of focusing on the transgressions of others. The second is that of concealing one's own transgressions.

As for "the two abyss-like dharmas," the first is that of contributing to the damage and destruction of right Dharma. The second is that of accepting offerings even as one breaks the moral precepts.

Of "the two dharmas leading to being burned," the first is that of continuing to wear the monastic's *kāṣāya* robe even when possessed of a defiled mind. The second is that of [continuing under such circumstances] to accept sustaining offerings from those who are pure in their observance of the precepts.

Monastics may be prone to developing "the two types of illnesses" that are difficult to cure. The first is that of possessing such overweening pride[13] that one thinks he can simply subdue his own mind [without availing himself of a teacher or the appropriate Dharma antidotes]. The second is that of obstructing and destroying the resolve of someone seeking to [cultivate the practices of] the Great Vehicle.

If the bodhisattva is able to completely abandon dharmas such as these, there are additional dharmas by which he may swiftly attain *anuttarāsamyaksaṃbodhi*. [If he avails himself of them,] he can then swiftly attain it. He may also acquire those that are praised by all buddhas, *pratyekabuddha*s, and arhats.

Question: Which dharmas are those that lead to rapid attainment of *anuttarāsamyaksaṃbodhi*? And which of them are praised by all buddhas, *pratyekabuddha*s, and arhats?

Response:

If one is able to practice the characteristic practices of the four truths,
one will swiftly attain the *bodhi* of the Buddha.
Also, if one practices four additional dharmas,
he will be praised by the three classes of *ārya*s.

What are the practices that are characteristic of cultivating the four truths? They are:

First, because one seeks to develop all good dharmas, one is energetically vigorous.

Second, one listens to, accepts, studies, and recites the Dharma of the sutras and then practices in accordance with their teachings.

Third, having renounced the three realms of existence as comparable to a site of human slaughter, one always seeks the means to avoid and transcend them.

Fourth, in order to benefit and bring peace and happiness to all beings, one strives to benefit one's own mind.

The "truth" [of "the four truths"] refers to being genuine and nondeceptive. Because [the four truths] lead to the attainment of *anuttarāsamyaksaṃbodhi,* they are not false.

Next, there are four dharmas that are praised by the three classes of *ārya*s. What are those four? They are:

First, even if abstaining from it will cost one's life, one will not do any bad deed.

Second, one always practices the giving of Dharma.

Third, one remains singlemindedly focused whenever receiving teachings on Dharma.

67c Fourth, if one produces a defiled thought, one is immediately able to correctly contemplate the defiled thought and the causes and conditions that initiated the defiled thought, [reflecting,] "As for these 'roots of defilement,' just what about them is designated as 'defiled'? What is it that becomes 'defiled'? In what circumstances does it arise? And precisely who is it that that generates this defilement?"

As one carries on right reflection in this way, one realizes that these factors are all false, devoid of any genuine substantiality, and devoid of any intrinsic existence of their own. Because one possesses a definite and resolute belief in the emptiness of all dharmas, because no dharmas whatsoever exist intrinsically, and because one carries on such right contemplation of the causes and conditions of defilement, one does not bring forth any sort of evil karmic action. As for all the other afflictions, one also contemplates them in this same manner.

The bodhisattva's acquisition of these dharmas that elicit the praises of the great men is a consequence of his abandoning all bad karmic actions rooted in the afflictions. His mind then completely develops the relinquishing mind. This is as described below:

> Having completely developed the relinquishing mind,
> one seeks to bestow both worldly and world-transcending benefit.
> As one seeks to bestow these forms of benefit,
> one's mind remains free of any weariness.

This bodhisattva completely develops the dharma of relinquishing. His desire to practice Dharma giving and to practice the giving of material wealth is due to his motivation to benefit beings. Whether he is striving to bring about worldly benefit or world-transcending benefit, so long as he has not yet succeeded, his mind still remains free of any weariness or any inclination to retreat.

[The bestowal of] "worldly benefit" entails a thorough understanding of the world's classical texts, cultural arts, professional skills, the implementation of clever expedients, and so forth. [The bestowal of] "world-transcending benefit" entails [providing instruction in the practice of] the dharmas of the [five] root faculties, [five] powers, [seven] limbs of enlightenment, and [eightfold] path [as practiced by those who have become] free of the contaminants. This is as described here:

> As one seeks in this manner to bestow the two kinds of benefit,
> one's mind remains free of weariness and neglectfulness.
> Through staying free of weariness and neglectfulness,
> one becomes able to acquire all of the profound dharmas.

> It is due to seeking it from within the classical works
> that one is able to acquire wisdom.

> One thereby develops a perfectly complete knowledge of the world's
> most superior and foremost dharmas.

In "remaining free of weariness and neglectfulness," "weariness and neglectfulness" refer to feelings of loathing. If in one's studies one remains free of loathing, then one's mind will remain free of weariness. If one remains free of weariness, then one will always be free of weariness as one seeks to acquire the dharmas found within the scriptures, the arts, medicine, professional skills, and the codes of propriety. If one remains free of weariness in these pursuits, then one will acquire wisdom and will perfect a deep knowledge of the dharmas appropriate for use in the world.

"Dharmas of the world" refers here to the local customs determining what is appropriate in any given situation for adapting to the minds of those in the world. One becomes well able to understand the dharmas necessary to maintain order in the world. One thereby becomes able to understand what is appropriate in addressing beings possessed of superior, middling, and inferior capacities. In guiding them, one accords with whatsoever is appropriate. One becomes skillful in understanding worldly affairs while also maintaining a mind deeply imbued with a sense of shame and a dread of blame.

As for "in guiding them, one accords with whatever is appropriate," this refers to the fact that, in addressing the needs of beings of superior, middling, and inferior capacity, each of them has what is most appropriate for use in instructing them.

As for "a sense of shame and a dread of blame," "shame" refers to a feeling of mortification regarding one's own actions whereas "dread of blame" refers to the potential for feeling mortified by [the critical judgments of] others.

There are those who hold that it is because of one's actions that one feels a sense of shame and that it is because of seeing others that one feels a dread of blame. Within the sphere of worldly dharmas, having a dread of blame is the primary priority. This is as described in a sutra [that says], "There are two dharmas of pristine purity that guard the world, namely a sense of shame and a dread of blame." This is as described in a verse:

> 68a Whenever there are people possessed of a dread of blame,
> they understand the Dharma, karmic transgressions, and merit.

> As for those devoid of a dread of blame, good people avoid them,
> for there is no evil that they will not do.

Question: Why do you so assiduously counsel bodhisattvas to develop a good understanding of the dharmas appropriate for use in the world?

Response: If the bodhisattva is knowledgeable about the dharmas of the world, it will be easy for him to gain access to beings in a way that is mutually pleasing. He will thereby be able to teach them and guide the development of their minds in a way that causes them to abide in the Great Vehicle.

If one does not understand the dharmas of the world, then he will be incapable of teaching even a single person. Therefore the dharmas of the world serve as an expedient path for teaching beings.

The bodhisattva who understands the dharmas of the world in this way has a mind that is well equipped with a sense of shame and dread of blame. This is as described here:

> When subjected to bad actions, remain respectful and generous.
> How much the more so in dealing with those that benefit oneself.
> One possessed of a dread of blame and an inclination to be respectful
> refrains from slighting or deriding those who are good.

Because this bodhisattva has a well-developed dread of blame, even in dealing with badly-behaved people, he is still able to behave respectfully, bestow offerings, welcome those who arrive, escort those who depart, and extend greetings. How much the more so would this be the case when dealing with good people possessed of meritorious qualities.

Because one is possessed of the two mental attitudes of a dread of blame on the one hand and respectfulness on the other, in dealing with those who are worthy and good but deficient in knowledge, one does not adopt a slighting or arrogant attitude toward them. One reflects: "There are those who are possessed of meritorious qualities, yet conceal their presence in the world just as ashes conceal hot coals. They should not be slighted merely because they feel disdain for such worldly concerns. If I were to slight them for such minor reasons, I would be guilty of a karmic offense."

Additionally:

In whatever endeavor one takes up,
although it may be difficult, one still completes it.
This being so, even in endeavors undertaken in the world,
they are still characterized by never retreating.

No matter what endeavors this bodhisattva takes up, whether that be building a stupa or a temple, arranging for a great Dharma assembly, or rescuing someone who has committed some crime—in all such difficult endeavors in the world, one's mind refuses to desist or retreat from the task. So long as any given endeavor has not yet been completed, it is essential to use the power of all sorts of expedients as well as the power of physical, verbal, and mental persistence to successfully complete the task.

It is not only with respect to endeavors related to the Dharma of the Buddha that one refuses to turn back in retreat, for even in worldly endeavors, one maintains this characteristic of refusing to turn back in retreat.

Question: Based on which causes and conditions is one able to succeed in such endeavors?

Response: If one is possessed of the power of patient endurance, he will be able to successfully complete his endeavors. This is as described here:

Having developed this power of great patient endurance,
one becomes deeply committed to making offerings to the buddhas.
Whatever teachings have been taught by the buddhas,
one is able to accept and uphold all of them.

Having developed this power of patient endurance, the bodhisattva uses this power to make offerings to the buddhas, to bow to them in reverence, and to freely offer up, as appropriate, robes, food, drink, and so forth.

Additionally, whatever the Buddha has taught one to do, whether that be upholding the moral precepts, cultivating *dhyāna* concentration, subduing one's own mind, or contemplating all dharmas in accordance with ultimate reality—one uses the power of patient endurance in all of these endeavors.

68b This is just as when one obtains a sharp knife. He should then use it for beneficial purposes and should not use it for unbeneficial purposes. As it is said:

It is through faith, compassion, kindness, and relinquishing,
through the capacity for tireless patient endurance,
through also being able to understand the significance [of teachings],
through serving as a guide for the minds of other beings,

through keeping a dread of blame enabling supreme endurance,
through making momentous offerings to the buddhas,
and through abiding in what the Buddha has taught—
it is through right practice of these ten dharmas

that one becomes able to purify the first of the grounds.
These then are what constitute the bodhisattva path.

It is due to the bodhisattva's ability to carry out these practices, beginning with faith and concluding with abiding in the Buddha's teachings, that he is able to purify the first ground.

These ten dharmas all take faith as what is foremost. "Faith" refers to the mind's reaching a definite resolve with respect to the causes and conditions of the Dharma of the buddhas, one that is enhanced by one's delight in it.

How does this come to be the case? It is because this bodhisattva's mind is pure in nature that he is able to develop such a deeply rooted power of faith.

Having acquired this power of faith, he then brings forth the mind of compassion toward beings, reflecting as follows: "The Dharma of all buddhas takes the great compassion as its very foundation. I now singlemindedly delight in the Dharma of the Buddha. Therefore, when in the midst of beings I should bring forth the mind of compassion."

As this compassion of his gradually increases, it develops into the great compassion.

Having developed the great compassion, one then brings forth thoughts of kindness toward other beings, reflecting as follows: "I should benefit other beings in a manner consistent with my capacity to do so. If I do this, then this would become the practice of kindness based on genuine compassion."

When one benefits beings, one is immediately able to practice relinquishing to the degree that one can give away all of his inward or outward possessions, reflecting as follows: "If I dispense with my possessions in this manner, doing so out of a wish to benefit beings and make them happy, this shall become genuine kindness. In addition, these beings will then become well-disposed to trust and accept my words."

One then becomes able to endure all manner of distressing situations in order to acquire valuable possessions with which to fulfill one's desire to practice such relinquishing. One then reflects in this manner: "If in doing this I were to become weary, then there would be nothing gained from my pursuit of wealth by involving myself in the means for mastering the world's various skills, arts, classical texts, and agriculture techniques. Therefore I should be tireless in learning the world's skills, arts, classical texts, agricultural techniques, and other such things."

Through such a capacity for patient endurance, one is able to understand the meaning and significance [of what one studies], whereupon one reflects as follows: "The flavor of worldly classics and texts derives from the meaningful ideas contained within them. If one becomes well able to understand the conceptual flavor of such classics, one is thereby able to gain a penetrating comprehension of all worldly dharmas."

If one becomes able to completely comprehend them, one can then serve as a guide for other beings of superior, middling, and inferior capacities.

One then reflects as follows: "If one has no sense of shame or dread of blame, he will be unable to inspire delight in other beings. In order to cause them to be delighted, I should act with a sense of shame and dread of blame."

One then reflects as follows: "If I have no capacity for patient endurance, then I will not be able to bring about either worldly or world-transcending benefit. It is through the capacity for patient endurance that one can serve as
68c a guide for all beings and cause them all to be delighted. It is because their minds are delighted that they will then trust and accept my words. Because they believe and accept my words, I can diligently implement skillful means by which I can serve as a guide for them."

One also reflects as follows: "If beings make offerings to the Buddha, then they will gain much benefit from this." Then, wishing to influence beings to make offerings to the Buddha, one immediately adopts this practice oneself by making offerings to the Buddha, his images, and his *śarīra* relics.

Because those beings believe and accept whatever one does, they then emulate one's practice of making offerings to the Buddha and thereby establish the causes and conditions for being reborn in the human and celestial realms and for abiding in the Dharma of the three vehicles.

It is in this manner that the bodhisattva sequentially develops his practice of these ten dharmas by which he is then able to purify the first bodhisattva ground.

Chapter 20

Mindfulness of the Buddhas

> When the bodhisattva dwelling on the first ground
> has completed what is to be practiced,
> due to the power of his roots of goodness, he will naturally
> be able to see several hundred buddhas.[14]

When, in this [above-discussed] manner, the bodhisattva subdues his own mind, he develops a deep love for the path to buddhahood. He then completely fulfills the first-ground practices in accordance with the way he learned them. Then, due to the power of his roots of goodness and merit, he is naturally able to see the present-era buddhas of the ten directions right before his very eyes.

Question: Is it solely through the power of roots of goodness and merit that one is then able to see buddhas or is there some other method by which one can do so?

Response:

> There is a deep *samādhi* that the Buddha
> explained for the sake of Bhadrapāla.
> If one acquires this *samādhi* treasure,
> one becomes able to see the buddhas.

Bhadrapāla was a lay bodhisattva well able to practice the *dhūta* austerities. It was for the sake of this bodhisattva that the Buddha spoke the *Pratyutpanna-samādhi-sūtra*.[15] The *pratyutpanna samādhi* is one in which one sees the buddhas right before one's very eyes. When the bodhisattva accesses this magnificently precious *samādhi,* even though he might not yet have gained the heavenly eye and heavenly ear, he is nonetheless able to see the buddhas of the ten directions and he is also able to listen to the Dharma of the sutras being taught by those buddhas.

Question: What means should one use to acquire this *samādhi*?

Response:

One should bring to mind the buddhas,
envisioning them as residing in a great assembly,
replete with all thirty-two major marks
and eighty secondary characteristics adorning their bodies.

In cultivating this *samādhi,* the practitioner brings to mind the buddhas with the thirty-two major marks and eighty secondary characteristics gracing their bodies, with *bhikṣu*s close by, with *deva*s making offerings, and with a grand and reverential assembly surrounding them. With focused mind, one envisions each of the major marks of those buddhas.

One also recollects the buddhas as those who are possessed of great vows, recollects their perfection of the great compassion and the fact that it has not been cut off, recollects their perfection of the great kindness through which they bring profound peace to beings, recollects their practice of the great sympathetic joy and their fulfillment of beings' aspirations, and recollects their practice of equanimity through which they have abandoned aversion and craving and do not abandon beings.

One also recollects their practice of the truthfulness basis of meritorious qualities by which they are never deceptive, recollects their practice of the relinquishment basis of meritorious qualities by which they have rid themselves of the miserliness defilement, recollects their practice of the thoroughgoing [quiescence][16] basis of meritorious qualities by which their
69a minds maintain a state of thoroughgoing quiescence, and recollects their practice of the wisdom basis of meritorious qualities through which they have acquired great wisdom.[17]

One recollects too their perfect practice of *dāna-pāramitā* by which they have become the lords of Dharma giving, their perfect practice of *śīla-pāramitā* by which their observance of the moral precepts is pure, their perfect practice of *kṣānti-pāramitā* by which their capacity for patient endurance is analogous to that of the earth, their perfect practice of *vīrya-pāramitā* by which their vigor is preeminent, their perfect practice of *dhyāna-pāramitā* by which they have destroyed all hindrances to meditative absorption, and their perfect practice of *prajñā-pāramitā* by which they have destroyed all obstacles to wisdom.

One recollects too:
Their mark of having the wheel insignia on the hands and feet, emblematic of their ability to turn the wheel of Dharma;
Their mark of securely planted feet, emblematic of their standing securely in every dharma;
Their mark of proximal webbing on fingers and toes, emblematic of the extinguishing of all afflictions;
Their mark of seven places of fullness, emblematic of their complete fulfillment of merit;
Their mark of soft and tender hands and feet, emblematic of their harmonious manner of proclaiming the Dharma;
Their mark of slender and long fingers and toes, emblematic of their cultivation and accumulation of every sort of good and sublime dharma during the long night [of previous lifetimes];
Their mark of having broad heels and wide eyes, emblematic of their vast learning;
Their mark of having a large and erect body, emblematic of their proclamation of the great and upright Dharma;
Their mark of having high arches, emblematic of their being lofty in all things;
Their mark of having upwardly spiraling bodily hairs, emblematic of their ability to cause beings to abide in the supreme and sublime dharma;
Their mark of having legs gradually growing in thickness like those of the *aiṇeya* antelope;
Their mark of long arms reaching past the knees, their arms appearing like golden gate bars;[18]
Their mark of the stallion-like retracted male organ, emblematic of their possession of the treasury of Dharma jewels;
Their mark of the golden-hued body emanating light of countless colors;
Their mark of fine and thin skin, emblematic of their proclamation of subtle and sublime Dharma;
Their mark of one hair per hair pore, emblematic of their revealing of the single-mark Dharma;

Their mark of the [mid-brow] white-down tuft adorning the countenance, due to which beings happily and tirelessly gaze at the Buddha's face;
Their mark of a lionlike upper torso, emblematic of the Buddha, like the lion, being one who is fearless;
Their mark of round and large shoulders, emblematic of their ability to make skillful distinctions regarding the nature of the five aggregates;
Their mark of fullness in the subaxillary region, emblematic of their possession of a full measure of good roots;
Their mark of distinguishing every flavor, emblematic of their having perfectly tasted the flavor of quiescence;
Their mark of having a square-set body, emblematic of having crushed the fear of births and deaths;
Their mark of the fleshy prominence atop the crown, emblematic of their heads never having to be lowered in reverence [to someone superior];
Their mark of the large tongue the color of real coral that is even able to cover the face;
Their mark of the Brahmā-like voice and the physical mark that reaches even to the Brahma Heaven;
Their mark of the lionlike jaw;
Their mark of the broad shoulders, these being emblematic of their ability to demolish [the views held by] non-Buddhist traditions;
Their mark of even teeth, emblematic of their practice of pure *dhyāna* meditation;
Their mark of their teeth being of even height, emblematic of their minds' equal regard for all beings;
Their mark of closely set teeth, emblematic of their abandonment of desires;
Their mark of having forty teeth, emblematic of their perfection of the forty dharmas exclusive to buddhas;
Their mark of blue eyes, emblematic of their looking on beings with minds imbued with kindness;
Their mark of having eyelashes like those of the royal bull, with the lashes long and in no way disarrayed;

Their obtaining of a rare physical form that beings look on without ever tiring of holding it in their gaze;
Their having bodies adorned with these thirty-two marks;
Their having the eighty minor characteristics like inlaid adornments on their bodies, emanating brilliant radiance;
Their complete fulfillment of merit;
Their transcendently supreme and awesome powers;
Their widespread illustrious esteem;
Their bodies' incense-like fragrance produced by purity in observing the moral precepts;
Their invulnerability to being moved by worldly dharmas;
Their ability to remain undefiled by any arising of afflictions;
Their ability to remain unsullied by others' verbal abuse;
Their ability to roam and sport through use of their spiritual powers;
The ability of the buddhas to be so intensely magnificent in the manifestation of their awe-inspiring powers that no one would dare obstruct them;
Their freely exercised sovereign mastery in using wisdom to proclaim the Dharma that is like the roaring of a lion;
Their ability to dispel the darkness of delusion by marshaling the power of vigor;
Their use of magnificent brilliance to everywhere illuminate the heavens and the earth;
Their utter invincibility in debate;
Their being such that everyone looks up to them and no one can look 69b
down on them;
Their constancy in regarding all beings with kindness;
Their possession of mindfulness as vast as the great oceans;
Their meditative absorption that is like Mount Sumeru [in its unshakability];
Their possession of patience comparable to the earth's [ability to endure anything];
Their ability to bring about growth in the merit planted by beings that is analogous [to the growth-enhancing capacity of] water's moisture;[19]

Their ability to bring forth roots of goodness in beings that, in its power, is like the rising of the wind;
Their ability to ripen beings that is like fire's ability to cook things;
Their possession of wisdom as boundless as empty space;
Their universal raining down of the great Dharma [rain] that is like [the rain that pours down from] immense dense clouds;
Their ability to remain unstained by worldly dharmas that is like lotus blossoms' [ability to rise from mud and yet remain unsullied by it];
Their ability, like lions pouncing on deer, to decisively refute [the doctrines of] non-Buddhist masters;
Their ability to bear a heavy burden that is like that of the great king of the elephants;
Their ability to lead a great congregation of followers that is like that of the great king of bulls;
Their possession of a retinue of pure followers that is like [the retinue of] a wheel-turning king;
Their utter supremacy in the world that is like that of the lord of the Mahābrahma Heaven;
Their ability to inspire fondness and delight that is like that of a bright moon in the clear night sky;
Their universal illumination that is able to burn as brightly as the brilliantly shining sun;
Their bestowal on beings of the causes and conditions for peace and happiness that is like [the generosity of] a humane father;
Their acting out of pity toward beings, protecting them in whatever way is appropriate, that is like the actions of a lovingly kind mother;
Their purity of conduct that is like [the purity of] the real gold in the heavens;
Their possession of the power of great strength that is like that of Indra in the heavens;
Their diligence in benefiting those in the world that is like that of a world-protecting lord;
Their ability to cure the disease of the afflictions that is like [the curative power of] a king of physicians;
Their ability to rescue one from disastrous circumstances that is like that of close relatives;

Their ability to accumulate a store of meritorious qualities that is like an immense treasury;
Their possession of immeasurably vast moral virtue;
Their possession of boundless meditative absorptions;
Their ineffable wisdom;
Their unequaled liberation;
Their knowledge and vision of liberation that is the equal of the unequaled;
Their incomparability in all things;
Their supremacy over everyone in the world due to which they are recognized as foremost among men;
And their perfection of great dharmas by which they are recognized as great men.

It is in this way that the bodhisattva engages in recollective contemplation of all buddhas in accordance with their possession of the qualities characteristic of the great men. [So, too, he recollects:]

That these buddhas have cultivated these meritorious qualities for a countless, boundless, inconceivable, and incalculable number of hundreds of thousands of myriads of *koṭi*s of *kalpa*s during which they have been well able to guard their physical, verbal, and mental karma;
That they are well able to completely sever all doubts with respect to the five categorical repositories of dharmas: past dharmas, future dharmas, present dharmas, unconditioned dharmas, and ineffable dharmas;
That, without falling into any error, they employ the four modes of reply: the definitive reply, the distinguishing reply, the counter-questioning reply, and the reply that sets aside the question;[20]
That they skillfully explain the dharmas of the thirty-seven enlightenment factors, namely: the faculties, the powers, the limbs of enlightenment, the path, the stations of mindfulness, the right efforts, and the foundations of psychic power;[21]
That they are well able to distinguish [each link comprising the chain of] cause and effect, namely: ignorance, actions, consciousness, name and form, the six sense faculties, contact, feeling, craving, grasping, becoming, birth, and aging and death;

That they are free of any attachment to the eye or visual forms, to the ear or sounds, to the nose or fragrances, to the tongue or flavors, to the body or touch, or to the mind or dharmas [as objects of mind];

That they skillfully expound the nine types of passages contained in the Dharma of the sutras, namely: sutras, *geya*s, prophetic teachings or expositions, *gāthā*s, *udāna*s, *nidāna*s, [short] discourses beginning with "Thus [spoke the Buddha]…," *vaipulya*s, and unprecedented events;

That they are not influenced by any of the negative influences such as: greed, hatred, delusion, arrogance, the view that conceives of the existence of true personhood, extreme views, wrong views, seizing upon views, seizing on rules and regulations, or doubts;

69c That they are not assailed by such afflictions as absence of faith, absence of a sense of shame, absence of a dread of blame, flattery, deviousness, frivolousness, neglectfulness, indolence, somnolence, animosity, miserliness, or jealousy;

That they have known and seen the truth of suffering, have cut off its origination, have realized cessation, have cultivated the path, have abandoned what is to be abandoned, have seen what is to be seen, have done what is to be done, have utterly destroyed the foes,[22] and have perfectly fulfilled their vows;

That they are venerated in the world, are as fathers to the world, and are lords of the world, are well come, are well gone, are possessed of the well-cultivated mind, are consummately skilled in meditative stillness, are well realized in the realization of cessation, and are well liberated;

That, as they abide in countless and boundless worlds throughout the ten directions, in worlds as numerous as the sands in the Ganges, [one envisions them] as if they were appearing directly before one's very eyes.

The bodhisattva should also envision in contemplation all of the buddhas as graced with their eighty secondary characteristics,[23] recollecting:

That their nails are copper-colored is emblematic of their practice of pure dharmas;

That their nails are prominent and large is emblematic of birth into the great clan;
That their nails are glossy and smooth is emblematic of a deep affection for beings;
That their fingers are round, tapered, and long is emblematic of the depth and duration of their practice;
That their fingers are fully fleshed is emblematic of fully developed roots of goodness;
That their fingers are tapered and long is emblematic of sequential accumulation of all dharmas of a buddha;
That their veins are hidden and invisible, but they do not hide the lineage of [the quality of their conduct in] body, speech, and mind;
That there are no thick knots in their veins is emblematic of their having broken up the knots of afflictions;
That their ankle bones are flat and inconspicuous is emblematic of their not hiding away the Dharma;
That their feet are not misaligned in their track is emblematic of their liberation of the multitudes who have fallen into deviant conduct;
That their gait is like that of the lion is emblematic of their being the lions among men;
That their gait is also like that of the king of elephants is emblematic of their being the elephant kings among men;
That their gait is also like the king of geese is emblematic of their flying high, like the wild goose;
That their gait is also like the king of bulls is emblematic of their being the most revered of all men;
That, when walking, they turn around to the right, is emblematic of their skillful proclamation of the right path;
That their posture is not hunched or crooked is emblematic of the fact that their minds are never crooked;
That their bodies stand solid and erect in their posture is emblematic of their praise of solidity and durability in upholding the moral precepts;
That their bodies gradually grew large is emblematic of their sequential exposition of Dharma;

That all parts of their bodies are large and majestic is emblematic of their ability to skillfully explain the great and sublime meritorious qualities;

That their bodies are perfectly developed is emblematic of their perfection in the Dharma;

That their strides are of equal length is emblematic of their equal-minded regard for all beings;

That their bodies are pristine in their cleanliness is emblematic of the purity of their three types of karma;

That their skin is fine and soft is emblematic of the naturally pliant character of their minds;

That their bodies remain free of all dust and dirt is emblematic of their good views that have abandoned all defilement;

That their bodies do not shrink through wasting [even in old age] is emblematic of their minds' always remaining unsinkable;

That their bodies are boundless and immeasurable is emblematic of the immeasurability of their roots of goodness;

That the flesh of their bodies is taut and finely textured is emblematic of their eternal severance of [karmically compulsory] later incarnations;

That all of their joints are smooth in their articulations is emblematic of their skillful explication of the twelve causes and conditions and their perfectly clear distinguishing of each of them;

That the hue of their bodies is not dark is emblematic of their knowledge and vision being free of any darkness;

That their waists are full all around is emblematic of their disciples' possession of fully developed conduct;

That their bellies are clear [of blemishes] and of fresh and immaculate appearance is emblematic of their being well able to completely know the serious faults of samsara;

That their bellies do not protrude is emblematic of their having crushed the mountain of arrogance;

That their bellies are flat and do not show is emblematic of the fact that their proclamation of Dharma is directed equally toward everyone;

That their umbilici are round and deep is emblematic of their penetrating comprehension of extremely deep dharmas;

That their umbilici have a rightward swirl is emblematic of their disciples' compliance with instruction;
That their bodies are in every way graceful in their refinements is emblematic of the thoroughgoing purity of their disciples;
That their awesomeness in deportment is utterly immaculate is emblematic of the incomparable purity of their minds;
That their bodies are free of blemishes is emblematic of their being completely free of any black dharmas;
That the softness of their hands is superior even to that of *tūla* cotton silk is emblematic of the experience of those receiving their instruction who feel as if their bodies have become as light as a wisp of down;
That the lines on their palms form a deep pattern is emblematic of the profoundly dignified nature of their awesome deportment;
That the lines on their palms are long is emblematic of their contemplative regard for the long-term future of those receiving their Dharma teaching;
That the pattern on their palms is lustrous and smooth is emblematic of 70a
their relinquishing of the affection of relatives and of their acquisition of the fruits of the great path;
That their countenances remain free of any long-faced expression is emblematic of the presence of exceptional circumstances in the moral precepts they establish;
That their lips are as red as *bimba* fruit is emblematic of their looking on the entire world as merely like an image reflected in a mirror;
That their tongues are soft and pliant is emblematic of their initial use of gentle speech in liberating beings;
That their tongues are thin and wide is emblematic of the purity and abundance of their meritorious qualities;
That their tongues are crimson red is emblematic of their Dharma's ability to cause common people to understand what they find difficult to understand;
That their voices are like thunder is emblematic of their not fearing the boom of a thunderclap;
That their voices are harmonious and gentle is emblematic of their proclamation of soft and gentle Dharma;

That their four central incisors are rounded [in their visible profile] and straight is emblematic of their proclamation of the Dharma of the straight path;

That their four central incisors are all sharp is emblematic of their liberation of those beings who are possessed of sharp faculties;

That their four central incisors are immaculately white is emblematic of their being foremost in purity;

That their four central incisors are evenly and equally set is emblematic of their standing on the level ground of the moral precepts;

That the profile of their rows of teeth gradually taper to those that are smaller [in height] is emblematic of the graduated sequence in their explanation of the dharma of the four truths;

That they have noses that are high and straight-ridged is emblematic of their standing atop the high mountain of wisdom;

That their nasal apertures are clear and clean is emblematic of the purity of their disciples;

That their eyes are wide and laterally long is emblematic of their wisdom's qualities of being vast and far-reaching;

That their eyelashes are not sparse or in disarray is emblematic of their skill in their differential assessment of beings;

That the whites and pupils of their eyes are as fresh and pristine as the petals of a blue lotus blossom is emblematic of their being such that even *deva*s and heavenly maidens are moved to gaze upon them fondly and bow down in reverence before them;

That their eyebrows are high and long is emblematic of the far-reaching spread of their fame;

That the hair of their eyebrows is smooth and glossy is emblematic of their thoroughgoing knowledge of the dharmas of mental pliancy;

That their ears are equal in their appearance is emblematic of the equality of all who listen to the Dharma;

That their faculty of hearing is undamaged is emblematic of their ability to liberate any being possessed of an undamaged mind;

That their foreheads are flat and of fine appearance is emblematic of their having skillfully abandoned all views;

That their foreheads are unrestricted in their wide breadth is emblematic of their having broadly refuted [the claims of] non-Buddhist traditions;
That their heads are in all respects perfectly developed is emblematic of their having thoroughly perfected [the goals of] their great vows;
That their hair is the color of the black bee is emblematic of their having transformed the pleasures associated with the five types of desire;
That their hair is dense and fine is emblematic of their having already put an end to the fetters;
That their hair, so pleasing in its appearance, is soft in texture is emblematic of their pliant and sharp wisdom's ability to know well the flavor of dharmas;
That their hair is not in disarray is emblematic of their words never being disordered;
That their hair is smooth and glossy is emblematic of their always being free of any sort of coarse speech;
That their hair has a marvelous fragrance is emblematic of their use of the fragrant blossoms of the seven branches of *bodhi* to teach and guide beings in whatever way is appropriate.
That their mark of virtue, peace, and joy appears in their hair.
And that their mark of virtue, peace, and joy also appears on the palms of their hands and on the soles of their feet.

It is in this manner that a bodhisattva should envision the buddhas residing in the midst of a great assembly, speaking on right Dharma, and sitting on the lion seat. The lion seat has feet made from *vaiḍūrya* inset with various jewels, a headrest made from real coral with marvelous red pearls, and a canopy made of hammered gold. It is draped with all sorts of soft, silky, and lustrous heavenly robes and is supported by bejeweled lions whose bodies are made of purple gold. Their eyes are amber and their tails are mother-of-pearl. They have carnelian tongues, four white-diamond tusk-teeth, hair made of real white silver, and long, full manes. That seat rests upon these four lions. They form [the base of] the throne that has armrests made from royal elephant tusks and a footrest made of the many sorts of jewels.

The buddhas receive there the reverential obeisance of the *deva*s, dragons, *yakṣa*s, *gandharva*s, *asura*s, *garuḍa*s, *kiṃnara*s, and *mahoraga*s. The
70b buddhas appear in this way on this throne. They wear the *saṃkakṣikā*[24] and the *nivāsana,*[25] neither too high nor too low, so that they cover the three regions of the body and are neatly arranged and straight all around. They wear a light-colored *saṃghāṭī* robe,[26] with the strips composing it clearly visible, neither too high nor too low, and not misaligned.

They abide in the midst of an audience adorned by the presence of the eight kinds of great *ārya*s,[27] surrounded by a great assembly of humans and *deva*s. When in attendance there, the dragons and golden-winged *garuḍa* birds all listen together to the teaching of Dharma, remaining free of any thoughts of mutual hostility.[28]

Everyone in the entire assembly is imbued with a deeply sincere sense of shame and dread of blame as, with reverential affection for the Buddha, they all listen singlemindedly to the discourse of the Buddha, accept and uphold it, reflect upon it, and practice in accordance with what is taught. Because their minds are focused as they listen and because their thoughts are pure, they are able to block any interference by the hindrances. Everyone in the great assembly gazes insatiably up at the Tathāgata, with all the hairs raised on their bodies, with their eyes filled with tears, with their minds afire with intensity, or with hearts filled with great joy.

Wherever people have become like this, one knows that their minds have become purified. They remain there motionless and silent, serenely still, and as if having entered *dhyāna* absorption. Their minds are free of either love or hatred and remain undistracted by any extraneous matters. They have thoughts of great compassion[29] by which they feel kindness and pity for beings, wishing to rescue them all. Their minds do not descend into flattery or deviousness, but rather have become utterly quiescent and pure as they distinguish what is good from what is bad. They have an immensely strong determination from which they neither fall away nor shrink back and they do not regard themselves as superior or others as inferior.

The buddhas are all observed abiding in such great assemblies, teaching Dharma that is easy to understand and easy to completely fathom. [Their audiences] listen with insatiable delight. Their voices are deep, are not subject to fading [even at a distance], are gentle, and are pleasing to the ear. Originating in the belly, through the interaction of the throat, tongue, nasopharynx, dental palate, teeth, and lips, the air is caused to become sounds and sentences that may be soft and pleasing to the ear, may be as powerfully strong as the earth-quaking thunder emanating from huge, dense rain clouds, may be like those fierce winds off the great ocean that drive up the surf, or may be like the voice of the *deva*s in the Mahābrahma Heaven. With voices such as these, they lead forth and guide those beings that are capable of being liberated.

They have abandoned any modes of expression associated with scolding that may involve contortion of the brow, the countenance, or the lips. Their speech is neither deficient in any way nor unnecessarily long and redundant. There is no doubt in what they proclaim and their words will certainly be beneficial. Their speech is entirely free of any deceptive statements, any statements vulnerable to refutation, or any other such statements. It is entirely free of these faults and it is heard equally well by those far and near.

The buddhas are freely able to answer the four types of challenging questions. They explain the four truths, thereby causing beings to gain the four fruits of the path. They establish points of meaning and make statements supported by reasons. They are completely equipped with all of the methods used in speaking. In the many different sorts of matters that they discuss, their meaning is easy to completely comprehend. Whatever they proclaim is entirely clear and never intentionally cryptic or convoluted. Their speech is neither too fast nor too slow. The beginnings and conclusions of each discourse are mutually compatible and invulnerable to anyone's challenges.

With speech such as this, they spread forth and proclaim the Dharma which is good in the beginning, middle, and end, imbued with meaning, beneficial, devoted solely to Dharma, and, in all respects, perfect.[30] It is able to cause beings to gain karmic rewards in in this very lifetime. Their discourse is not meaningful only for a time, is such that one can test it for oneself, and is such that will lead to the fulfillment of one's aspirations. Those possessed of profound and sublime wisdom realize it within themselves. It can extinguish in beings the raging fire set ablaze by the three poisons. It is able to rid one of all karmic offenses committed by body, speech, and mind, and it is also well able to open up and reveal the essence of moral virtue, the meditative absorptions, and wisdom.

It begins with mere naming that in turn provokes realization of meaning that then in its own turn causes one to be filled with joy. From this joy, there then arises bliss, and from this bliss, there then arises meditative concen-
70c tration. From this meditative concentration, there arises a wise knowing in accordance with reality, and from this wise knowing in accordance with reality, one then develops renunciation. Due to having developed this renunciation, one becomes able to destroy the fetters, and due to having destroyed those fetters, one then gains liberation.

In this very manner, this Dharma is caused to unfold in a sequence whereby:

It is well able to open forth and reveal the four bases [of meritorious qualities]: truth, relinquishment, quiescence, and wisdom;

It is able to reveal for beings the means by which they are caused to perfectly fulfill the *pāramitā*s of giving, moral virtue, patience, vigor, meditative concentration, and wisdom;

It is able to cause beings to sequentially enter and proceed through the Ground of Joyfulness, the Ground of Stainlessness, the Ground of Shining Light, the Ground of Blazing Brilliance, the Difficult-to-Conquer Ground, the Ground of Direct Presence, the Far-reaching Ground, the Ground of Immovability, the Ground of Excellent Intelligence, and the Ground of the Dharma Cloud;

It is able to make clear distinctions with regard to the *śrāvaka* disciple vehicle, the *pratyekabuddha* vehicle, and the Great Vehicle;

It is able to provoke realization of the fruits of the path gained by the stream-enterer, once-returner, nonreturner, and arhat;[31]

And it is able too to cause complete success in gaining wealth and happiness in the realms of humans and *deva*s.

This is what constitutes the treasury of meritorious qualities that provides all of the foremost forms of benefit.

It is in this manner that one uses right thought in the recollective mindfulness of all buddhas. One abides in a peaceful and quiet place, rids oneself of sensual desire, ill will, dullness and drowsiness, doubtfulness, regret and agitation, and singlemindedly carries on focused mindfulness in which one refrains from generating thoughts that obstruct or cause one to lose meditative absorption. One employs this sort of mind in one's focused mindfulness of the buddhas. If one's mind sinks, one should raise it up again. If one's mind becomes scattered, one should draw it back into a focused state. One then sees the entire great assembly as if it were always right before one's very eyes.

When one has not yet managed to enter concentrated meditative absorption, one should always praise the two types of phenomena that consist of the Buddha's major marks and secondary characteristics, using verses to celebrate the qualities of the buddhas and to cause one's mind to become well trained in this.

Accordingly, there are these lines of verse as follows:

> Referring to the marks and characteristics of the bhagavats
> and the karmic causes and conditions by which they acquired them,
> I shall use these marks and their corresponding karmic actions
> to set forth the praises of these great *ārya*s:
>
> The thousand-spoked wheel mark on the feet
> is associated with a pure retinue and giving.
> It is because of these causes and conditions
> that the many worthies and *ārya*s surround them.
>
> The mark of the stable stance of the feet
> arises from upholding without fail all goodness one has taken on.
> It is because of this that the legions of Māra's armies
> are unable to succeed in destroying them.
>
> Their fingers and toes join with proximal webs
> and their bodies have the mark of purple-golden coloration.
> Because of their skillful practice of the means of attraction,
> the great assembly naturally bows in deferential reverence.
>
> Their hands and feet are extremely soft
> and the body has the mark of fullness in the seven places.
> It is due to giving food that accords with others' wishes
> that they are naturally given many offerings.
>
> They have long fingers, broad heels,
> and the body has the mark of being large and upright.

This results from abandoning the causes and conditions of killing
and may lead to a life span lasting even up to a *kalpa* in length.

The hairs of the body grow in an upward and rightward spiral
and the feet have the mark of high arches.
By always advancing in good endeavors,
they thereby acquired the dharma of irreversibility.

71a They have the gradually tapering legs of the *aiṇeya* antelope
due to always delighting in study and recitation of scriptures.
It is through speaking the Dharma for others
that they rapidly realized the unsurpassable path.

As for having long arms that reach below the knees,
this is due to never being miserly in giving
anything one possesses to whoever seeks to acquire them.
Thus they can teach and guide others in ways suited to their wishes.

Genital ensheathment reflects a treasury of meritorious qualities
associated with skillfully reconciling those who are estranged.[32]
As a result, they acquire a great congregation of humans and *deva*s
and use the pure wisdom eye to create their sons.[33]

Their thin skin that radiates golden light
is associated with giving marvelous apparel and halls.
As a consequence, they acquire an abundance of fine robes
as well as pristine quarters, buildings, and viewing terraces.

The single hair in each pore
and the white hair tuft between the eyes
are associated with serving as a supreme protector.
Hence they are revered throughout the three realms of existence.

They have an upper body like that of a lion
with the two shoulders rounded and full.
These result from always using speech that is pleasing to others.
As a consequence, there is no one who opposes them.

The marks of subaxillary fullness and cognition of all tastes
stem from providing medical care and medicines for the sick.
As a consequence, *deva*s and humans all revere and love them
and their bodies remain ever free of disease.

The roundness of the mid-body and the crown's fleshy *uṣṇīṣa* sign
reflect the merit of giving with a harmonious and delighted mind.
As a consequence of exhorting and teaching even the stubborn,
they reign as sovereignly masterful kings of Dharma.

As for the voice like that of a *kalaviṅka* bird,
the broad tongue, and the voice like a Great Brahma Heaven *deva*,
they are from the speaking of words that are both gentle and true.
They therefore acquire the Great Ārya's eight voice qualities.[34]

Having first brought contemplative thought to bear
and then afterward spoken words of definite truthfulness,
they acquired the lionlike mark.
Hence all who see them trust them and defer to them.

That their teeth are white, straight, and close-set
is because they have always refrained from slighting
those who have previously given offerings.
Hence the minds of those in their retinue are agreeable and unified.

Above and below, they have a total of forty teeth
that, being close-set, have no gaps.
These result from never slandering and not lying.
Hence their disciples' [loyalty] cannot be destroyed.

The pupils and whites of their eyes are clearly delineated
and they have the mark of eyelashes like those of a royal bull.
These are caused by kindly thought and an amicable view of others.
Consequently all observers look on them with a tireless gaze.

Even though a wheel-turning king
who rules over four continents

possesses these major marks and secondary characteristics,
their radiance still cannot compare with that of a buddha.

I pray that the power of the merit from my setting forth praises
of the major marks and the secondary characteristics
71b may be able to cause everyone
to have purified minds as well as everlasting peace and happiness.

The bodhisattva should also engage in contemplative mindfulness of the buddhas by way of their eighty secondary characteristics. Accordingly, there are these lines of verse, as follows:

All buddhas possess the marvelous secondary characteristics,
eighty in number, with which their bodies are adorned.
You should all delight in them
and listen intently as I describe them.

The bhagavat*s* have round and slender fingers,
nails that are purplish red in hue,
convex in profile, smooth, and glossy,
characteristics of having everything in measureless abundance.

Their veins lie flat, their ankle bones are invisible,
their feet are not skewed in their track,
their gait is like that of the king of lions,
and they are incomparably awe-inspiring to all observers.

When walking, the entire body turns to the right.
They are serene in manner and refined in their deportment.
The parts of their squarely set bodies are orderly in their posture
and their dignified grace inspires fondness and happiness.

Their bodies are firm in tone, but extremely soft.
The articulations of their joints are quite visibly distinct.
When walking, they do not travel in a meandering manner.
All of their sense faculties are fully and perfectly developed.

The flesh on their bodies is extremely taut, finely textured,
freshly radiant, and especially immaculate.

Their physical posture is especially upright, refined,
and devoid of any feature subject to dispraise.

The belly is round, but does not visibly bulge.
The navel, though deep, does not appear to be an orifice.
Its creases manifest as a rightward spiraling swirl.
Their deportment is extremely pure.

The body is free of any blemishes
and the hands and feet are extremely soft.
The lines in the palms are deep and long,
continuous, straight, and lustrous.

The tongue is slender, the face is not too long.
The central incisors are white, rounded, slender, and sharp.
The hue of the lips is like that of the *bimba* fruit.
Their voice is as deep as the king of the wild geese.

The nose is prominent in profile and the eyes are bright and clear.
The eyelashes are close-set and fine, but not in disarray.
The brow is elevated, has eyebrow hair that is soft,
and it is straight and not crooked.

The hair of the brows, being even and straight,
is emblematic of being well aware of the faults in any dharma.
The hair of the brows is smooth and glossy,
a feature emblematic of skillfully liberating and aiding beings.

The ears are full, long, even in shape,
undamaged, and especially pleasing to the eye.
The forehead is broad and straight.
All of the head's features are perfectly formed.

The hair is fine, dense, never in disarray,
the color of the king of the black bees,
clean, pleasantly fragrant, immaculate,
and possessed of three of the marks.

This has been the description of the eighty secondary characteristics. Because these eighty secondary characteristics are interspersed with and
71c serve to adorn the thirty-two major marks, if one fails to take up contemplative mindfulness of both the thirty-two marks and the eighty secondary characteristics in one's praises of the Buddha's body, then one may lose forever the causal factors conducing to well-being and happiness in the present and future lives.

Chapter 21

Forty Dharmas Exclusive to Buddhas (Part 1)

It is in the above-discussed manner that the bodhisattva uses the thirty-two major marks and eighty secondary characteristics in his contemplative mindfulness of the Buddha's physical body. Now one should proceed to mindfulness of the dharmas exemplifying the Buddha's meritorious qualities, namely:

> One should also use the forty exclusive dharmas
> in one's contemplation of the buddhas,
> for the buddhas are their Dharma body
> and are not merely associated with their physical bodies.

Although the buddhas possess countless dharmas not held in common with any other persons, there are forty dharmas that, if borne in mind, will cause one to experience joyful happiness. And why [should one bear them in mind]? It is not the case that the buddhas are their form bodies, for they are rather to be identified with the Dharma body. This accords with this scriptural testimony: "You should not contemplate the Buddha merely in terms of his form body, for it is on the basis of Dharma that one should carry on such contemplation."

As for the forty dharmas exclusive to the buddhas, they are as follows:[35]

1. Sovereign mastery of the ability to fly;
2. [The ability to manifest] countless transformations;
3. Boundless psychic powers of the sort possessed by *ārya*s;
4. Sovereign mastery of the ability to hear sounds;
5. Immeasurable power of knowledge to know others' thoughts;
6. Sovereign mastery in [training and subduing] the mind;
7. Constant abiding in stable wisdom;
8. Never forgetting;
9. Possession of the powers of the *vajra samādhi;*
10. Thorough knowing of matters that are unfixed;

11. Thorough knowing of matters pertaining to the formless realm's meditative absorptions;
12. The completely penetrating knowledge of all matters associated with eternal cessation;
13. Thorough knowing of the nonform dharmas unassociated with the mind;[36]
14. The great powers *pāramitā;*
15. The [four] unimpeded [knowledges] *pāramitā;*
16. The *pāramitā* of perfectly complete replies and predictions in response to questions;
17. Invulnerability to harm by anyone;
18. Their words are never spoken without a purpose;[37]
19. Their speech is free of errors and mistakes;
20. Complete implementation of the three turnings [of the Dharma wheel] in speaking Dharma;
21. They are the great generals among all *ārya*s;
22–25. They are able to remain unguarded in four ways;[38]
26–29. They possess the four types of fearlessness;
72a 30–39. They possess the ten powers;
40. They have achieved unimpeded liberation.

These are the forty dharmas exclusive to the buddhas. We shall now discuss them more extensively, as below.

[1. Sovereign Mastery of the Ability to Fly]

As for "sovereign mastery of the ability to fly," all buddhas fly with sovereign mastery, entirely as they wish, and with a manner and speed that are limitless and unimpeded. How is this so? If the Buddha wishes to raise one foot and then the other, walking through space in just such a fashion, then he is immediately able to do so. If he wishes to simply step into space and depart in this manner or if he wishes to simply stand motionlessly in space and depart in this way, he is immediately able to do so.

If he prefers to just sit there peacefully in the full lotus posture and depart like that, then he is also able to leave that way. If he wishes instead to lie down peacefully and then depart, he is able to leave in that way as well.

If he decides to stand upon a precious lotus blossom extending to the very boundaries of empty space, one with a blue *vaiḍūrya* stem, real coral petals, pistils of yellow gold, wish-fulfilling pearls for its pedestal, and countless sorts of surrounding phenomena, one that appears like the sun on first rising—departing in just such a fashion—then he does just that.

Or if, alternatively, he wishes to create through spontaneous psychic transformation a palace like the palaces of the sun or moon, like the supremely marvelous palace of Indra, or like those of the Yāma Heaven *deva*s, the Tuṣita Heaven *deva*s, the Nirmāṇarati Heaven *deva*s, the Paranirmitavaśavartin Heaven *deva*s, the Brahma Heaven kings, or like the palaces of any of the other *deva*s, and if he then wishes to create any such palaces, sit down within them, and then depart in that fashion [in one of those flying palaces], then he is immediately able to do precisely that.

Then again, if he prefers to use any of the many other means [for flying from one place to another], then he is freely able to depart however he chooses. Hence it is said, "He is able to completely fulfill whatever wishes he makes." Consequently, with but a single step, the buddhas can pass beyond great trichiliocosms as numerous as the sands of the Ganges.

There are those who claim that the Buddha is able to move beyond some particular number of hundreds of thousands of lands in but a single mind-moment, whereas there are yet others who claim that, if anyone [supposed he could] know that the Buddha could depart such a distance with but a single step and in but a single mind-moment, then that would be [to infer that the Buddha's abilities] could be limited. But the sutras declare that the powers of the buddhas surpass all limits. One should therefore realize that the sovereign power of the buddhas to freely fly through empty space is limitless and boundless.

So how is this the case? Given that one of the great *śrāvaka* disciples using his sovereign mastery of the psychic powers is able in a single mind-moment to pass beyond a hundred *koṭi*s of Jambudvīpas, Aparagodānīya, Pūrvavidehas, Uttarakurus, Four Heavenly Kings Heavens, Trāyastriṃśa Heavens, Yāma Heavens, Tuṣita Heavens, Nirmāṇarati Heavens, Paranirmitavaśavartin Heavens, and Brahma Heavens—and given that there are a particular number of mind-moments in the wink of an eye and given that one might aggregate enough of these mind-moments to comprise a whole day, seven whole days, a whole month, a whole year, and so forth, on up to a full hundred years, and if in only a single day, such a *śrāvaka* disciple might pass through fifty-three *koṭi*s plus two million, nine hundred and sixty-six thousand, that large a number of great trichiliosms, any buddha would still be able in a mere mind-moment to exceed that number of great trichiliocosms passed through by such a *śrāvaka* disciple in the course of a full hundred years.

Then again, if one were to allow the passage of a single *kalpa* for each and every grain of sand in the Ganges—and if there was a great *śrāvaka* disciple foremost in psychic powers who, across the course of a life span of *kalpa*s as numerous as the Ganges' sands, passed through in each successive mind-moment just such a number of world systems [as described above]—and if he were to do this for a number of mind-moments equivalent to a day, month, or year, doing so with the free exercise of all of his powers even to the exhaustion of such a number of great *kalpa*s—all of those lands passed
72b through by that great *śrāvaka* disciple during that entire time could still be passed through by a buddha in but a single mind-moment. The buddhas may freely fly from one place to another with just such a speed as this.

In this, they cannot be obstructed by the Iron Ring Mountains, the ten jeweled mountains, the stations of the Four Heavenly Kings, the stations of the Trāyastriṃśa Heavens, the stations of the Yāma Heavens, Tuṣita Heavens, Nirmāṇarati Heavens, Paranirmitavaśavartin Heavens, Brahma World Heavens, Brahma Assembly Heavens, Great Brahma Heavens, Lesser Light Heavens, Limitless Light Heavens, Light and Sound Heavens, Lesser Purity Heavens, Measureless Purity Heavens, Universal Purity Heavens, Vast Fruition Heavens, Nonperception Heavens, Not Vast Heavens, No Heat Heavens, Delightful Vision Heavens, Sublime Vision Heavens, or the Akaniṣṭha Heaven.

[Nor can their flight be obstructed by] the great winds, by the great floods, or by the fires that occur at the end of the *kalpa*. Nor can it be obstructed by any heavenly dragon, *yakṣa, gandharva, asura, kiṃnara, mahoraga, deva,* Māra, Brahmā, *śramaṇa,* brahman, or anyone possessed of all the psychic powers. It is therefore said of the buddhas that they are unimpeded in their ability to fly.

Additionally, by virtue of the sovereign mastery of their flight, they are able to exercise that ability in any manner they wish, by sinking into or emerging from the earth, or by passing through the obstructions presented by stone cliffs, mountains, and such. The Buddha is superior in this ability to any of the other *ārya*s. Also, the Buddha is able to make his normal standing body reach in its height on up to the Brahma Heavens. *Śrāvaka* disciples are unable to match this. There are all manner of differences of this sort.

[2. (The Ability to Manifest) Countless Transformations]

As for the buddhas' sovereign mastery in "the ability to manifest transformations," in the matter of manifesting phenomena, they have immeasurable power to do this. The capacity to manifest transformations as possessed by the other classes of *ārya*s is both measurable and bounded whereas the buddhas' capacity to manifest transformations is measureless and unbounded.

The other *ārya*s are able, in but a single mind-moment, to manifest a single transformation body whereas the buddhas are able, in but a single mind-moment, to manifest countless phenomena in whatever way they wish.

This is as described in the *Sutra on the Great Spiritual Powers:*

> The Buddha may send forth from his navel a lotus blossom with transformation buddhas sitting atop it that then, in an orderly fashion, fill up all of space on up to the Akaniṣṭha Heaven. The many sorts of transformations created by the buddhas take all sorts of different forms and all sorts of different shapes and are all created in but a single mind-moment.

Also, *śrāvaka* disciples are able to perform transformations within a thousand lands whereas the buddhas are able to freely perform transformations within a countless and boundless number of lands and are additionally able to do much more than this, for the buddhas have gained the solid transformation *samādhi*. Also, the transformations performed by but one of the buddhas' bodies are able to occur in worlds as numerous as the sands of the Ganges.

Additionally, a buddha is able in a countless and boundless number of worlds of the ten directions to manifest a buddha being born, taking on a body, dropping to the earth, taking seven steps, leaving the home life, studying the path, defeating Māra's armies, achieving enlightenment, and turning the Dharma wheel. All of these phenomena are created in but a single mind-moment. All of these transformation buddhas are themselves also able to carry out the work of the buddhas. And the transformation-generated phenomena created by all of those buddhas are themselves countless and boundless.

[3. Boundless Psychic Powers of the Sort Possessed by *Āryas*]

Also, the buddhas have "boundless psychic powers of the sort possessed by *ārya*s." As for "the psychic powers possessed by *ārya*s," this refers to phenomena such as: radiating light from their bodies that may manifest as raging fire and also pouring forth rains; transforming their length of life however they wish, either lengthening it or shortening it; being able in a single thought to go to the Brahma Heaven; being able to perform transformations of various phenomena, being able to shake the great earth whenever they wish; or being able to ceaselessly radiate light capable of illuminating countless worlds.

72c Also, "psychic powers possessed by *ārya*s" are referred to as such because they are incomparably different from those possessed by common people, because of their being boundless, and because of their going beyond all limits. Although common people may possess some ability to perform transformations of various phenomena, their power to do so is so minor as to be beneath mention here.

A *śrāvaka* disciple may be able to split a thousand lands and then cause them to join back together again, may be able to lengthen his life span to a *kalpa* or somewhat less than a *kalpa* in duration and then be able to shorten it, but after having shortened it, he will be unable to make it long again. He may be able in a single mind-moment to go to the Brahma worlds of a thousand lands, may be able to freely perform transformations in a thousand lands, may be able to shake the earth in a thousand lands, may be able to ceaselessly radiate light from his body that can illuminate a thousand lands, and, even if his body is destroyed, he may retain the presence of his spiritual powers and their ability to perform transformations just as before, doing so in a thousand lands.

The lesser *pratyekabuddha* is able to perform a myriad transformations in a myriad lands. The middling *pratyekabuddha* is able to perform a million transformations in a million lands. A great *pratyekabuddha* is able to perform the sorts of transformations cited above, doing so throughout all lands in a great trichiliocosm.

The buddhas, the bhagavats, are able to perform transformations in worlds more numerous than the Ganges' sands wherein they send forth fire and water from their bodies. They are even able to grind to fine dust worlds as numerous as the Ganges' sands and then cause them to be restored. They are able to abide for a life span of countless *kalpa*s, are able to shorten that life span, and having shortened it, they are then able to lengthen it again. They are able to abide for an immeasurably long period of time. They are able to freely perform transformations such that, in the space of but a single mind-moment, they are able to go to countless and boundless worlds as numerous as the sands in the Ganges River.

They are able to cause their usual body, when standing, to reach all the way up to the Brahma worlds. They are also able to perform a transformation whereby countless and boundless *asaṃkhyeya*s of worlds are all caused to be transformed into gold, or into silver, or into *vaiḍūrya,* coral, mother-of-pearl, or carnelian. To sum up the essential point, they are freely able in accordance with their wishes to cause them to be transformed into a countless number of precious things.

They are also able in accordance with their wishes to transform the waters of the great oceans in worlds as numerous as the Ganges' sands into milk, ghee, yogurt, or honey. They are also able in but a single mind-moment to transform incalculably many mountains into real gold.

They are also able to shake the heavenly palaces of the desire realm and form realm heavens of countless and boundless worlds. They are also able in but a single mind-moment to cause gold-colored radiance to so universally illuminate an immeasurably great number of worlds that the light from all those suns and moons and heavenly palaces of the desire realm and the form realm no longer appear at all.

Although a buddha may have already passed into nirvana, afterward, he is still freely ever able in all those worlds to remain for however long he wishes, ceaselessly implementing his spiritual powers.

[4. Sovereign Mastery of the Ability to Hear Sounds]

As for "sovereign mastery in the ability to hear sounds," the buddhas have sovereign mastery in their ability to hear sounds however they please. Even if there were countless hundreds of thousands of myriads of *koṭi*s of musical sounds being simultaneously played and hundreds of thousands of myriads of *koṭi*s of beings simultaneously speaking—whether those sounds are far or near, the buddhas are freely able to hear whichever sounds they please.[39] 73a

If one were to cause all beings in great trichiliocosms as numerous as the Ganges' sands to simultaneously create any given number of hundreds of thousands of myriads of *koṭis* of kinds of music that filled up all those worlds, and if at the same time all beings in worlds as numerous as the Ganges' sands were to fill up all those worlds with the voice of Brahmā, if any buddha wished to hear only one single sound from among all those sounds, then that buddha would be freely able to hear that single sound while not hearing any other sound.

In the case of the sounds heard by *śrāvaka* disciples, if someone possessed of great spiritual powers were to block any given sound, then they would not be able to hear it. In the case of sounds heard by buddhas, even though there might be someone possessed of great spiritual powers seeking to block their hearing some sound, the buddhas are nonetheless able to hear it.

A *śrāvaka* disciple may be able to hear any sound within a thousand lands. The buddhas, the bhagavats, are able to hear even the most subtle sounds even from a distance spanning countlessly and boundlessly many world systems.

A *śrāvaka* disciple possessed of great spiritual powers and abiding in the Brahma World Heavens is able to issue such a great sound that it is capable of pervasively filling a thousand lands. As for the buddhas, the bhagavats, it matters not whether they are abiding here or in the Brahma World Heaven, or are instead in yet some other place—their voices are still able to fill up countlessly and boundlessly many world systems. If they wish to cause a particular being to hear the most subtle sound across a distance of countlessly and boundlessly many worlds, they can cause him to hear it and if they wish to prevent someone from hearing a sound, then that person will indeed be unable to hear it at all. Consequently, it is only the buddhas who have gained sovereign mastery with regard to the hearing of sounds.

[5. Immeasurable Power of Knowledge to Know Others' Thoughts]

As for "measureless power of sovereign mastery in the ability to know others' thoughts," the buddhas, the bhagavats, are completely aware of all the thoughts of all beings of the present existing throughout countlessly and boundlessly many worlds. Others may develop the ability to know someone else's thoughts, but only as represented by the words [contained in others' thoughts]. The buddhas, however, know others' thoughts in terms of the associated meanings of the words [contained in others' thoughts].

Moreover, others remain unable to know the thoughts of beings in the formless realm, but the buddhas are able to know them. Although others may possess the ability to know someone else's thoughts, if anyone possessed of great powers wishes to block that ability, then they will no longer be able to know others' thoughts.

Supposing that all beings had developed psychic powers to the same degree as Śāriputra, Maudgalyāyana, or a *pratyekabuddha*. Now suppose that they used all of their collective spiritual powers to block anyone from knowing someone's thoughts. In such a case, a buddha would still be able to break their spiritual powers and would still succeed in knowing that person's thoughts.

Additionally, a buddha is able to use his spiritual powers to completely know any being's superior, middling, and inferior thoughts, his defiled thoughts, and his pure thoughts. Moreover, he is able to know with regard to each thought, the condition taken as the object of that thought, is able to know also the sequential progression of each thought as it moves from one objective condition to another, and is able to comprehensively know all of the conditions associated with any given thought. Also, he is able to know any being's thoughts in accordance with their true character.

It is on these bases that the buddhas are acknowledged to have immeasurable powers to completely know the thoughts of others.

[6. Sovereign Mastery in (Training and Subduing) the Mind]

As for the buddhas' "*pāramitā* of being foremost in training and subduing the mind," they well know all of the *dhyāna*s, *samādhi*s, and liberations and well understand entry into them, abiding in them, and emerging from them. Whether a buddha is immersed in meditative absorption or not, should he wish to focus his mind on a single object, then he is freely able to focus upon it for however long he wishes and then is able to change from this object to focusing on some other condition, freely abiding in that focus for however long he wishes.

73b If the Buddha, abiding in his normal thoughts, wishes to cause others to remain unaware of his thoughts, then they would be unable to know them. Even if all beings had perfected the ability to know others' minds to a degree comparable to the ability to know others' thoughts as possessed by a king of the Great Brahma Heaven, a great *śrāvaka* disciple, or a *pratyekabuddha,* and they all then caused a single person to acquire their collective abilities in this, and this person then wished to know the normal thought of a buddha, so long as that buddha did not permit it, that person would still be unable to acquire that knowledge.

This is as described in the *Sutra on the Seven Expedients:*

> The practitioner:
> Well knows the signs of meditative absorption;
> Well knows the signs of abiding in meditative absorption;
> Well knows the signs of emerging from meditative absorption;
> Well knows the signs of stable and secure meditative absorption;
> Well knows the signs of the stations of practice in meditative absorption;
> Well knows the signs of the development of meditative absorption;
> And well knows what is and is not appropriate to the dharmas of meditative absorption.[40]

This is what is meant by the buddhas' "*pāramitā* of being foremost in training and subduing the mind."

[7. Constant Abiding in Stable Wisdom]

As for the buddhas' "constant abiding in stable wisdom," the buddhas' stable wisdom is constant and unshakable and their mindfulness is always maintained in their minds. And why is this the case? It is because they first know and then act, because they freely dwell on whichever object they choose while having no doubt in their actions, because they have cut off all afflictions, and because they have gone utterly beyond the realm[41] of movement itself.

This is as the Buddha told Ānanda:

> The Buddha, in this one evening, gains *anuttarāsamyaksaṃbodhi* and proceeds then to teach the path to the ending of suffering to everyone in the world, whether they be a *deva,* Māra, Brahmā, a *śramaṇa,* or a brahman, and then, in the end, finally enters the nirvana without residue.
>
> During the interim, the Buddha, with respect to every feeling, is aware of its arising, is aware of its abiding, is aware of its birth, and is aware of its cessation. With respect to all perceptions,[42] all tactile contact, all ideation, and all mental discursion, he is aware of their arising, aware of their abiding, aware of their birth, and aware of their cessation.

Māra the Evil One,[43] constantly and without resting, followed along after the Buddha both day and night for seven years yet was never in all that time able to come upon any shortcomings of the Buddha and was never able to observe an instance of the Buddha's mindfulness not abiding in a state of stable wisdom. This is what is meant by the Buddha's constant abiding in the practice of stable wisdom.

[8. Never Forgetting]

As for the dharma of "never forgetting," because the buddhas have gained the dharma of irreversibility, have reached a penetrating understanding of the five categorical repositories of dharmas,[44] and have acquired the unsurpassable Dharma, the buddhas never forget.

With respect to all that the buddhas have realized beneath the *bodhi* tree and have then subsequently acquired up to the time when they enter the nirvana without residue, no matter whether it be a *deva,* Māra, Brahmā, a *śramaṇa*, a brahman, or some other *ārya,* there is no one who is able to cause the buddhas to forget anything at all.

This is as described in the *Sutra on the Seal of Dharma,* "As for that which is realized at the *bodhimaṇḍa,* this is known as the genuine realization and there is no dharma superior to it."

This is also as described in the *Horripilation Sutra:*

> Śāriputra. If anyone could claim truthfully that they do not have any aspect of Dharma that they forget, I would be the one who could make that claim. How is this so? I alone do not forget anything whatsoever.

This is what is intended when it is said that the buddhas never forget Dharma.

[9. Possession of the Powers of the *Vajra Samādhi*]

As for the "*vajra samādhi,*" the *vajra samādhi* of all the buddhas, the bhagavats, is one of the exclusive dharmas, [so named:]

Because it cannot be destroyed by anything;
Because there is no place where it can be obstructed;
Because it is associated with right and universal knowledge;
Because it destroys all hindrances to Dharma;
Because it is able to equally penetrate [all dharmas];
73c Because it brings about the power to acquire the benefit of all meritorious qualities;
And because it is the most supreme of all *dhyāna samādhi*s.

As for its being called the "*vajra samādhi*" because there is nothing that can destroy it, it is like the precious *vajra* gem that cannot be crushed by anything at all. This *samādhi* is just like this. There is no dharma capable of destroying it. It is therefore known as the "*vajra samādhi.*"

Question: Why is it that it cannot be destroyed?

Response: This is because there is nothing anywhere that obstructs it. It is just as with Indra's *vajra* that meets no obstruction anywhere. This *samādhi* is just like that.

Question: Why is this *samādhi* said to have nothing anywhere that obstructs it?

Response: Because it possesses a right and utterly penetrating comprehension of all dharmas. All buddhas, abiding in this *samādhi,* are able to utterly penetrate all of the dharmas subsumed within the five categorical repositories of dharmas: all dharmas of the past, of the present, of the future, those that transcend the three periods of time, and those that are ineffable dharmas. It is for this reason that it is said to meet with no obstruction anywhere.

If it were the case that, while abiding in this *samādhi,* all buddhas still did not have an utterly penetrating comprehension of all dharmas, then that would be a case of still having obstructions. But, in truth, this is not the case. It is therefore said to not be obstructed by anything whatsoever.

Question: How is it that this *samādhi* brings about a penetrating comprehension of all dharmas?

Response: It is because this *samādhi* is able to open up all obstructive dharmas, namely the obstacle of the afflictions, the obstacles to meditative absorption, and the obstacles to knowledge. Because it is able to open up all obstructions, it is therefore said to bring about an utterly penetrating comprehension of all dharmas.

Question: How is it that this *samādhi* is able to open up all obstructions whereas other *samādhi*s remain unable to do so?

Response: This *samādhi* is well able to penetrate three[45] dharmas:

Because it is able to destroy the mountain of afflictions so that nothing remains of them;

Because it brings about the right and universal comprehension of all dharmas;

And because it brings about the thoroughgoing attainment of the liberation of the indestructible resolve.

It is for these reasons that this *samādhi* is said to be able to open up all obstructions.

Question: How is it that this *samādhi* is able to equally penetrate these three dharmas?[46]

Response: This is because, when one abides in this *samādhi,* one gains the power by which one is then able to acquire every sort of meritorious quality. None of the other *samādhi*s possess this sort of power. It is for this reason that this *samādhi* is able to "equally penetrate" [all dharmas].

Question: How is it that, abiding in this *samādhi,* one gains the power by which one is then able to acquire every sort of meritorious quality?

Response: This *samādhi* is the foremost among all meditative absorptions. It is because of this that, abiding in this *samādhi,* one is able to gain every sort of meritorious quality.

Question: How is it that this *samādhi* is foremost among all *samādhi*s?

Response: This *samādhi* is foremost among all meditative absorptions because it is produced through the possession of measurelessly and boundlessly many roots of goodness.

Question: How is it that this *samādhi* is produced through the possession of measurelessly and boundlessly many roots of goodness?

Response: This *samādhi* is possessed only by those who are equipped with all-knowledge. It has not been acquired by anyone else. Hence it is known as the "*vajra samādhi.*"

Chapter 22

Forty Dharmas Exclusive to Buddhas (Part 2)

Challenges to the Reality of Omniscience

Question: You claim that only those possessed of all-knowledge possess the *vajra samādhi* and no one else has it. If this *samādhi* was only possessed by someone who has all-knowledge and no one else possessed it, then this *samādhi* does not even exist. Why? Because there is no one who possesses all-knowledge. 74a

And why is this? It is because the dharmas that might be known are measureless and boundless whereas the knowledge that might know them is measurable and bounded. It should not be the case that this measurable and bounded knowledge could know measurelessly many phenomena.

For instance, on the present-day continent of Jambudvīpa, the number of beings dwelling in its waters and on its lands are beyond count. Also, consider the three categories of beings, whether male, female, or neither male nor female, those still in the womb, the children, the young and strong, the frail and old, and also the dharmas associated with their suffering, happiness, and so forth. Also, consider all of the mind and mental dharmas of the past, future, and present, as well as all good and bad karmic actions accumulated in the past, present, and future, all the karmic retributions undergone in the past, present, and future, all the births and deaths of the myriad creatures, and also all of Jambudvīpa's mountains, rivers, springs, ponds, grasses, trees, dense forests, roots, stems, branches, leaves, blossoms, and fruit. The things that can be known are limitlessly many.

The same is true for the other three continents. And just as this is the case with these four continents, it is also the case throughout all of the worlds of the great trichiliocosm. And just as this is the case with all of the worlds of the great trichiliocosm, so too is it also the case for all things that can be known in all other worlds.

As for the number of the worlds, that matter alone is measureless, boundless, and difficult to know. How much the more so is this the case for all of the sentient and insentient beings and all other categories of things on the Jambudvīpa continents in all those worlds.

For these reasons, one should realize that the things that can be known are countless and limitless and, because of that, it cannot be that there is anyone at all who is possessed of all-knowledge.

Suppose that one were to claim that the knowledge [of someone who is omniscient] is possessed of such great power that, because it is unimpeded with respect to those dharmas it cognizes, it is able to pervasively know all those dharmas in just the same manner as empty space is able to reach everywhere in its universal pervasion of all things. Suppose too that one were to claim that, because of this, it ought to be the case that there truly is such a thing as an omniscient person. If one were to make such a claim, this still could not be so, for even if knowledge could possess such a great power as this, even such great knowledge as this would still remain unable to know itself in just the same way that one's fingertip remains unable to touch itself. Therefore, there is no such thing as all-knowledge.

If, [in response to this,] one were to claim that there is yet some other knowledge possessed of the capacity to know this knowledge, this could not be the case, either. And why not? That is because this proposition would then fall into the fallacy of infinite regression. Knowledge either knows itself or is known by something other. They cannot both be true.

If, as you say, this knowledge is somehow possessed of measureless power, because of the fact that it still remains unable to know itself, one really cannot claim that it is possessed of measureless power. Therefore there is no such thing as some knowledge possessed of the ability to know all dharmas.

If there is no such thing as some knowledge possessed of the ability to know all dharmas, then there could not be anyone possessed of all-knowledge. And why is this the case? It is because anyone possessed of all-knowledge [could only be so by] availing himself of just such a [nonexistent] knowledge that knows all dharmas.

Furthermore, the dharmas that can be known are measureless and boundless. Even if one were to employ the combined knowing capacity of a hundred thousand myriads of *koṭi*s of wise men, they would still be unable to exhaustively know them all. How much the less could a single person do so? Therefore there is no such thing as any single person who is able to know all dharmas and there is no such thing as "all-knowledge."

If one were to claim that it is not on the basis of comprehensively knowing every mountain, river, being, or non-being that we speak of someone possessed of all-knowledge, but rather it is simply on the basis of exhaustively knowing all scriptures that one speaks of someone possessed of all-knowledge, this is also wrong. How so? It is because, within the sphere of the Buddha's Dharma, one does not speak of the concepts treated in the Vedas and other such scriptures. If the Buddha really were, [in this sense of the term,] someone possessed of all-knowledge, then he should make use of the Vedas and other such scriptures, but in truth, he does not use these, and so, because of this, the Buddha is not an all-knowing person. 74b

Moreover, the scriptures comprising the four Vedas are themselves measurable and limited in their scope and, even so, there is not even anyone capable of exhaustively knowing those scriptures, how much the less could there be anyone who exhaustively knows all the scriptures in existence? Therefore there is no such thing as a person possessed of "all-knowledge" [even in this limited sense of the term].

Moreover, there are scriptures that are able to cause the proliferation of desire and that devote themselves to such things as dance and music and such. If a person possessed of all-knowledge were to become knowledgeable with respect to these matters, then he would be subjected to the arising of desire. Scriptures of these sorts constitute the causes and conditions for the arising of desire. Where there is a given cause, there must necessarily be the corresponding result [ensuing from it]. If a person possessed of all-knowledge does not know these matters, then he could not be validly referred to as someone possessed of all-knowledge.

Furthermore, there are scriptures that are able to influence a person to become full of hate and to take delight in deceiving others, specifically such works as those classics concerned with ruling the world. Were one to become knowledgeable about such matters, then one would come to be possessed of hatred. How is the case? It is because, where there is such a given cause, then there must necessarily be the corresponding result ensuing from it. And were one to not know such matters, then one could not be validly referred to as possessed of all-knowledge. One should therefore realize that there really is no such thing as a person who is possessed of all-knowledge.

Additionally, it is not necessarily the case that a buddha could exhaustively know matters pertaining to the future. Take for instance my present challenge to the plausibility of there being anyone who is omniscient. The Buddha has no scriptural record of having predicted that in the future there would be this particular man of this particular caste from this particular clan in this particular place who would on these particular grounds challenge the plausibility of there being anyone who might be omniscient. If one were to claim that the Buddha exhaustively knows such things, why did he not speak of this matter? If he is the one who spoke these scriptures, then those scriptures should have a record of such matters, but he did not speak of these matters. Therefore one knows that he was not omniscient.

Moreover, if the Buddha exhaustively knew future matters, then he should have known in advance that, after Devadatta left home to become a monk, he would then create a schism in the sangha. If he had knowledge of that, then he should not have allowed Devadatta to become a monk. Also, the Buddha did not know that Devadatta would use a stick to pry loose a boulder [that would roll down and draw blood from the Buddha's foot]. If the Buddha had known of this matter in advance, then he should not have been walking in that place.

Additionally, the Buddha failed to know in advance that Ciñcā, the brahman woman, would slander him by accusing him of having had sexual relations with her. If the Buddha had known of this in advance, then he should have told the *bhikṣus* that, in the future, there would be just such an occurrence.

Also, there was the case of the *brahmacārin* who, because he was jealous of the Buddha, killed a *brahmacārin* woman named Sundarī in another place and then buried her in a trench in the vicinity of the Jeta Grove. The Buddha did not know of this matter. If he had known of this, then he should have sought among the brahmans to [find a way to] see that her life would be saved.

The Buddha went to that place beneath which Devadatta was about to set loose the falling boulder and he also failed to announce in advance

the incidents having to do with the brahman woman and the *brahmacārin* woman. Because he did not know of these matters, one should realize that the Buddha did not exhaustively know the future. Therefore he could not 74c
possibly have been omniscient.

Furthermore, the Buddha once entered a brahman village seeking food on the almsround but then had to leave with an empty bowl. He was unable then to know in advance that Māra would so turn the minds of the villagers against him that he would be unable to obtain anything to eat. If the Buddha had known of this matter, then he should not have entered that brahman village. Therefore one knows that the Buddha did not exhaustively know how matters would transpire in the future.

Moreover, because King Ajātaśatru wished to harm the Buddha, he released a drunken elephant used to guard the treasury.[47] Because the Buddha did not know of this matter, he entered the city of Rājagṛha on his almsround. If he had known of this matter in advance, then he should not have gone into the city. Therefore he did not have knowledge of future matters. Because he did not have knowledge of future matters, he therefore could not have been omniscient.

Additionally, the Buddha did not know of the causal circumstances involved in Agnidatta's invitation to the Buddha. Consequently he immediately accepted that invitation and then led the *bhikṣu*s to the state of Verañjā. Because this brahman had forgotten his prior issuance of that invitation, he caused the Buddha to eat only horse fodder. If the Buddha had known of this matter in advance, then he should not have accepted that invitation on account of which he spent the entire three months [of the rains retreat] surviving only on horse fodder. We know therefore that the Buddha did not have knowledge of future matters. Because he did not have knowledge of future matters, he therefore could not have been omniscient.

Also, because the Buddha accepted Sunakṣatra as a disciple, he could not have had knowledge of future matters. This man possessed an obdurately evil mind, made himself difficult to teach, and did not believe the words of the Buddha. If the Buddha had known of this, how could he have accepted him as a disciple? Because he accepted him as a disciple, then he could not have known future matters. Because he did not have knowledge of future matters, he therefore could not have been omniscient.

Furthermore, if the Buddha had been omniscient, then, in order to prevent inevitable future instances of moral transgressions, he would have formulated his moral precepts in advance. Because he had no prior knowledge of the causal circumstances that eventually led to the formulation of each particular moral precept, it was only after someone had committed such a transgression that he then subsequently laid down these moral regulations. This being the case, he could not have known of future matters. Because he did not have knowledge of future matters, he therefore could not have been omniscient.

Moreover, in the Dharma set forth by the Buddha, it is solely on the basis of seniority in years of monastic ordination that, within the community, one sits more toward the front and is accorded reverence and obeisance [by those of fewer years of seniority]. One is not acknowledged as of greater eminence merely on the basis of one's venerable age, one's noble birth, the stature of one's clan, one's meritorious qualities, the level of wisdom one has developed, the degree of learning one has achieved, the particular *dhyāna* absorptions one has entered, the fruits of the path one has gained, the fetters one has cut off, or the spiritual powers one has acquired.

If the Buddha had really been someone possessed of all-knowledge, then he would have accorded eminence, higher priority in the receipt of offerings, and stature in receipt of reverential obeisance on the basis of one's venerable age, one's noble birth, the stature of one's clan, one's meritorious qualities, the level of wisdom one has developed, the degree of learning one has achieved, the particular *dhyāna* absorptions one has entered, the fruits of the path one has gained, the fetters one has cut off, and the spiritual powers one has acquired. If the Buddha had made stipulations of this sort, then that would qualify as having established a well-regulated community.

Regarding the matter of years of monastic ordination seniority, this is the principle by which a practitioner of the path ordained for only five years is enjoined to accord reverential obeisance to a monk ordained for six years.

As for the issue of nobility of birth caste, the world has four classes of beings: brahmans, *kṣatriya*s, *vaiśya*s, and *śūdra*s. *Śūdra*s are enjoined to revere *vaiśya*s, *kṣatriya*s, and brahmans. *Vaiśya*s ought to pay obeisance to *kṣatriya*s and brahmans. *Kṣatriya*s are supposed to pay reverential obeisance to brahmans.

As for the status of clans, there are the artisan clans, the business and
trade clans, the merchant clans, the clans led by those of senior status, the 75a
clans of great officials, royal clans, and so forth. Among them, the members of lesser-status clans are supposed to revere members of the eminent clans. This being the case, when those from poor and base clans leave the home life to become monks, they should be enjoined to pay reverence to monks from wealthy and noble clans.

With respect to meritorious qualities, whoever has broken moral precepts should be enjoined to revere and bow in formal obeisance to those who uphold the moral precepts. Those who strictly observe the moral precepts should not be bowing in reverence to anyone who has broken the moral precepts.

Those who do not practice the twelve *dhūta* austerities[48] should bow in reverence to those who are practitioners of the twelve *dhūta* austerities. Those who are not perfectly complete in their practice of the *dhūta* practices should bow in reverence to those who are perfect in their practice of the *dhūta* austerities.

As for the matter of wisdom, people devoid of wisdom should bow in reverence to those possessed of wisdom. With regard to learning, those of shallow learning should bow in reverence to those who have achieved a high level of learning. Those who do not recite many scriptures should bow in reverence to those who are able to recite many sutras from memory.

As for the fruits of the path, the stream-enterer should bow in reverence to the *sakṛdāgāmin* and it should proceed in this fashion on up to [the circumstance where realizers of the first three fruits of the path are enjoined to] bow in reverence to the arhat. As for all of the common people, they should bow in reverence to anyone who has gained any of the fruits of the path. Those who have severed fewer of the fetters as well as those who have not yet severed any of the fetters should all bow in reverence to those who have severed many of the fetters.

Regarding the matter of spiritual powers, if one has not yet acquired any of the spiritual powers, he should then be bowing in obeisance to whomever has already acquired spiritual powers.

If the Buddha had skillfully set forth such sequentially ranked protocols regarding the making of offerings and the according of reverence, then his proclamations on these matters would be of a superior order. But, in truth, he did not do so. One can therefore know that the Buddha was not omniscient.

Furthermore, the Buddha was not even able to know all matters having to do with the present. If you were to ask me how I know that the Buddha did not have knowledge of present-era matters, then I would now inform you as follows:

There were beings whose fetters were but slight, who had no karmic obstacles, who were free of the eight difficulties, who were capable of practicing deep dharmas, and who were able to be successful in the cultivation of right Dharma, and yet the Buddha did not realize this. After the Buddha had attained enlightenment and was first on the verge of proclaiming the Dharma, he gave rise to the following doubt: "The Dharma that I have gained is extremely profound, recondite, far-reaching, sublime, quiescent, difficult to know, difficult to comprehend, and such as only the wise might be able to realize inwardly. The beings in this world are attached by their desires to worldly matters. That there might be any among them who might be able to cut off their afflictions, extinguish craving, and develop renunciation—this would be the rarest of possibilities. If I were to expound the Dharma, beings would fail to comprehend it. Such an endeavor would be but a useless experiencing of wearisome hardship."

And so the Buddha generated just such a doubt even though there were in fact beings whose fetters were but slight, who had no karmic obstacles, who were free of the eight difficulties, who were capable of practicing deep dharmas, and who were able to be successful in the cultivation of right Dharma. Because the Buddha was unable to know of the existence of such beings, one should therefore know that the Buddha failed to know matters having to do with the present time.

The Buddha also thought as follows: "Previously, when I was practicing ascetic austerities, the five *bhikṣus* made offerings to me and supported me. It is only appropriate that I first benefit them. Where are they now?" After he had this thought, a *deva* informed him, "They are now in Benares, in the place known as Deer Park."

Because of this, one knows that the Buddha did not even know of matters having to do with the present. If he failed to know of matters having to do with the present, then we can know from this that the Buddha could not have been omniscient.

Furthermore, after he had attained enlightenment, the Buddha accepted the invitation to expound on Dharma and then had this thought: "As I now proceed to proclaim the Dharma, who is it that ought to be the first to hear it?" He then had another thought, "Udraka Rāmaputra—this is a man of sharp wisdom, one who might easily become enlightened." 75b

By this time, that man had already died and yet the Buddha nonetheless went in search of him. A *deva* then informed him, "His life came to an end just last night." The Buddha thought again and, having reflected, he decided he wanted to liberate Ārāḍa Kālāma. A *deva* then told him, "This man died seven days ago."

If the Buddha had been omniscient, he should have known beforehand that these men had already died, but in truth he did not know these events had happened. Because the Buddha did not know about past matters, he could not have been omniscient.

The methods employed by an omniscient man would be such that he should strive to bring about the liberation of those capable of achieving liberation while setting aside those incapable of success in this.

Moreover, in place after place, the Buddha spoke in terms revealing the presence of doubts on his part. Take for example the city of Pāṭaliputra that he said was bound to be destroyed by one of three causes: by flood, by fire, or by a conspiracy between insiders and outsiders. If the Buddha had really been omniscient, then he should not have had instances where his speech was marked by the presence of doubts. One knows therefore that he could not have been omniscient.

Additionally, the Buddha inquired of the *bhikṣu*s, "What matter have you all come together to discuss?" He asked questions of this sort. If he were omniscient, then he should not have asked about matters of this sort. Because he was compelled to ask others [in order to know of these matters], then he could not have been omniscient.

Also, the Buddha engaged in self-praise while deprecating others. This is as described in the sutras, "The Buddha told Ānanda, 'I alone am foremost, without a peer, unequaled by anyone.'"[49]

He told the *bhikṣu*s, "The Nirgranthas and others of that sort are base and evil people who have perfected the five types of deviant dharmas. The Nirgranthas and such have no faith, have no sense of shame, have no dread of blame, and are people of but little learning who are indolent and possessed of only scant mindfulness and shallow wisdom."

He also discussed all manner of impermissible endeavors engaged in by *brahmacārins*, by Nirgranthas, and by the disciples and other followers of the non-Buddhist traditions.

Self-praise and deprecation of others is a behavior of which even common people of the world are ashamed. How much the more so should this be the case for someone who is omniscient? Because the Buddha engaged in behaviors of this sort, he could not have been omniscient.

Furthermore, comparing beginnings and endings, one finds that the Buddhist scriptures are self-contradictory. Take for instance the statements in the sutras in which, on the one hand, the Buddha claims, "*Bhikṣus*, I am one who has newly discovered the path." Then, on the other hand, he claims, "I have attained that path which has previously been attained by all buddhas of antiquity."

Even wise worldly people abandon any tendency to contradict themselves through chronological inconsistencies. How much the less should it be that a monastic possessed of all-knowledge could stumble into such chronological self-contradictions? Because the Buddha fell into chronological inconsistencies, one should realize that he could not possibly have been omniscient. Therefore your claim that the *vajra samādhi* is only acquired by omniscient men is wrong; this because there is no such thing as an omniscient person. Nor can one establish any case for the existence of some sort of omniscience *samādhi.*

Response: You should not speak this way. The Buddha truly is omniscient. And how is this so? In general, all dharmas are comprised of five categorical repositories of dharmas, namely: past dharmas, future dharmas, present dharmas, dharmas that transcend the three periods of time, and ineffable dharmas. It is only a buddha who completely knows all these dharmas in accordance with reality.

75c I shall now respond to your earlier challenge that asserts, because knowable dharmas are measureless and boundless, there are no omniscient people. Insofar as knowable dharmas might be measureless and boundless, the corresponding knowledge is also measureless and boundless. There is no fault in claiming that it is by means of measureless and boundless knowledge that one may know measureless and boundless dharmas.

As for your earlier assertion that knowing should somehow also involve a knowledge that knows [itself] and that this would entail the fallacy of infinite regress, I shall now respond, as follows:

It should be the case that dharmas are known by one's cognition. This cognition is similar to what is referenced when the world's common people describe themselves in this way: "I am a knowledgeable person," "I am someone with no knowledge," "I am someone possessed of only a coarse type of knowledge," or "I am someone who possesses subtle knowledge."

One should realize from these circumstances that it is with one's own cognitive ability that one knows [the character of one's own] knowledge. This being the case, there is no fallacy of infinite regress involved here. This is just a case of using one's own present cognitive ability to know one's past knowledge. It is in this way that one can exhaustively know all dharmas without any omissions.

Also, this is just like when someone counts others [in addition to oneself], thus reaching [for instance a total of] ten [people in all]. The capacity to know is just like that. For knowing to thereby know both itself and others is thus a concept free of any fault. This is also analogous to when a lamp is able to illuminate both itself and other things as well.

As for your contention that even the aggregated knowing capacity of a hundred thousand myriads of *koṭi*s of wise people could not exhaustively know all dharmas, how much the less might a single person be able to know them—this is wrong. How is this so? An omniscient person is able to know the many things. Although there may be some additional multitude of people, if they have no cognitive ability, they won't know much of anything.

This is comparable to a situation in which there was a group of a hundred thousand blind men. [Even together,] they still could not get hired as guides, but just one single person with good eyes might well be able to serve as a guide. Consequently, as regards your challenge to [the plausibility of omniscience on the part of] a single person, even in a situation where many knowers might be involved, they would still have no knowledge at all compared to the Buddha's capacities in this regard. Therefore your position as stated is erroneous.

As for your contention that, because the Buddha does not discuss the Vedas and other such non-Buddhist scriptures, he must therefore not be omniscient—I shall now respond to that as follows:

The Vedas are entirely lacking in the dharma of [liberation achieved through] skillful realization of nirvana.[50] They contain only all manner of conceptual elaboration. Since what the buddhas proclaim is all entirely devoted to the skillful realization of nirvana, even though the Buddha is already well aware of the contents of the Vedas and other such scriptures, the Buddha does not discuss such things because those [Vedic] teachings have no capacity to lead anyone to the skillful realization of nirvana.

Question: The Vedas *do* contain discussions of the skillful realization of nirvana. Before the arising of this world, all was darkness and nothing whatsoever existed. In the beginning there existed a great man who appeared like the rising of the sun. If one was able to see him, then one could be liberated from the difficulty of being subject to dying.

[The Vedas] contain yet more guidance on these matters. They state that, because one's person is but small, then one's spiritual soul is correspondingly small. However, if one's person is great, then one's spiritual soul will be correspondingly great in scope, for the body is the home of the spiritual soul that always abides within it. If one uses wisdom to untie the bonds restraining one's spiritual soul, one will then gain liberation. Therefore one should realize from this that the Vedas *do* contain teachings leading to liberation through attainment of nirvana.

Response: This is simply not so. Why not? The Vedic scriptures are tied up with the four inverted views. The world is impermanent and yet they posit the existence of a separate and permanent world. They claim that only one or two sacrifices to their *deva* [is insufficient and] conduces to falling away from it, but with a third sacrifice, one will not be subject to falling away from it. This scenario involves the inverted view that falsely ascribes permanence to what is itself impermanent.

76a The world is a place of suffering and yet the Vedas claim the existence of a sphere of eternal bliss. This is just an instance of the inverted view that falsely ascribes bliss to what is inherently bound up with suffering.

The Vedas also claim that one's soul may transform into one's son and be subject through prayer to an extended lifetime of a hundred years. But a "son" is another person, so how could it constitute a self? This is just an instance of the inverted view that falsely ascribes selfhood to what is not actually a self.

They also claim that one's body is possessed of the foremost level of purity and so incomparable in this respect that not even the purity of gold, silver, or precious gems can approach the purity of the body. This is just an instance of the inverted view that falsely ascribes purity to what is devoid of purity.

If one holds inverted views, then [one's views] are devoid of reality. [If such teachings] are devoid of reality, how could they possess [a path to] nirvana? Therefore the Vedas are devoid of any good methods for attaining nirvana.

Question: The Vedas assert that whoever is able to know the Vedas becomes purified and possessed of peace and security. How then can you state that they have no good methods for attaining nirvana?

Response: Although the Vedas assert that whoever knows the Vedas will gain peace and security, this is not ultimate liberation. Rather, this is but an envisioning of liberation projected onto another body. This claim bases itself on the idea that existence in the long-life heavens constitutes liberation. Therefore the Vedas truly contain no means to achieve liberation.

Furthermore, the teachings in the Vedas generally embody three types of concepts: The first involves chants and prayers. The second involves the utterance of praises. The third involves the principles of their dharma.

"Chants and prayers" refers to praying, "May I be caused to obtain a wife and sons, cows, horses, gold, silver, and precious jewels."

"Utterance of praises" refers to statements such as, "Oh, you, the spirit of fire with your black head, your red neck, and your yellow body—you abide eternally in the five great elements of living beings."

"Principles of their dharma" refers to teachings stating that one should do this and abstain from doing that.

Just as with their [erroneous teaching that] fire was first received from the Pleiades, so too, in truth, their methods of using chants and prayers and utterances of praises are all devoid of [any means to achieve] nirvana's liberation. How is this so? Covetous attachment to worldly pleasures, [offerings of] burning ghee, spells, and incantations—these are all devoid of genuine wisdom. Since these do not cut off the afflictions, how could [the Vedas] have [the means to achieve] liberation?

Question: The dharmas in the Vedas have come forth from antiquity and are deserving of the foremost degree of faith. As for your contention that they have no good methods by which one might reach nirvana, they are therefore not fit to be believed, this is wrong. Why? Whereas the Buddha's Dharma has only recently emerged into the world, the Vedas have come down from long distant antiquity and have always prevailed in the world. Therefore, given that ancient dharmas are deserving of belief and newly arisen dharmas are not deserving of belief, your claim that the Vedas are devoid of any good methods by which one might realize nirvana —this is wrong.

Response: Their relative antiquity is no justification for faith. Ignorance tends to come first whereas right knowledge comes only later. Erroneous views emerge first whereas right views emerge later. One cannot have faith in ignorance and erroneous views simply because they happened to emerge first nor can one deem right knowledge and right views to be unbelievable simply because they emerged later. This is analogous to there first being mud and only later lotuses, first being disease and only later a cure. Matters of these sorts are not worthy of being valued simply because they happened to appear first. Therefore, as for your contention that because the Vedas came first and the Buddha's Dharma came later the latter is unworthy of belief, this is a fallacy.

Furthermore, Dīpaṃkara Buddha and the other buddhas of the past all came into the world earlier. Their Dharma principles emerged in antiquity whereas the Vedas actually came forth only later. If you insist on relying on chronological primacy and long history as your bases for according esteem, then the buddhas and their Dharma should be most highly valued.

76b **Question:** You claim it is because the Vedas have no good methods for reaching nirvana that they are therefore not discussed in the Buddha's Dharma. But if the Buddha had really already known they are unable to lead to nirvana, why did he bother to become knowledgeable about them? If in fact he was not *already* knowledgeable about them, he could not have been omniscient. Both stances are faulty.

Response: Your claim is wrong. The Buddha knew from early on that the Vedas have no good methods for reaching nirvana. It is for this reason that he neither discussed them nor practiced what they teach.

Question: If it really was because the Buddha already knew there is no benefit to be had through the Vedas that he therefore instructed others not to cultivate their teaching, what was the point in his acquiring knowledge about them?

Response: People possessed of great knowledge should thoroughly distinguish between the correct path and the erroneous path. It is because one wishes to cause countless beings to go beyond dangerous and bad paths that one takes up the practice of the right path. This is analogous to a guide who skillfully distinguishes between errant paths and the right path.

The Buddha is just the same in this respect. Since he himself had already succeeded in escaping the dangerous path of birth, aging, and death and also wished to cause other beings to escape from it as well, he knew well the genuine eightfold path of the *ārya*s and also knew the dangerous and bad paths of the Vedas and other such teachings. It was in order to facilitate others' abandonment of deviant and bad paths and in order to encourage their practice of the correct path that, [with regard to the Vedas,] he merely became knowledgeable about them, but did not discuss them.

This is analogous to the situation with farmers who plant their fields and then, with the arrival of autumn, reap a harvest that may also happen to include a few useless weeds. The Buddha is like this as well. For the sake of achieving success in the unsurpassable path, he cultivates assiduously and vigorously and consequently gains the path of *bodhi* while incidentally gaining knowledge of the Vedas and other such erroneous paths. Hence there is no fault on his part in any of this.

As for your previous statement claiming that no single person can completely know the four Vedas, this challenge of yours is false. People of the world each have the power of memory. There are those who, in a single day, can only recite five verses from memory, whereas others can recite one or two hundred verses from memory. If a particular person who cannot even recite ten verses from memory then holds the opinion that nobody could be able to recite from memory a hundred or more than a hundred verses, this would be an untruthful claim. It is because people such as yourself are unable to completely know the Vedas that you then claim nobody knows them.

If someone observes that some other person was unable to ford a particular river and then claims that nobody can cross that river, this person's statement on the matter does not qualify as correct speech. Why not? It is because there will naturally be some other person possessed of great strength who can indeed cross that river. This case is just like that. Even if one supposes that other [ordinary people] would be unable to entirely know [the Vedas], what fault is there in stipulating that someone possessed of all-knowledge would know them?

Furthermore, the *pisuo*[51] *ṛṣi*s all study the Vedas and ought themselves to be able to reach all-knowledge. Thus if there are these persons who have completely studied the Vedas, how can you say that nobody can have all-knowledge?

I shall now respond to your [above-stated] claim that there are scriptures which [by their explication of the causes and conditions conducing to desire] are capable of causing one to feel desire or hatred. If one wishes to have a long life, he should abandon causes and conditions conducive to death. The Buddha, too, in this same way, wished to influence beings to cut off their desires and hatreds. This required that he know the causes and conditions that initiate the arising of desire and hatred.

Additionally, as for your contention that, if one is able to know the classical texts concerned with generating desire or hatred, one will then become afflicted with desire and hatred—this is a baseless claim. Although
76c the Buddha had knowledge of these texts, because he did not use them or implement their practices, he was without fault in this respect. So too, if a person merely knows the causes and conditions that precipitate death, this does not entail his dying [as a result]. Only if he were to implement the causes and conditions that precipitate death would he then die as a result. This case is just the same as that one.

I shall now address your contention that, if one does not know future matters, then one does not qualify as omniscient. This does not constitute as a valid challenge. We already know of instances involving challenges to the plausibility of omniscience. As stated in the sutras:

The Buddha told the *bhikṣus*, "The common person bereft of wisdom has three characteristics: He contemplates what he should not contemplate, discusses what he should not discuss, and does what he should not do."[52]

Everything of relevance is already comprehensively mentioned in that statement. You common people of this future time are all included in it. As it would have no particular benefit, what would be the point in his having distinguished and mentioned names and such [related to future events]?

If one were to claim [that there is a contradiction] if the Buddha knew there would be these challenges, yet failed to reply to them in advance, there would really have been no need for this, for, in this presently existing fourfold assembly there are already those well able to cut off doubts in their responses to challenges [such as this]. We now already have those well able to refute challenging inquiries. What then would be the point in [the Buddha himself] responding in advance to such things? Right now, among the *bhikṣus* you encounter in the present day, there are already those well able to refute the tenets posited by brahmans. Therefore there is no need [for the Buddha] to have responded in advance to such challenges.

Furthermore, there have already been prior responses to such challenges that are scattered in various places throughout the many sutras. Because people are unable to completely know the Dharma of the Buddha, they do not know where those passages are located.

I shall now address your challenge on the matter of the Buddha's having allowed Devadatta to leave the home life and become a monk. As for your opinion that, if the Buddha allowed Devadatta to leave the home life, he could not have been omniscient, this statement is wrong. When Devadatta left the home life to become a monk, it was not the Buddha who was involved in allowing him to become a monastic.

Question: Even if it was someone else who allowed him to become a monastic, why did the Buddha allow this to happen?

Response: The doing of good and the doing of evil each have the season in which they occur. It was not necessarily the case that, having left home, he would immediately embark on doing evil. After Devadatta left home to become a monk, he had all of the meritorious qualities that are associated with upholding the moral precepts. Therefore there was no fault in [permitting] his leaving the home life.

Additionally, for twelve years, Devadatta was pure in his observance of the moral precepts and also became able then to recite from memory sixty-thousand lines from the treasury of Dharma. The karmic reward from this is such that, in the future, [such cultivation] will not have been in vain. In fact, it will definitely benefit him later on.

I will now reply to your statement regarding Devadatta's prying loose of a boulder [in an attempt to murder the Buddha]. Because all buddhas have already perfected the dharma of not killing, nobody in any world can ever rob them of life.

Question: If the Buddha had actually perfected the dharma of not killing, why did the boulder shatter and [cause a piece] to come down [and strike him in the foot]?

Response: The Buddha had planted karmic causes associated with damage to the body for which he was bound to undergo this fixed retribution. He manifested the appearance of having to undergo it in order to demonstrate to beings that karmic retributions cannot be escaped. It was for this reason that he voluntarily came to that place.

I shall now respond to your contention that there was some problem in the Buddha's not having spoken in advance about the incident involving that woman, Ciñcā. There is nothing in that woman, Ciñcā's, disparaging of the Buddha that can serve as a causal basis for impugning his qualification as omniscient. If the Buddha had announced in advance, "In the future, that woman, Ciñcā, will come forth and slander me," then that woman, Ciñcā, would not in fact have come forth as she did. Furthermore, it was due to the karmic causes and conditions associated with the Buddha's having slandered others in a previous lifetime that he was now definitely bound to undergo [the corresponding retribution].[53]

I shall now address your challenge as to how it could have been that the Buddha failed to prevent the incident that occurred when Sundarī entered the
77a Jeta Grove.[54] This incident does not constitute a reason for impugning the Buddha's qualification as omniscient. The Buddha does not have some power by which he is able to cause every being's life to be an entirely happy one.

Also, the buddhas have all left behind disputation, do not elevate themselves, and are not attached to [making others] uphold moral precepts, consequently he did not act to prevent this incident.

Additionally, it was because of the ripening of karma from a previous life that he was definitely bound to undergo that seven days of slander. Moreover, when beings observed that the Buddha was neither perturbed over hearing himself slandered nor joyful when his innocence was made clear, they brought forth the resolve to follow the unsurpassable path, uttering this vow, "We too shall acquire just such a pure mind as this." Therefore there was no fault [in the Buddha's having acted as he did].

I shall now respond to your contention that, because the Buddha entered a brahman village and then left with an empty bowl, he was therefore not omniscient.[55] The Buddha [did not go to that village] for the sake of food and drink, [but rather because] he had contemplated the minds of the people there. It was only after he entered the village that Māra changed the villagers' minds.

Question: This is a matter about which the Buddha should have become aware in advance, thinking, "If I go into this village, Māra will change these peoples' minds."

Response: The Buddha in fact *did* know about this matter in advance [and entered that village anyway] in order to bring great benefit to those beings. It is not solely on the basis of receiving almsfood from them that the buddhas benefit beings and facilitate their liberation. There were those who welcomed him there with pure minds, bowed in reverence to him, and looked up to him with congenial gazes. All of these things already served great benefit. Why should it be an essential requirement that he be given food and drink? There are many different sorts of methods by which he was able to be of benefit to beings. Thus it was not in vain that he entered that village.

I shall now respond to your statement about the Buddha's having gone up the road on which there was a drunken elephant.[56] Although the Buddha already knew of this matter, there was a reason he deliberately went there. It was because this drunken elephant was definitely at a point where he could be brought across to liberation. The Buddha was also intent on preventing his falling into the karmic offense of harming a buddha.

Additionally, this elephant's body had the appearance of a black mountain. When the population there saw this elephant bow down its head in reverence to the Buddha, they all brought forth thoughts of reverence. It was for these reasons that the Buddha deliberately went up that road. Also, there was no error involved in the Buddha's having entered that road to encounter that elephant. Only if some unfortunate incident had transpired would you have a basis for bringing up this challenge.

As for your challenge regarding the Buddha's having gone to Verañjā, that was simply a case of having to undergo retribution for karmic deeds committed in a previous life.[57]

I shall now address your statement on the issue of the Buddha's having accepted Sunakṣatra as a disciple.[58] The Buddha has no need to guard against errors in actions of body, speech, mind, or livelihood.[59] It was because he is utterly without fear that he permitted Sunakṣatra to become a disciple.

Also, because this man always dwelled in close proximity to the Buddha, he was thus able to observe the display of all manner of spiritual powers and also saw the arrival of *deva*s, dragons, *yakṣa*s, *gandharva*s, *asura*s, kings, and others, all coming to make offerings to the Buddha and to pose respectful questions to him on all manner of extremely profound and essential dharmas. Hence his mind was thereby able to become purified. Because he was able to achieve purification of mind, this was a causal basis for his [eventual] benefit. Therefore, even though he was an evil man, the Buddha nonetheless accepted him as a disciple.

Question: This man had many evil thoughts about the Buddha. Therefore the Buddha should not have permitted him to become a disciple.

Response: Even if the Buddha had not accepted him as a disciple, the man still would have had those evil thoughts. Therefore there was no fault in the Buddha's permitting him to become a disciple.

I shall now respond to your challenge as to why the Buddha did not formulate the moral precepts in advance of [his disciples'] commission of
77b the corresponding transgressions. The Buddha did in fact formulate moral precepts in advance. He set forth the eightfold path of the *ārya*s that consist of right view, right thought, right speech, right action, right livelihood, right effort, right mindfulness, and right meditative concentration. Because he did

describe this path leading to the attainment of nirvana, he in fact had already formulated all of the precepts.

Furthermore, the Buddha described the three trainings wherein one thoroughly trains in moral virtue, thoroughly trains in [focusing] the mind, and thoroughly trains in wisdom. One should then realize from this that he had in fact already set forth all of the moral precepts.

Additionally, the Buddha told the *bhikṣus* that they should definitely not do any sort of evil. Does this not constitute prior formulation of moral precepts?

Also, the Buddha spoke of the path of the ten courses of good karmic action, namely abandoning killing, stealing, sexual misconduct, divisive speech, harsh speech, false speech, frivolous speech, covetousness, ill will, and wrong views. Does this not constitute prior formulation of moral precepts?

Twelve years earlier, the Buddha described in a single verse the *upoṣadha* dharma,[60] namely:

> To refrain from doing any sort of evil deed,
> to respectfully engage in every sort of good deed,
> and to purify one's own mind—
> This is the teaching of all buddhas.[61]

One should therefore realize that the Buddha in fact *did* formulate the moral precepts in advance.

Also, the Buddha stated that one should abandon even all of the most minor causes and conditions associated with evil, as stated in these lines:

> Abandon all evil actions of the body.
> Also abandon all evil speech,
> abandon all evil actions of the mind,
> and utterly abandon all other forms of evil.

On the basis of statements such as these, one should realize that the Buddha had already formulated the moral precepts in advance. Additionally, the Buddha had already described in advance the dharmas through which one guards against transgressions, as stated in these lines:

To guard the body is good indeed.
To be able to guard one's speech is also good.
To guard one's mind is good indeed,
and to guard against all errors is good as well.[62]
The *bhikṣu* guards against all errors
and thereby succeeds in abandoning all evil.

One should realize on the basis of these statements that the Buddha in fact *did* formulate the moral precepts in advance. Moreover, the Buddha also described in advance the characteristics of goodness, as stated in these lines:

Do not allow hands or feet to carelessly commit transgressions.
Restrain your words and take care in actions done.
One should take pleasure in guarding and focusing the mind.
It is on these bases that one is rightfully called a *bhikṣu.*[63]

One should realize on the basis of statements such as this that the Buddha in fact *did* formulate the moral precepts in advance.

Furthermore, because the Buddha described the dharmas by which one is a *śramaṇa,* one should realize he did in fact formulate the moral precepts in advance. There are four dharmas by which one is a *śramaṇa:* First, one does not respond in kind to hateful actions. Second, one remains silent in the face of scolding. Third, one is able to endure even being beaten with staves. And fourth, one maintains patience with those who have dealt one harm.

Moreover, the Buddha taught the four stations of mindfulness, namely the contemplation of the body, the contemplation of feelings, the contemplation of thoughts, and the contemplation of dharmas, doing so because they constitute the abode of the path to nirvana. Hence one should realize that he *did* formulate the moral precepts in advance.

The Buddha would not even permit the most subtle form of evil, how much the less would he condone any sort of evil karma in one's physical
77c actions or speech? For reasons such as these, one should realize that he did indeed formulate the moral precepts in advance.

This is analogous to a king's establishment of laws in which one is forbidden to do evil deeds. When, later on, there are transgressions against those laws, it is according to the relative gravity of the crime that corresponding punishments are imposed. The Buddha is just the same in this respect. He first made general statements describing the moral precepts. Later on, when offenses occurred, he described the specific characteristic factors by which the given action constituted an offense.

Where there were those who committed evil deeds, they were instructed and caused to repent. He instructed that, for a given offense, a given corresponding form of penance was to be performed or that either temporary expulsion or complete expulsion was stipulated so that the miscreant could not dwell together with the community, and so forth. It was only with the establishment of these sorts of cases that we came to have the subsequent formulation of moral precepts.

I shall now address your contention that superior position in the monastic community should be accorded on the basis of age, nobility of birth caste, status of one's clan, and so forth. In the dharmas of the path, issues of age, nobility of birth caste, status of one's clan, and so forth afford no benefit. How is this so? It is on the basis of being born into the Dharma of the Buddha that one qualifies as being born into nobility and into a fine clan. Seniority is determined on the basis of the number of years one has received the higher ordination and this is the rationale for being referred to as an elder.

As for your opinion that those who are merely older in years should be given priority in the receipt of offerings, is it not the case that those who first left the home life and received the ordination precepts are better regarded as of greater eminence?

Furthermore, from the time one receives the ordination precepts onward, there are no longer any distinctions on the basis of one's caste and such. It is only when *bhikṣus* receive the precepts of the higher ordination that they then qualify as having been born into the family of the buddhas. It is at this point that one loses any name associated with prior birth into a greater or lesser clan and everyone then belongs to this one single family.

As for your statements on upholding the precepts—those who first left the home life to become monastics and who have observed the moral precepts for the longest time and then proceed to uphold those moral precepts for a long time—it is because of their years of seniority in this that they should be accorded a superior position within the monastic community. This is as set forth in the original formulation of the moral precept code.

I shall now address your contention that those who are most strictly observant in their upholding of the moral precepts should not bow in reverence to those who have broken the moral precepts. Those who truly have broken the moral precepts should not even be allowed to dwell together with the community, how much the less should they receive reverential obeisance or offerings?

It is on the basis of their claim to be a *bhikṣu* that one pays reverence to them according to their order of seniority. This is similar to when one bows in reverence before a deity's image made of clay or wood, doing so as a means of bearing in mind that actual deity. The Buddha decreed that those of fewer years seniority should revere those who are seated in a superior position within the monastic order. It is through according with the Buddha's instructions in this that one acquires karmic merit.

I shall now respond to your statement that the according of reverence should be based on one's practice of the *dhūta* austerities. In this matter of those who take up the *dhūta* practices, there are five general types of practitioners among which it is difficult to make clear distinctions:[64]

78a First, there are those who are deluded and who, due to an absence of right knowledge, are driven by desire to practice these difficult dharmas;
Second, there are those possessed of only dull faculties who wish to acquire benefits as a result;
Third, there are those with evil intentions focused on deceiving others;
Fourth, there are those who are mentally ill;
And fifth, there are those who [take them up], thinking, "The dharmas of the *dhūta* austerities are praised by all buddhas, worthies, and *ārya*s because they accord with the path to nirvana."

Among these five classes of practitioners of the *dhūta* austerities, it is difficult to distinguish which are genuine and which are false.

Now, as for this matter of one's level of learning, just as with the *dhūta* austerities, it is difficult to distinguish clearly among those who have acquired abundant learning. How is this so? It could be that it is on the basis of delighting in the path that one has accrued much learning. Or perhaps it is only for the sake of receiving offerings that one has accrued much learning. It is difficult to make clear distinctions in matters such as these.

Additionally, in the Dharma of the Buddha, it is practice in accordance with one's words that is accorded esteem. One does not accord esteem merely on the basis of having engaged in much study or having become able to recite many scriptures. Also, according to the statements of the Buddha himself, if one practices but a single sentence of Dharma and is thereby able to derive self-benefit from that, this itself qualifies as abundant learning.

So too it is with this matter of wisdom. If one remains unable to implement a level of practice consistent with one's level of discourse, of what use is this wisdom? Consequently, it is not on the basis of one's degree of wisdom that one determines who is accorded a superior position in the monastic order.

This is analogous to the current way of doing things in the world. Although a younger brother may indeed be more learned or more wise, the elder brother is still not enjoined to pay him reverence. Therefore, after this same fashion, it is not on the basis of one's level of wisdom that one gains priority in the receipt of offerings or reverence. So it is then that, even though one may indeed have accrued much learning or wisdom, one should still accord reverence on the basis of who first received the ordination precepts. Were one to accord priority in the receipt of offerings to those of greater learning or a higher level of wisdom, this would inevitably result in discord within the community.

As for the other [criteria you propose for priority in according reverence], namely realization of the *śramaṇa*'s fruits of the path, severance of fetters, and acquisition of spiritual powers, those are the most difficult matters to know. Whether or not this person has attained a fruit of the path, whether he has cut off more fetters or fewer fetters [than this other person], and whether or not he has acquired spiritual powers—one cannot use such matters as the basis for superior position in the monastic order. Consider for instance those who have realized the same fruits of the path, cut off the same fetters, and acquired the same spiritual powers. Who among them should be accorded superior position in the monastic order? Consequently, it is by far the best to simply accord with the Buddha's instructions on these matters.

I shall now address your contention that the Buddha himself was beset by doubt about whether he should expound the Dharma.[65] The Buddha had no doubts at all even with regard to the most profound sorts of dharmas, how much the less might he have had doubts with regard to whether or not he should expound the Dharma? The Buddha never said that he would entirely forego his teaching of the Dharma. He merely indicated a preference for continuing to abide in serenity, refraining from becoming involved in numerous endeavors. There was no fault in his having simply waited till later to begin expounding the Dharma.

Also, the non-Buddhist partisans would say, "If the Buddha is such a great *ārya* that he remains silent and declines to involve himself in conceptual elaboration, what use could he have for assembling a following and offering to give teachings?" Then again, once he started teaching, this would inevitably turn into an endless endeavor. It was as if he was weighing the utility of proceeding to teach the Dharma and assemble a group of disciples when this could appear outwardly as if it were a mark of covetous attachment.

Due to these factors, the Buddha reflected, "Though my Dharma is extremely deep, the wisdom and skillful means that might be employed in teaching it would be measureless and boundless. Still, those who are actually amenable to gaining liberation are but few." Consequently, he thought to himself, "It would be better to remain silent." It was also to defend against the potential for mocking deprecation by non-Buddhist partisans that he instead influenced the Brahma Heaven King to [first] request the proclamation of Dharma. The Brahma Heaven King and others then immediately addressed the Buddha, saying, "Beings are surely worthy of pity. There are among them those of sharp faculties and but few fetters who would be easy
78b to teach and bring across to liberation."

Because of this, the Buddha acceded to the request of the Brahma Heaven King and others. It was as if someone who had just found a great treasury of jewels felt he should reveal their presence to others. In this same way, when *ārya*s themselves gain the benefits of the Dharma, they feel they should also use it to benefit others.

I shall now address your contention that, because the Buddha expressed a wish to discourse on the Dharma for Ārāḍa Kālāma and the others and therefore had not realized they had already died, [this contradicts the plausibility of his being omniscient]. The Buddha had not brought to mind the issue of whether or not they had already died, but rather was only considering the fact that, because these men's fetters were but scant, they would be capable of being instructed and brought across to liberation. It is in correspondence with the point upon which one's thought is focused that a corresponding knowledge arises. It was as a consequence of this that the Buddha first said this to himself and a *deva* then appropriately informed him.[66]

Also, since earlier on, when the Buddha had just abandoned the home life, he had gone to those men, [Ārāḍa Kālāma and Udraka Rāmaputra,] and had spent time with them, the *deva*s and other people could have entertained doubts in which they thought the Buddha had perhaps received the sublime Dharma from them and had then become enlightened in another location. Because the Buddha wished to cut off any doubts that they might have had, he immediately exclaimed, "Oh those men—they have for so long suffered such misfortune as this? How can it be that they have still not heard this sublime Dharma?"

By inferring the implications of this idea, one can deduce the nature of the matter of the five *bhikṣu*s. It was because the Buddha had only brought to mind the causes and conditions associated with their capacity to gain liberation that he had not yet considered precisely where they were currently dwelling. Afterward, once he had thought about where they were dwelling, he then knew where they were.

Therefore one should not look upon these issues as refuting the plausibility of there being an omniscient person.

I shall now address your stated doubt with regard to the causes for the destruction of the city of Pāṭaliputra. The precise causes and conditions by which this city would meet its destruction were still unfixed. To make a fixed pronouncement on the unfolding of unfixed causes and conditions would itself be a fault.

Also among the forty exclusive dharmas listed earlier, I stated that all buddhas are thoroughly cognizant of dharmas that are unfixed. In response then, I do not accept this challenge as valid.

I shall now address your contention about the Buddha's querying the *bhikṣu*s as to the contents of their conversation by asking, "So, what are you all gathered together to discuss?" It was because the Buddha was about to hold forth on some aspect of Dharma that he initiated the discussion by asking a question of this sort. It could have been that, because he wished to formulate another of the moral prohibitions, he directed them to talk about what they were discussing. Because he took all sorts of such instances as occasions for speaking Dharma, the Buddha's posing a question was free of any fault [in relation to the issue of his omniscience].

Furthermore it is a commonplace in the world, even when one is already well aware of what is happening, for one to go ahead and ask a question. For instance, on observing someone eating, one may ask, "Oh, so you're eating, are you?" Or, for instance, on a particularly cold day, one may ask, "Isn't it cold?"

In this same way, even though he already knew, the Buddha would nonetheless pose a question. Being but a means of conforming to convention, this is entirely free of fault.

I shall now address your judgment that anyone who praises himself and criticizes others could not possibly be an omniscient person. The Buddha entertained no desires with respect to himself and so was not the least bit covetous of receiving offerings. He did not hate other men and was not possessed of overweening pride. As for the reason for his having declared himself to be foremost among everyone in the world, it was because there were beings who were amenable to faith and possessed of acutely sharp faculties who, if they cast aside bad spiritual guides and took the Buddha as their teacher, they could then gain that peace and security that would see them through the long night [of subsequent rebirths]. It was for this reason that the Buddha did in fact praise his own personal qualities.

Additionally, there were those who, although they sought the path to the supreme bliss, were still indolent and unable to bring forth vigorous effort. Consequently the Buddha declared, "In this matter of gaining the most supreme benefit, one must not be indolent. I am the supreme spiritual guide in this world, the one who well proclaims right Dharma. It is only fitting then that you become assiduous and vigorous, for it is only then that you may gain the fruits of the path." And so it was that, for reasons such as these, the Buddha did indeed praise his own personal qualities. It was not
78c out of a wish to be accorded esteem, nor was it out of a wish to slight and deprecate others.

In cases where the Buddha rebuked evil men, it was for the sake of inducing them to get rid of evil dharmas. It was not because he detested other beings. In some cases, there were those seeking to achieve benefit through

Dharma, people whose minds were pure and of straightforward character, but who were locked in relationships with bad spiritual guides. In order to induce them to abandon these bad teachers, the Buddha would sometimes criticize and rebuke them. Even before he had achieved buddhahood, [in earlier lifetimes] he even sacrificed his own brain and the very marrow of his bones as gifts to others. How much the less could it be that, once he had already attained buddhahood, he would be inclined to berate and scold others?

I shall now respond to your contention that there were chronologically contradictory tenets in the Buddha's Dharma. There are no contradictions present in the Dharma of the Buddha between what came at the beginning and what followed later on. It is only because you and your cohorts do not understand the concepts involved in the Buddha's Dharma that you have the opinion that it is inherently contradictory.

This path leading to the realization of nirvana had not been either proclaimed or realized by anyone during the entire time between Kāśyapa Buddha's nirvana on forward to the present. It was for this reason that the Buddha declared, "I am he who has newly attained the path." In other places, he also said, "I have attained the ancient path." The path is that which was previously realized by Dīpaṃkara Buddha and the other buddhas of the past, namely the eightfold path of the *ārya*s that is able to lead one to nirvana. It is because, in all these cases, it is but a single path relying on but a single set of causes and conditions that it is referred to it as "the ancient path." One should realize from this that the Buddha did obtain all-knowledge.

Question: As for the so-called "all-knowledge," precisely what is it that constitutes all-knowledge? Is it really on the basis of knowing absolutely everything that it is referred to as "all-knowledge"?

Response: "All-knowledge" refers to knowing all that can be known. "What can be known" refers to the five categorical repositories of dharmas, namely all past, future, and present dharmas, the dharmas that transcend the three periods of time, and the ineffable dharmas. That which is used in knowing these five categories of dharmas is cognition. Hence it is both cognition and those things that it knows that are referred to as the "all" [in the term "all-knowledge"].

Question: As for this contention that it is both the faculty of cognition and those things it knows that together comprise the "all" [of all-knowledge], this is wrong. How so? This is but a singular dharma, this because that cognition that is capable of knowing is itself knowable as when people of the world speak of this person's cognitive ability as sharp whereas that person's cognitive ability is dull.

Response: Well, if as you state that "all" is itself just a singular entity, then it should be that those polar opposites such as "hot" and "cold" are but one thing. And so too it should be that "bright" and "dark," "suffering" and "happiness," and all polar opposites should in each case be but a single thing. But this is not the case. Therefore, one cannot claim that "all" is but a singular entity.

Question: That idea to which you are clinging is itself possessed of this same fault. If the faculty of cognition is one thing, then [that which it knows, namely] "suffering," "happiness," and so forth—those should all also be but singular entities, but in truth, they are not.

Response: I never claimed that everything that can be known is, [in aggregate,] but one single thing. Now that idea to which *you* are clinging is indeed that everything [that can be known] *is* somehow, [in its collective aggregate,] but a single thing. Therefore, [what I am saying] is not the same as that faulty concept you are proposing.

Furthermore, since you claim that [both of] these positions are equally at fault, that idea to which you are clinging is faulty. In a case where someone accepts that the idea he is proposing is faulty, his position is thereby refuted. Now, when you understand that the idea to which you have been clinging is faulty, you should not continue to claim that someone else is the party whose position is faulty. Hence, as for your contention that what I have set forth here is somehow possessed of the same fault that characterizes your position—this is wrong.

Moreover, if you claim that the two dharmas consisting of the faculty of cognition on the one hand and that which is known on the other are somehow but a single entity, then one should be able to use any particular knowable dharma to know phenomena like vases and robes and such, but in truth it is solely the faculty of cognition that can be used in the knowing of all things.

If you are going to claim that phenomena like vases and robes and such
are no different from the faculty of cognition—this vase and robe and so 79a
forth—they are entirely unable to know any phenomenon at all. It immediately follows that it ought to be the case that they are different [from the faculty of cognition] and it is truly the case that one uses the faculty of cognition to know everything.

Because your position is faulty in these ways in place after place, you cannot thus claim that the constituent phenomena forming the "all" of all-knowledge are all collectively but a single thing.

So, again, the faculty of cognition and that which is known, these two things—they are what constitute the "all" of "all-knowledge," this because they together constitute all dharmas. It is because of the Buddha's knowing of all of these dharmas that he is known as the Tathāgata and is renowned as one who is possessed of all-knowledge. This omniscient man became possessed of all-knowledge because of the *vajra samādhi*. Therefore the *vajra samādhi* is indeed something that can be established. As for your initial contentions that the *vajra samādhi* cannot be established and that "all-knowledge" is also not something that can be established, these contentions are both wrong.

Chapter 23

Forty Dharmas Exclusive to Buddhas[67] (Part 3)

[10. Thorough Knowing of Matters That Are Unfixed]

As for knowing well the unfixed dharmas, the Tathāgata's wisdom has achieved power within the sphere of all dharmas even at that point when they have not yet arisen, have not yet come forth, have not yet reached completion, have not become definitively fixed, and have not yet become clearly distinguishable. This is as stated in the *Sutra on the Buddha's Distinguishing of Karma:*

> The Buddha told Ānanda, "There are people who practice good deeds with the body, who practice good deeds through speech, and who practice good deeds with the mind, and yet, when their lives come to an end, they then fall into the hells. There are yet other people who practice evil deeds with the body, who practice evil deeds through speech, and who practice evil deeds with the mind, and yet, when their lives come to an end, they are nonetheless reborn in the heavens."
>
> Ānanda addressed the Buddha and asked, "Why do events occur in this way?"
>
> The Buddha replied, "It may have been that the causes and conditions associated with previous life karmic offenses or meritorious deeds had already ripened, whereas the karmic offenses or meritorious deeds of the present life had not yet ripened. Or, alternatively, when approaching the end of life, they gave rise to either right views or erroneous views that precipitated either wholesome or evil thoughts, this because the power of the thoughts produced as one approaches the moment of death—their power is immense."[68]

Additionally, the *Śuka Sutra* states:

> Śuka, son of a brahman, addressed the Buddha and asked, "Gotama, why is it that the brahman laity are in some cases able to cultivate meritorious deeds and roots of goodness in a manner superior to that of some of those who have left the home life and become monastics?"
>
> The Buddha replied, "For these sorts of matters, I do not present a fixed reply. There may be cases in which someone who has left behind the home life does not cultivate goodness and, as a consequence, in this endeavor, he does not equal the efforts of a given householder. This is a case in which a householder is able to cultivate goodness in a manner superior to that of a particular monastic."

Furthermore, the *Great Nirvana Sutra* states that the city of Pāṭaliputra is bound to be destroyed by one of three circumstances: by flood, by fire, or by a conspiracy between insiders and outsiders.

Also, [another example of an unfixed statement] arose because of a *brahmacārin* named Patikaputra about which the Buddha said:

> As for this naked ascetic, the *brahmacārin* named Patikaputra, if he fails to relinquish this statement, these thoughts, and these wrong views, then it will be impossible for him to come and appear before me. He will either be trapped by a broken rope or prevented from leaving by a broken body. In any case, he will never be able to arrive here in the presence of the Buddha.

Additionally, in the *Sutra on the Analogy of the Raft,* the Buddha said:

> This Dharma of mine is extremely deep. It is by resort to expedients that I enable even those who are shallow to easily reach an understanding of it. If there be anyone possessed of a straightforward mind who is willing to practice in accordance with the teachings, he will gain one of two kinds of benefit from this, either the cessation of the contaminants in this present lifetime or, in the event that he doesn't achieve the cessation of the contaminants, he will still succeed in attaining the path of the nonreturner (*anāgāmin*).[69]

Also, in the *Ekottara Āgama*'s *Shejiali Sutra,*[70] the Buddha told Ānanda:

79b

> As for whosoever deliberately undertakes the requisite karmic actions, none among them will fail to gain the karmic rewards and thus achieve

> success in the path, whether that be through receiving the results of present-life karma in this present life, whether that be through receiving them in the next birth, or whether that be through receiving them in subsequent lives.[71]

In addition, we also have this statement in the *Ekottara Āgama*'s *Afuluo Sutra:*[72]

> The Buddha told the *bhikṣus*, "When evil people die, they may become animals or they may fall into the hells. Good people will be reborn either in the heavens or among humans."

Also, the *Prince Fearless Sutra* states:

> Prince Fearless addressed the Buddha, saying, "Does the Buddha not have instances in which what he proclaims is able to cause others to become angry?"
>
> The Buddha replied, "Prince, this is an unfixed matter. It may happen that the Buddha, motivated by pity, will influence someone to become angry with the intended result that they will thereby plant the causes and conditions for goodness. This is analogous to a wet-nurse having to use a crooked finger to clear an infant's mouth of some dangerous object. Although it may inflict injury, it is done in order to prevent a calamity."[73]

There is also the statement recorded in the Abhidharma: "Beings fall into three groups. From the [karmically] indefinite group, they may fall into the definitely deviant group or the definitely righteous group."[74]

There are several thousand or even myriads of similar such types of unfixed phenomena that are cited within the four repositories of the Dharma.[75]

Question: If a person's wisdom is unfixed and characterized by indefinite thought that takes a given circumstance to perhaps be this way or perhaps not be this way, then this is not someone who is omniscient. One who is omniscient would not make two different statements [with regard to a single matter], but rather would instead be able to make definitive pronouncements, pronouncements that are utterly clear. Because of this, "thoroughly knowing unfixed matters" cannot be referred to as a dharma exclusive to the Buddha.

Response: Unfixed matters are such that they may either be this way or not this way. It is because they develop in accordance with a multiplicity of causes and conditions that one should not make definite pronouncements about them.

Moreover, were one to offer definite answers regarding indefinite phenomena, then that itself would indicate that one is *not* omniscient. Consequently, in assessing unfixed phenomena, it is essential to employ the knowledge of unfixed matters. Hence there is this exclusive dharma referred to as "the knowledge of unfixed matters."

Additionally, if one were to claim definitive knowledge with respect to all dharmas, then one would fall into the erroneous determinist fallacy. If all dharmas really were already definitely fixed, then all that one does would not require any human effort and skillful means to bring it about. This idea is as set forth here:

> If good or bad experiences were already definitely determined,
> then the character of a person's efforts should be fixed as well.
> There would be no need for any of the causal factors
> involved in the skillful means that one uses in one's cultivation.

Moreover, it is already manifestly clear that if one fails to take care with regard to one's personal behavior, then one will bring about manifold sufferings, whereas, if one is guarded with respect to one's personal behavior, then one will enjoy peace and benefit as a result of doing so.

Also, this is just as in all sorts of endeavors involved in carrying on one's livelihood wherein, on the one hand, one is required to endure a good deal of weariness and suffering to later acquire a reward in the form of all manner of wealth and happiness, whereas, on the other hand, someone else is able to simply remain still and silent in this present life, doing nothing whatsoever, only to then reap karmic rewards. So it is that there are these unfixed circumstances. It is because they are cognizant of these unfixed circumstances that we can know that the buddhas possess the knowledge of what is unfixed.

Question: Whether or not you personally take care and whether or not you make a direct personal effort, these unfixed circumstances will still occur. On the one hand there are those who skillfully defend against untoward developments and yet still end up being subjected to intense anguish while

on the other hand there are those who do not defend against such exigencies at all and yet do not encounter any intense anguish at all. Also, there are 79c
those who, in their diligence, undergo much weariness and pain, but still do not obtain the fruits of their efforts, whereas there are others who are not the least bit diligent and make no particular effort and, even so, they still manage to gain fruits [otherwise] associated with making an effort. These matters are all unfixed.

Response: Your statement simply serves to cooperate in the establishment of my position regarding unfixed matters. If these unfixed matters do indeed exist, then this wisdom that is cognizant of whatsoever is unfixed should exist. I never claimed that if someone failed to guard against untoward events they would always be subjected to suffering. Nor did I ever claim that, without the expenditure of effortful action, one would necessarily be able to enjoy fruitful results. There are those people who, despite making an effort, are still blocked from the enjoyment of happiness by karmic obstacles originating in earlier lifetimes. I never claimed that all cases were necessarily this way. Therefore the challenges that you have posed on this topic are wrong.

This is what is meant [when it is said] with regard to unfixed circumstances that it is the buddhas alone who possess complete knowledge of what is unfixed.

[11. Thorough Knowing of Formless Absorption Phenomena]

As for knowing the formless realm stations, *śrāvaka* disciples and *pratyekabuddha*s know a lesser portion of the beings and dharmas associated with the formless realm stations of existence whereas the buddhas, the bhagavats, have a perfectly complete knowledge of the beings and dharmas associated with the formless realm stations of existence.

Regarding these formless realm stations of existence, the buddhas know:

That a certain number of beings are born into this station;

That a certain number of beings are born into that station;

That a certain number of beings are born into the station associated with the first formless absorption;

That a certain number of beings are born into the second station;

That a certain number of beings are born into the third station;

That a certain number of beings are born into the fourth station;
That a certain number of beings have dwelled there for a particular amount of time since they were born there;
That a certain number of beings, after a particular period of time, will fall away from that realm;
That a certain number of beings will enjoy a maximum life span of a particular amount of time;
That a certain number of beings will have a definitely fixed life span;
That a certain number of beings will enjoy a life span the length of which is not definitely fixed;
That a certain number of beings will be born here after their lifetimes in the desire realm have come to an end;
That a certain number of beings will be born here after their lifetimes in the form realm have come to an end;
That a certain number of beings will return to be reborn here after their lifetimes in this formless realm have come to an end;
That a certain number of beings will be born here directly after their lives in the human realm come to an end;
That a certain number of beings will be reborn here directly after their lives in the heavens have come to an end;
That, when the lives of these particular beings end here, they will then take birth in the desire realm, that they will then take birth in the form realm, or that they will then take birth in the formless realm;
That, when the lives of these particular beings end here, they will then take birth in the celestial realm rebirth destiny, that they will then take birth in the human realm rebirth destiny, that they will then take birth in the *asura* realm rebirth destiny, or that they will then take birth in the rebirth destinies of the hell realms, the animal realms, or the hungry ghost realms;
That these particular beings will enter nirvana in that particular place;
That a particular group of beings are all merely common people;
That a particular group of beings are *ārya* disciples of buddhas;
That a particular group of beings are [buddhas'] disciples who are common people [that have not yet become *ārya*s];

That a particular group of beings will achieve success in the *śrāvaka* disciple vehicle;
That a particular group of beings will achieve success in the *pratyekabuddha* vehicle;
That a particular group of beings will all achieve success in the Great Vehicle;
That a particular group of beings will fail to achieve success in the *śrāvaka* disciple vehicle;
That a particular group of beings will fail to achieve success in the *pratyekabuddha* vehicle and will also fail to achieve success in the Great Vehicle;
That a particular group of beings will develop their practice to the point of reaching nirvana;
That a particular group of beings will fail to develop their practice to the point where they reach nirvana;
That a particular group of beings will pursue a superior level of practice;
And that a particular group of beings are all disciples of a particular buddha. 80a

The buddhas also know:
That this particular meditative absorption is one in which one is exposed to delectably blissful experiences;[76]
That in this particular meditative absorption there will be no exposure to delectably blissful experiences;
[That this particular meditative absorption] is wholesome or is merely neutral;
That in this particular meditative absorption one may successfully sever a certain number of fetters;
And that this particular meditative absorption is superior, is middling, or is inferior.

To summarize, only the buddhas, by employing their knowledge of all modes, are able to clearly distinguish which of these formless-realm meditative absorptions are greater or lesser, which are deeper or shallower, which involve mental dharmas, which involve dharmas not associated with the mind, which are acquired as resultant effects [of previous karma], which are not acquired as resultant effects [of previous karma], and so forth. This is what is meant when it is said that the buddhas thoroughly know the stations of existence corresponding to the formless meditative absorptions.

[12. The Knowledge of All Matters Related to Eternal Cessation]

As for [the completely penetrating knowledge of all] dharmas pertaining to cessation, the buddhas possess a penetrating knowledge of the *pratyekabuddhas* and arhats who have entered nirvana either in the past or present eras. This is as recorded in the sutras where it states:

> *Bhikṣus*, ninety-one *kalpas* prior to this "worthy *kalpa*" (*bhadrakalpa*), Vipaśyin Buddha appeared. After thirty-one *kalpas*, there followed two more buddhas, the first of whom was Śikhin and the second of whom was Viśvabhū. Then, in this worthy *kalpa,* Krakucchanda, Kanakamuni, and Kāśyapa Buddha emerged.[77]

Just such great knowledge and vision regarding all buddhas of the past should be discussed [more extensively] herein in relation to this sutra.[78] It also reaches to those *śrāvaka* disciples who have entered the nirvana without residue and extends also to the *pratyekabuddha* named "Success," to the one named "Floral Insignia," to the one named "Seer of Dharma," to the one named "Dharma Basket," to the one named "Delightful Vision," to the one named "Stainless," to the one named "Free of Gain," and to the other such *pratyekabuddhas* as well. So it is that the buddhas possess a completely penetrating knowledge of those who have entered the nirvana without residue.[79]

Additionally, in cases where they have not yet entered final nirvana, but rather still abide in the nirvana with residue, the buddhas possess a penetratingly comprehensive knowledge with regard to the utter ending of all conditions associated with taking birth. [These matters] also pertain to their penetrating knowledge of [the phenomena associated with] cessation.

This is as recorded in the sutras wherein it states:

> The Buddha told Ānanda, "I entirely know with respect to this person that he no longer has even the slightest darkness. This person has definitely

> put an end to these particular inward dharmas. When this person reaches the end of this life, he will enter nirvana."

This too is included in what is meant by "having knowledge of cessation."[80]

Also, regarding other people's penetrating comprehension of the four truths, he is able to know their circumstances. This too is included in what is meant by "having knowledge of cessation."

As it is said in the sutras:

> Why should I not simply resort to expedients to cause this person in this very place to gain the liberation associated with ending the contaminants?

And as the Buddha told Ānanda, "You delight in *dhyāna* concentration and delight in cutting off the fetters." These circumstances too are associated with what is meant by having a completely penetrating knowledge of cessation.

This is also as illustrated in the Buddha's statement to Śāriputra:

> I know nirvana, know the path leading to the realization of nirvana, and know those beings who will arrive at the realization of nirvana.[81]

Such sutras as we have cited herein should all be discussed at greater length. The ideas cited above are indicative of what is meant by all buddhas possessing the penetrating comprehension of all matters having to do with cessation.

[13. Thorough Knowing of Nonform Dharmas Unrelated to Mind]

As for thorough knowing of the nonform dharmas unassociated with the mind, roots of goodness associated with the moral precepts influence all of those nonform dharmas unassociated with the mind such as the moral regulations requiring wholesome actions and the moral regulations prohibiting bad actions. *Śrāvaka* disciples and *pratyekabuddha*s are unable to possess a completely penetrating comprehension of such matters. The buddhas, however, are so well able to penetratingly comprehend them that these become as manifestly clear to them as if they were right before their very eyes. This is because they have perfected the foremost power of wisdom with respect to dharmas unassociated with the mind.

Question: Moral regulations requiring wholesome actions and moral regu-
80b lations prohibiting bad actions are form dharmas. Why do you refer to them as "nonform" dharmas?

Response: Moral regulations requiring wholesome actions and moral regulations prohibiting bad actions are of two kinds, namely those involving actions and those not involving actions. Those involving actions are within the sphere of form dharmas whereas those not involving actions are "nonform" dharmas. As for those nonform dharmas not involving actions, employing his exclusive power of knowing, the Buddha is able to have a clear and present knowledge of them whereas others are compelled to rely upon inferential knowledge to understand them.

Question: Are the buddhas only able to thoroughly know the nonform dharmas unassociated with the mind while not being able to thoroughly know the dharmas associated with the mind?

Response: If one already possesses a penetrating comprehension of the unassociated dharmas, then there is no need even to bring up the associated dharmas. It is as if we were speaking of an archer able to pierce a single fine feather [floating through the air]. One would have no need in such a case to inquire if his arrow might be able to hit something large.

Furthermore, *śrāvaka* disciples and *pratyekabuddha*s are able to employ their sixth consciousness to know but seven among the seven hundred unassociated dharmas, namely: first, names; second, characteristic marks; third, meanings; fourth, impermanence; fifth, production; sixth, nonproduction; and seventh, crossing on beyond. The buddhas, however, are able to employ their sixth consciousness to know every one of them. The buddhas also know the marks of the four truths as well as the mundane dharmas. It is for these reasons that it is said that the buddhas thoroughly know the nonform dharmas unassociated with the mind.

[14. The Great Powers *Pāramitā*]

As for the powers *pāramitā,* [the buddhas] gain the power of the knowledge of all modes with respect to all knowable dharmas without exception and are assisted in this by the ten powers, the four fearlessnesses, and the four bases of meritorious qualities. Also, it is due to having gained the ten powers that the buddhas are therefore able to perfect the powers *pāramitā*. This power is increased in the sixteenth mind-moment [involved in achieving the direct seeing of the path]. All-knowledge is always present in the person of the Buddha until he attains the nirvana without residue. It is because of this that he gains the unimpeded knowledge of all dharmas.

[15. The Four Unimpeded Knowledges *Pāramitā*]

As for the *pāramitā* of the [four] unimpeded knowledges (*pratisaṃvid*), they are unimpeded knowledge with respect to dharmas (*dharma-pratisaṃvid*), meaning (*artha-pratisaṃvid*), language (*nirukti-pratisaṃvid*), and eloquence (*pratibhāna-pratisaṃvid*). [The buddhas] possess an unlimited penetrating comprehension of these four dharmas that is unimpeded in its implementation. As described in the sutras:[82]

> The Buddha told the *bhikṣus*, "There are four of the Tathāgata's disciples who have perfected the foremost power of mindfulness, power of wisdom, and power of endurance so consummately that they are like a skilled archer who can shoot any single tree leaf without difficulty. Even if these disciples were to all come forth and pose challenging questions on the four stations of mindfulness, setting aside the time required for drink, food, toilet, and sleep, I could always and incessantly respond to their questions for a hundred years during which the Tathāgata would always reply with inexhaustible eloquence and wisdom."

Here the Buddha, with his characteristically scant wish to do so, discussed his own implementation of these knowledges. Supposing that there were a number of great trichiliocosms as numerous as all the atoms in all four continents of all worlds in a great trichiliocosm, supposing also that all those world systems were filled with beings, all of whom were the likes of Śāriputra and the *pratyekabuddha*s, and suppose too that all these beings used their perfected knowledges and eloquence to pose difficult questions to the Tathāgata on the four stations of mindfulness, doing so to the exhaustion of lifetimes extending to a number of *kalpa*s as numerous as all the aforementioned atoms—the Tathāgata would still be able to reply to their questions on the meanings of the four stations of mindfulness, expounding on their meaning without redundancy and with inexhaustible eloquence.[83]

80c Now, as for the unimpeded knowledge with respect to dharmas, [the buddhas] are well able to distinguish all details involved in the designations of dharmas with an unimpededly penetrating comprehension.

As for the unimpeded knowledge with respect to meaning, they are able to bring to bear an unimpededly penetrating comprehension of the meanings associated with those dharmas.

In the case of their unimpeded knowledge with respect to language, the buddhas are able to accord with the languages and phrases through which the various sorts of beings are caused to understand those meanings, doing so with an unimpededly penetrating comprehension.

Regarding their unimpeded knowledge as it applies to eloquence, during that entire time in which they are answering questions, they are skillful and clever in speaking on Dharma and they are able to carry on in this fashion endlessly. Whatever topic all other worthies and *ārya*s are unable to treat exhaustively, it is only the buddhas who can reach the limits of that topic.

It is on these bases that we speak of the *pāramitā* of the unimpeded knowledges.

[16. The *Pāramitā* of Perfectly Complete Replies and Predictions]

Regarding the *pāramitā* of perfection in the answering of questions, the Buddha is well able to answer in all situations involving the posing of difficult questions. And why is this so? It is because, in the four types of responses, he remains utterly free of erroneous or disordered presentations, because he well knows the conceptual meanings, because he has perfected the *pāramitā* of preserving the undamaged meaning, and because he delights in a profound knowing of the natures of all beings, what they themselves practice, and what they themselves find pleasing. This is illustrated by the instance in which Śāriputra addressed the Buddha, saying:

> Bhagavat, when the Buddha discourses on the good Dharma, many are the beings who, upon hearing this, then gain realizations. Having gained

such realizations, their minds become free of all craving. And because they become free of all craving, they no longer have anything in the world that they indulge. And once they no longer have anything at all that they indulge, their minds achieve a state of inward cessation.

The Buddha exhaustively knows, without exceptions, the unsurpassable aspects of the good Dharma. There is no one who is superior to him in this regard.

Question: You spoke of the four types of replies. What are those four?

Response:
First, the definitive reply.
Second, the distinguishing reply.
Third, the counter-questioning reply.
And, fourth, the reply that sets aside the question.
In the case of the definitive reply, this is illustrated by the instance where a *bhikṣu* asked the Buddha:

> Bhagavat, is it or is it not the case that there could be some form that is eternal and unchanging? Bhagavat, is it or is it not the case that there could be any feelings, perceptions, formative factors, or consciousnesses that are permanent and unchanging?

The Buddha replied:

> *Bhikṣu,* there is no form that is permanent and unchanging. There are no feelings, perceptions, formative factors, or consciousnesses that are permanent and unchanging.

Cases such as these illustrate the "definitive reply."
The distinguishing reply is illustrated by the instance where Potaliputta,[84] the *brahmacārin,* inquired of Samiddhi,[85] asking:[86]

> In instances where a person deliberately performs actions of body, speech, or mind, what sorts of karmic retributions ensue therefrom?

Samiddhi responded with a definitive reply, saying:

In instances where persons deliberately perform actions of body, speech, or mind, they are bound to undergo retributions involving suffering and anguish.

But this should have involved a distinguishing reply. This *brahmacārin* later came and asked the Buddha about this matter, to which the Buddha replied:

Potaliputta, in instances where someone deliberately performs actions of body, speech, or mind, this karma may result in undergoing painful retributions, in undergoing pleasurable retributions, or in undergoing retributions that are neither painful nor pleasurable. Pain-inducing actions result in undergoing painful retributions. Pleasure-inducing actions result in undergoing pleasurable retributions. Actions that are neither pain-inducing nor pleasure-inducing result in undergoing karmic retributions that are neither painful nor pleasurable.

Scriptural passages such as these illustrate instances of the distinguishing reply.

The counter-questioning reply is illustrated by that instance in which the *brahmacārin* named Śreṇika inquired of the Buddha and the Buddha replied:

"I shall now return the question to you whereupon you may reply in accordance with your own idea on this matter. Śreṇika, what do you think? Do physical forms constitute the Tathāgata, or not? Or is it that feelings, perceptions, formative factors, or consciousnesses constitute the Tathāgata?"

81a He replied, "No, Bhagavat. They do not."

[The Buddha then asked him,] "Is the Tathāgata apart from form, feelings, perceptions, formative factors, or consciousnesses, or not?"

He replied, "No, Bhagavat. He is not."

These types of passages from scripture should be more extensively discussed. They illustrate what is meant by the counter-questioning reply.

As for the reply that sets aside the question, this applies to the response to questions regarding the fourteen classic erroneous views, namely:

Is the world eternal?

Is the world non-eternal?

Is the world both eternal and non-eternal?

Is the world neither eternal nor non-eternal?
Is the world bounded?
Is the world unbounded?
Is the world both bounded and unbounded?
Is the world neither bounded nor unbounded?
Does the Tathāgata exist after his nirvana?
Does the Tathāgata not exist after his nirvana?
Does the Tathāgata both exist and not exist after his nirvana?
Does the Tathāgata neither exist nor not exist after his nirvana?
Is the body identical with a spiritual soul (*jīva*)?
Is the body different from a spiritual soul?

As stated above, even in an instance where all beings possessed the wisdom and eloquence of the *pratyekabuddha* and they inquired of the Buddha on these four matters, the Buddha would in all cases adapt to their needs in answering their questions, offering replies that are neither excessive nor deficient. It is for these reasons that the buddhas are said to possess the *pāramitā* of perfection in the answering of questions.

[17. Invulnerability to Harm by Anyone]

There is no one whatsoever who can harm the Buddha. This is because he has gained that dharma by which one cannot be killed. There is no one who can cut off any part of the Buddha's body. He has sovereign mastery over whether he will live or die. This is as stated in scripture, wherein it states, "Were one to seek some method by which to inflict harm on the Buddha—there simply is no such possibility at all."

Question: Is the life span of a buddha fixed or is it unfixed?

Response: There are those who claim that it is unfixed. But if a buddha's life span were actually fixed, what difference then would there be between his case and that of all others who have fixed life spans? Still, in truth, the life span of a buddha is not fixed. That there is no one who can harm a buddha—now *that* is extraordinary. There are those who say that the life span of a buddha is fixed. However, whereas others whose life spans are fixed are indeed subject to having hands, feet, ears, and nose sliced off, the Buddha [is unique in that he] is entirely free of any such vulnerability.

Question: How is it that the buddhas have this exclusive dharma of being invulnerable to being harmed?

Response: The inconceivability of the buddhas can be understood by resort to analogy. Suppose for instance that all beings throughout the worlds of the ten directions were to have a given amount of power. Now, if a single *māra* could possess a certain amount of power, also suppose that each and every one of those beings throughout the ten directions was caused to possess powers like those of Māra, the Evil One. Even if all of those beings then joined in wishing to inflict harm on the Buddha, they would still be unable to move even a single hair on the Buddha's body. How much the less might they actually succeed in harming the Buddha?

Question: Well, if that is the case, how then could Devadatta have succeeded in injuring the Buddha?

Response: This question was already answered earlier. The Buddha wished to show beings the character of the three poisons. Even though Devadatta had previously upheld the moral precepts and cultivated goodness, because he was attached to receiving offerings, he then committed immensely evil deeds.

[The Buddha] also allowed this to happen to enable [beings] to realize that the mind of the Buddha does not vary in the way it regards any human or *deva*. His having compassion and pity for Devadatta on the one hand and Rāhula[87] on the other was the same as his equal regard for his own left and right eyes.

The Buddha always spoke of the mind of uniformly equal regard for everyone. He revealed his equality of regard at this time. When the *deva*s and people observed this, they were struck by the extraordinary nature of this and thus felt even stronger resolute faith.

In addition, because of this, the *deva*s of the long-life heavens could see that the Buddha was still bound to undergo retribution for bad karmic actions done in previous lives. Had he not undergone it now, they might have thought that bad actions could be free of corresponding karmic retributions. Because
81b the Buddha wished to cut off their wrong views, he thereby revealed his own undergoing of this karmic retribution.

Furthermore, the Buddha's mind is no different in the presence of pain or pleasure. His mind is free of any concept of a self. This is because it is ultimately empty. Because his sense faculties have all been made pliant and imperturbable by change, he has no need to use expedients to separate from pain and enjoy pleasures. This is as described in the bodhisattva canon where it states, "It was merely as an expedient that the Buddha manifested as subject to this experience." One should infer the broader implications of this.

The above points illustrate what is meant by the Buddha's exclusive dharma of being invulnerable to being killed or harmed.

[18. Their Words Are Never Spoken without a Purpose]

In speaking on the Dharma, their words are never empty. All words spoken by the buddhas have a corresponding intended effect. Therefore, when the buddhas speak on Dharma, their words are never empty. And how is this so? Before the buddhas begin to speak on Dharma, they first contemplate from root to branch where beings' minds abide and whether their fetters are thick or only scant. Thus they know the origins of their meritorious qualities in previous lives, observe the nature and strength of their karmic roots, and know:

Where and when beings [will encounter] obstacles;
Whether they are susceptible to liberation through gentle teaching methods;
Whether they are susceptible to liberation through harsh teaching methods;
Whether they are susceptible to liberation through a combination of gentle and harsh teaching methods.[88]
Whether they need only a little bit of instigation to gain liberation;
Whether they require extensive distinguishing instructions to gain liberation;
That there are those who gain liberation through [teachings on] the aggregates, the sense bases, the sense realms, or the twelve links of conditioned co-production;
Whether they may gain access [to liberation] through the gateway of faith or through the gateway of wisdom;

That this person should gain liberation through the teaching of a buddha;
That this person should gain liberation through the teaching of a *śrāvaka* disciple;
That this person should gain liberation through some other set of conditions;
That this person should be able to gain success in the *śrāvaka* disciple vehicle;
That this person should be able to gain success in the *pratyekabuddha* vehicle;
That this person should be able to gain success in the Great Vehicle;
That this person has long practiced habitual greed, habitual hatred, and habitual delusion;
That this person has practiced habitual greed and hatred;
And that this person has practiced habitual greed and delusion.

In this way, they distinguish and determine with regard to each and every situation:

That this person has fallen into an annihilationist view;
That this person has fallen into an eternalist view;
That this person is for the most part attached to the view that seizes on the existence of a real self in association with the body [or any of the other four aggregates];[89]
That this person is most often habitually attached to extreme views;
That this person is most often habitually attached to the views that seize upon either prohibitions or on opinionated views;
That this person is for the most part habitually arrogant;
That this person is for the most part habitually inclined toward feelings of inferiority and the tendency to flattery and deviousness;
That this person's mind is mostly inclined toward doubt and regret;
That this person has developed a fondness for refined literary expressiveness;
That there are those who prize refinement in meanings and principles;
That there are those who delight in profundities;
That there are those who enjoy topics that are merely superficial;

That, in previous lifetimes, this person has accumulated the Dharma provisions requisite to success in the path;
That this person is accumulating the Dharma provisions for the path in this present lifetime;
That this person has only accumulated roots of goodness conducive to enjoying karmic rewards [from previous meritorious actions];
That this person has only accumulated roots of goodness associated with thorough understanding;
That this person should be able to rapidly become enlightened;
And that this person will require a long time before he can become enlightened.[90]

The Buddha first engages in investigative contemplation and assessment of individual circumstances and then, according with whichever approach is appropriate to instigate someone's liberation, he then speaks Dharma for them and thereby brings about their liberation.

It is as a consequence of this that every instance of the Buddha's speaking of Dharma is free of any merely empty discourse. This is as described in a sutra: "The Bhagavat first knows and sees and only then speaks Dharma. It is not the case that he speaks Dharma without first knowing and seeing."

[19. Their Speech Is Free of Error]

Regarding the absence of errors and mistakes [in their speech], when the buddhas speak Dharma, they do not commit any errors or make any mistakes. "Absence of errors" refers to there being no instances in which the meaning of what they say is contradictory. "Absence of mistakes" means they make no mistakes with regard to meanings.

It is because they do not make mistakes with regard to causes and conditions as they relate to the path that they are said to not make mistakes. It is
because they do not commit errors with regard to causes and conditions as 81c
they relate to the fruits of the path that they are said to not commit any error.

It is because they are not deficient that they are said to not make mistakes and it is because they are not excessive that they are said to not commit any error.

This is accomplished through their possession of a penetrating comprehension of the four unimpeded knowledges, through their constant harmonization of mindfulness and stable wisdom, and through their utter abandonment of views associated with annihilationism, eternalism, acausality, erroneous causality, or other such wrong views.

In the Dharma that they speak, there is no cause by which people become perplexed. In whatsoever they say, there are no faults involving inconsistencies between what is set forth in the beginning and in the end.

Scriptures accordant with these concepts should be discussed more extensively herein. As it says in one of the sutras:

> *Bhikṣus*, when I speak Dharma for you, it is good in the beginning, good in the middle, and good in the end. The phrasings are good and the meanings are good. It possesses a singular purity free of any debasing admixture and it is perfectly complete in its proclamation of *brahmacarya*.[91]

[20. Complete Use of the Three Turnings in Speaking Dharma]

As regards the matter of [the Buddha's] speaking of Dharma involving rarities, whomever they undertake to teach is immediately enabled to realize the fruits of the path. This is a rarity.

Whenever they provide a reply or offer a prediction, their statements are always genuine and do not differ [from actual circumstances]. This too is a rarity.

The Buddha has the path as the subject of his discourse. This path as it is proclaimed by the Buddha is not admixed with afflictions and is able to bring about the severance of the afflictions. This too is a rarity.

Whenever the Buddha speaks, benefit ensues from it and it never involves mere empty words. This too is a rarity.

Whenever a person applies mental diligence and vigor to the cultivation of the Buddha's Dharma, he can cut off the unwholesome dharmas and bring about increase in the good dharmas. This too is a rarity.

There are three additional rarities: the rarity of displaying spiritual powers, the rarity of foretelling the content of others' thoughts, and the rarity of being able to accomplish the transformational teaching of others. It is on the basis of these three sorts of rarities in the proclaiming of Dharma that the Buddha's discourse on Dharma is said to be characterized by rarities.[92]

[21. They Are the Great Generals Among All *Āryas*]

Regarding [the Buddha's] eminence as the most superior spiritual guide among all the *ārya*s, buddhas know what the minds of beings course in, know what they delight in, know whether their fetters are deep or shallow, know whether their faculties are sharp or dull, and know whether their wisdom is superior, middling, or inferior. It is because they know these matters well and know them with penetrating comprehension that they are the most superior spiritual guides among all the *ārya*s.

They are also able to well know the characteristics of the four truths, and to well know all the general and specific characteristics of all dharmas.

It is also because, when they speak on the Dharma, their words are not empty and because, when they speak on the Dharma, they commit no errors and make no mistakes that they are therefore the most superior spiritual guides among all the *ārya*s.

Question: But the other four groups are also able to speak on the Dharma and thus refute the teachings of the non-Buddhists and thereby cause them to enter into the Dharma of the Buddha. Why then does one only speak of the Buddha as the most superior spiritual guide?

Response: This should be explained by an analogy. Suppose all beings possessed the wisdom powers of a *pratyekabuddha*. If all of these beings did not receive the intentional assistance of the Buddha and yet wished somehow to bring about the liberation of but a single person, this would be a complete impossibility. When all of these persons spoke Dharma, they would still be unable to cause the severance of a tiny fraction of even one of the formless realm fetters.

If, on the other hand, the Buddha wished to bring about the liberation of some being and then proceeded to say something, even those burdened with the erroneous views of the non-Buddhists, the dragons, the *yakṣa*s, and the various other sorts of beings who do not understand the language of the

Buddha—these would all still be caused to understand. Then all of these would in turn be able to teach countless other beings. And so this proceeds even to the point that, today, whenever those within the community of *śrāvaka* disciples cause beings to abide in the four fruits of the path, they are all emblematically representative of the Tathāgata as the most superior of all spiritual guides.

It is for these reasons that the Buddha is known as the most superior
82a spiritual guide, and it is for these reasons that this is regarded as an exclusive
dharma not held in common with the other *ārya*s.

[22–25. They Are Able to Remain Unguarded in Four Ways]

As for the four unguarded dharmas, the buddhas are unguarded in their physical actions, are unguarded in their verbal actions, are unguarded in their mental actions, and are unguarded with respect to the means for sustaining life. And why is this? These four matters are not protected from others' [knowledge]. They do not think, "Regarding my [actions of] body, speech, and mind, and my [means of sustaining] life—I fear that others might come to know about them."

And why is this? This is because, during the long night [of previous lifetimes], they have cultivated every sort of pure karmic deed and have always well seen, well known, and well severed every one of the dharmas associated with the afflictions. And this is because they have perfected every sort of peerless root of goodness, because they have so well practiced whatever dharma is amenable to practice, because they have reached the point where there is nothing about them the least bit worthy of criticism, and because they have utterly perfected the *pāramitā* of equanimity.

Now, on this matter of their "equanimity," when their eyes view form, they relinquish any thoughts of either distress or delight. And so it goes [with the other sense faculties and objects] up to and including the mind faculty's engagement with dharmas [as objects of mind]. In this connection, one would ideally also discuss here citations from such scriptures as the *Poheti* and *Uttara* sutras.[93]

[26–29. They Possess the Four Types of Fearlessnesses]

Now, as for the four types of fearlessness....

Question: There is a single dharma known as "fearlessness." How is it that we here have four of them?

Response: It is because there are four matters in which there is an absence of doubt or fear that we therefore speak of four of them, as follows:[94]

First, as the Buddha told the *bhikṣus*:

> I myself here utter these truthful words, "I am a man possessed of all-knowledge." If anyone here, whether he be a *śramaṇa,* brahman, *deva,* Māra, Brahmā, or other person possessed of worldly knowledge were to challenge this statement in a manner consistent with Dharma, claiming that I do not indeed possess a direct knowledge of this Dharma, I would not then experience in this challenge even the slightest sign of fearfulness, and it is because of not experiencing any such sign that I have become established in security and fearlessness in this regard.

This is the first type of fearlessness. It is a result of exhaustively knowing all dharmas in accordance with reality.

As for the second type of fearlessness, the Buddha said,

> I myself here utter these truthful words, "I have brought all of the contaminants to an end." If any *śramaṇa,* brahman, *deva,* Māra, or Brahmā were to claim that these contaminants have not indeed been brought to an end, I would not then experience in this challenge even the slightest sign of fearfulness.[95] It is because of not experiencing any such sign that I have become established in security and fearlessness in this regard.

This is the second type of fearlessness. It is a result of having thoroughly cut off all afflictions and having also cut off the habitual propensities associated with past afflictions.

As for the third [type of fearlessness], [the Buddha said:]

> I have proclaimed which dharmas constitute obstacles to realization of the path. If anyone herein, whether he be a *śramaṇa,* brahman, *deva,*

> Māra, Brahmā, or other person possessed of worldly knowledge were to challenge this statement in a manner consistent with Dharma, claiming that, even though one might avail oneself of these dharmas, they would not be able to cause an obstacle to the path, I would not then experience in this challenge even the slightest sign of fearfulness. It is because of not experiencing any such sign that I have become established in security and fearlessness in this regard.

This is the third type of the fearlessness. It is a result of having thoroughly known those dharmas that constitute obstacles to the achievement of liberation.

As for the fourth [type of fearlessness, the Buddha said]:

> Whoever practices the path I have proclaimed, practicing it in accordance with the way I have explained the Dharma, will succeed in reaching the end of suffering. If any *śramaṇa,* brahman, *deva,* Māra, Brahmā, or other person possessed of worldly knowledge were to challenge this statement in a manner accordant with Dharma, claiming that, although one might practice a dharma such as this in a manner consistent with the way it has been explained, one would be unable to reach the path that brings about the end of suffering, I would not then experience in this challenge even the slightest sign of fearfulness. It is because of not experiencing any such sign that I have become established in security and fearlessness in this regard.

This is the fourth type of fearlessness. It is a result of thoroughly knowing the path leading to the extinguishing of suffering.

82b All four of these types of fearlessness are referred to as "fearlessnesses" because they all involve leaving behind such characteristic signs as fearfulness, terror, or horripilation. They are also termed "fearlessnesses" because they are able to maintain within the great assembly an awe-inspiring power of virtue extraordinary in its excellence. They are also called "fearlessnesses" because they so well know how to respond to all sorts of questions. Here, one should extensively discuss citations from the *Sutra on the Convocation of the Devas*.[96]

Question: If the buddhas are indeed possessed of all-knowledge, then they should be fearless in relation to all dharmas. Why is it then that we speak only of these four types [of fearlessness]?

Response: These serve to raise the major essential topics in order to introduce the most important instances. All other instances are similar to these.

[30–39. They Possess the Ten Powers]

As for the ten powers of the Buddha, "power" refers to the inexhaustible energetic strength that assists them and makes them invulnerable to interference by anyone. Although there are ten designations in this regard, in truth, this involves a single type of knowledge that, because it takes ten different circumstances as objective conditions, [these ten exemplary manifestations] are known as "the ten powers."

Because the knowledge of the Buddha takes all things as its objective conditions, it should be that there are countless powers. But it is because these ten powers are adequate to bring about the liberation of beings that we only speak of "the ten powers." Through merely introducing these ten powers, one can then know the others by inference.

The first power is [the Buddha's] definite and completely penetrating knowledge with respect to all dharmas of what does and does not constitute the cause. This is the first power. [This was the basis for, as cited earlier,] the Buddha's having said [in reference to the *brahmacārin* named Patikaputra]:

> If this crazy person does not relinquish these claims, does not relinquish these perverse views, and does not relinquish these thoughts, then, as for his being able to arrive here in the presence of the Buddha—this is an utter impossibility.

[This is also the basis for] the Buddha's having said to Ānanda:

> It is utterly impossible that two buddhas might arise in the world at the same time. However, it is indeed possible for a single buddha to come forth into the world.[97]

This was said solely with respect to the circumstance of a single buddha emerging in a single world. In truth, in all of the countless and limitless worlds throughout the ten directions, there are countless hundreds of thousands of myriads of *koṭi*s of buddhas simultaneously emerging throughout those worlds.

Additionally, the sutras state:

> It is impossible that bad physical, verbal, and mental karmic actions might have excellent and desirable results. However, it is indeed possible that good physical, verbal, and mental karmic actions may have excellent and desirable results.[98]

Here one should extensively discuss related scriptural citations from among the five categorical repositories of Dharma.

The second power is [the Buddha's] knowing in accordance with reality and with distinguishing clarity the place, the circumstances, and the karmic retributions associated with all past, future, and present karmic deeds along with all the dharmas that are involved in experiencing [those retributions].

If the Buddha wishes to know with regard to any being their past karmic deeds and their past karmic retributions, he is able to immediately know them. So too, he is immediately able to know:

With respect to past karmic deeds, their retribution in the present;
With respect to past karmic deeds, their retribution in the future;
With respect to past karmic deeds, their retribution in the past;
With respect to past karmic deeds, their retribution in both the past and the future;
With respect to past karmic deeds, their retribution in both the past and the present;
With respect to past karmic deeds, their retribution in both the future and the present;
With respect to past karmic deeds, their retribution in the past, the future, and the present;
With respect to present karmic deeds, their retribution in the present;
With respect to present karmic deeds, their retribution in the future;
With respect to present karmic deeds, their retribution in both the present and the future;
And with respect to future karmic deeds, their retribution in the future.

There are all manner of such distinctions regarding the dharmas involved in undergoing karmic retributions. There are four dharmas categorizing such karmic retributions, namely:

Undergoing blissful experiences in the present followed by undergoing suffering in future lifetimes;
Undergoing suffering in the present followed by undergoing blissful experiences in future lifetimes;
Undergoing blissful experiences in the present followed by blissful experiences in the future; 82c
And undergoing suffering in the present followed by undergoing suffering in the future as well.[99]

As regards [the Buddha's knowing] "the place," this refers to his knowing for any karmic deed the time and place [of its occurrence] as well as the precise place in which this retribution will be undergone.

As regards [the Buddha's] knowing "the circumstances," this refers to knowing the corresponding causes and conditions, knowing the three corresponding types of bad karmic roots, knowing whether the deed was primarily performed by oneself, or knowing whether the deed occurred for the most part through the instigation of someone else. The Buddha entirely knows all such causes and conditions associated with good and bad karmic deeds.

As regards [the Buddha's knowing] "the karmic retributions," he knows that all karmic deeds have their corresponding karmic retributions. For instance, good karmic deeds may result in being reborn in a good place or in attaining nirvana, whereas bad karmic deeds may result in being reborn in any of the wretched destinies.

The Buddha knows entirely with respect to all these karmic deeds their roots, their branches, their associated causes and conditions, and whether they were done at one's own behest or at the behest of others. It is because this power of knowledge does not diminish that it is referred to as a "power."

The third power is the Buddha's knowing in accordance with reality the *dhyānas*, the meditative concentrations, the liberations, and the *samādhis*, together with their corresponding marks of defilement and purity.

"*Dhyānas*" refers to the four *dhyānas*. "Meditative concentrations" refers to the four formless realm meditative concentrations, the four immeasurable minds, and other such states, all of which are referred to as "meditative concentrations." "Liberations" refers to the eight liberations. As for "*samādhis*," all of the other meditative concentrations aside from the *dhyānas* and the liberations are referred to as "*samādhis*."

There are others who claim that the three gates to liberation—meditative concentrations still characterized by initial ideation (*vitarka*) and discursive thought (*vicāra*), meditative concentrations characterized by the absence of initial ideation and the presence of discursive thought, and meditative concentrations devoid of both initial ideation and discursive thought—these may all be referred to as "*samādhis*."

There are yet others who claim that "meditative concentrations" are relatively minor [meditative states] whereas "*samādhis*" are relatively major. Therefore, one may refer to all meditative concentrations realized by any buddha or bodhisattva as constituting a "*samādhi*."

All four of these constituent categories are subsumed within all explanations of "*dhyāna-pāramitā*."

As for "defilement," this refers to [meditative states characterized by] the experience of delectably pleasurable (*āsvādana*) sensations whereas "purity" refers here to not indulging delectably pleasurable sensations.

Then again, "defilement" may refer to any meditative concentration still characterized by the contaminants (*āsrava*) whereas "purity" may refer to any meditative concentration characterized by the absence of the contaminants.

As for the distinctions among the *samādhis*, liberations, and so forth, [the Buddha] knows with distinguishing clarity these sorts of *dhyāna* meditation states.

The fourth power is [the Buddha's] knowing in accordance with reality the relative superiority or inferiority of the faculties of other beings and other personages.

"Other beings" refers to common persons. "Other personages" refers here to the stream-enterer and the other classes of worthies and *āryas*. There may be others who interpret "beings" as a reference not only to common persons, but also even to those practitioners still involved in the learning stages, this because all of these have still not succeeded in putting an end to all of the contaminants. For them, "other personages" is a reference reserved for arhats and such, this because they have utterly ended all afflictions.

Yet others point out that both "beings" and "other personages" are but a single category and it is only the designations themselves that differ.

As for their "faculties," in this context they refer to faith, vigor, mindfulness, concentration, and wisdom and *not* to the sense faculties such as the eye and so forth [as the word might otherwise signify].

"Superior," as it applies to these faculties, refers to faculties that are fiercely sharp and which have the capacity to enable the attainment of enlightenment. "Inferior," on the other hand, refers to [faculties] that are dim, dull, and inadequate to enable one to take up [the practice of] the path.

The Buddha knows the relative superiority and inferiority of these two types of faculties and knows these matters in accordance with reality and in a manner free of any sort of error.

The fifth power is [the Buddha's] knowing in accordance with reality that in which the minds of other beings and other personages delight. "That in which they delight" refers to whatever endeavors they esteem and are inclined to engage in. For instance, there are those people who esteem wealth and worldly pleasures, whereas there are others who deeply esteem karmic merit and the practice of good dharmas. The Buddha knows all of these matters in accordance with reality.

The sixth power is the Buddha's knowing in accordance with reality the different types of natures of beings in the world as well as the countless [distinctions among those] natures. "Different types of natures" refers to the myriad variations in these natures. "Countless natures" is a reference to the
countless distinctions in each and every one of these types of natures. As for 83a
the term "nature," it is because one's mind has always habitually practiced [particular sorts of endeavors] and has always delighted in practicing and cultivating them throughout one's past lives right up until the very present—it is for this reason that they therefore form the basis of one's "nature." The Buddha knows in accordance with reality these two categories of natures, the good and the bad.

The seventh power is [the Buddha's] knowing in accordance with reality the paths leading to all destinations. As for "the paths leading to all destinations," those are the means by which one may succeed in acquiring all meritorious qualities. These paths are referred to as "the paths leading to all destinations."

These include, for instance, the five-factor *samādhi,*[100] the fivefold awareness *samādhi,*[101] the eightfold path of the *ārya*s, all dharmas subsumed by the path of the *ārya*s, or the four bases of psychic power, the latter as cited in a sutra that says, "If a *bhikṣu* cultivates the four bases of psychic power, there is no benefit that he will not acquire."

There are others who claim that this may also refer to the four *dhyāna*s, as cited in a sutra:

> When a *bhikṣu* gains the four *dhyāna*s, his mind comes to abide with stability and purity in a single place in which he then succeeds in ridding himself of all afflictions and in destroying all obstacles. It then becomes well regulated so that it becomes serviceable and no longer subject to movement or distraction.

The eighth power is the [Buddha's] immediate ability to know past-life matters whenever he chooses to direct his awareness to events from previous lives. If the Buddha wishes to recall any of the countless and limitless lifetimes of either himself or all other beings, he then knows all of these matters entirely. There are no instances in which he is unable to know some particular matter even beyond a number of *kalpa*s equal to the number of sands in the Ganges River.

He knows where this person was born, what his name was, whether he was of noble or lowly caste, what he drank and ate, how he sustained his life, whether he experienced suffering or happiness, the types of endeavors in which he engaged, the karmic retributions that he underwent, what his mind engaged in, and from whence he originally came. He knows all such matters.

The ninth power is the [Buddha's] ability to see with the heavenly eye purified beyond the power of man's eyes the beings of the six destinies taking on bodies in accordance with their karmic deeds.

A *śrāvaka* disciple possessed of great powers uses the heavenly eye to see the lands contained within a small chiliocosm and also sees when the beings therein are born and when they die.

A lesser *pratyekabuddha* sees the lands of a thousand small chiliocosms and sees when the beings therein are born and when they die.

A *pratyekabuddha* possessed of middling powers sees the lands contained in a hundred myriads of small chiliocosms and sees when the beings therein are born and when they die.

A *pratyekabuddha* possessed of great powers sees the lands contained in a great trichiliocosm and sees the destinies to which they proceed when they die and are reborn.

The buddhas, the bhagavats, see a countless, boundless, and inconceivable number of worlds and also see when the beings therein are born and when they die.

As for the tenth power, it is the [Buddha's] ending of all contaminants, including the contaminant of sensual desire, the contaminant of [craving for] existence, and the contaminant of ignorance, these together with the utter ending of all afflictions or affliction-associated energetic propensities. This is the tenth power.

[They Have Achieved Unimepeded Liberation]

As for unimpeded liberation, there are three types of liberations. The first is the liberation from the obstacles of the afflictions. The second is the liberation from the obstacles to meditative concentration. The third is the liberation from the obstacles to [the knowledge of] all dharmas. Among these, an arhat who has achieved liberation through wisdom gains liberation from the obstacles of the afflictions. Both the doubly liberated arhat and the *pratyekabuddha* succeed in achieving both the liberation from the obstacles of the afflictions and the liberation from the obstacles to the *dhyāna* concentrations.

It is only the buddhas who have completely achieved all three of these liberations, namely liberation from the obstacles of the afflictions, liberation 83b
from the obstacles to acquisition of the *dhyāna* concentrations, and the liberation from the obstacles to [the knowledge of] all dharmas. It is because he brings together all three of the liberations that the Buddha is designated as having achieved unimpeded liberation. This [unimpeded liberation] always accompanies the mind all the way up to the point of entry into the nirvana without residue.

These forty dharmas exclusive to the buddhas provide a general introduction to an entryway into the dharmas of the Buddha. They are discussed here because this allows beings to thereby acquire an understanding of them. However, those [exclusive dharmas] that remain undiscussed herein are innumerable and boundless. Specifically, these include the following:

1. [The Buddha] never departs from wisdom.
2. He never errs in knowing the right time.
3. He has extinguished all habitual karmic propensities.
4. He has gained the meditative concentration *pāramitā.*
5. All of his meritorious qualities are possessed of extraordinary supremacy.
6. He has perfected the *pāramitā* of always according in his actions with what is appropriate to the circumstances.
7. No one is able to view the very top of [the light rays radiating from] the crown of his head.
8. No one is his equal.
9. No one is able to surpass him.
10. He is superior to all beings in the world.
11. His attainment of the path is not learned from anyone else.
12. He never turns away from the Dharma.
13. Whoever else might claim to be a buddha is forever unable to enter the presence of the Buddha.
14. He has perfected the dharma of never retreating.
15. He has acquired the great compassion.
16. He has acquired the great kindness.
17. He is the foremost among all whose teachings one may accept in faith.
18. He is the foremost among those [who are worthy of] fame and offerings.
19. No guru who is a contemporary of the Buddha is equal to the Buddha.
20. No guru gains a community of disciples equal to that of the Buddha.
21. The supreme refinement of his appearance causes all who see him to be delighted.
22. Whoever is sent forth as an emissary of a buddha cannot be harmed by anyone.

23. No one is able to injure anyone whom the Buddha has set out to liberate.
24. From the very moment he first brings forth a thought, he is able to sever all thought-related fetters.
25. He never misses the right time [to provide appropriate instruction to] beings who are capable of achieving liberation.
26. In the sixteenth [mind-moment involved in the acquisition of] wisdom, a buddha attains *anuttarāsamyaksaṃbodhi.*
27. He is the foremost among the world's fields of merit.
28. He emanates measureless radiant light.
29. His actions differ from those of anyone else.
30. He possesses the [physical] marks that are associated with a hundredfold generation of merit.[102]
31. He has measureless and boundless roots of goodness.
32. When he enters the womb—
33. When he is born—
34. When he achieves buddhahood—
35. When he turns the wheel of the Dharma—
36. When he relinquishes the possibility of the long life span—
37. And when he enters nirvana—[on all these occasions,] he is able to cause all the worlds throughout the great trichiliocosm to shake.
38. [On all of the above occasions], he sets quaking the countless palaces of the *māra*s, causing them to lose their awesome power and be struck with terror.
39. [When he achieves buddhahood], the world-protecting heavenly kings, Śakra, ruler of the *deva*s, the Yāma Heaven King, the Tuṣita Heaven King, the Nirmāṇarati Heaven King, the Paranirmitavaśavartin Heaven King, the Brahma Heaven King, the *deva*s of the Pure Abodes, and the other *deva*s—they all simultaneously assemble and request the turning of the Dharma wheel.
40. The Buddha's body is as solid as the body of Nārāyaṇa.[103]
41. When the moral precepts have not yet been formulated, he is the one who first formulates the moral precepts.
42. Whenever he takes up any endeavor, his power in accomplishing this is superior to that of any man.

83c 43. During the entire time the Bodhisattva is residing in his mother's womb, she loses all thoughts of defiling attachment for men.

44. His power is such that he is able to bring about the rescue and liberation of all beings.

There are measurelessly and innumerably many dharmas such as these that are exclusive to the Buddha. Because it would interfere with the explanation of other matters, there is no need to present an extensive discussion of them here. Although these dharmas as found in the Dharma of the *śrāvaka* disciples do resemble dharmas of the Buddha, due to dissimilarities in the degree of superiority or inferiority, there are distinct differences [in how they are described].

Moreover, to summarize, all of the dharmas of the buddhas are measureless, limitless, inconceivable, of the foremost degree of rarity, and such that no other being is able to have them in common [with any buddha]. Even if all the countless beings in the worlds of all the great trichiliocosms throughout the ten directions possessed wisdom comparable to the king of the Great Brahma Heaven, comparable to a great *pratyekabuddha,* or comparable to Śāriputra, and one were somehow able to collect all this wisdom together in a single person—even if that one person then wished to approach the most minutely small fraction of these forty dharmas exclusive to the buddhas—this would still be an utter impossibility. He could not even measure up to but one part in a hundred thousand myriads of *koṭi*s of parts of just a single one of those dharmas.

The buddhas possess the power of just such an immeasurable and limitless number of meritorious qualities. And why is this so? It is because they have securely established themselves in the four bases of meritorious qualities for a countless number of great *kalpa*s during which they have deeply practiced the six *pāramitā*s and have become well able to completely equip themselves with all dharmas practiced by the bodhisattva. Because [these dharmas] are not held in common with any other beings, so too, the fruits resulting [from their practice] are not held in common with any beings, either.

Chapter 24

Verses Offered in Praise

Now that, in this way, we have reached the end of this explanation of the forty dharmas exclusive to the buddhas, one should take the aspects emblematic of these forty exclusive dharmas and use them in one's own practice of mindfulness of the Buddha. One should also use verses to praise the Buddha, doing so as if one were standing directly before him, speaking to him. If one proceeds in this manner, then one may succeed in entering the mindfulness of the Buddha *samādhi.* Accordingly, there are verses, as follows:

> O greatly vigorous Lord of the Āryas—
> Now, in the presence of the Buddha,
> I shall praise with reverential mind
> these forty dharmas possessed only [by buddhas].[104]
>
> As for his supernatural powers and travel through flight,
> their power when enacted is utterly limitless.
> Among the psychic powers of the other *ārya*s, 84a
> there are none at all that can equal these.
>
> Among the *śrāvaka* disciples, he holds sway with sovereign mastery,
> using his measureless knowledge of others' thoughts.
> Thus he is well able to train their thoughts
> by according with their minds as he appropriately responds to them.
>
> His mindfulness is as expansive as the great ocean
> while also being tranquil and calmly secure.
> In all the world, there is no dharma
> able to cause him to become perturbed.
>
> The jewel of the *vajra samādhi*
> that is praised by all buddhas—
> he has acquired it and it resides within in his heart
> just as the worthies embrace the straightforward mind.

He thoroughly knows the unfixed dharmas
and the matters associated with the four formless absorptions
that are so subtle they are difficult to distinguish.
He exhaustively knows them all without exception.

Regarding whether a being has already died in the past,
dies now in the present, or will die at some point later in the future,
it is solely the Bhagavat, and he alone,
whose wisdom is able to fully comprehend such things.

He knows well all matters related
to the formless dharmas unassociated with the mind
that everyone else throughout all worlds
remains entirely unable to know.

The Bhagavat's great awesome powers,
his measureless meritorious qualities,
and his boundless wisdom
are all unmatched by anyone at all.

In the four types of responses to questions,
he is so preeminent that he has no peer.
As for all the challenging questions that beings present,
he replies to them all with utter ease.

If anywhere in any world
there is someone wishing to harm the Buddha,
this circumstance never comes to pass,
for he has gained the dharma by which he cannot be slain.

If at any point throughout the three periods of time
there is anything that he says,
those words are definitely not set forth in vain,
but rather always bring great fruits as a result.

Of all the dharmas that he proclaims,
none of them are not especially rare.
He is never in error as regards their significance,
how much the less might he ever err in words and phrases.

For the three types of *ārya* disciples
that differ as either superior, middling, or inferior,
and include the eight classes in four pairs,[105] and the others,
he is the foremost great spiritual guide.

In actions of body, speech, and mind, and in sustaining his life,
he is ultimately and always pure
and hence, in all of these,
he never again needs to act in a guarded way.

When he himself proclaims his possession of all-knowledge,
his mind remains utterly free of any doubt or fear
such that he might think, "If someone comes and challenges me,
I fear there may be something I do not know."

When declaring his characteristic of having ended the contaminants, 84b
thus reaching the utmost elimination of the contaminants,
his mind remains utterly free of any doubt or fear
that there might be residual contaminants that are not yet ended.

When proclaiming his knowledge of the obstructive dharmas,
he has no doubt at the prospect of being challenged
that, though one might indulge in these dharmas,
they might not actually then constitute an obstacle.

As for the eightfold path of the *ārya*s that he has proclaimed,
his mind is free of any doubt or fear
that someone might rightly claim of this eightfold path
that it is unable to lead one to reach liberation.

He knows in accordance with reality that this is a cause,
this is its result, and this other factor does not constitute [a cause].
It is for these reasons that he is said to be omniscient
and that his fame spreads immeasurably far.

All actions carried out throughout the three periods of time,
the fixed retribution associated with these actions,
and their unfixed karmic results—
He thoroughly knows all of these different matters.

As for all coarse, subtle, deep, and shallow phenomena
within all of the *dhyāna* absorptions and *samādhi*s,
he is able to entirely know them all.
In the realm of *dhyāna* absorptions, no one is his equal.

He first knows with regard to the faculties of beings,
their distinctions as either superior, middling, or inferior,
knows what they delight in, and knows their individual natures,
whereupon, adapting to what is fitting, he teaches them the Dharma.

He cultivated the path and gained its benefits
while also teaching and guiding others.
It is in this manner that the community of disciples
gains the wholesome benefit that accords with reality.

His knowledge of past lives is measurelessly vast
and the vision of his heavenly eye has no bounds.
Among all humans and *deva*s,
no one is able to know their limits.

He abides in the *vajra samādhi,*
having extinguished the afflictions and karmic propensities,
and also knows the utter ending of the human contaminants.
Hence this is known as the power of having ended the contaminants.

The obstacle of afflictions, the obstacles to *dhyāna* absorptions,
and the obstacles to the knowledge of all dharmas—
he has gained liberation from all three obstacles
and hence is known as one who has gained unimpeded liberation.

The forty exclusive dharmas
have measureless meritorious qualities
of which no one could present an expansive explanation.
I have hereby now concluded this general explanation.

Even if, for an entire *kalpa,* the Bhagavat
spoke in praise of these dharmas of the buddhas,
he would still be unable to completely describe them.
How much the less might I do so in the absence of such wisdom.

The shade of the Bhagavat's great kindness
has been thoroughly gathered together through countless deeds.
It is because of the four bases of meritorious qualities
that he has gained the Buddha's measureless Dharma.

As for these four supreme bases of meritorious qualities
of which the Bhagavat has spoken with praise—
I shall now return to these 84c
in setting forth praises of the Tathāgata.

He is completely endowed with the thirty-two marks,
each mark of which requires a hundredfold generation of merit.
As for the eighty marvelous secondary characteristics,
who residing in the three realms could possibly possess them?

Were one to multiply by a hundred all the karmic rewards
produced by the merit created by all the beings
residing within a great trichiliocosm,
each of the marks has just such a quantity of merit [as its cause].

It would require just such a quantity of merit
as well as its associated karmic rewards,
multiplied yet another hundred times
to produce a buddha's mid-brow white hair mark.

It would require for each and every one of thirty marks
all of their corresponding merit and karmic rewards,
multiplied yet again a thousand more times,
to produce the fleshy *uṣṇīṣa* sign atop a buddha's crown.

The meritorious qualities of the Bhagavat
are such that they could never be measured.
Any attempt to do so would be like someone using a ruler
to measure the endless expanse of empty space.

From the moment he brought forth the great resolve
for the sake of bringing about the liberation of all beings,
he persevered for countless *kalpa*s with solid resolve.
It was because of this that he then achieved buddhahood.

Intensely diligent in his zeal to achieve the fulfillment
of such a magnanimous vow,
throughout an immeasurably great number of *kalpa*s,
he has cultivated all the difficult ascetic practices.

Just as with all buddhas of the ancient past
who taught these four bases of meritorious qualities,
only after countless *kalpa*s were they then perfected
so that now he has succeeded in securely abiding within them.

Their foundation lies in preservation of the actual truth,
for which he relinquished even his own body and loved ones,
his riches, treasures, and the happiness associated with wealth.
It is through this that he achieved its complete fulfillment.

Throughout measurelessly many *kalpa*s,
in every instance, he has first thoroughly contemplated
the dharmas that are seen, heard, sensed, and known,[106]
and then, afterward, has explained them for the sake of others.

Where others had not observed (some aspect of Dharma) and such,
as well as in situations where they were beset by doubts,
he was then able to explain these matters in accordance with reality.
Those whom he benefited in this way were measurelessly many.

He would not discuss the confidential matters of others.
Even if resented or ridiculed for this, he still refused to betray them.
His thoughts always dwelled in a state of stable wisdom
as he adapted his teachings to lead others to peace and security.

As for the foremost and most genuinely sublime truth,
nirvana is truly supreme,
for all else, in every case, is false.
The Bhagavat has achieved[107] its complete fulfillment.

[He made gifts of] beverages, food, bedding, and such,
halls, buildings, marvelous residences, viewing terraces,
highly prized elephants, horses, and vehicles, and also
relinquished female companions of especially fine appearance.

[He gave away] gold, silver, pearls, jewels, and such, 85a
villages, cities, and towns,
entire states, and exalted official positions,
and gave away [his dominion over] the four continents as well.

[He relinquished] cherished sons, beloved wives,
his limbs, his head, and his eyes,
and made gifts by slicing off his flesh, removing bones and marrow,
or even giving away his entire body.

Doing so out of pity for beings,
he gave them all, having none that he continued to cherish.
He did so aspiring to go beyond samsara
and not out of some quest to secure his own bliss.

All of the stars and constellations throughout empty space,
and all the grains of sand in this entire earth—
when the Tathāgata was still a bodhisattva,
the number of times he gave in such ways exceeded even these.

He never resorted to actions contrary to Dharma
as he sought out wealth to be used in giving.
He never engaged in giving unaccompanied by knowledge and
never engaged in giving that was invasive or distressing to others.

He never gave bad things as gifts
because he coveted some other fine thing [in return].
He never gave with an ingratiating deviousness
and never engaged in forceful giving because of coveting something.

He never gave with a hateful or doubting mind,
never did so with perverse intent or with derisive laughter,
never did so out of disgust or disbelief,
and never gave with the face turned away, or in other such ways.

He had no discriminating mind [by which he judged],
"This one is worthy and that one is unworthy."
Because he only relied on the mind of compassion,
it was with equal regard for everyone that he practiced giving.

He did not slight other beings,
considering them to not qualify as fields of merit.
On seeing *ārya*s, his mind was reverential.
On seeing those who have broken the precepts, he felt pity for them.

He did not elevate himself above others,
treat others as mere inferiors,
engage in giving for the sake of praise,
give in expectation of rewards, or give in other such ways.

He never gave with regrets or with worry-filled misgivings
and never gave with thoughts of disdain or disrespect.
He never gave with a mind affected by irritability or hostility
and never gave simply as a protocol-dictated formality.

He never gave with a disrespectful mind,
never gave by simply tossing the gift on the ground,
never gave deliberately seeking to cause distress,
and never gave out of a jealousy-driven struggle for supremacy.

He would never tease a supplicant,
never failed to present a gift with his own hands,
did not slight the recipient with a merely paltry gift,
and did not give excessively in order to enhance his own esteem.

His giving was never motivated by intentions associated with
either the *śrāvaka* disciple vehicle or the *pratyekabuddha* vehicle.
His giving was never limited to concern for only a single lifetime
and he never engaged in giving done at the wrong time.

For countless *kalpa*s, the Bhagavat
practiced every form of rare giving,
85b always doing so for the sake of the unsurpassable path
and not merely in order to seek his own happiness.

Throughout the duration of all buddhas' Dharma,
he became a monastic, practiced renunciation,
cultivated the Dharma of all buddhas,
and proclaimed the Dharma for the sake of all humans and *deva*s.

He taught just such a dharma of giving as this
that is supreme among all types of giving,
just as, among all the stars and the moon,
it is the light of the sun that is supreme.

Such supremacy in the relinquishment basis [of meritorious qualities]
surpasses that of any *deva* or human,
just as it is the Bhagavat
who is superior to everyone in the world.

He was therefore able to perfect
such supreme practice of the relinquishment basis.
His fame shall endure for countless *kalpa*s,
flowing on and spreading ceaselessly.

For countless *kalpa*s, the Bhagavat
preserved and upheld the precepts of moral purity
and opened the gates of the *dhyāna* absorptions
for the sake of acquiring the deep quiescence basis.

He began by abandoning five characteristics[108]
and later practiced the eight liberations.
He entered and purified the three *samādhi*s,
and also dwelled in the three liberations.

The Bhagavat well distinguishes
the sixty-five kinds of *dhyāna*s.
There is no *dhyāna* whatsoever
that he has not formerly produced.

Even when abiding in these meditative absorptions,
he did not indulge in their delectably pleasurable states.
Due to the various meditative absorptions,
the Bhagavat gained three types of spiritual superknowledges.

He used these in the liberation of beings
and so became supreme in all things.
For countless *kalpa*s, with a mind of equal regard,
the Bhagavat widely spread his kindly transformative teaching.

An *asaṃkhyeya* of beings
was thereby caused to abide in the Brahma World Heavens
because he was able to use skillful means
in thoroughly teaching the *dhyāna* absorptions.

While still a bodhisattva, the Bhagavat
for incalculably many lifetimes, always
remained free of any entanglement in the affliction of covetousness.
Thus he was able to come and go in the world.

Of those who succeeded in encountering him in the past,
countless such beings thereby achieved rebirth in the heavens.
As for that quiescence that
all bodhisattvas of the past were able to practice,

when still a bodhisattva, the Bhagavat
also practiced, doing so in a manner no different from theirs.
Thus, as regards the realization of quiescence,
that supreme basis [of meritorious qualities], it was entirely fulfilled.

All those forms of wisdom
possessed by the Bhagavat while he was still a bodhisattva—
He relied on such wisdom in his quest for *bodhi*
so that, as a karmic result, he has now developed this wisdom.

85c Just as people rely on the earth for the production
of all the food that it supplies,
[so, too,] as in life after life, the Bhagavat
relinquished the ten courses of dark and bad actions
and always practiced the path of the ten good actions,
these [deeds] were all due to the power of wisdom.[109]

He renounced the five desires and the five hindrances
and thus acquired all the various *dhyāna* absorptions.
He accomplished this for the number of lifetimes in countless *kalpa*s
and did not acquire this from others.
This is excellent indeed, O Great Honored One of the Āryas.
All of this was due to the power of wisdom.

It is because of the Bhagavat that beings,
countless in number, have taken rebirth in the six heavens.
So too has he enabled them to reach the Brahma world.
All of this was due to the power of wisdom.

Throughout the course of his births and deaths, the Bhagavat,
even when confused and perturbed by sufferings and pleasures,
never lost the resolve to attain *bodhi.*
All of this was due to the power of wisdom.

Throughout the course of samsara, the Bhagavat
did not delight [in worldly existence] and yet still always remained.
He delighted in nirvana, yet did not seize on its [final] realization.
All of this was due to the power of wisdom.

When sitting peacefully there in the *bodhimaṇḍa,*
he overcame Māra and his armies
and proceeded to liberate all the classes of beings.
All of this was due to the power of wisdom.

When he originally strove in quest of *bodhi,*
he accumulated countless provisions for the path.
If merely hearing of them causes one to be confused and perturbed,
how much the less might one be able to take on their practice.
That the Bhagavat was able to patiently endure such things
was in every case due to the power of wisdom.

That, in lifetime after lifetime, he was able to naturally know
the classic texts as well as all the arts and skills
while also being able to teach them to others
was in every case due to the power of wisdom.

He drew close to countless buddhas
and from them all drank the sweet dew nectar of their teachings,
He consulted them and inquired about the many different topics
and then also pursued additional distinguishing [clarifications].

He was never the least bit miserly
with the wisdom of the sutras' Dharma,

but rather offered it even to servants, youths, and menials,
allowing them to freely receive his fine explanations.
Because of this, [the fame of] the Bhagavat's
supreme wisdom basis [of meritorious qualities] spreads on afar.

Throughout his former lifetimes, as the Bhagavat
pursued his quest for the realization of *bodhi,*
he practiced the great kindness and compassion
toward all beings.

Relying on the foremost wisdom,
he always marshaled his great strength
to take up and do all the countless kinds
of rare and difficult endeavors.

In all of the many worlds,
he exhaustively contributed all his efforts for countless *kalpa*s.
86a One could never come to the end of them through verbal description,
nor could one even reach it through mathematical calculation.

All of his endeavors of such sorts
surpass those done by any human or *deva.*
Even in all the many worlds,
there is nothing comparable to his extraordinary marvels.

The fruits reaped through such great deeds
reach complete fulfillment in the realization of all-knowledge.
He is the king of those able to destroy samsara
and dwells securely in the place of the Dharma King.

Chapter 25

Teachings to Aid the Mindfulness of the Buddha *Samādhi*

The bodhisattva should rely on these
forty exclusive dharmas
in his mindfulness of the buddhas' Dharma body,
for the buddhas are not their form bodies.

These [preceding] verses have sequentially and summarily explained six categories of meanings associated with the forty exclusive dharmas.[110] In doing so, the practitioner therefore first takes up the mindfulness of the Buddha's form body and then takes up the mindfulness of the Buddha's Dharma body.

Why is this the case? The bodhisattva who has only recently brought forth the resolve [to attain buddhahood] should first take up the practice of mindfulness of the Buddha in reliance on the thirty-two marks and eighty secondary characteristics [of the Buddha's form body], doing so in the manner described earlier.

Then, as one's practice progressively penetrates more deeply, one will develop a middling degree of strength in that practice. One should then rely on the Dharma body in his mindfulness of the Buddha.

Then, as one's mind progressively penetrates yet more deeply, one will then achieve a supreme degree of power in the development of this practice. At that point, one should then take up mindfulness of the Buddha in accordance with the true character of [all dharmas][111] and remain free of any sort of attachment in doing so.

One must not become deeply attached to the form body.[112]
One also refrains from becoming attached to the Dharma body.
One should thoroughly realize that all dharmas
are as eternally quiescent as empty space.

As this bodhisattva develops a superior degree of power [in this practice], he refrains from developing a deep attachment to the Buddha on the basis of either the form body or the Dharma body. Why not? Through one's resolute belief in the dharma of emptiness, one understands that all dharmas are like empty space.

Empty space is defined by the absence of obstruction. The causal circumstances associated with obstruction include phenomena like Mount Sumeru, Yugaṃdhara Mountain, the rest of the ten jeweled mountains, the Iron Ring Mountains, Black Mountain, Stone Mountain, and the others. There are all sorts of other such causal bases for the existence of obstructions.

Why is this [a point at issue]? Because this person has still not yet gained the heavenly eye; if he brings to mind buddhas abiding in the worlds off in the other directions, the various mountains will block them from his view. Consequently, The bodhisattva who has only recently brought forth the resolve [to attain buddhahood] should use the sublime characteristics described by the ten names as bases for his mindfulness of the Buddha. This is as described in these lines:

> The bodhisattva who has only recently brought forth the resolve
> uses the sublime features described by the ten names
> in practicing mindfulness of the buddhas that is free of fault,
> seeing them just as if they were images in a mirror.

As for "the sublime features described in the ten names," those ten names are:

Tathāgata,[113]
Worthy of Offerings,
The Right and Universally Enlightened One,
Perfect in the Clear Knowledges and Conduct,
Well-Gone One,
Knower of the Worlds,
Unsurpassable Trainer of Those to Be Tamed,
Teacher of *Deva*s and Humans,
Buddha,
Bhagavat.

As for "free of fault," the phenomena that one contemplates are beheld as empty and like space itself. Thus [one's contemplation] is free of any fault with regard to the Dharma. And how is this so? It is because all dharmas, from their very origin on forward to the present, have been unproduced and quiescent. Just as this is true [with respect to these dharmas], so too is this also true of all other dharmas.

By taking these names as the object [of his contemplation], this person 86b
develops his practice of the dharma of *dhyāna* meditation. Having done so, he is then able to take these characteristic signs themselves as the object of his contemplation.

At this time, this person then immediately acquires these signs in his practice of the dharma of *dhyāna* meditation and experiences what is referred to as the direct personal experience of an especially extraordinary bliss. One should realize that when this occurs, one has acquired the *pratyutpanna samādhi.* Because of developing this *samādhi,* one is then able to see the buddhas.

As for "as if they were images in a mirror," once the bodhisattva has developed this *samādhi,* it is as if one is seeing one's own face in a clean, brightly lit mirror or like seeing the image of one's own body in a clear, still pool of water.

Initially, whichever buddha one first brings to mind, it is that very image that one sees. After one has seen this image, if one wishes to see buddhas in other regions, then, in accordance with whichever region one brings to mind, one obtains an unimpeded vision of those very buddhas. Hence, regarding this person:

> Although he does not yet possess the spiritual superknowledges
> by which he could fly to visit them,
> he is nonetheless able to see those buddhas
> and has an unimpeded ability to listen to their Dharma.

For this bodhisattva who has only recently brought forth the resolve [to attain buddhahood], neither Mount Sumeru nor any other mountain can present an obstacle and, even though he has not yet acquired any of the spiritual superknowledges, the heavenly eye, or the heavenly ear, and even though he has not yet developed the ability to fly from this country to that country, through the power of this *samādhi,* even while still abiding in this country, he is able to see the buddhas, the bhagavats, abiding in the other regions and is able to hear the Dharma as they are speaking it. Through always cultivating this *samādhi,* he becomes able to see all of the buddhas throughout the ten directions just as they really are.

Question: Through which dharmas is one able to bring forth this meditative absorption and how can one acquire it?

Response:

> One draws close to the good spiritual guide,
> brings forth nonretreating vigor,
> develops extremely solid and durable wisdom,
> and develops the power of unshakable faith.

It is through utilizing these four dharmas that one is able to bring forth this *samādhi.*

As for "drawing close to the good spiritual guide," someone able to instruct a person in the acquisition of this *samādhi* qualifies here as "the good spiritual guide." One should bring forth reverential respect and assiduous diligence and, in drawing close [to the good spiritual guide], one must not allow any indolence, diminishment in motivation, or relinquishing of effort to take place. If one acts accordingly, one will then be able to hear the teaching of the deep meaning of this *samādhi.*

Sharp wisdom, wisdom characterized by penetrating comprehension, and undiminishing wisdom are what qualify as "solid and durable" [wisdom]. One's faculty of faith is deeply and firmly established, so much so that, no matter whether it be a *śramaṇa* or a brahman or a celestial *māra* or Brahmā or anyone else in the world—none of them could cause it to quaver even slightly. This is what is meant by an unshakable power of faith. It is these very four dharmas described here that are able to bring forth this *samādhi.*

Furthermore:

> With a sense of shame, dread of blame, cherishing reverence,
> and offerings to those who proclaim the Dharma
> presented as if they were given to the bhagavats themselves,
> one thereby becomes able to bring forth this *samādhi.*

As for "with a sense of shame, dread of blame, and cherishing reverence," one brings forth a profound sense of shame and dread of blame in relation to those who teach the Dharma. With sincere reverence and affectionate delight, one makes offerings to them as if they were the buddhas themselves. In this way, these four dharmas are able to produce this *samādhi*.

Another preliminary set of fourfold dharmas is as follows: 86c

First, for a period of three months, one strives to refrain from sleeping and, with the exception of using the toilet and eating and drinking, one refrains from sitting down;

Second, for that period of three months, one avoids, even for the duration of a finger snap, indulgence in any thought seizing on the existence of a self;

Third, for that entire three months, one strives to always walk and never rest;

Fourth, for that entire three months, when also engaged in the giving of Dharma, one refrains from seeking offerings from others.

These are the four. There are four more such dharmas, as follows:

First, one becomes able to see the buddhas;

Second, one reassures and encourages others to listen to the teaching of this *samādhi;*

Third, one is never envious or jealous of anyone who is putting the resolve to attain *bodhi* into practice;

Fourth, one is able to accumulate the dharmas of the bodhisattva path.

These are the four. There are four more such dharmas, as follows:

First, one makes buddha images that may also include painted images;

Second, one should carefully write out copies of the sutra that discusses this *samādhi* and then encourage others who have a resolute faith in it to study and recite it aloud once they have obtained it;[114]

Third, teach those of overweening pride[115] to abandon their overweening pride[116] and then influence them to pursue the attainment of *anuttarāsamyaksaṃbodhi;*

Fourth, one should devote oneself to the protection and preservation of the right Dharma of all buddhas.

These are the four. There are four more such dharmas, as follows:

First, one avoids speaking;

Second, both lay and monastic practitioners are to refrain from dwelling together with others;

Third, one always anchors one's mind on the characteristic sign that has been chosen as the object of one's mental focus;[117]

Fourth, one delights in dwelling far apart from others, in a location that is vacant, serene, and silent.

These are the four. The first of the fivefold sets of associated dharmas is as follows:

First, abiding in the unproduced-dharmas patience (*anutpattika-dharma-kṣānti*), one renounces all conditioned dharmas, does not delight in any of the destinies of rebirth, refuses to accept any of the non-Buddhist dharmas, and remains so disgusted with all worldly desires that one does not even bring them to mind, how much the less might one draw physically close to them;

Second, even as one's mind always cultivates and practices countless dharmas, it remains in a state of one-pointed concentration; one remains free of the obstacle of hatred toward any being and one's mind always accords with the practice of the four means of attraction;

Third, one becomes able to perfect kindness, compassion, sympathetic joy, and equanimity while also refraining from exposing others' transgressions;

Fourth, one becomes able to accumulate a multitude of dharmas proclaimed by the Buddha while also being able to carry them out in accordance with the way they were taught;

Fifth, one purifies one's physical, verbal, and mental actions as well as one's views.

These are the five. There are five more associated dharmas, as follows:

First, one delights in according with the practice of giving as praised in the sutras, doing so without miserly thoughts. One delights in speaking on profound dharmas, withholds nothing due to stinginess, and also remains able to dwell in those very dharmas oneself;

Second, one abides in patience, mental pliancy, and delight when abiding in close proximity to others and, if subjected to harsh speech, scolding and cursing, whippings, beatings, being tied up, or other such experiences, one simply attributes it to one's own karmic conditions and does not hate others for doing this;

Third, one always delights in listening to teachings that explain this *samādhi,* in reading and reciting them, in thoroughly understanding them, in explaining them for others, and in causing them to circulate and spread ever more widely even as one diligently practices and cultivates [this *samādhi*];

Fourth, one's mind remains free of any jealous feelings toward others, one refrains from elevating oneself and looking down on others, and one strives to rid oneself of the hindrance of drowsiness;

Fifth, one maintains a mind of pure faith in the Buddha Jewel, the Dharma Jewel, and the Sangha Jewel, offers up deeply sincere service to those of senior, middling, and lower station, always remembers and never forgets even the smallest kindnesses of others, and always abides in truthful speech.

These are the five. In addition, there are the following lines:

As for those *samādhi* dharmas
in which monastic bodhisattvas train,
householder bodhisattvas 87a
should also know these dharmas.

If a householder bodhisattva wishes to cultivate this *samādhi* [he should observe the following twenty guidelines]:

1. One should proceed with a mind of deep faith;
2. One should not seek any sort of karmic reward;
3. One should give up all personal and extra-personal things;
4. One should take refuge in the Three Jewels;
5. One should uphold the five moral precepts purely and in a manner free of any transgression or deficiency;
6. One should perfect the practice of the ten courses of good karmic action while also influencing others to abide in these dharmas;
7. One should cut off all sexual desire;
8. One should repudiate the five types of desire;
9. One should refrain from any feelings of jealousy toward others;

10. One should not nurture an affectionate attachment for either one's spouse or one's children;
11. One should always maintain an aspiration to leave the householder's life to become a monastic;
12. One should always take on and observe the layperson's precepts of abstinence;[118]
13. One's mind should delight in the opportunity to abide within the precincts of a temple;[119]
14. One should be well possessed of a sense of shame and a dread of blame;
15. One should bring forth thoughts of reverential respect toward *bhikṣus* who are pure in upholding the moral precepts;
16. One should not act in a miserly way with the Dharma;
17. One should maintain a mind of deep affection and reverence toward those who teach the Dharma;
18. One should think of teachers of Dharma as if they were one's father, mother, or great teaching master;
19. One should respectfully present all manner of delightful gifts as offerings to the Dharma teaching masters;
20. One should feel gratitude for the kindnesses that have been bestowed upon one and one should repay those kindnesses accordingly.

If a householder bodhisattva abides in meritorious qualities such as these, he will then be able to learn this *samādhi*.

As for [the guidelines appropriate to] a monastic bodhisattva's cultivation of dharmas pertaining to this *samādhi,* they are as follows:

1. One remains free of any defect as regards observance of the moral precepts;
2. One maintains uncorrupted observance of the moral precepts;
3. One maintains unsullied observance of the moral precepts;
4. One maintains pure observance of the moral precepts;
5. One maintains undiminished observance of the moral precepts;
6. One does not seize on the moral precepts themselves [as constituting the very essence of moral virtue];

7. One does not rely on the moral precepts [alone as the sole component of one's practice];
8. One realizes that the moral precepts cannot finally be apprehended at all [as inherently existent entities];
9. One never retreats from one's observance of the moral precepts;
10. One upholds the moral precepts in the manner that is praised by the *ārya*s;
11. One upholds the moral precepts in the manner that is extolled by the wise;
12. One accords with the *prātimokṣa* precepts;
13. One perfects the bases for the awe-inspiring deportment;
14. One remains immensely fearful of committing even the most minor transgression of the precepts;
15. One purifies the actions of body, speech, and mind;
16. One maintains purity in right livelihood;
17. One completely upholds all of the moral precepts;
18. One maintains resolute belief in the extremely profound dharmas;
19. One is able to patiently acquiesce in the dharma of the nonapprehension [of any dharma whatsoever] and is able to not be frightened even by the dharmas of emptiness, signlessness, and wishlessness;
20. One remains diligent in bringing forth vigor [in one's practice];
21. One always maintains ever-present mindfulness;
22. One maintains a mind of solid faith;
23. One is well possessed of a sense of shame and a dread of blame;
24. One does not covet offerings;
25. One remains free of jealousy toward others;
26. One abides in the meritorious qualities associated with practicing the *dhūta* austerities;
27. One abides in the subtleties of Dharma practice;
28. One takes no delight in speaking the coarse language of the world;
29. One avoids gathering in groups for [idle] conversation;
30. One knows to repay kindnesses one has received;
31. One acknowledges those who bestow kindnesses and those who repay kindnesses;

32. Toward one's monastic preceptors and monastic Dharma teachers, one brings forth thoughts of sincere reverence and appreciation for the rarity of being able to encounter them;[120]
33. One does away with any arrogance one might be harboring;
34. One overcomes the self-cherishing mind;
87b 35. Because a good spiritual guide can only rarely be encountered, one strives with diligence to look after his needs;
36. With regard to the source from which one first learned about this Dharma, whether by obtaining a sutra text from someone or by hearing someone recite it, one thinks of them with the same regard as one would maintain for one's own father or mother, one's good spiritual guide, or a great teaching master, and with regard to them, one also feels a sense of shame, dread of blame, affection, and reverence;
37. One always delights in dwelling in a forest hermitage;
38. One does not delight in dwelling in a city or village;
39. One does not covet the opportunity to frequent the homes of benefactors[121] and good spiritual friends;
40. One does not maintain a stinting covetousness for one's own physical survival;
41. One remains ever mindful of death;
42. One does not hoard offerings;
43. One does not indulge any defiling attachment for possessions;
44. One remains free of cravings;
45. One guards and preserves right Dharma;
46. One is not attached to one's robes or bowl,
47. One does not hoard leftover things;
48. One prefers to eat only food that has been obtained on the almsround;
49. On the almsround, one moves along seeking alms according to the proper sequence;[122]
50. One always maintains a sense of shame and dread of blame and always feels remorse [for one's past transgressions];
51. One refrains from hoarding gold, silver, precious jewels, or money and also avoids indulging in unwholesome remorsefulness;[123]
52. One's mind remains free of entangling defilements;

53. One always puts the mind of kindness into practice;
54. One cuts off all feelings of anger;
55. One always puts the mind of compassion into practice;
56. One cuts off affectionate attachments;
57. One always seeks ways to benefit and bring peace to the entire world;
58. One always feels pity for all beings;
59. One always delights in [meditative] walking;
60. One does away with lethargy and sleepiness.

The monastic bodhisattva who abides in dharmas such as these should cultivate and practice this *samādhi*. Additionally:

> One should also train in this same manner
> in the other dharmas pertaining to the cultivation of *samādhi*.

In order to be able to bring forth this *pratyutpanna samādhi,* one should also cultivate the other supportive dharmas. And what are these? They are:

1. One takes the Buddha's kindness as one's objective focus and always mindfully contemplates him as if he were directly before one;
2. One does not allow one's mind to become scattered;
3. One anchors one's attention directly before one;
4. One guards the gates of the sense faculties;
5. With respect to food and drink, one is easily satisfied;
6. One always cultivates *samādhi* in both the first and last watches of the night;
7. One abandons the obstacle of the afflictions;
8. One brings forth all of the *dhyāna* absorptions;
9. In one's practice of *dhyāna* meditation, one does not indulge in the delectably pleasurable meditation states;
10. One demolishes through separation the appearance of attractive forms;[124]
11. One acquires the sign of unloveliness;[125]
12. One does not desire the five aggregates;
13. One does not become attached to the eighteen sense realms;
14. One does not indulge any defilement in relation to the twelve sense bases;

15. One does not presumptuously rely on one's [superior] caste origins;
16. One destroys any arrogance;
17. One's mind always remains empty and quiescent in relation to all dharmas that one encounters;
18. One imagines all beings as one's close relatives;
19. One does not seize on the moral precepts themselves [as constituting the very essence of moral virtue];
20. One does not make discriminating distinctions regarding the meditative absorptions;
21. One should diligently pursue abundant learning;
22. One does not become arrogant because of this abundant learning;
23. One remains free of doubts with respect to any of the dharmas;

87c 24. One does not oppose the buddhas;

25. One does not act in a manner that is contrary to the Dharma;
26. One does not do anything that contributes to the destruction of the Sangha;
27. One always goes to pay one's respects to worthies and *ārya*s;
28. One distances oneself from foolish common people;
29. One delights in discussion of world-transcending topics;
30. One cultivates the six dharmas of mutual harmony;[126]
31. One always cultivates the five bases of liberation;[127]
32. One rids himself of the nine bases for generating the affliction of anger;[128]
33. One cuts off the eight dharmas associated with indolence;[129]
34. One cultivates the eight types of vigor;[130]
35. One always contemplates the nine signs [of the deterioration of the corpse];[131]
36. One has realized for himself the eight realizations of great men;[132]
37. One perfects all of the *dhyāna* concentrations and *samādhi*s;
38. One has no covetous attachment to these *dhyāna* concentrations and realizes they have no apprehensible reality;[133]
39. When listening to Dharma, one does so with a focused mind;
40. One demolishes the perception of the five aggregates [as inherently existent phenomena];

41. One does not abide in the perception of phenomena [as inherently existent];
42. One is deeply fearful of samsara's births and deaths;
43. One contemplates the five aggregates as like enemies;[134]
44. One contemplates the sense bases as like an empty village;
45. One contemplates the four great elements as like venomous serpents;
46. One brings forth the contemplation of nirvana as quiescent, secure, and happy;[135]
47. One contemplates the five desires as worthy of being spat upon and one's mind delights in escaping from them;
48. One never opposes the teachings of the Buddha;
49. One has no disputes or quarrels with any other being;
50. In teaching beings, one influences them to dwell securely in all of the meritorious qualities.

In addition:

> The bodhisattva should understand
> the benefits that result from such a *samādhi*.

The bodhisattva should also understand the benefits that result from practicing this *pratyutpanna samādhi*.

Question: What are the resulting benefits gained by cultivating this *samādhi*?

Response: One obtains the resulting benefit of becoming irreversible with respect to the unsurpassable path. Additionally, as for what the sutra says about these resulting benefits, we have the following:[136]

> The Buddha told Bhadrapāla Bodhisattva, "By way of analogy, suppose there was a person who was able to crush to dust all the earth in all worlds in a trichiliocosm and was also able also to crush to dust all the grasses, trees, flowers, leaves, and everything else throughout all of the worlds in a great trichiliocosm.
>
> "Bhadrapāla, let us consider now that each and every one of those motes of dust were to constitute one world in which a single buddha dwells, and suppose then that one filled to overflowing just such a number

of worlds with sublimely marvelous precious jewels and presented all of these jewels as an offering to them.

"Bhadrapāla, what do you think? By performing such an act of giving, would this person gain a great deal of merit or not?"

"Indeed, O Bhagavat, he would reap a great deal."

The Buddha said, "Bhadrapāla, I will now tell you truthfully that if there was a son of good family who heard of this *samādhi* in which all buddhas appear before one and he were then to be neither startled nor frightened by hearing of it, the merit he would reap from that alone would be immeasurably vast. How much the more so would this be the case if he were to have faith in it, accept it, uphold it, read [teachings in which it is explained], recite them, and explain them for others. How much the more so yet would this be the case if he were to actually cultivate it with
88a concentrated mind even for the time it takes to tug a single squirt of milk from the udder of a cow.

"Bhadrapāla, let me tell you: Even this person's merit would surpass one's ability to measure it. How much the more so would this be so in the case of someone who was actually able to succeed in acquiring this *samādhi*."

The Buddha continued, telling Bhadrapāla, "If a son or daughter of good family who receives, upholds, reads, recites, and explains [teachings on this *samādhi*] for others were on the verge of falling into the fires arising at the end of the *kalpa,* those fires would immediately become extinguished.

"Bhadrapāla, whosoever sustains this *samādhi*—supposing that he were to encounter some difficulty with officialdom, or supposing that he were to encounter hostile thieves, lions, tigers, wolves, fearsome beasts, fearsome dragons, any of the venomous serpents, or any other such threat, whether from *yakṣa*s, *rākṣasa*s, *kumbhāṇḍa*s, *piśāci*s, and such, or from humans, nonhumans, or any other sort of entity—that any of those entities might succeed in physically harming him, taking his life, or causing him to break the precepts—this would be an utter impossibility.

So too would this also be the case with respect to those who might be reading, reciting, or teaching this to others. In those cases too they would remain free of any destructive affliction, with the sole exception of instances where they were already bound to undergo compulsory karmic retributions.[137]

"Furthermore, Bhadrapāla, when a bodhisattva accepts, upholds, reads, or recites the sutra on this *samādhi,* if he happens to contract some sickness of the eye, ear, nose, tongue, mouth, or teeth, some disease instigated by wind or cold, or any other such disease, that he might then lose his life because of any of these diseases would be an utter impossibility with the sole exception of instances where he was already bound to undergo compulsory karmic retributions.

"Also, Bhadrapāla, if a person were to accept, uphold, read, or recite the sutra on this *samādhi,* the *deva*s themselves would protect him. So too would he be protected by the dragons, *yakṣa*s, *mahoraga*s, humans, nonhumans, the Four Heavenly Kings, Śakra, ruler of the *deva*s, the Brahma Heaven King, and the buddhas, the bhagavats. They would all join in remaining protectively mindful of this practitioner.

"Furthermore, this person would be one of whom the *deva*s would all be affectionately mindful, and so too would this be so for other such beings up to and including the buddhas themselves who would also remain affectionately mindful of this practitioner.

"Additionally, this person would be one whom the *deva*s praise, and so too, he would be one whom other beings up to and including all buddhas would praise as well.

"Also, this bodhisattva would be one whom the *deva*s would all wish to see coming to visit them, and so too with the others on up to the buddhas themselves who would all wish to see him coming to visit them.

"Furthermore, the bodhisattva who accepts and upholds the sutra on this *samādhi* will naturally become able to hear whichever other sutras he has not yet heard.

"Additionally, this bodhisattva who gains this *samādhi* will become able to acquire all of these beneficial experiences even in his dreams.

"Bhadrapāla, were I to attempt to describe the merit of this bodhisattva who accepts, uphold, reads, and recites the sutra on this *samādhi,* doing so even for an entire *kalpa* or somewhat less than a *kalpa,* I would still be unable to come to the end of it. How much the less would this be possible in the case of someone who actually succeeds in perfecting this *samādhi*?

"Bhadrapāla, if some man with strong body and speed like the wind ran for a hundred years without resting, always proceeding to the east, south, west, north, the four midpoints, above, and below, what do you think? Would anyone be able to know the number of miles he traveled in all those regions throughout the ten directions?"

Bhadrapāla replied, "That would be an incalculable number. Except for the Tathāgata, someone like Śāriputra, or an *avaivartika* [bodhisattva], nobody would be able to know such a number."

88b "Bhadrapāla, suppose that, on the one hand, there was a son or daughter of good family who filled up with real gold all the area traveled by that man and then give it all away as gifts. Suppose too that, on the other hand, there was someone who merely heard of this *samādhi* and then engaged in four types of rejoicing and dedication of merit to *anuttarāsamyaksaṃbodhi* and the constant pursuit of abundant learning, [doing so by reflecting as follows]:

Just as all buddhas of the past when practicing the bodhisattva path rejoiced in this *samādhi,* so too do I now rejoice in it;
Just as the bodhisattvas of the present now rejoice in this *samādhi,* so too do I now rejoice in it;
Just as all future buddhas during their practice of the bodhisattva path shall rejoice in this *samādhi,* so too do I now rejoice in it;
And in just that fashion as this *samādhi* was practiced by all past, future, and present bodhisattvas, so too do I now also rejoice in all of that, and just as they all did so for the sake of pursuing abundant learning [essential to the path], so too do I now rejoice in this *samādhi* for the sake of the quest for such abundant learning.

"Bhadrapāla, if one were to attempt to compare the previously described merit with the merit from this rejoicing, it could not approach a hundredth part or even one part in a hundred thousand myriads of *koṭis* of parts. The futility of this comparison simply could not be adequately described through any form of calculation or analogy. The benefits resulting from this *samādhi* are just so immeasurable and boundless as this."

In addition:

As for the stations in which one may abide in this *samādhi*
as well as the distinctions pertaining to lesser, middling, and greater,
the many different characteristics such as these
should all be taken up for a discussion of their meaning.

The stations in which one may abide in this *samādhi* as well as its lesser, middling, and greater characteristics—all such things should be distinguished and known and these matters should then be explained.

Regarding "the stations in which one may abide in it," this *samādhi* may be acquired in the first *dhyāna,* the second *dhyāna,* the third *dhyāna,* or the fourth *dhyāna* and one may acquire strength in it while in the first *dhyāna.*

It may be that someone who is "lesser" is able to bring forth this *samādhi.* Here, "lesser" may refer to the fact that a person is possessed of only a lesser degree of strength [in this practice]. "Lesser" may also refer to abiding [in the *samādhi*] for a shorter period of time. "Lesser" may also refer to the practitioner's seeing a relatively smaller number of buddha worlds. Distinctions regarding "middling" and "greater" may be made in just the same way.

In discussing this *samādhi,* one may speak of it as:

Sometimes involving the presence of ideation (*vitarka*) and the presence of discursion (*vicāra*);
Sometimes involving the absence of ideation and the presence of discursion;
Sometimes involving the absence of ideation and the absence of discursion;
Sometimes involving the presence of joy (*prīti*);
Sometimes involving the presence of bliss (*sukha*);
Sometimes involving neither suffering nor bliss;
Sometimes involving the presence of breathing;
Sometimes involving the absence of breathing;
Sometimes definitely being of a wholesome nature;
Sometimes involving the presence of the contaminants;
Sometimes involving the absence of the contaminants;
Sometimes connected with the desire realm;
Sometimes connected with the form realm;
Sometimes connected with the formless realm;

Sometimes not connected with the desire realm;
Sometimes not connected with the form realm;
And sometimes not connected with the formless realm.

This *samādhi:*
Is a mental dharma;
Is [a dharma] associated with the mind;
Is a dharma that occurs along with the mind;
Is a nonform [dharma];
Is a nonmanifest [dharma];
Is able to take an object;
Is not karma [per se];
Is associated with karmic activity;
Is coexistent with karmic activity;
Is not the result of karmic actions from a previous life except when it is the result of a particular cause;[138]
Can be cultivated, can be known, and can be realized;
Can be realized both with the body and by means of wisdom;
Can be subject to severance or may be invulnerable to severance;
Should be severed when contaminants are present;
88c And is invulnerable to severance when free of the contaminants.

Similar distinctions of this sort may also be made with respect to the knowledge and vision associated with this *samādhi*. Also, it is not necessarily conjoined with the seven limbs of enlightenment.[139] Ideally, all of these distinctions should be discussed herein.

Furthermore, it is through the cultivation of this *samādhi* that one may succeed in seeing the buddhas. Accordingly, it is said that:

> After one has succeeded in seeing the buddhas,
> one proceeds with diligent resolve to present offerings [to them].
> As one's roots of goodness are thus able to grow,
> one becomes able to rapidly teach beings.

"Making offerings" refers to having a pure mind imbued with reverence and delight as one brings to mind the countless meritorious qualities of the Buddha. When one praises him in various ways, this constitutes the making of verbal offerings. When one makes formal reverential bows and presents flowers, incense, and other such things, this constitutes the making of physical offerings.

Because of these actions, one's karmic merit grows ever greater just as a seed starts to grow when it is planted in earth and receives moisture from the rain. "Rapidly teaching" refers to influencing beings to abide in the three vehicles. It is in this way that the bodhisattva brings about the growth of his roots of goodness.

> Through availing oneself of the first two dharmas of attraction,
> one is able to attract beings [to the Dharma].
> One resorts to the latter two dharmas of attraction
> for those not yet fully able to believe and accept [Dharma teachings].

"The first two" refers to "giving" and to "pleasing words" whereas "beneficial actions" and "joint endeavors" constitute "the latter two dharmas" [of the four means of attraction]. Because this bodhisattva who abides on the first ground is as yet unable to completely comprehend everything, [there may be certain aspects of the teaching] that he can only accept on faith.

> He then takes all of his roots of goodness
> and dedicates them to the realization of buddhahood.
> This is comparable to when others smelt gold
> and then refine it, whereupon it thereby becomes amenable to use.

It is through being smelted by the fire of wisdom that, in all the endeavors undertaken by the bodhisattva, his roots of goodness ripen and then finally become amenable to use.

Chapter 26

The Analogy Chapter

This bodhisattva should learn of the characteristic features
of the grounds and then attain the fruits of their cultivation.
It is in order to attain all aspects of the grounds
that he is therefore diligent in the practice of vigor.

"Characteristic features" refers here to their appearances. It is due to [learning about them] that one is then able to know them. "Attain" refers here to bringing them to a state of complete development. It is because of this dharma [of "complete development"] that one refers to completely developing this dharma.

"Cultivation" refers to [the two types of cultivation, namely] cultivation associated with acquisition and cultivation associated with practice. As for always bearing in mind "the fruits," it is from the cause that one achieves the accomplishment of an endeavor that is referred to as its "fruits."

This bodhisattva who aspires to acquire the practices specific to the ten grounds should learn well their characteristic features and then acquire the fruits of their cultivation. "Learning" refers to hearing [these teachings] from buddhas, bodhisattvas, and one's superiors.

"It is in order to gain all aspects of the grounds" means that it is for the sake of successful acquisition of the aspects of these grounds that one diligently practices vigor. The characteristic aspects of the first ground that are of concern here are as described earlier in this text:

The bodhisattva who abides on the first ground
has much that he is able to endure.
He is not fond of struggle or disputation,
and, for the most part, his mind is joyous and pleased.

He always delights in purity. 89a
He has a compassionate mind and feels pity for beings.

He has no thoughts of hatred or anger,
and, for the most part, practices these seven things.[140]

Thus, the seven dharmas consisting of the capacity for endurance, non-disputation, being joyous and pleased, purity, compassion, an absence of hatred in the mind, and such—these are all characteristic features of the first ground. It is the complete development of these seven dharmas consisting of the "capacity for endurance" and so forth that define their "acquisition." Furthermore, these seven dharmas comprising the characteristics of "capacity for endurance" and so forth—they are all acquired on the first ground. This is as described in verse, as follows:

Having densely planted one's roots of goodness,
having thoroughly practiced the practices,
having well accumulated all the provisions,
having made offerings to all buddhas,

having become protected by the good spiritual guide,
having completely developed the resolute intentions,
having become compassionately mindful of beings,
and having resolute belief in the unsurpassable Dharma—[141]

Once one has become completely equipped with these eight dharmas,
at one's own behest, one should bring forth a vow, saying,
"After I have accomplished my own liberation,
I shall return and liberate other beings."

For the sake of gaining the ten powers,
one enters the congregation of those at the stage of certainty.[142]
Then one is born into the family of the tathāgatas
that is free of any transgressions.

One immediately turns away from the worldly path
and enters the supreme path that goes beyond the world.
It is because of this that one gains the first ground.
This ground is referred to as the "Ground of Joyfulness."[143]

Therefore, one should understand that the definite resolve one has developed for the sake of attaining *bodhi* is what constitutes the essence of one's cultivation in gaining the first ground. From that initial bringing forth of the resolve all the way to one's attainment of the *samādhi* in which all buddhas manifest before one—all of the meritorious qualities thoroughly described as pertaining to that intervening period are what are able to bring forth all of these meritorious qualities. And after they have arisen, their cultivation, accumulation, and growth are what define the first ground.

As for "the fruits of their cultivation," we have previously already emphasized in place after place that, when one acquires however much merit, one is not to dedicate that merit for the sake of reaching the grounds of either *śrāvaka* disciples or *pratyekabuddha*s. Now we should state this yet again. When the bodhisattva acquires the fruition of the first ground, he is able to acquire several hundreds of meditative concentrations and other such results.

As for the "aspects" of the first ground, this refers to all the many dharmas that jointly establish the first ground. This is what is meant here by "all aspects." This is analogous to the yeast, rice, and other ingredients that, when mixed together, are able to make wine. These are what constitute the causes and conditions for the making of wine. So too it is with all the dharmas that are able to contribute to the establishment of the first ground. These are what constitute the "aspects" of the first ground. These are as follows:

> The power of faith becomes ever more superior
> as one perfects the mind of great compassion.
> One feels kindness and pity for all types of beings
> and tirelessly cultivates the mind of goodness.
>
> One finds joyous delight in sublime dharmas,
> always draws close to the good spiritual guide,
> maintains a sense of shame, dread of blame, and reverence,
> and makes one's mind gentle and harmonious.
>
> One delights in contemplating dharmas and stays free of attachment,
> singlemindedly strives to acquire abundant learning,
> and refrains from coveting offerings of benefits and support, 89b
> while staying far from base cheating, flattery, and deception.
>
> One does not defile the family of the buddhas
> and does not damage moral precepts or cheat the buddhas.

One deeply delights in all-knowledge[144]
and remains as unmoving as an immense mountain.

One always delights in cultivating the practice
of ever more superior sublime dharmas.
One delights in the world-transcending dharmas
and does not delight in worldly dharmas.

Even as one cultivates the Ground of Joyfulness,
one is able to cultivate what is difficult to cultivate.
Therefore one is always singleminded
in the diligent practice of these dharmas.

The bodhisattva is able to perfect
such supremely sublime dharmas as these.
It is this then that constitutes secure abiding
on the bodhisattva's first ground.[145]

Question: What use is there for the bodhisattva in learning of these characteristic features of the first ground and other related matters?

Response: This bodhisattva should thoroughly know the skillful means associated with the characteristic features of the first ground and the other associated dharmas. Therefore he should learn about them.

Question: Should the bodhisattva come to thoroughly know only the skillful means associated with these dharmas or should he also thoroughly know other associated skillful means as well?

Response: He should not only thoroughly know the skillful means associated with all of these dharmas but should also thoroughly know the skillful means associated with other dharmas.

Question: If that is the case, then could you perhaps set forth a summary discussion [of these additional topics]?

Response:

There are dharmas able to assist [in acquisition of] the ground.
There are dharmas running counter to [acquisition of] the ground.

There are dharmas able to give rise to the ground.
There are dharmas able to destroy the ground.

There are the characteristic features and fruits of each ground.
There are those things gained as one abides on each ground.
There are aspects of each ground that facilitate its purification.
There are things gained in advancing from one ground to another.

There are things that increase as one abides on each ground.
There are factors through which no one can cause one's retreat.
From the point where the bodhisattva [begins to] purify the grounds
to the point he reaches the ground of the countlessly many buddhas,

when engaged in all these endeavors,
he should thoroughly know the associated skillful means,
should inquire of those who are skilled in such matters,
and should rid himself of arrogance.

As for "dharmas assisting acquisition of the first ground," these include such factors as faith, moral virtue, learning, relinquishing, vigor, mindfulness, and wisdom. It is dharmas of this sort along with the other dharmas that accord with the first ground that constitute what is meant here by "assisting dharmas."

"Dharmas running counter [to acquisition of the ground]" include disbelief, breaking of precepts, having but little learning, covetousness, indolence, chaotic thoughts, absence of wisdom, and any other dharmas that fail to accord with the first ground and do not assist its acquisition.

As for "dharmas able to destroy the ground," these include any that might cause one to retreat from and abandon cultivation of this ground, any that might obstruct it, and any that might cause it to not manifest. These would be comparable in their effect to the utter destruction of the myriad things that occurs at the very end of the *kalpa*.

What are the dharmas said to have the ability to rob one of the resolve to attain *bodhi*? This is a matter that has already been explained [earlier in this text].

As for "dharmas able to give rise to the ground," this refers to those 89c
that are able to bring forth the first ground and those that are able to bring

about successful establishment in the first ground. These are the dharmas preventing one from being robbed of the resolve to realize *bodhi.* These were explained earlier as well.

The meanings of "characteristic features," "acquisition of fruition," and "the aspects of the ground" were explained above.

As for "dharmas facilitating purification," if one uses these dharmas, one will be able to purify the first ground. As previously explained,[146] they are as follows:

> The bodhisattva who abides on the first ground
> has much that he is able to endure.
> He is not fond of struggle or disputation,
> and, for the most part, his mind is joyous and pleased.
>
> He always delights in purity.
> He has a compassionate mind and feels pity for beings.
> He has no thoughts of hatred or anger,
> and, for the most part, practices these seven things.

It is by resort to dharmas such as these seven that one is able to purify the first ground.

"Advancing from one ground to another" refers for example to when one advances from the first ground to the second ground, and from the second ground to the third ground. So too it is with the rest [of the grounds]. [That one is able to proceed] from the first ground to the second ground is due to acquiring ten types of mind including refraining from deviousness, and so forth. [And that one is able to proceed] from the second ground to the third ground is due to acquiring the ten types of mind through which one acquires resolute faith, and so forth. It is due to acquiring just such various sorts of mind and various types of dharmas that one is then able to advance from one ground to the next ground.

As for "things that increase as one abides on each ground," this includes for example the fact that the first ground is characterized by much cultivation of the perfection of giving (*dāna-pāramitā*), the second ground is characterized by much cultivation of the perfection of moral virtue (*śīla-pāramitā*) and an increase in the strength of faith and other such dharmas, and the third ground is characterized by much cultivation of abundant learning and increasing strength in giving, moral virtue, faith, and other such dharmas. The same process occurs on each of the other grounds as well.

Regarding "factors through which no one can cause one's retreat," this refers to the capacity that develops as one dwells on this ground through which no *śramaṇa* or brahman, and no celestial *māra*, Brahmā, or anyone else in the world can possibly cause one to turn back from it. Why [can't they cause one to turn back]? It is because one has gained the power of great meritorious qualities, because one has deeply penetrated to the very bottom of the nature of all dharmas, and because one has developed great resolute faith.

As for "from the point where the bodhisattva [begins to] purify the grounds to the point he reaches the ground of the countlessly many buddhas," this refers to the fact that, if the bodhisattva finishes the complete purification of all the grounds, he will then succeed in reaching the Buddha ground.

"When engaged in all of these endeavors," in every case, "he should thoroughly know the associated skillful means."

Regarding "inquiring of those who are skilled in such matters," it is on the basis of having completely perfected one's cultivation of right Dharma that one qualifies as "one who is skilled in such matters."

As for what is meant here by "right Dharma," in summary, this refers to:

First, faith;

Second, vigor;

Third, mindfulness;

Fourth, meditative concentration;

Fifth, wisdom;

Sixth, moral virtue in body, speech, and mind; and

Seventh, freedom from greed, hatred, and delusion.

Regarding "ridding himself of arrogance," when one regards oneself as superior to those who truly *are* superior, this is known as "great arrogance." When one regards oneself as superior to those who are one's equals and thus elevates oneself in one's own mind, this is what is known as "arrogance." When, with regard to those compared to whom one is in fact vastly inferior one instead regards oneself as being only slightly inferior, this is what is known as "arrogance even in inferiority."

Question: You have stated that one should come to thoroughly know the
90a skillful means associated with all of these dharmas. Assuming that one does gain all of these skillful means, of what use are they?

Response:

If the bodhisattva thoroughly knows with regard to all the grounds
their characteristic features and their acquisition,
so long as he has not yet attained buddhahood,
he will never turn back from the first ground.

"Characteristic features" refers to the seven [above-listed] dharmas that assist advancement through the grounds. "Acquisition" refers to [avoidance of] the eight [above-listed] dharmas that run counter to acquisition of the grounds.[147] The eight dharmas that destroy cultivation are those one should not practice. If the bodhisattva thoroughly knows these dharmas, so long as he has not yet attained buddhahood, he will never turn back.

Question: As for this bodhisattva who well knows all of these dharmas but will never retreat so long as he has not yet attained buddhahood, what sort of analogy would serve to describe his circumstance?

Response:

It is as if there was a guide possessed of immense powers
who knew well the characteristics of the good road
and knew how best to get from this place to that place,
knew what was appropriate when encountering a turn in the path,

knew the provisions and implements to be taken on the trip,
knew how they were all to be adequately prepared,
knew how in the midst of that dangerous road
one ensures that the group can remain safe and secure

and succeed in reaching the great city,
being able all the while to cause everyone to escape calamities.
[Success in this] would be because of this great guide,
because of his being well able to know the path,

because of his knowing well the changes in the terrain,
and due to having completely prepared the provisions for the path.
The bodhisattva thoroughly knows the path,
the good and bad aspects in this place and that place

so that he can himself cross beyond the dangers of samsara
while also leading many other beings across,
thereby causing them to arrive at a safe and secure place
in the city of unconditioned nirvana,

enabling them all to avoid the many anguishing calamities
encountered within the wretched destinies.
The power of a bodhisattva's skillful means
is the result of his ability to thoroughly know the path.

As for "the characteristics of the good road," this refers to knowing where there is abundant firewood, forage grasses, and water; knowing where there
are no bandits, lions, wolves, tigers or any other sorts of fearsome beasts or 90b
venomous insects; knowing where it is neither too cold nor too hot; knowing where there are no fearsome mountains, crevasses, abysses, precipitous river gorges, hazardous ravines, deep thorny underbrush, jungles, or deep coves blocking the path; knowing where there are no steep ascents and plummeting descents; knowing where the path is level, straight, flat, direct in its connections, and having but few forks in the road; and knowing where it is wide, able to accommodate many people, and frequented by many travelers. It refers as well to knowing where traveling is not inordinately wearisome or exhausting, and to knowing where there is an abundance of flowers, fruit, and things one can eat. It is just such circumstances as these that define what is meant by "the characteristics of the best road." Whatever features are opposite to these characteristics are signs of a bad road.

"This place" refers to a location where the band of travelers stops, eats, and rests. "That place" refers to a different place that is reached after departing from this place, or it may also refer to the different places passed through between two overnight stops. "Turn in the path" refers to where one sees that there is a fork in the path. As for [the path that] "reaches the great city," it is this path that should be traveled, whereas all other paths must be avoided.

"Provisions" refers to supplies that are eaten along the road such as balls made of wheat and honey.

The "immense powers" [as possessed by this guide] refers to great strength, the possession of abundant resources in wealth, and a thorough understanding of the methods required to maintain order.

"Adequate preparation" refers to gathering together an abundance of food and drink so that they will encounter no shortages.

"Safety" refers to ensuring that there will be no frightful experiences involving encounters with bandits.

"Security" refers to ensuring that there will be no sickness, intensely painful incidents, or ruinous calamities.

"Great city" refers here to being able to reach a great city accommodating a large population.

This great guide thoroughly understands all of the signs along the road and is himself personally free of any troublesome difficulties while also being well able to prevent the entire group from encountering any troublesome difficulties. This is a result of his thorough familiarity with the path. There are no encounters with intense cold or heat, hunger or thirst, bandits, fearsome beasts, poisonous insects, fearsome mountainous terrain, treacherous rivers, deep chasms, or other such calamities. And why is this? This is because he thoroughly knows all of the good and bad signs along the entire road.

This comparison is used as an analogy for one's progression through the Ground of Joyfulness and the rest of the ten grounds, for it is comparable to when someone who has embarked on a path refrains from resting and thereby becomes able to reach a great city. So too, the bodhisattva travels in this way through the ten grounds and thus succeeds in arriving at the Buddha Dharma's entry into the great city of nirvana.

This route is comparable to that good road along which there is an abundance of firewood, forage grasses, water, and such. As a consequence, the traveler does not encounter shortages in those things. "Forage grasses" refers to that situation wherein someone traveling by horse does so on a road where, because there are excellent fields of grass along the way, the horse's strength remains robust. The meritorious qualities associated with the path of the ten grounds are just like this.

Because the four supreme bases [of meritorious qualities] consisting of truth, relinquishment, quiescence, and wisdom facilitate the arising of all the meritorious qualities, they are analogous here to those forage grasses. How is this so? If a person esteems truthfulness in his endeavors, then he delights in speaking in a manner that accords with the truth. One should draw close to those who speak the truth. One sees that truthfulness is beneficial and thus delights in according with truth in his endeavors. Hence he deeply abhors false speech, renounces false speech, sees the faults inherent in false speech, and does not wish to even hear it. Due to causes and conditions such as these, one acquires the supreme basis of truthfulness. The other three supreme bases [of meritorious qualities] consisting of relinquishment and the rest should be similarly understood.

Just as, in traveling that good road, in order to reach the great city, it is essential that the elephants, horses, cattle, donkeys, and such obtain foraging grass through which they are provided with strength, so too it is that the bases of truthfulness, relinquishment, quiescence, and wisdom enable one to reach the Buddha Dharma's entry into the great city of nirvana.

"Firewood" is analogous here to the wisdom associated with extensive learning, [the wisdom associated with] contemplation, and [the wisdom associated with] cultivation by which one is able to perfect the works of great wisdom. Just as firewood is able to cause a fire to burn and also cause it to
become fiercely intense, so too is the wisdom of learning, contemplation, and 90c
cultivation able to produce the great wisdom that one is then able to cause to grow. In just the same manner as fire is able to burn, is able to cook, and is able to provide illumination, so too is the fire of wisdom able to burn up the afflictions, ripen one's roots of goodness, and illuminate the four truths of the *ārya*s. Just as fire is analogous to wisdom, firewood is analogous to the various dharmas that are capable of generating wisdom.

"Abundant water" refers to there being numerous flowing rivers and canals one can freely use to satisfy everyone's needs in a way that mere springs, wells, and ponds could not sufficiently serve.

Then again "abundant water" is analogous to when people board boats and then follow the current until they reach a great city. The water contained in wells, springs, reservoirs, and ponds is simply unable to serve in this capacity. As stated in the sutras:

> Faith serves as the great river and merit serves as its banks. Just as a river is able to relieve heat, quench thirst, rinse away filth, and produce power [for waterwheels and such], faith in good dharmas is similarly able to extinguish the fire of the three poisons, rinse away the filth of the three types of bad actions, quench the thirst associated with the three realms of existence, and contribute power to good dharmas undertaken for the sake of nirvana.

Just as that good road has an abundance of roots and medicinal herbs along its course by which the traveler will not encounter shortages of those things, so too it is with the path of the ten grounds.

In this case, "roots" signifies whatever is cherished by [virtue of] one's resolute intentions. Just as when roots are established, sprouts, a trunk, branches, leaves, and an abundance of fruit grow forth, so too, when one's resolute intentions cherish the path, they then bring about the growth of right recollective mindfulness, great vows, and the other meritorious qualities.

"Medicinal herbs" here signifies the *pāramitā*s. Just as the medicinal herbs are able to extinguish all manner of toxins, the medicinal herbs of the *pāramitā*s are able in this same manner to extinguish the poisons of greed, hatred, and delusion and do away with the sickness associated with the afflictions.

[When one possesses these *pāramitā*s] it is analogous to when one travels a good road and makes sure not to lose his passport.[148] He is then able to travel safely along the road.[149] Just as when a traveler who has not lost his passport is able to go wherever he wishes without being obstructed by anyone, so too, on the path of the ten grounds, so long as one does not lose his passport, the roots of goodness gathered while ascending through the grounds are able to freely assist the increase and growth of the roots of goodness that one currently possesses.

One is then also able to teach those beings who presently abide in the paths of *śrāvaka* disciples, *pratyekabuddha*s, and *deva*s of the desire realm and form realm, thereby influencing them to abide in the path to buddhahood. Then, no matter whether it be Māra or some proponent of a non-Buddhist tradition, one cannot be interfered with or disturbed by anyone. This is what is meant by "not losing one's passport."

Just as that good road is free of mosquitoes, horseflies, and the various sorts of poisonous insects, the path of the ten grounds is free of the sounds of sorrow, worry, weeping, and crying. Just as that good road is free of difficulties wrought by bandits, so too is the path of the ten grounds free of the five hindrances' gang of evil thieves. This is just as described by the Buddha when he told the *bhikṣus*, "The thieves in this village are the so-called "five hindrances."[150] Just as thieves start by stealing peoples' possessions but then later move on to murder, so too it is with the thieves of the five hindrances. They start by stealing one's roots of goodness, but then later cut off the life of one's wisdom with the result that one falls into negligence and finally dies. 91a

Just as that road is free of lions, tigers, wolves, and the various other sorts of fearsome beasts, so too is the path of the ten grounds free of hatred, anger, fighting, and disputation. Just as lions and the other sorts of fearsome beasts enjoy tormenting and harming other beings, so too do hatred, anger, and such arise in order to afflict others in this same way. Just as those fearsome beasts eat flesh and drink blood, so too do hatred, hostility, and such consume the flesh of the wisdom that arises from abundant learning. And so too do they drink the blood of the wisdom that arises from cultivation and the other [forms of wisdom][151] in this same manner.

And just as that good road is free of terribly extreme cold and heat, so too, because on the path of the ten grounds one does not fall into the hells of cold and ice, it is free of terribly extreme cold. And because one does not fall into the hot hells, it is free of terribly extreme heat.

Just as that good road is free of deep chasms and other such difficulties, so too is the path of the ten grounds free of the difficulties inherent in the ascetic practices of the non-Buddhist traditions such as:

Coating the body with ashes;
Plunging into ice;
Pulling out one's hair;
Bathing three times each day;
Standing on one foot;
Eating one meal the first day, then one meal every two days, and so forth until one goes a month on only one meal;
Taking a lifelong vow of silence;
Always holding up one arm;

Always practicing endurance by subjecting one's body to the five kinds of fire;
Lying down on beds of nails:
Plunging into fire;
Plunging into water;
Throwing oneself off of high cliffs;
Burning one's body by standing in a deep cauldron of cattle excrement;
Going straight off in one direction without avoiding any difficulties one might encounter;
Always wearing wet clothes;
Lying down in water;
Or subjecting oneself to any of the other sorts of physical or mental sufferings.

None of these lead to right wisdom. Because [the path of the ten grounds] is free of such things, it is said to be free of difficulties.

Just as that road is free of deviating pathways, so too it is with the path of the ten grounds. It is because it is free of evil actions of body, mouth, or mind that it is said to be free of deviating pathways.

Just as that road is free of thorny underbrush, so too it is with the path of the ten grounds. It is because it is free of the thorny underbrush of karmic obstacles that it is said to be free of thorny underbrush. Just as when thorns pierce one's feet, one is then prevented from traveling along that road, so too, the thorny underbrush of karmic obstacles impede one's ability to practice the Dharma of the Buddha and thus reach nirvana.

Just as that road is straight and direct, so too it is with the path of the ten grounds. It is because it is free of any ingratiating flattery, deviousness, cheating, or deception that it is said to be straight and direct.

Just as that road has but few forks in it, so too it is with the path of the ten grounds, for it has but few variant paths. How is this so? Those who have set out along the path of the Great Vehicle travel but little on the pathways of *śrāvaka* disciples and *pratyekabuddha*s. Hence there is but little involvement with variant paths. Where there may be cases in which a bodhisattva travels along in the path of those two vehicles, one should realize that he has not yet established himself on the grounds of a bodhisattva. Because he has not yet entered the right and fixed position,[152] he engages in those peripheral practices.

Just as that good path is free of jungles that obstruct the way, so too it is with the path of the ten grounds. It is free of the jungles of evils associated with the five objects of desire.

Question: Why did you not just state that it is free of *all* jungles associated with the five objects of desire, but instead only stated that it is free of the jungles of "evils" [associated with the five objects of desire]?

Response: For one who has set out in the Great Vehicle, the causes and conditions of one's merit conduce to possession of the foremost objects of the five desires. Consequently one cannot say that they are utterly nonexistent. It is just that those associated with evil are nonexistent.

Moreover, in the case of a deep jungle, it is difficult to enter, difficult 91b
to pass through, and possessed of a multitude of difficult obstructions. The objects of the five desires as encountered by the bodhisattva are not of this sort. He is not like the foolish common person who creates all manner of transgressions in association with the objects of the five desires. Because this is the case, it was only stated here that [the path of the ten grounds] is free of [such evil] jungles.

Just as that road is wide, accommodating of many people, and not conducive to mutual interference, so too is the path of the ten grounds able to accommodate many people, for the countless hundreds of thousands of myriads of *koṭi*s of beings could all bring forth the resolve to embark upon this unsurpassable path and there would still be no mutual interference among these hundreds of thousands of myriads of *koṭi*s of beings. In fact, all beings could bring forth the resolve to attain *anuttarāsamyaksaṃbodhi* and they could all still travel together along this path and there would still be no mutual interference.

Just as that road is one along which many people travel, so too it is with the path of the ten grounds. When they were still cultivating the bodhisattva path, past and present buddhas as numerous as the sands of the Ganges all traveled along this path.

Just as that good road admits of travel without weariness or exhaustion, so too it is with the path of the ten grounds, for this path is associated with abundant bliss produced through cause and effect. For instance, bliss is enjoyed when one is often born into the realms of humans and *deva*s and then enjoys one's karmic rewards there. Because [the practitioner] delights in the abandonment of desire, he then experiences joy and bliss, the bliss of *dhyāna* concentration, the bliss that is free of joy, and the bliss experienced in abiding in this present moment. Because one acquires these various sorts of bliss, one is free of weariness or exhaustion.

Just as that path has along its course an abundance of flowers, fruit, and roots, so too does the path of the ten grounds also possess an abundance of roots, flowers, and fruit. "Roots" refers here to the three types of good roots. "Flowers" refers to the flowers of the seven limbs of *bodhi*. This is as stated in the sutras where it says, "The seven types of flowers are the seven limbs of *bodhi*." "Fruit" refers to the four fruits of the *śramaṇa*.

Because one is free of any of these faults that would obstruct the attainment of meritorious qualities as one courses along this good path, one is said to have abandoned evil.

Just as that guide knows with respect to that road that one should stop and eat here, that one should spend the night here, and that one should then stop for the night there, so too it is with a bodhisattva as he travels through the ten grounds wherein he knows in which place one may stop for the night and knows in which place one may eat.

"Where one may stop for the night" refers to those places where buddhas of the present now dwell. "Where one may eat" refers to where one can cultivate the practice of good dharmas.

Just as eating is able to benefit all of one's faculties and also assists the fulfillment of one's life span, so too it is with good dharmas. They are able to increase faith and the rest of those faculties[153] while also assisting the fulfillment of one's wisdom life.

"Spending the night in another place" is a reference to going from the dwelling place of that buddha to the dwelling place of yet another buddha. Also, one may interpret "another place" as signifying the places in between this buddha's land and that buddha's land.

"Knowing well where to make a turn in the road" refers for example to when a guide recognizes that a road has become unsafe and so then takes a turn. So too it is with a bodhisattva. He knows that this particular path takes one into the realm of the *śrāvaka* disciples, that this other path takes one into the realm of the *pratyekabuddha*s, and that this other path takes one to the realization of buddhahood. Having realized this, he relinquishes the paths of *śrāvaka* disciples and *pratyekabuddha*s and thenceforth travels solely along the path to buddhahood.

Just as that good road has much to eat and drink along the way, so too the path of the ten grounds provides sustenance through the abundant practice of giving, moral virtue, and cultivation of the *dhyāna* concentrations.

Just as that guide has great power because he has abundant wealth and is well able to use the means for maintaining order, so too does the bodhisattva also have great power because he has wealth and the means for maintaining order.

"Wealth" here refers to the seven kinds of wealth, namely: faith, [adher- 91c
ence to] moral precepts, a sense of shame, a dread of blame, relinquishing, learning, and wisdom.

"Means for maintaining order" refers to the ability to defeat all challenges from any *māra* or from any of the various sorts of *śramaṇa*s, brahmans, or non-Buddhist treatise masters. This is what is meant by "awesome strength."

Just as that great city is deemed to be safe and secure because it is free of bandits, pestilence, the causes of violent death, and the many different sorts of distress, so too is the great city of nirvana deemed to be safe and secure; this because it is free of *māra*s, non-Buddhists, the contaminants, greed, hatred, neglectfulness, death, sorrow, grief, suffering, anguish, and lamentation.

Just as that great city, because it has an abundance of food and drink, is deemed to be bountiful, so too is the city of nirvana deemed to be bountiful because it has an abundance of deep *dhyāna* absorptions, liberations, and *samādhi*s.

Just as that great city, because it is able to accommodate many people, is said therefore to be a great city, so too is the city of nirvana deemed to be great because it is able to accommodate many beings. If one could cause all beings to enter the nirvana without residue through their nonacceptance of any dharmas [as inherently existent], the nature of nirvana would still neither increase nor decrease.

Just as that guide is deemed to be a guide because he is able to lead many groups of people to safety and security by showing them the good road, so too is a bodhisattva also deemed to be a great guide, for he is able to lead forth beings, showing them the Dharma of the Buddha, showing them nirvana, and guiding them out from the hazardous road of samsara so that they successfully reach nirvana.

And just as that guide, because he so well knows the signs all along that road, is able to ensure that he himself as well as the rest of his group do not encounter any calamities, so too it is with the bodhisattva. Because he himself does not course in desire, ill will, or the other hindrances; because he does not practice bad ascetic practices; because he does not fall into the deep pit of aging and death; and because he also does not fall into the hot hells, the cold hells, or the realms of the hungry ghosts, he is deemed to be one who does not encounter calamities himself while ensuring that his followers do not encounter calamities, either.

It is for these reasons that the verse says that it is due to knowing well the signs along the path that [the guide] does not encounter any calamities himself, nor do any of the others encounter calamities, either.

Chapter 27

A Summarizing Discussion of the Bodhisattva Practices

We have now come to the end of the general explanation
of the bodhisattva's Ground of Joyfulness
The bodhisattva who abides herein
often becomes a monarch who rules over Jambudvīpa.

He is ever distant from the defilements of greed and desire,
and never fails in his recollection of the Three Jewels.
His mind always aspires to become a buddha
and to rescue and protect all beings.

The first ground is known as the Ground of Joyfulness. We have come to the end of its general explanation. All of the measureless and boundless dharmas of all buddhas take this very ground as their foundation. Were one to take up an expansive discussion of it, that too would become measureless and boundless. Hence we speak here of a "summarizing" explanation.

The bodhisattva who abides on this ground will often serve as a powerful wheel-turning monarch reigning over the entire continent of Jambudvīpa. Due to having cultivated the causes and conditions for this ground in previous lives, he has a resolute belief in the practice of giving and is free of the
defilement of miserliness. Because he always gives to the Three Jewels, he 92a
never fails in his recollection of the Three Jewels. He always bears in mind his resolve to become a buddha and to rescue and protect all beings. Good thoughts such as these are always in his mind.

Additionally:

If he aspires to leave behind the home life
and then diligently practices vigor,
he is able to acquire several hundred meditative concentrations,
and is able to see several hundred buddhas.

He is able to shake a hundred worlds,
and his ability to travel [to other worlds] is also of this sort.
If he wishes to emanate radiant light,
he is able to illuminate a hundred worlds.

He creates transformation bodies of several hundred kinds of people
and can remain for a life span of a hundred *kalpa*s.
He is able to selectively investigate several hundred dharmas
and is able to manifest a hundred transformation bodies,

He is able to transformationally create a hundred bodhisattvas
that manifest as his retinue.
Those of sharp faculties can exceed these numbers
through relying on the Buddha's spiritual powers.

Having already explained the first ground's characteristic features,
its fruits, its powers, and the dharmas used in its purification,
We shall now also present an explanation
of the second ground, the Ground of Stainlessness.

"Fruits" refers to the acquisition of several hundred meditative absorptions, the ability to see several hundred buddhas, and so forth. "Powers" refers to the ability to manifest as several hundred [kinds of] beings, and so forth. The meanings implicit in the rest of the verse have already been explained. Hence we shall not proceed with an explanation of the rest of the verse but rather shall now discuss the second ground, the Ground of Stainlessness.

Question: You wish to present an expansive discussion of the dharmas practiced by the bodhisattva. There are still many [additional] meanings pertaining to the first ground. It is to be feared that, if the discussion becomes ever more expansive, those attempting to study this will become prone to indolent thoughts that could impair their ability to study and recite this. Therefore, for the sake of those unable to [memorize and] recite a more [extensive explanation], you should now [instead] present a summarizing explanation of the dharmas practiced by the bodhisattva.

Response:

All dharmas of the bodhisattva—
these dharmas should all be practiced.
All forms of evil should be relinquished.
This is what constitutes the summarizing explanation.

Dharmas such as those explained in preceding chapters are able to produce and are able to instigate growth in the dharmas pertaining to the [bodhisattva] grounds. Also, if dharmas such as those explained in previous chapters have been explained elsewhere, one should cause all of those dharmas to arise as well. One should abandon all endeavors involving bodhisattva transgressions. This is what constitutes the summarizing explanation of what the bodhisattva should practice. This is as taught in the *Dharmapada:*

To refrain from doing any manner of evil,
to respectfully perform all varieties of good,
and to carry out the purification of one's own mind—
This is the teaching of all buddhas.

There is one dharma that subsumes the path to buddhahood and that is what the bodhisattva should practice. And what is that singular teaching? It is what is referred to as being singleminded and non-neglectful in the cultivation of good dharmas. As the Buddha told Ānanda, "It is due to not being neglectful that I attained *anuttarāsamyaksaṃbodhi.*" This is as described here:

It is through non-neglectfulness that one becomes a buddha,
one who is unmatched by anyone anywhere in the world.
If one is simply able to refrain from neglectfulness, 92b
what endeavor could one fail to achieve?

There are also two dharmas that are able to subsume the path to buddhahood, namely:

First, non-neglectfulness;
And second, wisdom.

These are as described below:

Non-neglectfulness and wisdom—
The Buddha spoke of these as gateways to benefit.
One does not see instances wherein one avoids neglectfulness,
and yet those endeavors still fail to succeed.

There are also three dharmas that are able to subsume the path to buddhahood, namely:

First, training in the supreme moral virtue;
Second, training in the supreme mind;
And third, training in the supreme wisdom.

These are as described below:

Moral virtue produces superior *samādhi,*
samādhi produces wisdom,
and wisdom scatters the afflictions
just as wind blows away floating clouds.

There are also four dharmas that are able to subsume the path to buddhahood, namely [the four bases of meritorious qualities]:

First, the truth basis;
Second, the relinquishment basis;
Third, the quiescence basis;
And fourth, the wisdom basis.

These are as described below:

By perfecting truth, relinquishment, and meditative concentration,
one acquires the pure benefits of wisdom.
One who vigorously pursues the path to buddhahood
should gather together these four dharmas.

There are also five dharmas that are able to subsume the path to buddhahood, namely:

First, the faculty of faith;
Second, the faculty of vigor;
Third, the faculty of mindfulness;
Fourth, the faculty of meditative concentration;
And fifth, the faculty of wisdom.

These are as described below:

> Through the faculty of faith and the faculty of vigor,
> mindfulness, concentration, and wisdom are solid and durable.
> Once these dharmas are joined with the great compassion,
> one will never retreat from the path to buddhahood.
>
> Just as a person who acquires the five sense faculties
> is then able to completely comprehend the five sense objects,
> similarly, if one acquires faith and the rest of the [five] faculties,
> he is then able to know the [true] character of all dharmas.

There are also six dharmas that are able to subsume the path to buddhahood, namely the *pāramitās*:

Giving,
Moral virtue,
Patience,
Vigor,
Dhyāna concentration,
Wisdom.

These are as described below:

> If [one practices] the six perfections as explained,
> one will overcome the afflictions,
> will always bring about the growth of the roots of goodness,
> and, before long, will succeed in attaining buddhahood.

There are also seven dharmas that are able to subsume the path to buddhahood, namely the so-called "seven right dharmas":

Faith,
A sense of shame,
A dread of blame,
Extensive learning,
Vigor,
Mindfulness,
Wisdom.

These are as described below:

One who aspires to acquire the seven right dharmas
should delight in meditative concentration pursued with vigor.
If one rids himself of the seven wrong dharmas,
he will be able to know all the meritorious qualities.

Such a person will be able to rapidly acquire
the unsurpassable *bodhi* of the Buddha,
extricate those sunken in samsara,
and cause them then to reside in the safe and secure abode.

92c There are also eight dharmas that are able to subsume the path to buddhahood, namely the so-called "eight types of thought of great men," namely:

Having but few desires,
Being easily satisfied,
Renunciation,
Vigor,
Mindfulness,
Meditative concentration,
Wisdom,
Delighting in the avoidance of mere conceptual elaboration.

These are as described below:

If someone forms the definite resolve
to abide in the eight types of thought of great men, and then,
in order to pursue the path to buddhahood,
rids himself of the bad forms of ideation and reflection,

by proceeding in this manner, before long,
he will swiftly gain the unsurpassable path.
This is just as when someone practices goodness:
He is certainly bound to gain the sublime fruits [of the path].

There are also nine dharmas that are able to subsume the path to buddhahood, namely:

Great patience,
Great kindness,
Great compassion,

Wisdom,
Mindfulness,
Solid resolve,
Non-greed,
Non-hatred,
Non-delusion.

These are as described below:

> If one is well equipped with great patience,
> great kindness, and great compassion,
> and is also able to abide in wisdom,
> mindfulness, and solid resolve—
>
> If with resolute intentions one enters the good roots
> of non-greed, non-hatred, and non-delusion—
> If one is able to act in this manner,
> the path to buddhahood will then be in the palm of one's hand.

There are also ten dharmas that are able to subsume the path to buddhahood, namely the ten courses of good karmic action. [In the case of the first of them, these include]: not killing any being oneself, not instructing others to kill, not praising any killing that one observes, and not delighting in any killing [carried out by others]. And so the list continues similarly until we come to [the tenth], not holding wrong views. One then dedicates the merit [of adhering to these ten courses of good karmic action] to the attainment of *anuttarāsamyaksaṃbodhi*. These are as described below:

> One does not harass or harm any living being,
> nor does one engage in any robbery or theft,
> nor does one indulge in sexual transgressions with another's wife.
> These are the three concerned with the karmic actions of the body.
>
> One does not engage in false speech, divisive speech,
> harsh speech, or frivolous speech,
> nor does one indulge covetousness, ill will, or wrong views.
> These are the seven actions of the mouth and the mind.

> If one acts in this manner, then one is able to open
> the gate to the unsurpassable path to buddhahood.
> If one wishes to attain buddhahood,
> one should practice in accordance with this initial gateway.

The bodhisattva should bring forth dharmas such as these, and then, having brought them forth, he should guard them. Having guarded them, he should then increase them so that every single good endeavor subsequently brings about an ever-increasing devotion to that form of goodness.

One should also realize that there is one bad dharma that one who pursues the path to buddhahood should urgently abandon. We refer here to the need to abandon neglectfulness.[154] This is as described here:

> If one is unable to cross beyond
> samsara's dangerous wretched destinies,[155]
> this is something worthy of rebuke
> and is the worst of all offenses.

> Although one delights in wealth's pleasures,
> one may still be reborn into a poor and lowly family
93a in which one is unable to plant any roots of goodness
> and in which one becomes a slave or a servant of others.

> This is all brought about by the causes and conditions
> associated with neglectfulness.
> Therefore one who is wise
> urgently leaves it behind as if it were a lethal poison.

> If one has not yet developed the great compassion
> and gained the unproduced-dharmas patience and irreversibility
> and yet still indulges in neglectfulness,
> this is synonymous with bringing on one's own death.[156]

There are also two faults that one should urgently abandon, namely:
First, longing for the grounds of *śrāvaka* disciples;
Second, longing for the ground of *pratyekabuddha*s.

As the Buddha said:

If one falls down onto the grounds of the *śrāvaka* disciples
or onto the ground of the *pratyekabuddha*s,
for the bodhisattva, this is synonymous with dying
and is also synonymous with complete failure.

Even though one might fall into the hells,
one should still not feel any terror.
However, if he were to fall into the two vehicles,
the bodhisattva should then feel immensely fearful.

Although one might fall into the hells,
this would not forever block one's path to buddhahood.
However, if one were to fall into the two vehicles,
this would forever block one's path to buddhahood.

The Buddha has stated that one who loves his life,
would feel immensely fearful if faced with decapitation.
In this very same way, one who wishes to become a buddha
should feel immensely fearful of entering the two vehicles.[157]

There are also three faults that one should urgently abandon, namely:
First, hating bodhisattvas;
Second, hating the bodhisattva practices;
Third, hating any extremely profound Great Vehicle scripture.

These are as described below:

Those of lesser wisdom may, over but minor conditions,
come to hate bodhisattvas,
hate the bodhisattva path,
or hate the sutras of the Great Vehicle.

Because they do not understand them, they have no faith in them
and then fall down into the great hells.
There, struck with fear, they scream in terror.
This is a situation that one should abandon.

There are also four faults that one should urgently abandon, namely:
First, flattery;

Second, deviousness;
Third, being quick-tempered;
Fourth, being bereft of kindness or pity.

These are as described below:

One who describes himself as a bodhisattva
who has a mind much given over to flattery and deviousness,
who is quick-tempered and intolerant,
and who does not act with a mind of kindness and pity—
This is to draw near to the Avīci Hells
and depart far from the path to buddhahood.

There are also five faults that one should urgently abandon, namely:
First, desire;
Second, ill will;
Third, lethargy and sleepiness;
Fourth, excitedness and regretfulness;[158]
Fifth, doubtfulness.

These are the five hindrances that may cover over a person's mind which are as described below:

If a person falls into neglectfulness,
the hindrances will cover his mind,
93b making even birth in the heavens difficult to achieve,
how much the less might one then attain the fruits of the path?

If one is diligent in the practice of vigor,
one can then tear through the hindrances.
If one is able to tear through the hindrances,
then, whatever one wishes for, it will all be obtained.

There are also six faults that are opposite to the six *pāramitā*s and that one should urgently abandon:
First, miserliness;
Second, breaking the moral precepts;
Third, anger;
Fourth, indolence;

Fifth, excited agitation;
Sixth, delusion.

These are as described below:

> Having the stain of miserliness defiling one's mind,
> breaking the moral precepts, indulging in indolence,
> being as ignorant as a cow or sheep,
> being as fond of hatred as a venomous serpent,
>
> or having a mind as scattered as that of a monkey—
> If one fails to abandon the hindrances,
> then, even gaining a celestial rebirth would be extremely difficult,
> how much the less could one succeed in attaining buddhahood?

There are also seven faults that one should urgently abandon:
First, delighting in pursuing many different endeavors;
Second, delighting in excessive study and recitation;
Third, delighting in sleep;
Fourth, delighting in talking;
Fifth, coveting offerings;
Sixth, always wanting to make people laugh;
Seventh, being so confused and befuddled in cultivating the path that one's mind follows the influence of craving.

These are as described below:

> Inferior persons may delight in activities
> or delight in much recitation of non-Buddhist scriptures.
> Ignorant people may delight in sleeping
> or delight in much talking amid groups of people.
>
> Although they aspire to become a buddha,
> they are deeply attached to receiving offerings.
> These slaves to craving have become confused
> with regard to the path to buddhahood.
>
> All such people as these who engage in what is bad
> nonetheless claim to be bodhisattvas.

There are also eight dharmas that one should urgently abandon, namely:
First, wrong views;
Second, wrong intentional thought;
Third, wrong speech;
Fourth wrong [physical] actions;
Fifth, wrong livelihood;
Sixth, wrong effort;
Seventh, wrong mindfulness;
Eighth, wrong meditative concentration.

These are as described below:

Wherever there are people who are so foolish
that they practice the eightfold wrong path,
pursue the study of deviant scriptures,
become fond of chasing after deviant spiritual guides,

and abandon the profound and sublime qualities
of the *ārya*s' eightfold path,
[these are people who] are solidly and deeply attached to afflictions,
and yet still may wish to succeed in realizing *bodhi*—

People who are so deluded as this
are like those who would wish to cross over a great ocean
by abandoning a fine, solid, and durable ship,
seeking instead to make the crossing by carrying stones.

There are also nine dharmas that one should urgently abandon, namely:
First, failing to hear [the teachings on the attainment of] *anuttarā-samyaksaṃbodhi*;
Second, having heard them, failing to have faith in them;
Third, having acquired faith in them, failing to take them on;
93c Fourth, having taken them on, nonetheless still failing to retain them through recitation;
Fifth, though one has also begun to retain them through recitation, one nonetheless still does not understand their meaning;
Sixth, having understood their meaning and significance, one nonetheless fails to explain them [for others];

Seventh, having explained them [for others], one nonetheless fails to accord with their explanation in one's own practice;
Eighth, having begun to practice in accordance with their explanation, one is still unable to always put them into practice;
Ninth, having become able to always put them into practice, one is unable to thoroughly practice them.

These are as described below:

Foolish people do not wish to even hear
[teachings on] the unsurpassable, right, and true path,
or, having heard them, they are unable to have faith in them,
or they are unable to retain them through recitation,

or they do not understand their meaning or explain them for others,
or they do not cultivate in accordance with how they were taught,
or they are unable to always or thoroughly put them into practice.
Moreover, they have no mindfulness or stable wisdom.

Such foolish people as these
cannot obtain the fruits of the path.
In this, they are like people who, having committed karmic offenses,
cannot succeed in gaining rebirth in the heavens.

There are also ten dharmas that one should urgently abandon, namely those comprising the ten courses of bad karmic actions. These are as described below:

Foolish people, when still young,
begin to crave descending into the five desires,
abandoning the ten courses of good karmic action,
and engaging in the ten courses of bad karmic action.

Although the bliss of the heavens is in their own hands,
they still cast it aside and reject it,
just as, due to greedily pursuing the benefit of but little money,
one might somehow abandon a great treasury of jewels.

Question: When you were explaining the characteristic aspects of the unsurpassable path, for many different reasons, you criticized and scolded empty-vow bodhisattvas, self-proclaimed bodhisattvas, and those who are bodhisattvas in name only. If those three types of individuals do not qualify as bodhisattvas, then, through the perfection of which dharmas does one qualify as a genuine bodhisattva?

Response:

> It is not merely by making empty vows
> by proclaiming oneself to be a bodhisattva,
> or by being a bodhisattva only in name.
> To state it briefly, it is those who are able to perfect
> thirty-two dharmas
> who then truly qualify as bodhisattvas.

If one brings forth the resolve by which he seeks to pursue the path to buddhahood and then claims himself to be a bodhisattva, merely emptily assuming the name but not cultivating the meritorious qualities, the mind of kindness and compassion, the *pāramitā*s, and the other practices, this sort of person does not actually qualify as a bodhisattva, for he is comparable to some model city made of mud being referred to as "the jeweled city." In this, he only deceives himself, cheats all buddhas, and cheats all of the world's beings as well.

If a person comes to possess thirty-two sublime dharmas while also being able to bring forth the [bodhisattva's] vow, this is someone who qualifies as a genuine bodhisattva. What then are these thirty-two dharmas? They are:

1. He strives with resolute intentions to bring about every form of peace and happiness for all beings;
2. He is able to enter into the wisdom of all buddhas;
3. He knows through his own self-examination whether or not he is capable of becoming a buddha;
4. He does not hate or loathe anyone;
5. His resolve to succeed in the path is solid;
6. He does not form friendships or trusting relationships on false pretenses;
7. He always serves as a close friend to beings even up to the point of his entry into nirvana;

8. Whether others are personally close or distant from him, his mind remains the same [in the way he treats them]; 94a
9. He does not retreat from good endeavors to which he has assented;
10. He never cuts off his great kindness for all beings;
11. He never cuts off his great compassion for all beings;
12. He always pursues right Dharma and his mind never becomes weary or prone to laziness;
13. He is diligent in bringing forth vigor and he has insatiable resolve;
14. He is possessed of extensive learning and comprehension of its meanings;
15. He always reflects upon his own faults;
16. He does not deride others for their shortcomings;
17. In all matters he observes or hears, he always cultivates the resolve to attain *bodhi;*
18. In giving, he seeks no reward;
19. His observance of the moral precepts is not motivated by the desire to take rebirth in any particular place;[159]
20. He exercises patience in his interactions with all beings and thus remains free of any hatred or obstructiveness toward them;
21. He is able to diligently and vigorously cultivate all roots of goodness;
22. He does not take on rebirths corresponding to the formless realm meditative absorptions;[160]
23. His wisdom is inclusive of appropriate expedient teaching methods;
24. His skillful means are those that lie within the four means of attraction;[161]
25. His kindness and pity for others do not differ with respect to those who observe the moral precepts versus those who break the moral precepts;
26. He is singlemindedly attentive when listening to the Dharma;
27. He remains singlemindedly focused when dwelling in a forest hermitage;
28. He does not delight in any of the many different sorts of endeavors that are admixed with worldly priorities;
29. He does not covet or retain any attachment for the Small Vehicle;

30. He perceives that the benefit brought about by the Great Vehicle is immense;
31. He stays away from bad spiritual guides;
32. He draws close to good spiritual guides.

As the bodhisattva abides in these thirty-two dharmas, he is able to perfect seven additional dharmas. Specifically, they are:

The four immeasurable minds;[162]
The ability to roam about, delighting in the use of the five spiritual superknowledges;
Constant reliance on wisdom;
Never forsaking either good or evil beings;
Decisiveness in all pronouncements;
Definite truthfulness in all statements;
Insatiability in the accumulation of all good dharmas.

These constitute the thirty-two dharmas with their seven additional dharmas. Any bodhisattva who perfects these dharmas qualifies as a genuine bodhisattva.

Chapter 28[163]

Distinctions in the Second Ground's Courses of Karmic Action

> The bodhisattva who has already succeeded
> in the complete fulfillment of the first ground
> and then wishes to reach the second ground
> should bring forth ten types of resolute intentions.[164]

Those bodhisattvas who have already reached the first ground, the Ground of Joyfulness, next bring forth ten types of resolute intentions for the sake of reaching the second ground. It is because of these ten kinds of resolute intentions that one is able to reach the second ground. This is comparable to when someone wishes to go up to an upper-story balcony and must rely on the stairs to do so.

Question: What then are these ten kinds of resolute intentions that serve as means for reaching the second ground?

Response:

> The straight mind, the capable mind,
> the pliant, the restrained, and the quiescent minds,
> the truly sublime, the unmixed, and the noncovetous minds,
> the happy mind, and magnanimous mind make ten in all.

The bodhisattva who has already completely fulfilled the practices of the 94b
first ground and now wishes to reach the second ground proceeds to develop these ten kinds of resolute intentions as the appropriate means, namely:[165]

1. The straight mind,
2. The capable mind,
3. The pliant mind,
4. The restrained mind,
5. The quiescent mind,
6. The truly sublime mind,

7. The unmixed mind,
8. The unattached mind,
9. The expansively happy mind,
10. The magnanimous mind.

Now, as for the straight mind, this is one that has abandoned flattery and deviousness. Because the mind has abandoned flattery and deviousness, it becomes characterized by pliancy. Pliancy refers to not being unyielding or gruff and ill-mannered. The bodhisattva who acquires this pliant mind develops many different *dhyāna* absorptions and also cultivates all good dharmas.

Once one has contemplated the true character of all dharmas, his mind then becomes capable. Because the mind has become capable, one develops the restrained mind.

The restrained mind is one that is well able to restrain the eye and the other sense faculties. This is as stated in the sutras: "What is it that comprises the path of goodness? It is one wherein the *bhikṣu* restrains his eye sense faculty and so forth until we come to his restraining of the mind faculty." It is due to restraint of the six sense faculties that we refer to "the restrained mind."

Once the mind has become restrained, it is then easy to bring forth the quiescent mind. Now, as for the quiescent mind, this refers to being able to extinguish greed, hatred, delusion, and the other afflictions. Having first restrained the mind, one is able to block [the arising of those afflictions] and bring about a state of quiescence.

There are others who claim that acquisition of the *dhyāna* absorptions itself constitutes the quiescent mind. This is as described in the sutras where it says:

> If a person thoroughly knows the characteristic features of the *dhyāna* absorptions, then he will not desire the delectability [of their pleasurable meditative states]. This then is what is meant by the quiescent mind.

Once one has acquired the quiescent mind, he will then definitely bring forth the truly sublime mind. "The truly sublime mind" is a state in which, whatever one wishes to accomplish in the *dhyāna* absorptions and spiritual powers, one will be able to put them to use in a manner that conforms to one's wishes. This is like having real gold that one is able to use however one wishes.

Once the practitioner has acquired these types of mind from the straight mind on through to the truly sublime mind, in order to preserve and protect these kinds of mind, he delights in bringing forth the unmixed mind. The unmixed mind is one in which one abstains from getting involved with either householders or monastics. This practitioner has this thought, "Acquiring these types of mind depends entirely on the power of the *dhyāna* absorptions. It is by means of these types of mind that one acquires the measureless benefits of the second ground. If I allow [these types of mind] to become admixed with the affairs of these many other people, then I will lose these benefits.

"And why would this be so? If one allows his practice to become admixed with the affairs of other people, then, because of the eye faculty and the rest of the six sense faculties, one may sometimes then revert to the production of unwholesome dharmas. Why? Because, when one draws close to dharmas able to provoke lust, hatred, or delusion, [the sensations experienced through] the sense faculties may stir up the fires of the afflictions. It would be due to having ignited the fires of the afflictions that one would then lose these benefits."

It is because of having perceived these sorts of faults that one then develops the unmixed mind and realizes that he should not allow his practice to become admixed with the affairs of householders or other monastics.

Having already developed this unmixed mind, this practitioner next develops the unattached mind. The unattached mind is that through which one does not become attached to any householders or monastics, including even one's father, one's mother, one's older or younger brother, one's preceptors, one's teachers, or one's elders. One reflects thus, "If I become attached to householders or monastics, then this will surely involve the interactions involved with going thither and exchanging mutual greetings. In such circumstances, how could I possibly avoid the arising of mixed mind states?
Therefore, if I wish to ensure that the benefits of the *dhyāna* absorptions 94c
continue to abide, doing so through preservation of the unmixed mind, then I should relinquish any thoughts of attachment for either householders or monastics."

Question: The Dharma of the bodhisattva prescribes that one should not forsake beings and should not entertain any thought of forsaking them. This is as stated in the *Bodhisaṃbhāra* [*Treatise*]:

From the very beginning, the bodhisattva exerts vigor
in the power of every form of skillful means
through which he should influence all beings
to abide in the Great Vehicle.

Even were one to teach beings as numerous as
the sands of the Ganges to abide in arhatship,
that would not equal [the merit of] instructing even one person
to abide in the Great Vehicle, for this would be the superior deed.

If one encounters someone possessed of only lesser strength
who is thus incapable of bringing forth Great Vehicle resolve,
one should, as a secondary priority, teach them to abide instead
in the *śrāvaka* disciple or *pratyekabuddha* vehicles.

If they find themselves incapable of abiding
in either *śrāvaka* disciple or *pratyekabuddha* vehicles,
then one should instruct such beings
in a way that causes them to cultivate the causal bases of merit.

If, however, they cannot take on any of the three vehicles
and cannot take on [causal bases] for human or celestial bliss, either,
then one should always resort to present-world endeavors
to benefit them in a manner corresponding to the situation.

If, even then, there happen to be those beings who
cannot accept benefit as offered by the bodhisattva,
one must still refrain from forsaking these beings,
but should bring forth great kindness and compassion for them.[166]

Also, why is it that you claim that the bodhisattva takes on the unmixed mind and brings forth the unattached mind? If the bodhisattva has no attachment to other beings, then that just amounts to abandoning them. How then could he liberate them?

Response: One should accord with the practice of the mind of equanimity as prescribed by the bodhisattva path. And why? It is because of the mind of equanimity that this person then develops the expansively happy mind.

Thus, one reflects, "If I relinquish these many sorts of disturbances, then I will be able to acquire the *dhyāna* absorptions and it is because of the *dhyāna* absorptions that I will bring forth that sublime dharma of expansive happiness. Once I have acquired this dharma, I will then be able to benefit beings in ways that are ten million times more beneficial than what I can do right now."

Consequently, in order to bring about far greater benefit for other beings, one temporarily uses the mind of equanimity to provisionally abandon the many disturbances so that one can then acquire the *dhyāna* absorptions, the five spiritual powers, and the associated qualities with which one can benefit beings.

So, why is it that the bodhisattva engages in these sorts of skillful means? In order to acquire the magnanimous mind, the bodhisattva reflects, "Because the great man delights in providing great benefit, he does not settle for providing merely minor benefit. Therefore I should now seek to acquire the dharmas of great men and then cultivate the corresponding course of training. I should then pursue just such a diligent application of vigor for the sake of being able to provide such great benefit, namely by acquiring the *dhyāna* absorptions, the spiritual powers, the extinguishing of the sufferings, the liberations, and so forth."

Given the above, the challenge that you have presented here is wrongly conceived.

Question: One already possesses the straight mind and other such dharmas on the first ground. Why then do you yet again state that the bodhisattva wishing to gain the second ground must develop these ten types of mind? 95a

Response: Although one has already come into possession of these dharmas on the first ground, one still does not deeply delight in them and still has not yet solidly established them. One's mind is always joyous on this ground. One then becomes ever more solidly established [in these dharmas] and then develops the capacity to put them to use. Therefore, this challenge of yours is wrong.

Question: In the case of those who deeply delight in these dharmas and become ever more solidly established in them, what sorts of circumstances result from this?[167]

Response:

If this person succeeds even one time in acquiring
deep delight and solid establishment in these types of mind,
then he will never again have to apply further effort in this,
for they will then become like servants who always follow after him.

They will become like a servant that, from the time of his birth, then always follows along after his master. So too, once the bodhisattva has acquired deep delight in and solid establishment of these [ten types of] minds, they will immediately and always accompany him and never again require the application of special effort to cause them to arise. Thereafter, it requires only the most minor sort of causal circumstance for them to come forth yet again. Why is this so? It is because the roots [of goodness associated with these types of mind] have penetrated down so deeply that stems and branches continuously push forth [forever after].

Question: If the bodhisattva succeeds in acquiring these ten types of mind, what sorts of fruits will he gain?

Response:

If one acquires these types of mind,
then one will abide directly on the second ground
and will become completely equipped with a threefold stainlessness:
[Nominal;] in terms of bad karma; and in terms of the afflictions.

If the bodhisattva succeeds in acquiring these ten types of mind consisting of the straight mind as well as the others, he will then immediately qualify as abiding on the second bodhisattva ground.

The first type of stainlessness is the name of this ground, [i.e., the "stainlessness" ground]. The second type of stainlessness refers to the abandonment on this ground of the defilements associated with the karmic transgressions occurring in the ten courses of bad karmic action. The third type of stainlessness refers to abandonment of the defilements associated with greed, hatred, and the other sorts of afflictions.

It is for these reasons that this is called "the Ground of Stainlessness." Furthermore, regarding the meaning of "stainlessness":

The bodhisattva abiding on this ground
naturally abstains from engaging in bad actions.
Because he deeply delights in good dharmas,
he naturally practices the courses of good karmic action.

Question: Given that [this bodhisattva] naturally abstains from the ten courses of bad karmic action and naturally engages in the ten courses of good karmic action, how many of the actions comprising these two classes of courses of karmic action are physical, how many are verbal, and how many are mental?

Response:

The [bad] physical and mental actions are each of three types 95b
and the [bad] verbal actions are fourfold. So too with good actions.
The brief explanation then is of this sort.
This is a subject that should be distinguished [further].

There are three types of bad physical karmic actions, namely killing, stealing, and sexual misconduct. There are four types of bad verbal karmic actions, namely false speech, divisive speech, harsh speech, and scattered or inappropriate speech. There are three types of bad mental karmic actions, namely covetousness, ill will, and wrong views.

There are also three types of good physical karmic actions, namely abandoning killing, stealing, and sexual misconduct. The good verbal karmic actions are also fourfold, namely abandoning false speech, divisive speech, harsh speech, and scattered or inappropriate speech. There are three types of good mental karmic actions, namely noncovetousness, refraining from ill will, and right views.

Whether the physical, verbal, or mental courses of karmic action are good or bad is a topic requiring further discussion so as to cause people to clearly understand such matters.

First, "killing" as a course of bad karmic action involves the following factors:

The existence of another being;
The knowledge that there is this being;
The deliberate infliction of physical injury;
The loss of life due to this infliction of physical injury.

If one brings forth these physical karmic actions, this is what is known as "killing," the first of the courses of bad karmic action. It is the abandoning of these factors that defines the good karmic action of refraining from killing.

As for "stealing," it involves the following factors:

There is something belonging to someone else;

One knows that this thing belongs to someone else;

One produces a thought intent on stealing it;

One's hand grasps this thing, picks it up, and then moves it away from its current location;

Whether one openly robs or surreptitiously steals the object, one then reckons, "This is my possession" and thinks, "This is mine."

These are the factors defining the act of stealing. It is the abandoning of these factors that defines the good karmic action of refraining from stealing.

As for "sexual misconduct," [it involves the following factors:]

There is a woman;[168]

She is under the protection of parents, under the protection of her clan, under the protection of her caste, under the protection of worldly convention or law, or under the protection of the moral precepts;

In the case of another man's wife, one may even know of the potential for such obstacles as being whipped, beaten with clubs, tormented, or afflicted with bodily injury;

Even in the midst of any of these circumstances, one nonetheless produces thoughts of lust and then actually commits one of the types of offending physical karmic actions.

In circumstances involving one's own wife, [the following factors constitute transgressions of this precept:]

She may have formally taken a [temporarily restricting] moral precept;

She may be pregnant;

She may still be nursing an infant;

The act may involve a restricted orifice.[169]

These are the factors defining the act of sexual misconduct. It is the abandonment of these factors that defines the good karmic action [of refraining from sexual misconduct].

As for "false speech," [it involves the following factors:]
There is some deceptive sign;
There is the mental intent to deceive;
There is the perception that this action would constitute a deceptive falsehood;
There is the acquiescence in some circumstance constituting a deceptive falsehood;
There is the desire to deceive;
There is the knowledge that the circumstances are of this sort and yet one describes them as being otherwise.

These are the factors defining the action of false speech. It is the abandonment of these factors that defines the good karmic action of abstaining from false speech.

As for "divisive speech," [it involves the following factors:]
One wishes to cause others to separate;
One says something about this person to that person or says something about that person to this person in order to cause them to separate;
Those who previously were close are then caused to separate;
If they become separated, one is subsequently happy that they have separated, rejoices that they have separated, or is pleased that they have separated.

Factors such as these define an act of divisive speech. It is the abandonment of these factors that defines the good karmic action of abstaining from divisive speech.

As for "harsh speech," this is inclusive of all of the types of worldly speech that are inclined to cause anger or torment in others such as:
Harsh speech,
Injurious speech,
Bitter speech,
Coarse speech,
Abusive speech.

Factors such as these define an act of harsh speech. It is the abandonment of these factors that defines the good karmic action of abstaining from harsh speech. 95c

As for "scattered or inappropriate speech,"[170] [it may involve the following factors:]

Speaking [of particular topics] at an inappropriate time,
Nonbeneficial speech,
Speech contrary to Dharma,
[Rambling] speech having neither beginning nor end,
Unreasonable speech.

Factors such as these define the action of scattered or inappropriate speech. It is the abandonment of these factors that defines the good karmic action of "abstaining from scattered or inappropriate speech."

As for "covetousness," [it involves the following factors:]

There are things belonging to someone else which that person wishes to keep such as his fields, lands, or wealth;
One's mind is influenced by covetousness;
One wishes to obtain that thing.

In whichever circumstance of this sort one refrains from coveting, refrains from envy, and refrains from wishing to obtain such an object, these factors constitute the good karmic action of "noncovetousness."

As for "ill will," [it may involve the following factors] directed toward some other being:

One produces thoughts of hatred,
Or one produces thoughts inclined toward obstructiveness,
Or one becomes angry,
Or one thinks, "Why not beat him up, tie him up, or murder him?"

Factors such as these define what is meant by "ill will." It is the abandoning of these factors that defines the good karmic action of "refraining from ill will."

As for "wrong views," this refers to claims such as these:

There is no point in practicing giving;
There is no point in repaying others for kindnesses they have bestowed;
There are no corresponding karmic effects of good or bad karmic actions;
There is no [rebirth into] the present life and no [rebirth] into future lives;

There is no need to respect one's parents;
There are no *śramaṇa*s or brahmans who are able to know of [rebirth into] this life or into future lives or who personally gain utterly clear and penetrating comprehension and realizations.

Factors such as these define what is meant by "wrong views."
As for right view, this is reflected in such views as:
There is giving [that should be done];
It is right to repay others for kindnesses they have bestowed;
There are corresponding karmic effects resulting from good and bad actions;
There is [rebirth into] the present life and into future lives;
The world does indeed have *śramaṇa*s and brahmans who know [of rebirth into] this life and into future lives and who personally gain utterly clear and penetrating comprehension and realizations.

Factors such as these define the good karmic action of right view. It is in this manner that this bodhisattva enters the right view course [of good karmic action].

> The courses of good karmic actions and of bad karmic actions
> each involve twenty specific types of distinctions.
> Knowledge of factors such as point of origin and such
> each involve twelve different types of distinctions.

With respect to the ten courses of bad karmic action and the ten courses of good karmic action, the bodhisattva knows twenty distinctions pertaining to their many different distinguishing aspects. He also thoroughly knows twelve kinds of distinctions pertaining to each of these twenty distinctions that include their point of origin and so forth.

For each of these component actions within the path of the ten bad karmic actions there are twenty distinguishing factors. For instance, in not abandoning the karmic offense of taking some other being's life, we have these factors:

First, it is an action that is not good.
Second, it is connected with the desire realm's planes of existence.
Third, it involves the contaminants.

Fourth, it is not a mental dharma.
Fifth, it is not associated with the mind.
Sixth, it does not follow the actions of the mind.
Seventh, it may or may not arise in conjunction with the mind.

What all is implied by "arising in conjunction with the mind"? [This involves the following:]

There is a truly existent being;
One knows it is a being;
One uses some physical action to take its life.

These factors define what is meant by "arising in conjunction with the mind."

What is meant by "not arising in conjunction with the mind"? In an instance where a person [merely] wished to kill a being, grab him, pull him forth, throw him down, and pin him to the ground, but only later was able to bring about his death, this would be a case of "[killing] not arising [directly] in conjunction with the mind."

Also, it might be that the body does not move and the mouth does not speak and one only brings forth the thought, "From this day on, I shall become someone who kills beings." This instance of the karmic offense of killing is one wherein [the actual act of taking a life] does not take place directly in conjunction with the mind.

Also, in an instance where this [ideational] non-abandonment of taking others' lives always accumulates habitual karmic propensities that continue
96a to increase whether one is asleep or awake, this too qualifies as an instance where [the act of killing] does not arise in conjunction with the mind.

Eighth, it may be [an offense] involving either form or nonform.

That initial case [directly above] in which the act of killing occurred in conjunction with the mind—that is one that involved form. That second [immediately subsequent] example of the karmic offense of killing as well as the third and the fourth—these are all instances not involving form.

Ninth, it may involve performing an action or it may not involve performing an action.

That which involves form is one that does involve performing an action whereas any others do not involve the performing of an action.

Tenth, it may or may not involve the presence of objective conditions.

That involving form does involve objective conditions whereas the rest are circumstances devoid of objective conditions.

Question: Are these states of mind that are possessed of objective conditions or devoid of objective conditions?

Response: They do not necessarily involve objective conditions.

Question: If these states of mind do not necessarily involve objective conditions, and we have a case of the body not moving and the mouth not speaking wherein there is only the production of the thought, "From this day forward, I shall be one who takes the lives of beings," how can it be that karmic offenses such as these do not involve an objective condition?

Response: If it is an instance wherein the karmic offense of killing takes place, then this mind should indeed have associated objective conditions. However, now, in truth, the karmic offense of killing is not [merely] mental. If the mind was what actually commits the karmic offense of killing, then that would itself involve a physical action. But, in truth the mind's actions are not physical actions. Therefore, this [merely mental] karmic offense of killing beings is not defined by the presence of objective conditions. Rather, [an actual] karmic offense of killing occurs in conjunction with the mind and arises within the physical body. It is because this [merely mental] instance does not involve any action that it is referred to as being one not involving objective conditions.

Eleventh, it may involve performing a karmic action.

Twelfth, it may not correspond to the commission of a karmic action.

Thirteenth, it may occur in a manner not in direct linkage with the commission of a karmic action.

Fourteenth, it may or may not be generated in conjunction with the commission of a given karmic action.

This is analogous to the case involving arising in conjunction with the mind and is no different than that. The only difference here is that it is not arising in conjunction with mind, but is instead arising in conjunction with volition.[171]

Fifteenth, it may not be a karmic result of actions carried out in previous existences.
Sixteenth, it is not to be cultivated.
Seventeenth, it is to be well understood.[172]
Eighteenth, it should be realized by wisdom and is not realized by the body.
Nineteenth, it can be severed.[173]
Twentieth, it can be known and seen.

[Now, as for the application of these factors to] the karmic offense of "not abandoning stealing," the karmic offense of "not abandoning sexual misconduct," and the karmic offense of "not abandoning false speech," these are just the same as when they were applied to the karmic offense of "killing" except that these involve:[174]

One instance that occurs in conjunction with the mind and two instances that do not occur in conjunction with the mind;
One instance that involves form and two instances that do not involve form;
One instance that involves the performance of an action and two instances that do not involve the performance of an action;
One instance that involves objective conditions and two instances that do not involve objective conditions.

As for "not abandoning divisive speech" and "not abandoning harsh speech," [the relevant distinctions] are just the same [as with the above-discussed actions].

In the case of "not abandoning scattered or inappropriate speech," [the relevant distinctions are as follows:]

It may be karmically bad;
It may be karmically neutral;
That which arises from bad intentionality is karmically bad;
That which arises from neutral intentionality is karmically neutral;

It may occur in connection with the desire realm;
It may occur in connection with the form realm.

As for that which occurs in connection with the desire realm, it is scattered or inappropriate speech arising in a desire-realm body and mind that occur in connection with the desire realm;

The basis for being categorized as "connected with the form realm" is similarly determined.

The remaining factors relevant to "scattered or inappropriate speech" are similar to those set forth earlier with regard to "false speech."

As for "covetousness," [the relevant distinctions are as follows]:[175]
It arises in connection with the desire realm;
It is a mental dharma influenced by the contaminants;
It is not associated with the mind;
It does not follow the actions of the mind;
It occurs in conjunction with the mind;
It is formless;
It does not involve an action;
It does involve an objective condition;
It does not correspond to a karmic action;
It does not follow and correspond to karmic action;
It does not arise in conjunction with karmic action;
It is not itself a karmic result from actions committed in a prior existence except when it is a karmic result of a [prior] cause;[176]
It cannot be cultivated;
It should be thoroughly understood;
It should be the object of wisdom-based realization;
It may involve realizations pertaining to the body;
It is subject to severance;
It is subject to being perceived and understood.

As for "ill will," [the relevant distinctions are as follows:]
It may be associated with the mind;
It may not be associated with the mind;
In instances where it is associated with the mind, it is included in the obsessions;

In instances where it is not associated with the mind, it is included among the latent afflictions;[177]
The cases are just the same with reference to its following or not following actions of the mind.

96b As for instances in which it occurs in conjunction with the mind or, alternatively, does not occur in conjunction with the mind, it is when it occurs in beings possessed of ideation that it occurs in conjunction with the mind and it is when it occurs in beings not possessed of ideation that it does not occur in conjunction with the mind.

Just as it is with occurrences associated with the mind, with occurrences following actions of the mind, with occurrences arising in conjunction with the mind, so too it is with occurrences associated with karmic actions, with occurrences following karmic action, and with occurrences in conjunction with the arising of karmic action.

And just as it is with occurrences unassociated with the mind, with occurrences not following actions of the mind, and with occurrences not arising in conjunction with the mind, so too it is with occurrences unassociated with karmic actions, with occurrences not following karmic action, and with occurrences not in conjunction with the arising of karmic action.

The remaining distinctions that could be made here [with regard to "ill will"] may be deduced from the earlier discussion of "covetousness."

[The distinctions that could be made regarding] "wrong views" are just the same as those already described above with regard to "ill will."

As for "abandonment of taking others' lives" among the ten courses of good karmic action, [the relevant distinctions are as follows:]

It is good in nature.
It may occur in connection with the desire-realm planes of existence.
It may be unconnected to the three realms of existence.[178]

In instances connected to the desire realm, one abides in a desire-realm body and abandons taking other beings' lives. This is what is meant by being "connected to the desire realm."

In instances "unconnected to the three realms of existence," this corresponds to actions included in the eightfold path of the *ārya*s engaged in by those at and beyond the stages of training who practice "right action" by abandoning the killing of beings.

It may involve the contaminants.
It may not involve the contaminants.

When it is "connected to the desire realm," it involves the contaminants. When it is "unconnected to the three realms," it is free of the contaminants.
It is not a mental dharma.
It is not a dharma associated with the mind.
It is not [a dharma that] follows the mind.
It may arise in conjunction with the mind.
It may not arise in conjunction with the mind.

What all is implied by arising in conjunction with the mind? This is a circumstance like that of someone who is walking along, sees a bug, and thinks, "Through physical actions that abandon killing, I shall refrain from injuring it." This is what is meant by a good action of abandoning killing arising in conjunction with the mind.

How is it that the good action of abandoning killing other beings does not occur in conjunction with the mind? Take an instance where there is a person whose body does not move, whose mouth does not speak, and who only thinks, "From this very day forward, I shall no longer kill beings." This is a case in which [the action itself] does not occur in concert with the mind.

Then again, we may have a person who, from early on, has abandoned the killing of beings. Whether sleeping or awake, when his mind takes various other circumstances as objective conditions, in thought after thought, as he refrains from killing beings, his merit always increases and at the same time, this does not take place in conjunction with the mind.

This may or may not involve form. One instance involves form and two other instances do not involve form. One instance involves the performance of an action and two other instances do not involve the performance of an action. One instance involves objective conditions and two other instances do not involve objective conditions.
It may constitute an action.
It may not occur in conjunction with an action.
It does not follow an action.

In instances where it may occur in conjunction with an action or may not occur in conjunction with an action, the determining factor is just the same [as in the case explained above] involving the issue of whether the action occurs in conjunction with the mind or does not occur in conjunction with the mind. The only difference is with regard to the presence of mind versus the presence of volition.

It is not itself a karmic result from actions committed in a prior [existence] except when it is a karmic result of a prior cause.
It can be cultivated.
It can be thoroughly understood.
It can be the object of physical realization or wisdom-based realization.
It may be subject to severance or may not be subject to severance.

If it is associated with the contaminants, then it may be subject to severance. If it is unassociated with the contaminants, then it is not subject to severance. So too with respect to its amenability to being known and seen.

[The relevant distinctions applicable to] "abandonment of stealing," "abandonment of sexual misconduct," "abandonment of false speech," "abandonment of divisive speech," and "abandonment of harsh speech" are all similar.

As for [the good karmic action of] "abandonment of scattered or inappropriate speech," [the relevant distinctions are as follows:]

It may be connected to the desire realm.
It may be connected to the form realm.
It may not be connected to any of the three realms.

When connected with the form realm, it is with a desire-realm body and mind that one abandons scattered and inappropriate speech. So too, when connected with the form realm, [it is with a form-realm body and mind that one abandons scattered and inappropriate speech]. When not connected with any of the three realms, [the distinguishing factors] are as explained above in the discussion of the good karmic action of abstaining from killing.

It may be associated with the contaminants.
It may be unassociated with the contaminants.

When associated with the contaminants, it is connected [with the three realms]. When unassociated with the contaminants, it is not connected [with any of the three realms]. The other applicable distinctions are as explained in the above discussion of "abandoning false speech."

As for [the good karmic action of] "abandonment of covetousness," [the relevant distinctions are as follows:] 96c

It is good in nature.
It may be connected with the desire realm.
It may not be connected to any of the three realms.

When connected to the desire realm, this may be a desire realm common person refraining from covetousness or else this may be someone who is a worthy or an *ārya* practicing the good karmic action of abstaining from covetousness. This is what is meant by being "connected with the desire realm."

When not connected to any of the three realms, this is an instance of refraining from covetousness that is a good karmic action unassociated with the contaminants done by either a worthy or an *ārya*.

This may be associated with the contaminants.
It may be unassociated with the contaminants.

When it is connected with the desire realm, it is associated with the contaminants. When not connected to any of the three realms, it is unassociated with the contaminants.

This is a mental dharma.
It is associated with the mind.
It may follow actions of the mind.
It may arise in conjunction with the mind.
It is formless.
It does not involve performance of an action.
It has objective conditions.
It is not a karmic action.
It is associated with karmic actions.
It may follow karmic actions.
It may arise in conjunction with karmic actions.
It is not itself a karmic result from actions committed in a prior [existence] except when it is a karmic result of a prior cause.
It can be cultivated.
It can be thoroughly known.
It is amenable to physical realization.
It is amenable to wisdom-based realization.

It may be subject to severance.
It may not be subject to severance.

When associated with the contaminants, it is subject to severance. When unassociated with the contaminants, it is not subject to severance. So too with the distinctions regarding amenability to being directly known and seen.

As for [the good karmic action of] "abandoning ill will," [the relevant distinctions are as follows:]

It is good in nature.
It may be connected with the desire realm.
It may be connected with the form realm.
It may be connected to the formless realm.
It may be that it is not connected with any of the three realms.

When connected with the desire realm, it is in a desire realm existence with roots of goodness arising [from previous practice] of restraint from ill will. When connected with existence in either of the other two realms, the bases are just the same.

As for when it is "not connected to any of the three realms," all other instances [aside from the above] are "not connected [to any of the three realms]."

This may be associated with the contaminants or it may be unassociated with the contaminants.

When connected to any of the three realms, it is associated with the contaminants. All other instances are unassociated with the contaminants.

It is a mental dharma.
It may be associated with the mind.
It may be unassociated with the mind.

When opposing obsession, roots of goodness arising from refraining from ill will are associated with the mind. When opposing latent tendencies, roots of goodness arising from refraining from ill will are unassociated with the mind. The distinctions are the same with respect to following actions of the mind and arising in conjunction with the mind.

It is formless.
It does not involve performance of an action.

It may have objective conditions.
It may not have objective conditions.

When it is associated with the mind it has objective conditions. When it is unassociated with the mind it does not have objective conditions.

It is not a karmic action.
It may be associated with a karmic action.
Or it may not be associated with a karmic action.
It may follow the enactment of a karmic action.
Or it may not follow the enactment of a karmic action.
It may arise in conjunction with a karmic action.
Or it may not arise in conjunction with a karmic action.

[The distinctions applicable to this arising or not arising in conjunction with a karmic action] are the same as those that applied above when discussing mind.

It is not a karmic result from actions [committed in a prior existence] except when it is a karmic result of a prior cause.
It can be the object of physical realization or wisdom-based realization.
It may be subject to severance or may not be subject to severance.

When associated with the contaminants it is subject to severance. When unassociated with the contaminants, it is not subject to severance. So too with regard to its amenability to being known and seen.

As for [the good karmic action of] "right view," [the relevant distinctions are as follows:]

It is good in nature.
It may be connected with the desire realm.
It may be connected with the form realm.
It may be connected with the formless realm.
It may not be connected with any of the three realms.

When connected to the desire realm, it involves thoughts corresponding to right views produced in the desire realm by common persons, worthies, or *ārya*s. When connected to the form realm and when connected to the formless realm, the circumstances are just the same.

When not connected to any of the three realms, these are right views unassociated with the contaminants as held by worthies or *ārya*s.

It may be associated with the contaminants.

It may be unassociated with the contaminants.

When connected to any of the three realms, it is associated with the contaminants. When not connected [to any of the three realms], it is unassociated with the contaminants.

It is a mental dharma.

It is a dharma associated with the mind.

It follows actions of the mind.

It arises in conjunction with the mind.

It is formless.

It does not involve the performance of an action.

It may have objective conditions.

It is not a karmic action.

It may be associated with a karmic action.

It may follow the enactment of a karmic action.

It may arise in conjunction with a karmic action.

It is not a karmic result from actions [committed in a prior existence] except when it is a karmic result of a prior cause.

It can be the object of physical realization or wisdom-based realization.

It may be subject to severance or may not be subject to severance.

97a When associated with contaminants, it is subject to severance. When unassociated with the contaminants, it is not subject to severance.

The differentiations here are the same with respect to amenability to knowing and seeing.

This [above discussion illustrates] what is meant by the application of twenty distinguishing factors such as "goodness," and so forth [to the understanding of the ten courses of good karmic action and the ten courses of bad karmic action].

As for the twelvefold discussion of "origins" and so forth, it is as follows:[179]

1. From what did it originate?
2. What does it produce?

3. From what cause did it originate?
4. For whom is it a cause?
5. What are the associated conditions?
6. For what is it a condition?
7. What does it take as an objective condition?
8. What is the benefit?[180]
9. What factors are dominant?
10. For whom is this dominant?
11. What losses does this incur?
12. What karmic effects does this entail?

In the case of the karmic offense of "killing," [these discussions are as follows:]

As for "From what did it originate?", it arises from the three types of bad karmic roots and additionally arises from wrong thought. Further, it arises from whichever thought the act of taking a being's life next followed upon. It originated from this thought.

As for "What does it produce?", these are all of the dharmas proximate to the karmic offense of killing whether those dharmas have already arisen, are now arising, or eventually will arise. So too with these causes and conditions.

As for "What does it take as an objective condition?", it takes a living being as its objective condition. Additionally, whichever thought precipitated the taking of that being's life—it also takes this thought as a condition.

As for "For what is it a condition?", all of the peripheral dharmas caused by the karmic offense of killing, whether already arisen, now arising, or eventually arising—these are all conditions associated with the karmic offense of killing.

As for "What losses does this incur?", this includes having a bad reputation in the present lifetime, being the object of others' distrust, and so forth.

As for "What karmic effects does this entail?", these include falling into the hell realm, the animal realm, the hungry ghost realm, the *asura* realm, and other wretched destinies wherein one undergoes suffering and anguish.

As for "What factors are dominant?" and "For whom is this dominant?", these are the same as with above statement on the bases of origination.

These distinctions are the same in their application to stealing, sexual misconduct, false speech, divisive speech, harsh speech, scattered or inappropriate speech, covetousness, ill will, and wrong views. There are only differences with regard to what in each case serves as an objective condition.

For instance, in the case of stealing, it is the object that one appropriates to one's own use that serves as the objective condition. Sexual misconduct takes a being as the objective condition.

False speech, divisive speech, harsh speech, and scattered or inappropriate speech all take words as their objective condition.

Covetousness takes as its objective condition the particular object that one would appropriate to one's own use.

Ill will takes a being as the objective condition.

Wrong views take words as their objective condition.

All of the remaining distinctions are deducible from the differentiations described above.

"Refraining from killing beings" arises from the three types of good karmic roots as well as from right mindfulness. It also arises from the thought arising just prior to the act of refraining from killing a being.

As for "What does it produce?," these are all of the dharmas arising from this dharma, whether they have already arisen, are now arising, or eventually will arise. So too with the associated causes and conditions.

As for "What does it take as an objective condition?," it takes a living being as its objective condition.

As for "For what is it a condition?," all of the peripheral dharmas caused by the act of not killing whether already arisen, now arising, or eventually arising—these are all conditions associated with the act of not killing.

As for "dominant factors," the roots of goodness are dominant and right mindfulness is also dominant. Also whichever thought was followed by the restraint from killing a particular being—that thought was also dominant.

As for "For whom is this dominant?," this is determined by all of the dharmas peripheral to the act of not taking a being's life, whether they have already arisen, are now arising, or will eventually arise.

As for "What is the benefit?," being opposed to the karmic offense of killing—this is the benefit.

As for "What karmic effects does this entail?," these are whichever karmic effects are opposite to those entailed by killing beings.

These distinctions are the same in their application to not stealing, to not committing sexual misconduct, to not committing false speech, to not engaging in divisive speech, to not engaging in harsh speech, to not engaging in scattered or inappropriate speech, to noncovetousness, to refraining from ill will, and to right views. There are only differences with regard to what 97b
in each case serves as an objective condition.

For instance, in the case of not stealing, it is the object that one might otherwise appropriate to one's own use that serves as the objective condition.

Refraining from sexual misconduct takes a being [otherwise susceptible to one's sexual misconduct] as the objective condition.

Refraining from false speech, divisive speech, harsh speech, and scattered or inappropriate speech all take words as their objective condition.

Noncovetousness takes as its objective condition the particular object that one might otherwise desire to have available to one's own use.

Refraining from ill will takes a being as the objective condition.

Right views may take words as the objective condition or may take meaning as the objective conditions. Those associated with the contaminants take words as objective conditions. Those unassociated with the contaminants take meanings as the objective condition.

It is in this manner that this bodhisattva should distinguish and know with respect to the practice of the ten courses of good karmic actions the [twenty] analytic discussions of "goodness" and so forth as well as the twelve analytic discussions of "origination" and so forth.

In addition, he should know:

> The bases for the seven types of bad karmic actions,
> how they may arise from greed, hatred, or delusion,
> and also the application of four types of distinctions
> of which two each are linked to karmic actions and to beings.

This bodhisattva knows that seven courses of bad karmic action may arise from greed, hatred, or delusion, and thus applies these distinctions to circumstances in the world. He is also aware of four categorical distinctions applicable to these seven types of bad karmic deeds.

This karmic offense of killing may arise from greed, hatred, or from delusion. [Consider the case in which killing] arises from greed. Suppose for example that a person sees some being, produces a thought of greed, and then, due to these causes and conditions, because he wishes to enjoy the use of that being's visual forms, sounds, fragrances, tastes, or touchables, or because he wants its tusks, horns, fur, hide, sinews, flesh, bones, marrow, and such—this person then, due to having this covetous thought, takes this being's life. This is a case of the karmic offense of killing arising from greed.

In a case where someone kills a being due to hating and being displeased [with that being], this is an instance of killing arising from hatred.

In a case where someone beset by wrong views fails to realize the effects of good and bad karmic actions as they unfold in subsequent lives and then, because of that, kills some being, this is an instance of the karmic offense of killing arising from delusion. In some cases, the killer may kill due to regarding the act as productive of merit. Or he may kill out of a desire to liberate [the being he is killing] from suffering. These cases are reflective of customs in the country of Parthia in the west and other such places.

There are yet other instances of killing motivated by the idea that it may serve as a cause and condition for the acquisition of merit. Thus one may wish to achieve rebirth in the heavens through the karma of killing. This latter situation is exemplified by a practice in East India of sacrificing beings in the temple of their *deva,* wishing through such deeds to be reborn in the heavens. These are all cases of killing occurring because of delusion.

There are yet other individuals who, because of greed, take the possessions of others, thinking: "This is because I deserve to freely acquire whichever fine visual forms, sounds, fragrances, flavors, or touchables appeal to me." This is just a case of stealing arising from greed.

There are yet other people who, due to hatred and dislike of others, steal the wealth and possessions of others, wishing thereby to cause them anguish. These are cases of stealing arising from hatred.

Then again, there are people who, holding wrong views and failing to realize the karmic retribution involved, steal the possessions of others. This is stealing arising from delusion. This is exemplified by brahmans who state, "All the wealth and treasures of the world are rightfully mine. It is only because of the relative weakness of my power that all of these inferior classes of people have been able, using methods contrary to our dharma, to take

these things for their own use. If I now seize them, this is just a case of someone retrieving his own possessions. Hence there is no karmic transgression in doing this." When someone uses such rationalizations to steal the belongings 97c
of others, this too is just a matter of stealing arising from delusion.

When someone commits sexual misconduct because of desire and attachment to sexual gratification, this is an instance of sexual misconduct arising from greed.

If someone motivated by hatred and aversion toward someone else thinks, "Because this fellow violated my mother, wife, sister, or daughter, I shall get back at him by sexually defiling his mother, wife, sisters, and daughters," this is an instance of sexual misconduct arising from hatred.

In someone holding wrong views and not realizing the karmic retributions involved violates [some woman], this is an instance [of sexual misconduct] arising from delusion. This is exemplified by a man who claims, "There is really no such thing as sexual misconduct between humans. Why? All women were born for the enjoyment of men and thus are just like any other thing we exploit for our own use. Thus, if one has a need for it and therefore becomes involved in this kind of affair, then there is no karmic offense of sexual misconduct involved here." When someone relying on this sort of rationalization goes ahead and indulges his sexual desire in this way, that is a case of sexual misconduct arising from delusion.

Just as it is with the karmic offense of stealing, so too it is with false speech. When someone tells lies because of greed for wealth, then this is referred to as false speech arising from greed. When someone deceives someone else in order to cause them anguish, this is referred to as false speech arising from hatred. When someone with wrong views who does not understand the karmic retributions involved tells a lie, this is referred to as false speech arising from delusion.

Divisive speech, harsh speech, and scattered or inappropriate speech are the same [as the above discussion of "false speech"] in that these three courses of bad karmic action also have these same foundational bases. From this, one can distinguish the arising of the karmic effects resulting from all seven physical and verbal karmic deeds.

Question: Is it or is it not the case that all instances of not abandoning killing beings constitute the karmic offense of killing? Are all instances of the karmic offense of killing necessarily instances of not abandoning killing?

Response: There are instances of not abandoning killing that constitute instances of the karmic transgression of killing beings and there are also instances of not abandoning killing that do not qualify as instances of the karmic transgression of killing beings.

This being the case, which of these instances of not abandoning killing constitute instances of the karmic transgression of killing? Taking for example a case where there is a being, one knows it is a being, one deliberately kills it, and in taking its life, one produces the associated physical karmic action—this is an instance of not abandoning killing also constituting an instance of the karmic offense of killing.

What would be an example of failure to abandon killing not qualifying as an instance of the karmic offense of killing? Take for instance a case where this person did in fact previously engage in the causes and conditions of killing but the being somehow did not die. Further, take the case in which someone makes no bodily movement and utters no words but merely thinks, "From this day on, I shall kill beings." Both of these instances qualify as cases of failure to abandon killing that do not actually entail the karmic offense of killing. This involves two categorical distinctions through which one makes a total of four distinctions, two for each of these two subcategories of the so-called "good" and "bad."

> This is not just a matter of "good" versus "bad,"
> but also of two types of karma, "physical" versus "mental."
> One should also know
> that there are still other distinctions.

There are other subsidiary physical actions aside from the actual killing of beings, stealing, or sexual misconduct, actions that, in the case of killing, include such abuses as beating, tying up, imprisoning, whipping, striking with staves, dragging [through the streets], and so forth. Because they fall short of actually inflicting death, these sorts of bad physical karmic actions are not subsumed under [the karmic offense of] taking life, and so forth [with the subsidiary physical actions associated with stealing and sexual misconduct].

[So too,] among the actions that are good, actions such as welcoming eminences on arrival, escorting them off when they leave, pressing the palms together, bowing down in reverence, greeting with half bows, assisting with bathing, massage, and proffering of gifts, none of these good physical karmic actions are subsumed under non-killing, and so forth [with the wholesome subsidiary physical actions associated with stealing and sexual misconduct].

[So too,] among the karmic actions of the mind, [the same principle 98a
applies] to all of the rest of the unwholesome [mental] dharmas aside from covetousness, ill will, and wrong views, dharmas such as not guarding or focusing the mind, the fetters, and so forth.

[So too,] among the karmic actions of the mind, [the same principle applies] to all of the rest of the good [mental] dharmas aside from noncovetousness, refraining from ill will, and right views, dharmas such as guarding and focusing the mind, faith, observance of moral precepts, learning, meditative concentration, equanimity, wisdom, and so forth.

> Seven of the karmic deeds are also courses of karmic action
> and three of the courses of karmic action are not karmic deeds.

These seven "karmic deeds" that consist of killing, stealing, sexual misconduct, false speech, divisive speech, harsh speech, and scattered or inappropriate speech are themselves both "karmic deeds" and "courses of karmic action." Covetousness, ill will, and wrong views are "courses of karmic action," but are not "karmic deeds" as such, for these three phenomena correspond to [intentional] thought, this type of [merely mental] activity.

Question: How is it that the previous seven endeavors qualify both as "karmic deeds" and "courses of karmic action"?

Response: It is due to progressively increasing habitual practice of these endeavors that one therefore arrives in the hell realm, the animal realm, and the realm of the hungry ghosts. It is because of this that they are referred to as "courses of karmic action." Because these seven are also endeavors that one can perform, they are also referred to as "karmic deeds."

As for the three which are "courses of karmic action" but not "karmic deeds" as such, this is because they serve as the foundation for those which do constitute bad karmic deeds. Consequently these three are referred to only as "courses of karmic action" but not as "karmic deeds."

The same principle applies in the sphere of the "good" [courses of karmic action]. Abandonment of killing, of stealing, of sexual misconduct, of false speech, of divisive speech, of harsh speech, and of scattered or inappropriate speech are all both "karmic deeds" and "courses of karmic action." The other three consisting of noncovetousness, refraining from ill will, and right view are all "courses of karmic action," but are not "karmic deeds" as such, for these three phenomena correspond to [volitional] thought, this type of [merely mental] activity.[181]

Question: How is it that [within the ten courses of good karmic action] the first seven are both "karmic deeds" and "courses of karmic action"?

Response: They are referred to as "courses" [of karmic action] because it is due to always practicing these endeavors that one becomes able to arrive in good circumstances within the realms of humans and *devas*. It is because these seven are karmic deeds amenable to being performed that they are also referred to as "karmic deeds."

Question: How is it that [within the ten courses of good karmic action] the remaining three are only "courses of karmic action," but are not "karmic deeds"?

Response: These three serve as the foundation for those that do qualify as good karmic actions. It is because the practice of all good karmic deeds comes forth from within them that they are referred to as "courses of karmic action," while not being referred to as "karmic deeds" as such.

Furthermore:

> [Observances of] moral precept dharmas are karmic deeds.
> karmic deeds may or may not be [observances of] moral precepts.
> Qualification as a "karmic deeds" or as a "course of karmic action"
> is a matter involving the application of four types of distinctions.

Physical and verbal karmic deeds may be [observances of] moral precepts. Mental actions may be karma, but they are not themselves [observances of] moral precepts.

As for the four types of categorical distinctions made with respect to qualification as either "karmic actions" or "courses of karmic action," they are as follows:

There are "karmic deeds" that are not "courses of karmic action."
There are "courses of karmic action" that are not "karmic deeds."
There are "karmic deeds" that are also "courses of karmic action."
There are [actions] that are neither "karmic deeds" nor "courses of karmic action."

As for those "karmic deeds" that are not "courses of karmic action," these are three types of bad physical deeds not subsumable within the sphere of "courses of karmic action," namely the wielding of fists to strike, whips to lash, cudgels to beat, and so forth. So too in the case of the three corresponding types of good physical deeds not subsumable in one of the categories of "courses of karmic action," namely: welcoming eminences on arrival, bowing down in reverence, and so forth. These two subcategories of good and bad deeds are not subsumable within the "courses of karmic action."

There are those who state that [these two subcategories of good and bad deeds] *are* also "courses of karmic action." Why? [They claim that] because these two types of deeds may have times when they lead one to [rebirth in] good or bad stations of rebirth, they are therefore "courses of karmic action." However, because this is not a fixed matter, we do not claim here that they constitute "courses of karmic action."

As for those that are "courses of karmic action" but which are not "karmic deeds," because the final three bad karmic deeds [of the ten courses of bad karmic action] and the final three good karmic deeds [of the ten courses of good karmic action] are, by nature, associated with the presence [or absence of] afflictions, they are not "karmic deeds" as such. However, because they 98b
are able to instigate the production of karmic deeds, they do therefore constitute "courses of karmic action."

[Among these,] the three that are good, because they are, by nature, roots of goodness, they are not "karmic deeds" as such. But, because they are able to instigate the production of good karmic deeds, they do therefore constitute "courses of karmic action."

As for those that are both "karmic deeds" and "courses of karmic action," they are the seven deeds consisting of killing or not killing and the others [as well as their opposites].

As for those that are neither "karmic deeds" nor "courses of karmic action," they are all of the dharmas [not otherwise subsumed in the first three of these four categories].

In addition:

> If a bodhisattva still at the border with the first ground
> uses three kinds of purity
> to abide securely in the ten courses of good karmic action,
> he will then be able to bring forth decisive resolve.

Once this bodhisattva comes to dwell on the second ground, he then distinguishes with utter clarity these ten good and bad courses of karmic action. Having come to know these matters, he applies three kinds of purity to his abiding in the ten courses of good karmic action, namely:

He does not personally kill any being;
He does not instruct others to kill any being;
And he does not delight in the karmic offense of killing.

In this same way, he also [applies these three kinds of purity to the rest of the courses of good karmic action] up to and including "right view."

Question: A bodhisattva dwelling on the first ground already abides in the ten courses of good karmic action. Why is this matter being discussed yet again here [in the context of the second ground]?

Response: It is not that he does not abide in the ten courses of good karmic action when dwelling on the first ground. However, due to the application of these three kinds of purity, such practice becomes ever more superior and ever more greatly increased here [on the second ground]. Previously, when still abiding on the first ground, although he might indeed become a monarch reigning over all of Jambudvīpa, he was still unable at that point to implement these three kinds of purity. It is for this reason that we discuss the three kinds of purity here. The bodhisattva who abides here on the second ground knows these distinctions as they apply to all sorts of karmic actions and thus brings forth decisive resolve.

> All the world's wretched destinies
> are produced from the ten bad deeds.
> All the world's good destinies
> are produced because of the ten good deeds.

"All the world's wretched destinies" refers to:

The three types of hell realm destinies, namely the hot hells, cold hells, and hells of blackness;

The three types of animal realm destinies, namely the animals that live in the water, the animals that live on land, and the animals that fly through the air;

And the different types of ghost realm destinies, namely the hungry ghosts, the ghosts who eat impure things, and those with flaming mouths, *asura*s, *yakṣa*s, and so forth.

All of these arise from engaging in the ten courses of bad karmic action.

It is because of the presence of relatively superior, middling, or inferior causes and conditions that all of the world's good destinies are produced. Whether it be the *deva* realm or the human realm, they all arise from the practice of the ten courses of good karmic action. They are all included within the three realms of existence wherein there are the twenty-eight *deva* realms and, in the case of the human realm, these are all those peoples that inhabit the four continents.

Having come to definitely know such matters, [this bodhisattva] reflects, "I wish that I myself will be born within these good stations of rebirth and wish also that I may be able to influence other beings to be reborn in these good stations of rebirth."

> Therefore I should abide
> within the ten courses of good karmic action
> while also influencing other beings
> to immediately abide within these courses of good karmic action.

Whether one is reborn in the good stations of rebirth or is instead born into bad stations of rebirth, this is all due to the ten courses of good karmic

98c action or ten courses of bad karmic action. [Hence one reflects,] "I realize that this world exists on the basis of all of the karmic causes and conditions and that there is no fixed subjective agent [involved in its creation].[182] Therefore, I should first ensure that I myself have become established in the practice of the ten courses of good karmic action and then, afterward, I should influence other beings to also abide in the practice of the ten courses of good karmic action."

Question: Why is it that one must first see that he himself abides within the ten courses of good karmic action and only later influences others to abide therein as well?

Response:

It is not easy for one who engages in bad deeds
to influence others toward goodness,
for, if one does not practice goodness oneself,
others will not believe and accept [one's teaching].

If someone who is a bad person does not practice goodness himself even as he wishes to influence others to practice goodness, this will be a very difficult to accomplish. Why? If this person does not practice goodness himself, other people will not believe in or accept his instruction. This is as described in a verse:

If one is not good oneself,
one will be unable to influence others toward goodness.
If one has not reached quiescence oneself,
one will be unable to influence others to reach quiescence.

It is for this reason that you should
first practice goodness and quiescence yourself
and then afterward instruct other people
to influence them to practice goodness and reach quiescence.

It is in this way that this bodhisattva should practice good dharmas.

From the Avīci Hells
on up to the summit of existence,

one distinguishes the effects of ten courses of karmic action
as well as the places in which one undergoes their retribution.

In just this manner, one should rightly realize that, from down below in the Avīci Hells all the way on up to the station of neither perception nor nonperception, all of these are but places wherein one undergoes the resulting retribution from all of the many different sorts of good and bad karmic deeds. Among these [stations of rebirth]:

It is by habitually practicing the worst of the ten courses of bad karmic action that one is reborn in the Avīci Hells;
When the extent of evil karma is somewhat less, one is reborn instead in the Great Broiling Hell;
When somewhat less than that, one is reborn in the Lesser Broiling Hell;
When somewhat less again, one is reborn in the Great Screaming Hell;
When even less, one is reborn in the Lesser Screaming Hell;
When yet less than that, one is reborn in the Saṃgata Hell;
When less again, rebirth is in the Great Road Hell;
A yet lesser level brings birth in the Black Line Hell;
When lesser yet, one is reborn in the Living Hell;
Yet another increment less brings rebirth in the Sword Forest Hell or other lesser subsidiary hells for which one should also make ever finer distinctions [in these subcategories of hell realm retributions].

It is through practicing an intermediate level of the ten courses of bad karmic action that one is reborn into the animal realm. One should also make ever finer distinctions regarding [the levels of karmic retribution as manifested within] the animal realm.

It is through practicing a relatively lesser level of the ten courses of bad karmic action that one is reborn into the realm of the hungry ghosts.

This represents only a general discussion of these matters. We should present a more expansive range of differentiating distinctions among these. There are the *asura*s and *yakṣa*s born into the ghost realms, *nāga* kings reborn into the animal realm wherein the bliss they enjoy may be identical to that experienced by the *deva*s. All of these beings take these rebirths because of bad karma and then, having taken such rebirths, they may also enjoy the karmic fruits of their past good karmic actions.

99a In the case of those who have practiced only the very lowest level of the ten courses of good karmic action, they take rebirth in Jambudvīpa within poverty-stricken low-caste clans, namely among the *caṇḍāla*s, or in remote regions, or as artisans, or as people of low social stature.

With a somewhat more superior level [of practice of the ten courses of good karmic action], one may be reborn into merchant-class families. When somewhat more superior, one is reborn into brahman clans. When more superior yet, one is reborn into a *kṣatriya* clan. When more superior than that, one is reborn into a family of high governmental officials. When more superior yet, rebirth occurs into royal families.

When one's practice of the ten courses of good karmic action has been at a yet more superior level, one is reborn on the continent of Aparagodānīya. When more superior yet, rebirth is on the continent of Pūrvavideha. and when superior to that, rebirth is on the continent of Uttarakuru.

When more superior yet, rebirth is into the abodes of the Four Heavenly Kings. At increasing levels of superiority to that, rebirth is into the Trāyastriṃśa Heaven, the Yāma Heaven, the Tuṣita Heaven, and the Nirmāṇarati Heaven. At the most superior level of practice of the ten courses of good karmic action, one is reborn in the Paranirmitavaśavartin Heaven.

Here we should make all kinds of distinctions with regard to the minor and major differences. For instance, among humans, there are minor kings, major kings, the kings ruling over all of Jambudvīpa, and wheel-turning kings. The abode of the Four Heavenly Kings has Four Heavenly Kings. In the Trāyastriṃśa Heaven, there is Śakra, ruler of the *deva*s. In the Yāma Heaven, there is the Suyāma *Deva* King. In the Tuṣita Heaven, there is the Saṃtuṣita Heaven King. In the Nirmāṇarati Heaven, there is the Skillful Transformations Heaven King. In the Paranirmitavaśavartin Heaven, there is the Paranirmitavaśavartin Heaven King. Beyond this, one must utilize volition associated with cultivation of the *dhyāna* absorptions to gain rebirth into the higher [celestial] realms.

Question: If in fact it is essential to utilize volition associated with the *dhyāna* absorptions, why was it just stated that, in every case, it is because of the ten courses of good karmic action that one gains every place of rebirth all the way up to the station of neither perception nor nonperception?

Response: Although one must cultivate the *dhyāna* absorptions to gain rebirth in the stations of either the form or formless realm, one must still first become solidly established in the practice of the ten courses of good karmic action. Only after this can one succeed in the cultivation of the *dhyāna* absorptions. It is for this reason that [acquisition of] those stations relies upon the great benefit provided by the ten courses of good karmic action. It is for this reason as well that it was stated here that, in every case, it is because of the ten courses of good karmic action that one attains every station of rebirth all the way up to the station of neither perception nor nonperception.

How is this so? After having first cultivated purity in the ten courses of good karmic action, by separating from sensual desire and cultivating the first *dhyāna* with relatively inferior volition, one may succeed in taking rebirth in the Brahmakāyika Heaven. By cultivating the first *dhyāna* with relatively middling volition, one may take rebirth in the Brahmapurohita Heaven. And by cultivating the first *dhyāna* with relatively superior volition, one may succeed in taking rebirth in the Mahābrahma Heaven.

By cultivating the second *dhyāna* with relatively inferior volition, one may take rebirth in the Lesser Light Heaven. By cultivating the second *dhyāna* with relatively middling volition, one may succeed in taking rebirth in the Limitless Light Heaven. And by cultivating the second *dhyāna* with relatively superior volition, one may succeed in taking rebirth in the Sublime Light Heaven.

By cultivating the third *dhyāna* with relatively inferior volition, one may succeed in taking rebirth in the Lesser Purity Heaven. By cultivating the third *dhyāna* with relatively middling volition, one may succeed in taking rebirth in the Limitless Light Heaven. And by cultivating the third *dhyāna* with relatively superior volition, one may succeed in taking rebirth in the Universal Purity Heaven.

By cultivating the fourth *dhyāna* with relatively inferior volition, one may take rebirth in the Anabhraka Heaven. By cultivating the fourth *dhyāna* with relatively middling volition, one may take rebirth in the Puṇyaprasava Heaven. And by cultivating the fourth *dhyāna* with relatively superior volition, one may take rebirth in the Bṛhatphala Heaven.

By cultivating the nonperception absorption with relatively middling volition, one may succeed in taking rebirth in the Nonperception Heaven.

By repeated cultivation of contaminant-free concentration in the fourth
99b *dhyāna* with relatively inferior volition, one may take rebirth in the "Non-extensive"[183] or Avṛha Heaven. By repeated cultivation of contaminant-free concentration in the fourth *dhyāna* with [more] superior volition, one may take rebirth in the "Non-hot" or Atapās Heaven. By repeated cultivation of contaminant-free concentration in the fourth *dhyāna* with [yet more] superior volition, one may take rebirth in the "Delightful Vision" or Sudarśana Heaven. By repeated cultivation of contaminant-free concentration in the fourth *dhyāna* with [even more] superior volition, one may take rebirth in the "Sublime Vision" or Sudṛśa Heaven. By repeated cultivation of contaminant-free concentration in the fourth *dhyāna* with the most superior volition, one may take rebirth in the Akaniṣṭha Heaven.

By cultivating the concentration associated with the station of infinite space with the corresponding volition, one may take rebirth in the Infinite Space Heaven. By cultivating the concentration associated with the station of infinite consciousness with the corresponding volition, one may take rebirth in the Infinite Consciousness Heaven. By cultivating the concentration associated with the station of nothing whatsoever with the corresponding volition, one may take rebirth in the Station of Nothing Whatsoever Heaven. By cultivating the concentration associated with the station of neither perception nor nonperception with the corresponding volition, one may take rebirth in the Neither Perception nor Nonperception Heaven.

The above discussion shows the stations to which beings go and from which they come as they undergo birth and death in the world, [as determined by their differing levels of cultivation of either the ten courses of bad karmic action or the ten courses of good karmic action].

Chapter 29[184]

Distinctions Pertaining to *Śrāvakas* and *Pratyekabuddhas*

Question: Do these ten courses of good karmic action function solely as causes and conditions for rebirths among humans and *deva*s or do they also confer other additional benefits?

Response: They do have [additional benefits, as below]:

> All of those cultivating the *śrāvaka* disciple vehicle,
> the *pratyekabuddha* vehicle, or the Great Vehicle,
> in every instance rely upon the ten courses of good karmic action
> to provide immense benefit for them.

Generally speaking, there are only three vehicles that serve as means for escaping samsara's cycle of births and deaths: the *śrāvaka* disciple vehicle, the *pratyekabuddha* vehicle, and the Great Vehicle. These three vehicles all rely upon the ten courses of good karmic action to provide immense benefit for them. And how is this the case? These ten courses of good karmic action enable the practitioner to reach the grounds of the *śrāvaka* disciples, also enable him to reach the ground of the *pratyekabuddha*s, and also enable him to reach the ground of the buddhas.

Question: Which kinds of beings do these ten courses of good karmic action enable to reach the grounds of *śrāvaka* disciples?

Response:

> Those reliant on learning from others, who have no great compassion,
> who are frightened by existence within the three realms,
> who delight in but a minor measure of meritorious qualities,
> and whose resolve is too inferior and weak—

Those whose minds delight in renunciation,
who always contemplate the impermanence of the world,
and who also know that all dharmas
have no self—

Those who do not for even a single mind-moment
wish to take on any rebirths,
and who always disbelieve that the world
is possessed of a stable and secure nature[185]—

Those who contemplate the great elements as like venomous snakes,
the aggregates as like knife-wielding thieves,
and the six sense bases as like a mere empty village,
and who do not delight in worldly wealth or pleasure—

Those who esteem solid observance of the moral precepts
and, for the sake of gaining the *dhyāna* absorptions,
always delight in sitting in *dhyāna* meditation
and in cultivating good dharmas—

99c Those who look only to nirvana
to serve as the foremost rescuer and protector,
who always seek the wisdom that puts an end to suffering,
and who delight in accumulating the practices leading to liberation—

And those who only esteem the accomplishment of self-benefit
as they come forth through one or another of the supreme bases.
The courses of good karmic action cause these people
to have the ability to reach the grounds of *śrāvaka* disciples.

[Stanza 1 Commentary]

As for these [*śrāvaka* disciples] who accord with what is taught them by others,[186] they listen to what is taught them by others and practice in accordance with that, but are not otherwise able to develop wisdom of their own.

Question: Are the ten courses of good karmic action able in every case to cause all who hear the teachings from others to become *śrāvaka* disciples?

Response: No, that is not the way it is. For those who do not have the great compassion, the ten courses of good karmic action are indeed able to cause them to reach the grounds of the *śrāvaka* disciples. However, in the case of the bodhisattvas who have heard the Dharma from the buddhas, because they are possessed of the great compassion, the ten courses of good karmic action cannot influence them to enter onto the grounds of the *śrāvaka* disciples.

Question: Is it the case then that whosoever does not possess the great compassion can be caused by the ten courses of good karmic action to reach the grounds of the *śrāvaka* disciples?

Response: No. It is not that way. For those who are frightened at the prospect of continued existence within the three realms, the ten courses of good karmic action are indeed able to cause them to reach the grounds of the *śrāvaka* disciples. For all of those others who are not fearful of existence in the three realms, the ten courses of good karmic action are able to cause them to gain rebirth in good stations of existence among humans and *deva*s. This is because they delight in [continued existences within] the three realms.

Question: The ten courses of good karmic action are able to cause all who are frightened at the prospect of continued existences within the three realms to reach the grounds of the *śrāvaka* disciples. That being the case, bodhisattvas too are fearful of continued existence in the three realms. It is just that, in their diligent and vigorous striving for nirvana, they do so for the sake of both themselves and other beings. Therefore it must be that the ten courses of good karmic action are also able to cause even the bodhisattvas to reach the grounds of the *śrāvaka* disciples.

Response: It is not necessarily the case that everyone who is fearful of continued existence in the three realms is bound to fall down onto the grounds of the *śrāvaka* disciples. Who then is bound to fall? Those who delight in cultivation of but a minor measure of [the requisite] meritorious qualities and who take on but a minor measure of the six *pāramitā*s as it was taught them by the buddhas—it is people of this sort who are bound to fall down onto the grounds of the *śrāvaka* disciples.

In the case of a person who is able to acquire the meritorious qualities of the buddhas and who is able as well to thoroughly train in their wisdom, the ten courses of good karmic action will definitely propel them directly to the realization of buddhahood.

Among those who rely upon what they have been taught by others, who are fearful of continued existence in the three realms, and who acquire only a minor measure of the meritorious qualities—these people are of two different types. There are those for whom the ten courses of good karmic action are able to cause them to reach the grounds of the *śrāvaka* disciples and there are those who are thereby caused to reach the ground of the *pratyekabuddha*s.

Question: Among these [two types of persons] who rely upon what they have been taught by others, who are fearful of continued existence in the three realms, and who acquire only a minor measure of the meritorious qualities, how is it that the ten courses of good karmic action cause some of them to reach the grounds of the *śrāvaka* disciples, whereas others are instead caused to reach the grounds of the *pratyekabuddha*s?

Response: Those of [relatively] inferior and weak resolve end up becoming arhats whereas those whose resolve is somewhat more solid become *pratyekabuddha*s.

[Stanza 2 Commentary]

Question: Is it the case then that the ten courses of good karmic action cause all such people whose resolve is inferior and weak to reach the grounds of the *śrāvaka* disciples?

Response: No, that is not the way it is. Why? This refers to those whose resolve is relatively weak, but who still do delight in renouncing samsara. It is not the case that this refers to those whose resolve is weak but who do not delight in renunciation [of samsara], either.

100a **Question:** Through contemplation of which matters can one know whether one's mind delights in renunciation?

Response: If one contemplates conditioned dharmas as impermanent and contemplates all dharmas as having no self, one should then realize that he definitely delights in renunciation.

[Stanza 3 Commentary]

Question: Now that we know the bases for delighting in renunciation, since the bodhisattva also contemplates in the same way conditioned dharmas as impermanent and all dharmas as having no self, why do the ten courses of good karmic action not cause this person to fall down onto the grounds of the *śrāvaka* disciples?

Response: Because these people [who are drawn to the *śrāvaka* disciple and *pratyekabuddha* vehicles] have brought forth deep renunciation and have distanced themselves from the great compassion, they do not wish for even a single mind-moment to take on any further rebirths and they do not believe that the world is characterized by stability or security. As the Buddha told the *bhikṣu*s in a sutra:

> Just as even a small amount of excrement is smelly, defiled, and unclean, how much the more so a lot of it, so too, even a single mind-moment of rebirth existence is suffering, how much the more so a lot of it? *Bhikṣu*s, you should train in the severance of rebirths. Do not allow yourselves to undergo any more of them.[187]

Because *śrāvaka* disciples believe and accept these instructions, they do not wish for even a single mind-moment to undergo any further rebirths. These individuals additionally think thus, "The world is impermanent. Whether it be the endeavors one pursues or the life span one experiences, these are all characterized by instability and insecurity. Given that death is always pursuing people, who can know the time of their own death? At the time of one's death, one cannot know what kind of karmic retribution one will undergo or what sort of thoughts will arise.[188] Because all such matters are unstable and insecure and because they cannot be trusted, one should urgently strive to put an end to suffering."

The bodhisattva, on the other hand, does not act in this manner, but rather commits himself to undergoing rebirths as numerous as the sands of the Ganges across the course of countless *asaṃkhyeya kalpa*s for the sake of attaining *anuttarāsamyaksaṃbodhi* and liberating beings.

Thus the verse says [of *śrāvaka* disciples] that they "do not for even a single mind-moment delight in taking on any rebirths." The [ten] courses of good karmic action enable these individuals to reach the grounds of the *śrāvaka* disciples.

[Stanza 4 Commentary]

Question: What sorts of endeavors do these people delight in cultivating and accumulating that they therefore so dislike undergoing further rebirth?

Response: Because, in contemplating the four great elements of earth, water, fire, and air, these people are fond of regarding them with animosity, and because they regard them as forming what is unlovely, foul-smelling, defiled, and ungrateful for kindnesses,[189] they therefore see them as analogous to poisonous snakes.

Because the five aggregates of form, feeling, perception, formative factors, and consciousness are able to rob one of one's wisdom life, they contemplate them as analogous to hostile bandits.

Because the sense bases of eye, ear, nose, tongue, body, and mind are destitute of permanence, unshakability, immutability, and indestructibility, and because they are devoid of self and are devoid of anything belonging to a self, they perceive them as like an empty village.

[They realize that] even if one were to have the advantage of every sort of natural endowment and life-enhancing provision for enjoyment, because those things are impermanent, false, deceptive, and do not abide for even a moment, they are not moved to delight in this. Hence people of this sort think of all stations of rebirth as devoid of any stability or security and they look only to the single dharma of nirvana as their rescuer and protector. This is as described in a sutra:

> *Bhikṣu*s, the world is entirely ablaze, that is to say: The eye is ablaze, visual forms are ablaze, eye consciousness is ablaze, eye contact is ablaze, and whatever feeling is produced with eye contact as the causal condition—that too is ablaze.
>
> And with what is it ablaze? It is ablaze with the fire of desire, the fire of hatred, the fire of delusion, the fire of birth, aging, sickness, death,

grief, lamentation, anguish, and torment. So too is this the case with the 100b
ear, nose, tongue, body, and mind faculty.[190]

[Stanzas 5–6 Commentary]

They contemplate all conditioned dharmas as ablaze and regard only nirvana's dharma of quiescent cessation as able to provide a source of rescue. Because they so esteem this single dharma of nirvana, they abandon all other endeavors in favor of diligent practice of sitting in *dhyāna* meditation.

Question: If one contemplates all conditioned dharmas as ablaze and the quiescent cessation of nirvana as the only source of rescue and protection, is it the case then that the ten courses of good karmic action are able in every case to cause these people to reach the grounds of the *śrāvaka* disciples?

Response: No, that is not so. Consider the moral precepts formulated by the Buddha. It is for the sake of attaining the *dhyāna* absorptions that these moral precepts are esteemed as so important. [Hence we refer here instead to] those with resolute aspiration who refrain from transgressing against the precepts, who abandon all other endeavors, who delight solely in sitting in *dhyāna* meditation, who seek the wisdom that extinguishes suffering, and who always diligently cultivate the causes and conditions for liberation. It is people of this sort who have come forth from cultivating one or two of the supreme bases [of meritorious qualities] in previous lives that the ten courses of good karmic action thus enable to reach the grounds of the *śrāvaka* disciples.

And how does this come about? If one upholds the moral precepts purely, one's mind becomes free of any regrets. Because one's mind is free of regrets, one becomes suffused with joyfulness. Having gained this state of joyfulness, one's body experiences a state of pliancy. Because one's body experiences this state of pliancy, one's mind becomes blissful. Because one's mind becomes blissful, one focuses the mind and gains meditative absorption. Because one focuses the mind and gains meditative absorption, one develops wisdom that accords with reality. Because one develops wisdom that accords with reality, one immediately develops disenchantment. From disenchantment, one develops detachment, and from detachment, one attains liberation.[191]

[Stanza 7 Commentary]

As for "coming forth from one or perhaps two of the supreme bases [of meritorious qualities]," this is exemplified by Venerable Rāhula who came forth from the supreme basis of truthfulness, by Venerable Sīvalī[192] who came forth from the supreme basis of relinquishment, by Venerable Revata who came forth from the supreme basis of quiescence, and as exemplified by Venerable Śāriputra who came forth from the supreme basis of wisdom.

Then again, it may perhaps be that one comes forth from the two supreme bases consisting of truthfulness and relinquishment, that one comes forth from the two supreme bases consisting of truthfulness and quiescence, that one comes forth from the two supreme bases consisting of truthfulness and wisdom, that one comes forth from the two supreme bases consisting of relinquishment and quiescence, that one comes forth from the two supreme bases consisting of relinquishment and wisdom, or that one comes forth from the two supreme bases consisting of quiescence and wisdom.

It is in this way that the ten courses of good karmic action may enable one to reach the grounds of the *śrāvaka* disciples.

100c **Question:** What sorts of people do the ten courses of good karmic action cause to enter the grounds of the *pratyekabuddhas*?

Response:

In the ten courses of good karmic action
practiced by *śrāvaka* disciples, they are even more superior.
They cultivate deep *dhyāna,* don't rely on others' teaching,
and are always fond of abiding in seclusion, far from others.

They always delight in the thorough cultivation
of the extremely deep dharma of causes and conditions.
They remain detached from the power of skillful means
as well as from the mind of great compassion.

They pursue lesser aspirations and lesser endeavors.
They abhor and disdain boisterous chatter,
always enjoy abiding in secluded places,
and are possessed of awe-inspiring virtue and deep solemnity.

They delight in serving as fields of merit
and always contemplate what by nature promotes transcendence.
They accomplish those endeavors that are principled
and accord reverence to the Lords [of the Dharma].

Having already perfected anchoring of the mind,
the knowing mind focuses on whatever is taken as the object.
They always delight in *dhyāna* concentration
and in this possess the power of men of intermediate capacities.

They delight in the dharmas of the monastic
and in them the mind of goodness does not shrink or sink away.
Those who gain the light of wisdom
may come forth from two of the supreme bases.

Or perhaps they come forth from three of the supreme bases.
The ten courses of good karmic action
enable persons of this sort
to reach the ground of the *pratyekabuddha*s.

[Stanza 1 Commentary]

As for "In the ten courses of good karmic action practiced by *śrāvaka* disciples, they are even more superior," they surpass that level of accomplishment in the ten courses of good karmic action reached by the *śrāvaka* disciples, but still do not approach the level of accomplishment in such dharmas as practiced by the bodhisattvas.

They reflect in this manner, "The *śrāvaka* disciple practitioners respond to and accord with what they are taught by others in their practice of the path, after which they attain personal realizations of wisdom. As for myself, I am not thus inclined, for I do not delight in following others. Therefore I should cause the practice of the ten courses of good karmic action to become even more superior. For this reason I shall delight in the ten courses of good karmic action without relying on others and this shall enable me to reach the ground of the *pratyekabuddha*s."

Having reflected in this manner, they always delight in seclusion, thinking thus, "If I forever delight in the boisterousness [of the common crowd], then that is bound to lead to the accumulation of all manner of evil and

unwholesome dharmas due to close proximity to circumstances that can
101a cause defilement, can cause hatred, and can cause delusion. In this seclusion, I should cultivate the extremely deep dharma of causes and conditions."

[Stanza 2 Commentary]

They additionally reflect in this way, "If I do not cultivate the extremely deep dharma of causes and conditions, then I will be unable to gain that wisdom that is not reliant on the teachings of others. Why should I not now always cultivate the extremely deep dharma of causes and conditions so that I can later gain the wisdom that is not reliant on the teachings of others?"

"Extremely deep" refers in this context to that which is difficult to fathom and that with regard to which one cannot reach an utterly penetrating comprehension. One can completely fathom all of the scriptures, texts, skills, and arts possessed by all common people across the beginningless course of samsara. It is only the extremely deep dharma of causes and conditions that one cannot completely fathom. [The difficulty of fathoming it] is comparable to a rabbit's or other small creature's inability to fathom the very bottom of a great ocean.

If one possesses skillful means and the mind of great compassion while also increasingly cultivating the extremely deep dharma of causes and conditions, then he can proceed directly toward the attainment of *anuttarāsamyaksaṃbodhi*. However, if one abandons these two requisites while increasingly cultivating the extremely deep knowledge of causes and conditions, then he will instead become a *pratyekabuddha*.

"Skillful means" refers here to perfecting in a manner free of error all the different sorts of thought used in teaching beings while also not seizing on merely superficial aspects of extremely profound dharmas.

"Great compassion" refers here to abiding in a deep and kindly sympathy for beings, one that is superior even to that of *śrāvaka* disciples and *pratyekabuddha*s, how much the more so common people.

[Stanza 3 Commentary]

As for "pursuing lesser aspirations and lesser endeavors," and "abhorring and disdaining boisterous chatter," those possessed of these qualities can reach the ground of the *pratyekabuddha*s.

If one is inclined toward great aspirations and great endeavors, if one enjoys gatherings of many people, and if one is protected by skillful means and great compassion, then it will become easy to reach *anuttarā-samyaksaṃbodhi.*

Why is this so? One who pursues pratyekabuddhahood, possessed as he is of lesser aspirations, thinks, "One need only see to one's own liberation."

As for his "pursuing lesser endeavors," this practitioner devotes himself solely to the perfection of his own roots of goodness and does not extend his concern to other people. Because this person abandons the endeavor of teaching beings, he does not draw near to any of the many sorts of commotion.

The bodhisattva, being inclined toward great aspirations and great endeavors, thinks, "I should liberate all beings." It is because of this great aspiration that he then takes on the great endeavor of teaching beings. This teaching of beings is no minor endeavor. If one abhors boisterousness and talkativeness, then he will not succeed in this work. Therefore the bodhisattva enters into the midst of such commotion and resorts to discourse appropriate to such commotion, but he still has nothing to which he is attached.

Moreover, it is because [the *pratyekabuddha* practitioners] reject the cultivation of genuine meritorious qualities that they are said to have "lesser aspirations." It is because they take on but few responsibilities that these are referred to as "lesser endeavors." It is because of their abhorrence and disdain for commotion that they are said to have "lesser aspirations." And it is because they delight in residing in solitude that they are said to engage in "lesser endeavors."

As for persons such as these who have lesser aspirations, engage in lesser endeavors, do not delight in the commotion and chatter of the multitudes, and who delight in proximity to far away, fearsome, and very remote places, their determination is extremely great. These individuals reflect thus, "If I dwell in a faraway, fearsome, and very remote place, then nobody will come there, and thus, by virtue of that abiding at a great distance, the mind itself will also be able to abide at an especially great distance. If one does not dwell extremely far from those who delight in frivolousness, then outsiders will not find it difficult to come and go there."

[Stanza 4 Commentary]

101b People of this sort do not live together with other beings. Although they have abandoned beings, they still wish to influence beings to plant roots of goodness and do wish to be of great benefit to them. Hence they reflect in this manner, "How might I not live together with other beings and yet still benefit beings?" Having pondered in this manner, they realize, "I should benefit beings by serving as a field of merit for them, doing so by accepting offerings from them. Thus, even though I do not live together with other beings, I shall still be able to be of great benefit to them."

Continuing in this vein, this person reflects, "How then might I become a field of karmic merit for others?" He then immediately sees and realizes the following, thinking, "If I deeply delight in serving as a field of merit and in always contemplating whatever naturally leads to transcendence, then, later on, the means for serving as a field of merit will spontaneously come forth and whatever dharmas naturally lead to transcendence will spontaneously come forth as well."

These [dharmas that naturally lead to transcendence] are what we refer to as the observance of moral precepts, cultivation of *dhyāna* absorptions, development of wisdom, and so forth.

He also has this thought, "How might I be able to swiftly reach that ground in which I may become a field of merit and acquire the dharmas leading to transcendence? I should become one who is grounded in right contemplation, should accomplish all endeavors that are manifestly principled and of meaningful significance, and should make offerings to and demonstrate reverence for the Lords [of the Dharma]. If I proceed in this manner, then before too long I shall swiftly acquire that ground on which I can serve as a field of merit and shall also acquire the dharmas that naturally lead to transcendence.

"Why should I proceed in this manner? I should accomplish those endeavors that are principled and should rightly contemplate dharmas for this shall enable me to realize the wisdom that is not reliant on the teachings of others.

"Furthermore, it is because of making offerings to and revering the Lords [of the Dharma] that one's roots of goodness are able to increase and grow ever more fully developed. Due to such growth in one's roots of goodness, wisdom too shall then become extremely deep and full in its development.

"It is because of wisdom's becoming extremely deep and full in its development that one is then able to gain an utterly penetrating comprehension of the true character of all phenomena. When one is able to gain an utterly penetrating comprehension of the true character of all phenomena, one can then generate disenchantment. It is from this disenchantment that one is then able to generate detachment. It is through this detachment that one gains liberation. And it is because of gaining liberation that the roots of goodness one has accumulated in the past and later on finally enable one to serve as a field of merit. Afterward, one then attains the realization of the dharmas naturally leading to transcendence."

As for "the Lords," this is a specific reference to all buddhas, the bhagavats. During the time that one is planting roots of goodness, this matter [of reverence for the buddhas] is the very greatest of all causes and conditions in that endeavor.

[Stanza 5 Commentary]

This practitioner continues pondering these matters, thinking, "Now, how exactly will I be able to swiftly succeed in those endeavors that are principled and of meaningful significance?"

This person then immediately understands and sees, "If I anchor the mind in a single place, directly know what it takes as its object, and always delight in the cultivation of the *dhyāna* absorptions, [my aims may be accomplished in this way]."

If this practitioner is able to anchor his mind in a single place, he is then able to gain *samādhi*. Due to acquiring *samādhi,* all principled endeavors can then be accomplished. This is as described in the sutras, "By gaining *dhyāna* concentration, one becomes able to know in accordance with reality and see in accordance with reality."

If one has already practiced anchoring of the mind, then he will swiftly enter *samādhi*. It is through this ability to swiftly enter *samādhi* that one becomes an adept in the *dhyāna* absorptions, one who always abides in meditative absorption.

If one becomes able in this manner to cultivate these dharmas, then this itself constitutes offerings and reverence to the buddhas. If someone were to make offerings of incense, flowers, and the four requisites to the buddhas, this would not truly qualify as making offerings to the buddhas. Rather, if one can singlemindedly draw close to and cultivate the path of the *ārya*s, doing so without falling into neglectfulness, this would truly constitute offerings and reverence to the buddhas. As stated in the sutras, at the time of his
101c *parinirvāṇa,* the Buddha told Ānanda:

> The raining down of *māndārava* flowers and powdered *candana* incense accompanied by the music of the *deva*s—this does not truly qualify as offerings and reverence to the Tathāgata. Ānanda, if a *bhikṣu, bhikṣuṇī, upāsaka,* or *upāsikā* were to singlemindedly and without neglectfulness draw close to and cultivate the dharmas of the *ārya*s, it is this that would truly constitute the making of offerings to the Buddha. Therefore, Ānanda, you should cultivate and train in this true offering to the Buddha.

Many meritorious qualities such as these characterize the practitioner of intermediate strength who delights in leaving the household life and who does not allow his devotion to goodness to retreat or fall away.

Those of the most superior strength are able to succeed in attaining buddhahood whereas those possessed of a lesser degree of strength become *śrāvaka* disciples. Hence it is those of intermediate strength who become *pratyekabuddha*s.

[Stanzas 6–7 Commentary]

Because they delight in leaving behind the household life they are able to perfect a multitude of meritorious qualities. And why is this so? If one continues to abide within the household, one is unable to have but few desires and take on but few endeavors. One is unable to remain physically and mentally detached or acquire the *dhyāna* absorptions.

If one's resolve retreats and sinks into impurity, one will be unable to successfully accomplish many endeavors, one will be unable to understand the extremely deep dharma of causes and conditions, one will be unable to achieve the realization of the nature of transcendence, and one will be unable to truly make offerings to and revere the buddhas in a manner that accords with the Dharma.

Beings such as these possess an intermediate level of strength. They think, "I am a person of intermediate strength. If I always delight in leaving the household life and maintain a resolve that does not retreat or fall away, all the meritorious circumstances that I wish for will naturally come forth for me."

He also reflects, "Being one of middling capacities, which of the fruits of the path should I delight in acquiring?" He immediately realizes that he should acquire the fruit of wisdom. And why? Because wisdom can bring about brilliant illumination. This is as stated in the sutras where it says, "*Bhikṣu*s, of all the different sorts of illumination, the light of wisdom is supreme."[193]

He then also thinks, "How should I go about acquiring this light of wisdom in which I delight?" He then realizes that it will come forth through perfection of either two or three of the supreme bases [of meritorious qualities]. As for the twofold acquisitions of the supreme bases, those combinations were already discussed above.

As for threefold acquisitions of the supreme bases, those may consist of truth, relinquishment, and quiescence; may consist of truth, relinquishment, and wisdom; or may consist of truth, quiescence, and wisdom. [He thinks,] "Therefore I should cultivate and accumulate these supreme bases. Once I have cultivated and accumulated these [supreme bases], I shall gain the light of wisdom and thus that wisdom that I have vowed to gain will naturally arrive here for me."

When someone possessed of such characteristics as these cultivates and accumulates these path-assisting dharmas in this way, the ten courses of good karmic action will enable him to reach the ground of the *pratyekabuddha*.

Chapter 30[194]

[Distinctions Pertaining to] the Great Vehicle

Question: As you have already explained, the ten courses of good karmic action enable one to reach the grounds of the *śrāvaka* disciples and *pratyeka-buddhas*. Which sorts of beings can the ten courses of good karmic action also cause to reach the ground of buddhahood?

Response:

The way they practice the ten courses of good karmic action
is superior to that of the two other classes of practitioners,
for they engage in measureless extraordinary cultivation 102a
superior to that of anyone else in the world.

They bring forth vows that are both solid and good,[195]
perfect the great compassion that cannot be impeded,
thoroughly take on the practice of skillful means,
and patiently endure every sort of pain and anguish.

They do not abandon any being,
deeply cherish the wisdom of the buddhas,
and delight in those who completely and thoroughly practice
the buddhas' powers and sovereign masteries.

They are able to refute all ideas involving wrong views
and accept and protect the buddhas' right Dharma.
They are valiant, able to endure, and vigorous,
and are possessed of solid resolve in teaching beings.

They do not covet or become attached to their own happiness
or to living a measurelessly long life.
They are supreme in all their endeavors
and free of fault in all the works they do.

> They possess every kind of purity
> and come forth through the practice of all the supreme bases.
> The courses of good karmic action enable these persons
> to reach the ground of the bhagavats who possess the ten powers.

As for "the way they practice the ten courses of good karmic action is superior to that of the two other classes of practitioners,"[196] this refers to the fact that the bodhisattvas have become superior to the *śrāvaka* disciple and *pratyekabuddha* aspirants in the quality of their cultivation of the ten courses of good karmic action. "Becoming superior" [in their cultivation of the ten courses of good karmic action] means that the bodhisattvas cultivate them with singleminded focus, that they always cultivate them, that they cultivate them to benefit themselves, that they cultivate them to benefit others, and that they cultivate them purely.

"Cultivating them with singleminded focus" means that they employ full mental intention in their cultivation.

"Always cultivate them" means that they never rest in their cultivation of them.

"Cultivating them to benefit themselves" means that they do this to establish the causes and conditions for birth among humans and *deva*s and to establish the causes and conditions for the attainment of nirvana.

"Cultivating them to benefit others" means that, as the bodhisattvas cultivate the ten courses of good karmic action, they dedicate the merit to the benefit and peace of all beings. It is for this reason that they can liberate an incalculable number of beings.

"Cultivating them purely" means theirs is undamaged practice, unmixed practice, unsullied practice, practice in which one has sovereign mastery, perfectly complete practice, practice free of covetousness and attachment, and practice that is praised by the wise.

"Damaged" practice refers here to that in which some aspects of the practice are cultivated whereas others are left aside and not practiced. Practice that is opposite to this is "undamaged" practice.

"Mixed" practice refers here to that wherein one encourages others to practice what one does not practice oneself. Practice that is opposite to this is "unmixed" practice.

"Sullied" practice is practice that occurs in conjunction with afflictions and karmic offenses. Practice that is opposite to this is "unsullied" practice.

As for "sovereign mastery," because they are tied down by agricultural work, wives, children, or material possessions, those who are prone to breaking the precepts are unable to achieve a state of sovereign mastery [in their practice]. Having no such [encumbering] circumstances, those who uphold the precepts may freely achieve a state of sovereign mastery in which they are not tied down by anything at all.

"Perfectly complete" practice refers to exhaustively complete observance of all the major and minor moral precepts that blocks off the afflictions, that involves constant mindfulness of the need to preserve them and guard against transgression, that serves as a cause and condition for the *dhyāna* absorptions, that is dedicated to realization of buddhahood, and that enables one to unite with ultimate reality and the nature of dharmas. This is what is meant by "perfectly complete" in this context.

Practice "free of covetousness and attachment" does not direct its focus toward worldly priorities, does not seize on merely superficial aspects of the moral precepts, and remains free of any tendency to elevate oneself and disparage others. 102b

As for practice "praised by the wise," in the Dharma of *śrāvaka* disciples, it is because it does not follow the cycle of births and deaths and is implemented solely for the sake of nirvana that it is referred to as "praised by the wise."

In this Dharma of the Great Vehicle, its practitioners do not even dedicate their practice to success in the *śrāvaka* disciple vehicle or the *pratyekabuddha* vehicle, how much the less could their practice be dedicated to samsara? Rather, it is dedicated solely to the realization of *anuttarāsamyaksaṃbodhi*. This is what is meant by practice of the ten courses of good karmic action that is "praised by the wise."

Question: What are the marks of cultivation that qualify it as "good" cultivation?

Response: It is that which incorporates countless extraordinary qualities into cultivation of the ten courses of good karmic action in a manner superior to the cultivation practiced by anyone else in the world. This is what is meant by "good" cultivation.

Question: How do the bodhisattvas, employing this sort of cultivation, cultivate in a manner "superior to anyone else in the entire world"?

Response: It is on the basis of five aspects of their cultivation that the bodhisattvas' cultivation is "superior to that of anyone else in the world":197

First, their vows;
Second, their solid resolve;
Third, their resolute intentions;
Fourth, their thoroughgoing purity;[198]
And fifth, their use of skillful means.

As for "their vows," the vows implemented by the bodhisattvas do not even exist among all common people, *śrāvaka* disciple practitioners, or *pratyekabuddha* practitioners. It is for this reason that the vows implemented by the bodhisattvas are superior to those of anyone else in the world. This is as described in the questions of the woman Vimaladattā in the *Mahāprajñā-pāramitā-sūtra,* in which the Buddha, because of Maudgalyāyana, said:

> From the point of his initial generation of the vow all the way on forward to his arrival at the *bodhimaṇḍa,* the bodhisattva is able to serve the entire world's *deva*s and humans as a field of merit, doing so in a manner that is superior to all *śrāvaka* disciples or *pratyekabuddha*s.

This is also as set forth in the *Pure Vinaya Sutra,* in which Mahākāśyapa said in the Buddha's presence:

> The Bhagavat has here so well described this rarity, that is to say, the bodhisattva's initial generation of the vow which is superior to that of all *śrāvaka* disciples and *pratyekabuddha*s.

This also accords with a verse in which it is proclaimed that:

> As for the bodhisattva's initial generation of his resolve
> conjoined to the great kindness and great compassion
> for the sake of the unsurpassable path,
> it is just this very resolve that is supreme.
> It is therefore the case that, because of this vow,
> he abides in a position superior to those in the world.

As for his "solid resolve," the bodhisattva maintains it even in the midst of every sort of pain and torment, that is to say he maintains it even in the Living Hells, Black Line Hells, Unification Hells, Lesser Screaming Hells, Great Screaming Hells, Lesser Roasting Hells, Great Roasting Hells, Avīci Hells, Boiling Excrement Hells, Sword Forest Hells, River of Coals Hells, Arbuda Hells, Nirarbuda Hells, Ahaha Hells, Apalāla Hells, Huhuva Hells, Utpala Hells, Kumuda Hells, Sumanā Hells, Puṇḍarīka Hells, and the Padma Hells. He maintains it even when tortured and whipped in these various cold and hot hells.

He maintains it even in the midst of the anguish and torment in the animal realms, the hungry ghost realms, the *asura* realms, and the realms of humans and *deva*s in which beings devour each other, exist in a state of mutual fearfulness, and go hungry when food has become too expensive.

And he maintains it when he falls back from and loses celestial realm rebirth and when he then encounters jealousy, the torment of hatred, separation from those one loves, association with those one detests, birth, aging, sickness, death, sorrow, lamentation, misery, and the like.

Thus he maintains his resolve even in the midst of all these sufferings in
the six destinies of rebirth. Whether observing them, whether hearing them 102c
occur, or whether actually undergoing them himself, the bodhisattva still continues to cultivate the ten courses of good karmic action for the sake of realizing *anuttarāsamyaksaṃbodhi*. During that entire time, his resolve continues on and never deteriorates.

It is on these bases that this bodhisattva, by cultivating the ten courses of good karmic action with solid resolve, thereby surpasses everyone else in the entire world. This is as described here:

> Even when in the hells, among the animals,
> the hungry ghosts, the *asura*s,
> the *deva*s, or the humans, the sufferings of these six destinies,
> are still incapable of shaking their resolve.
>
> Therefore the bodhisattvas,
> through such solid resolve as this,
> are superior to the entire world
> in their cultivation of the ten courses of good karmic action.

Regarding their "resolute intentions," they also possess great intentions, useful intentions, affectionate intentions, and mindful intentions. The bodhisattvas rely on such types of intentions as these in their cultivation of the ten courses of good karmic action and, in this, they are superior to everyone in the entire world with the exception of the buddhas, the bhagavats, and those bodhisattvas of long-enduring practice. This is as described here:

> They possess resolute intentions, useful intentions,
> and intentions that strive to benefit the world,
> it is through their use of these types of intentions
> that the bodhisattvas surpass the entire world.

As for "their thoroughgoing purity,"[199] in cultivating the courses of good karmic action, the bodhisattvas maintain the three types of karmic purity to a degree not found in such cultivation as carried on by anyone else.[200] Consequently, they are superior in this to everyone else in the entire world. This is as described here:

> The bodhisattvas are treasures of the human realm
> completely possessed of resolute intentions and pure intentions.
> It is because of the power of these good dharmas
> that they are unequaled by anyone in the world.

As for "their use of skillful means," the bodhisattvas use the power of skillful means to cultivate good dharmas that others do not possess. Consequently, they are superior in this to everyone else in the entire world.

Regarding their "measureless" cultivation,[201] it is on the basis of five types of causes and conditions that the cultivation of the bodhisattva qualifies as "measureless," namely:

First, immeasurability of time;
Second, immeasurability of roots of goodness;
Third, immeasurability of objective conditions;
Fourth, immeasurability of ultimate ends;
And fifth, immeasurability of dedication of merit.

As for "immeasurability of time," the cultivation of the courses of good karmic action as practiced by the bodhisattvas exceeds the very bounds of time. Because it exceeds the bounds of time, their cultivation of the courses of good karmic action is itself measureless. Therefore, in this, they are superior to everyone else in the entire world. This is as described here:

> As for the cultivation of the courses of good karmic action
> as practiced by the bodhisattvas, those lions among men,
> because its duration surpasses the bounds of calculable time,
> their cultivation of goodness is the most superior of all.

As for "immeasurability of roots of goodness," bodhisattvas cultivate measureless and boundless roots of goodness. Because the courses of good karmic action they cultivate in reliance upon these roots of goodness are also immeasurable, the bodhisattvas are in this respect superior to everyone else in the world.

As stated in the Great Vehicle Dharma's *Pure Vinaya Sutra:*

> The Buddha told Kāśyapa, "It is as if the four great seas were filled to the brim with buttermilk. Just so extensive are the bodhisattva's conditioned roots of goodness and provisions for the path."

Because this merit is dedicated to the knowledge that cognizes the uncon- 103a
ditioned, it is able to provide immense benefit to all beings. Therefore, even though the bodhisattva abides in the midst of conditioned existence, he is able to surpass everyone else in the world in this respect. This is as described here:

> [Accumulated] for the sake of all beings
> as well as for the sake of buddhahood,
> their roots of goodness are immeasurable.
> Because of this, they are superior to all others in the world.

As for the "immeasurability of objective conditions," in his accumulation of roots of goodness, the bodhisattva does not take as his objective condition a merely measurable number of beings. He does not say that the roots of goodness he has cultivated are for benefiting some particular number of beings. Rather, the bodhisattva simply takes all beings as the objective condition for his accumulation of roots of goodness. Therefore, since the bodhisattva takes a measureless number of beings as the objective condition on which he focuses, the courses of good karmic action that he cultivates are also measureless. Consequently, he is superior in this respect to everyone else in the world. As stated in the *Pure Vinaya Sutra:*

> The Buddha told the *devaputra*s, "This is just as in the case of the great bodhisattva possessed of the mind of kindness and compassion who strives to benefit others. This resolve of his is able to cause countless beings to receive benefit and happiness. So too it is with the bodhisattva who is deeply earnest in bringing forth his resolve. Being like this in his diligent application of vigor, he can thereby teach measurelessly many *asaṃkhyeya*s of beings, enabling them to gain the bliss of nirvana."

This is as described here:

> The bodhisattva adorns himself
> with measurelessly many fine meritorious qualities,
> all for the purpose of liberating beings
> from their measureless great suffering.

As for "immeasurability of ultimate ends," "the ten ultimate ends" were already discussed during the explanation of the first ground when discussing the making of [the ten bodhisattva] vows.[202] It is because of this immeasurability of ultimate ends that the courses of good karmic action as cultivated by the bodhisattva are measureless. He is therefore superior in this respect to anyone in the world. This is as described here:

> The bodhisattva's cultivation of the courses of good karmic action
> comes forth from the ten ultimate ends.
> Therefore it is superior to that of everyone else
> and such that no one is able to ruin it.

"Immeasurability of dedication of merit" is as described earlier in the explanation of the first ground. The karmic fruits of the bodhisattva's dedication of merit are measureless. Because the karmic fruits of dedication of merit are measureless, the courses of good karmic action he cultivates are also measureless. He is therefore superior in this respect to anyone in the world. This is as described here:

On the basis of measureless causes and conditions,
they cultivate the courses of good karmic action.
Because they dedicate this to [the realization of] the buddha vehicle,
they are therefore the most superior of all.

As for the "extraordinary" nature of their cultivation,[203] it is because of five causes and conditions that the bodhisattvas' cultivation of the courses of good karmic action is said to be "extraordinary":

First, because of their capacity to endure;
Second, because of their vigor;
Third, because of the solidity of their resolve;
Fourth, because of their wisdom;
Fifth, because of the karmic fruits.

As for [the extraordinary nature of] their capacity to endure, [they reflect,] "I ought to become one who is the most revered among all *deva*s and humans, one
who is possessed of all-knowledge." If one is able to have a capacity such as 103b
this, this is extraordinary. Were someone to use his finger to lift a great trichiliocosm's worlds and hold them aloft in space for a hundred thousand myriads of *kalpa*s, even this might be considered possible to do and not worthy of being deemed truly difficult. Yet if one makes the vow: "I shall become a buddha," it is this that is extraordinary and extremely difficult. This is as described here:

As for he who, for the sake of a buddha's measureless dharmas,
would make the vow: "I shall become a buddha,"
this person is one who is beyond compare,
how much the less could there be anyone who might surpass him?

Regarding [the extraordinary nature of] their vigor, there are many people who can bring forth the resolve to attain *anuttarāsamyaksaṃbodhi* but who are then unable to vigorously practice the six *pāramitā*s. If someone can bring forth the resolve to attain *anuttarāsamyaksaṃbodhi* and then also be able to vigorously practice the six *pāramitā*s, this is what is meant by truly having the capacity to take on the attainment of the measureless meritorious qualities. It is because of the extraordinary nature of their vigor that the courses of good karmic action they cultivate are also extraordinary in nature. This is as described here:

Their practice of great vigor is so extraordinary that,
having merely contemplated it, the common man is frightened.
The bodhisattva actually practices it.
How could this not be regarded as extraordinary?

As for [the extraordinary nature of] their solidity of resolve, there are those who bring forth vigorous resolve to cultivate the path to buddhahood. However, if upon encountering obstacles, their resolve is not solid, they will be unable to succeed. Therefore, if they bring forth vigor and become securely established in extraordinarily solid resolve, they will succeed in their endeavors and demolish all obstacles. It is this that is the most extraordinary accomplishment in bodhisattvas' cultivation of the courses of good karmic action. This is as described here:

If one has no solidity of resolve,
he will be unable to succeed in even minor endeavors.
How much the less could one attain buddhahood
and become the one unsurpassed by anyone in the world?

As for [the extraordinary nature of] their wisdom, this capacity to endure, this vigor, and this solidity of resolve all take wisdom as their foundation. Therefore it is the wisdom of the bodhisattva that is the most extraordinary. Because it is able to produce this capacity to endure, this vigor, and this solidity of resolve, wisdom is itself deemed to be extraordinary. It is because this wisdom is extraordinary that the courses of good karmic action that are cultivated are also extraordinary. This is as described here:

If someone has the capacity to endure
in pursuing his aspiration to realize the Buddha's Dharma,
and if he possesses vigor and has achieved solidity of resolve,
all of these capacities take wisdom as their foundation.

As for [the extraordinary nature of] the karmic fruits they achieve, due to their cultivation of the courses of good karmic actions, they gain all the measureless and boundless dharmas of the buddhas. Therefore [the karmic fruits] are extraordinary in nature. This is as described here:

By practicing this goodness, one realizes buddhahood,
acquires the power of its measureless meritorious qualities,
and then serves as the teacher of all beings.
Who, on hearing this, could fail to practice them?

Regarding their "solid" vows,[204] it is for five reasons that the bodhisattva 103c
is deemed to have made solid vows, namely:

First, his resolve does not turn back toward the *śrāvaka* disciple vehicle;
Second, his resolve does not turn back toward the *pratyekabuddha* vehicle;
Third, his resolve does not turn back in favor of the endeavors of the followers of non-Buddhist paths;
Fourth, his resolve does not turn back due to any of the works of Māra;
And fifth, his resolve does not turn back due to an absence of [conducive] causes and conditions.

This is as described here:

One might hear of the liberations won through the two vehicles
and think, "Why not take up these paths instead?"
If one has not yet entered the station [of irreversibility],[205]
then one might fall away from the bodhisattva path.

Or one might covet the endeavors of followers of non-Buddhist paths,
or one might be destroyed by the works of Māra,
or else, due to an absence of conducive causes and conditions,
one might voluntarily abandon the bodhisattva path.

As for the "goodness" of their vows,[206] it is for five reasons that the bodhisattva's vows are said to be "good" vows, namely:

First, they reflect a prior assessment of gains or losses;
Second, they are based on a knowledge of the path;
Third, they reflect a knowledge of the fruits of the path;
Fourth, they reflect an absence of any selfish attachment to one's own pleasure;
Fifth, they reflect the wish to extinguish the immense sufferings endured by all beings.

Vows made in this manner are deemed to be good vows. This is as described here:

> One first observes the faults and misery of the world
> and the immense benefit bestowed by the path to buddhahood.
> One knows and practices the unsurpassable path
> as well as its measureless fruits.
>
> One relinquishes the bliss of entering one's own quiescent cessation,
> and wishes to rid beings of their sufferings.
> One who brings forth such peerless vows as these
> is someone who is praised by all buddhas.

Regarding "the great compassion" that cannot be impeded,[207] there are five grounds for knowing a bodhisattva is possessed of the great compassion, namely:

First, because he is devoted to benefiting and conferring happiness on countless beings, he does not covet or selfishly cherish any of the life-sustaining requisites;

Second, he does not selfishly cherish his own physical well-being;

Third, he does not selfishly cherish his own life span;

Fourth, he is not concerned with the extensively long period of time involved;

Fifth, he maintains a mind of equal regard and motivation to benefit both adversaries and friends.

This is as described here:

> He has no covetous attachment for any of those things
> that people cherish, whether personal or external.
> In order to be of benefit to beings,
> he would even sacrifice his body and life.
>
> The countless *kalpa*s spent amid samsara
> are for him like the mere blinking of an eye.
> He acts with uniformly equal regard for both enemy and friend.
> These are the factors defining a bodhisattva's great compassion.

As for [their compassion's] being "unimpeded,"[208] there are five reasons why a bodhisattva's compassion might [otherwise] become impeded, namely:

First, by the sufferings of the hell realms;
Second, by the sufferings of the animal realms;
Third, by the sufferings of the hungry ghost realms;
Fourth, by evil people's ingratitude [for kindnesses bestowed on them];
Fifth, by the faults and evils encountered amid samsara.

If even these five circumstances fail to impede his resolve, then he qualifies as possessing the unimpeded great compassion. This is as described here:

> If even the foremost sufferings encountered in the hell realms,
> the sufferings met in the animal realms or hungry ghost realms,
> [the ingratitude of] evil people, and samsara 104a
> still fail to impede him, he is one possessed of the great compassion.
> The bodhisattva who is able to be one who is like this
> has been declared by the Buddha to possess unimpeded compassion.

Regarding "thoroughly taking on the practice of skillful means,"[209] there are five bases for a bodhisattva's qualification as "thoroughly taking on the practice of skillful means," namely:

First, he knows the correct place and time;
Second, he knows what delights the minds of others;
Third, he knows what will cause others to turn and enter the path;
Fourth, he knows what constitutes the correct sequence of events;
Fifth, he knows how to lead and guide beings.

As for "knowing the correct place and time," he knows that, in this particular place, one should explain Dharma in this particular way and knows that, at this particular time, one should explain the Dharma in this other way. He knows that, in this particular place, one should employ these specific causes and conditions to bring about the liberation of these particular beings. And he knows that, at this particular time, one should employ just these particular causes and conditions to bring about the liberation of these other beings. Having assessed these specific factors in advance, the bodhisattva then proceeds to act accordingly. This is as described here:

If one takes up the intent of the Bhagavat
wishing then to explain it for others,
one should first know these two factors,
and then speak in accordance with the correct time and place.

Should one fail to know the correct time and place
and yet wish to proclaim the intent of the buddhas,
he will [not only] fail to accomplish the intended benefit,
but moreover may thus commit a blameworthy error.

As for "knowing what delights the minds of others," this involves knowing, due to their mental dispositions, which endeavors and which experiences will cause them to be pleased. Having known this in advance, the bodhisattva acquires a penetrating understanding of what beings know and delight in and then brings forth the appropriate skillful means to facilitate their liberation. If one acts in this way, then his efforts will not be in vain. This is as described here:

The bodhisattva knows with respect to beings
the difficult-to-assess intentions present in their mental dispositions,
and, having already first known the character of their intentions,
he gradually influences them to dwell in the Buddha's intent.

Through thoroughly knowing the affairs of the world,
he benefits himself while also benefiting others.
One who is able to proceed in this manner
is said to be adept in the practice of skillful means.

As for their "knowing what will cause others to turn and enter the path," this refers to knowing whatever may induce the minds of common persons following non-Buddhist paths to turn away from them and instead enter the path of the Buddha. It also refers to knowing whatever will induce beings to turn away from evil deeds and instead engage in good deeds. And it also refers to knowing whatever will induce followers of the *śrāvaka* disciple and *pratyekabuddha* paths to turn away from them and instead enter into the Great Vehicle.

This refers as well to knowing with respect to those already abiding within the Buddha's Dharma just what will prevent them from entering into non-Buddhist paths. Having first come to know these matters, one then implements the practice accordingly. This is as described here:

> If one is able to induce beings
> to abandon non-Buddhist paths
> while also inducing those devoted to what is bad
> to enter the Buddha's way to the supreme quiescent cessation,
>
> and if one knows with respect to beings
> the superior, middling, or inferior character of their minds,
> and, having known this, one is then able to lead and guide them,
> this is what is meant by being adept in the practice of skillful means.

As for "knowing what constitutes the correct sequence," take for instance 104b
the priorities in the *śrāvaka* disciple vehicle wherein they first speak of giving, then of upholding the moral precepts, then of being reborn in the heavens, then of the faults and misery in pursuing the five kinds of sensual pleasures, then of the suffering and distress of the household life, and then of the benefits and bliss of abandoning the home life [in favor of the monastic path]. Following this, they explain the truth of suffering, then the truth of its origination, then the truth of its cessation, and then the truth of the path. After this, they speak of the stream-enterer's fruit of the path, the fruit of the *sakṛdāgāmin,* the fruit of the *anāgāmin,* and the fruit of arhatship. They next speak of the indestructible liberation and then speak of those that are unimpeded.

Beyond that, within the *pratyekabuddha* vehicle, they also speak of the faults and misery inherent in the self and everything deemed to be possessed by the self and speak as well of the immense benefit in the abandonment of such faults and misery. They then speak of the life of the householder as possessed of serious faults and of leaving behind the household life as beneficial.

They next explain that the many sorts of disputation and conceptual elaboration involve serious faults, that solitary practice bestows wholesome benefits, that village life involves serious faults, that abiding in a forest hermitage brings wholesome benefits, that one should renounce the many desires and the many sorts of [worldly] endeavors and instead delight in having but few wants and but few endeavors. [They teach that] one is to carefully guard the sense faculties, know moderation in drink and food, maintain vigilance at all times throughout the first watch and the last watch of the night,[210] contemplate an object, focus on its characteristics, and take delight in dwelling in an empty hut.

They esteem the upholding of the moral precepts, the cultivation of *dhyāna* absorptions, and the development of wisdom. They refrain from displaying idiosyncratic or strange personal appearances. Although they do inspire happiness in others [who observe them on the daily almsround], they are only concerned with benefiting themselves. They delight in profound dharmas and acquire wisdom that does not rely on [teachings provided by] others.

According to the Great Vehicle's priorities regarding the correct sequencing of events, one first speaks of the perfection of giving, then the perfection of moral virtue, then the perfection of patience, then the perfection of vigor, then the perfection of meditative concentration, and then the perfection of wisdom.[211]

[The Great Vehicle also] first speaks of the truthfulness supreme basis [for the generation of meritorious qualities], then the relinquishment basis, then the quiescence basis, and then the wisdom basis.

Then again, they also first praise the generation of the resolve to attain *bodhi,* then the ten vows, and then the ten ultimate ends. They then praise the renunciation of whatsoever dharma might conduce to retreat from the resolve to attain *bodhi,* then they praise cultivation of those dharmas that prevent retreat from the resolve to attain *bodhi,* followed by promoting vigor buttressed by solid resolve, solidly established capacity for endurance, and then solidity in sustaining one's vows.

Yet again, [the Great Vehicle:]

First speaks of the dharmas that enable acquisition of all the [bodhisattva] grounds;

Next speaks of the dharmas that enable dwelling on the grounds;

Next speaks of the dharmas that enable acquisition of the deepest aspects of the grounds;

Next speaks of the dharmas by which one abandons defilements on the grounds;

Next speaks of the dharmas enabling purification of the grounds;

Next speaks of the dharmas conducive to abiding for a long time on the grounds;

Next speaks of the dharmas enabling one to reach the most extreme limits of each of the grounds;
Next speaks of the dharmas enabling nonregression from the grounds;
Next speaks of the fruits associated with each of the grounds;
And then speaks of the powers associated with the fruits of each of the grounds.

Then again, it may be that [the Great Vehicle]:
First speaks of the Ground of Joyfulness;
Next speaks of the Ground of Stainlessness;
Next speaks of the Ground of Shining Light;
Next speaks of the Ground of Blazing Brilliance;
Next speaks of the Difficult-to-Conquer Ground;
Next speaks of the Ground of Direct Presence;
Next speaks of the Far-reaching Ground;
Next speaks of the Ground of Immovability;
Next speaks of the Ground of Excellent Intelligence;
And then speaks of the Ground of the Dharma Cloud.

These [various three vehicle sequences] are as described below:

[*Śrāvakas*] first speak of giving, next of upholding moral precepts,
and then their karmic fruition in gaining rebirth in the heavens.
Next, impermanence, the faults of the household life, 104c
and then the immense benefits achieved by leaving the home life.

Next, they speak of the unsurpassed dharma of the four truths,
the severance of the fetters, and attaining the four fruits [of the path].
This sequence of skillful means
induces people to abide in the first of the [three] vehicles.

[*Pratyekabuddha*s] first speak of the faults in samsara
and then speak of the benefits associated with nirvana,
guarding and restraining the sense faculties,
maintaining the moral precepts, the *dhyāna* absorptions,

the wisdom not reliant on [the teachings] of others,
the excellent qualities associated with delighting in dwelling alone,

relying upon oneself, not relying on others,
delighting in striving for one's own benefit and happiness

while still not abandoning others,
and deeply cultivating the dharmas of the *dhūta* austerities.
In the case of those who cultivate this mid-level vehicle,
such are the features of the dharmas they teach.

[The Great Vehicle] refers to the forty exclusive dharmas
in describing the measureless qualities of the Buddha,
speaks as well of all of the dharmas that he practiced
when he was a bodhisattva

in order to be of benefit to beings,
speaking of these dharmas according to their correct sequence,
describing self-benefit as well as the benefiting of others,
explaining all of his different sorts of meritorious qualities,

explaining also with regard to all the Buddha's sons
the ten grounds in which they delight.
Those who seek Dharma as set forth in the Great Vehicle
achieve liberation in accordance with just such a sequence as this.

"Leading and guiding beings" involves adapting to whatever subjects beings delight in, and then, having understood precisely what those subjects are, using those very subjects as the means by which one leads and guides them. By adapting to whatever they delight in, allowing for their individual strengths, one influences them toward the achievement of liberation. This is as described here:

There may be cases where there are beings
amenable [to being led and guided] through profound classics,
through recondite subjects, through trades or artisanal skills,
through techniques involving mantras, through pleasing words,

through skillful discourse, through resources or wealth,
or through giving, moral virtue, meditation, or wisdom.
After [the bodhisattva] has assessed such factors,
he leads them to enter into the Great Vehicle.

He might manifest in a woman's body
to lead and guide men,
or he might manifest in the body of a man
to lead and guide women,

first showing the many pleasures of the five types of sensual desire,
and, afterward, speaking of the faults inherent in those desires,
thereby leading every sort of person
to then abandon the five types of sensual desire.

It is just such a skillful implementation of [his awareness of] these five matters that constitutes the bodhisattva's "adeptly taking on the practice of skillful means."

Regarding "patiently enduring every sort of pain and anguish,"[212] this refers to the case of a person who, through an incalculable number of *kalpa*s in the cycle of births and deaths, can endure all sorts of pain and anguish as he cultivates the ten courses of good karmic action that enable this person to eventually abide in *anuttarāsamyaksaṃbodhi.*

Question: Every person delights in happiness and detests suffering. How 105a
then could such a person be able to endure [such an immense amount of] pain and anguish?

Response: There are five reasons for his ability to accomplish this:
First, delight in nonself;
Second, resolute belief in emptiness;
Third, assessment of the nature of worldly dharmas;
Fourth, contemplation of retributions resulting from karmic actions;
Fifth, mindfulness of an incalculable number of *kalpa*s already spent fruitlessly undergoing pain and anguish.

These are as described here:

He delights in the dharmas of nonself and emptiness,
and also understands the retributions resulting from karmic actions
as well as gain, loss, and the rest of the eight worldly dharmas
that one must certainly endure while dwelling in the world.

He is also mindful of his past lives
in which he endured in vain a measureless amount of suffering,
[thinking,] "How much the more so should I be willing to undergo it
when this would be for the sake of realizing buddhahood?"

As for "They do not abandon any being,"[213] sometimes there are beings who engage in the most extreme sorts of pernicious evil, who are utterly devoid of meritorious qualities, and whom it is impossible to benefit. Nonetheless, the bodhisattva still never thinks to abandon such beings.

Question: If these sorts of evil people cannot be brought to liberation, why should one not simply abandon them?

Response: There are five reasons, namely:

First, because of disdain for the dharmas of petty people;
Second, because of esteem for the dharmas of the great men;
Third, because of fear of cheating the buddhas;
Fourth, because of gratitude for the kindnesses one has received;
Fifth, it is because of these works within the world that one transcends the world.

These are as described here:

Because of one's aspiration to liberate beings,
one brings forth the resolve to carry a heavy burden.
Thus, even in the midst of evil adversaries,
one's mind should never be inclined to abandon them.

To disdain petty people and esteem those who are great[214]
is [to conceive of] some difference between the petty and the great.
When in the midst of beings, one should not allow
one's mind of kindly sympathy to withdraw or cease.

In the midst of [others'] urgent difficulties
wherein one has no personal interests, one still provides help.
When it is the time to bear a heavy burden,
one does not shrink from or diminish one's efforts in that work.

In a case where one has brought forth the unsurpassable resolve,
but may still have instances in which one abandons beings,
either due to mental weariness or anguish
or because of being harmed by evil men,
those are instances of cheating and deceiving
all buddhas of the ten directions and three periods of time.

The buddhas, the honored ones within the world,
for the sake of bestowing benefit on beings,
engaged in all manner of austerities
in their cultivation of the path to buddhahood.
For *kalpa*s in number as the sands of the Ganges, the buddhas
sacrificed happiness as they performed meritorious karmic deeds.

Were one to abandon even a single evil person,
that would be to turn one's back on the kindness of the buddhas.
Therefore one must not abandon in mid-course
even those beings who are evil.

In an instance where someone,
throughout countless *asaṃkhyeya*s of *kalpa*s,
cultivates the path to buddhahood, 105b
the great compassion is the very root of that endeavor.

If due to thoughts rooted in desire
or thoughts founded on hatred or fear,
one were to abandon even one being who could attain liberation,
this would be to sever the root of the Buddha path.

Therefore [one should realize that] the courses of good karmic action can enable one who does not abandon [any beings] to eventually reach *anuttarāsamyaksaṃbodhi*.

As for "deeply delighting in the wisdom of the buddhas,"[215] if one deeply delights in the wisdom of the buddhas, then he will thereby swiftly attain *anuttarāsamyaksaṃbodhi*. There are five reasons why [the bodhisattva] feels deep delight in the wisdom of the buddhas, namely:

First, the wisdom of the buddhas is unequaled by any other;

Second, the wisdom of the buddhas is able to cause someone to become one who is honored throughout the world;
Third, the buddhas use the wisdom of the buddhas to bring about their own liberation;
Fourth, the wisdom of the buddhas also enables the liberation of others;
Fifth, the wisdom of the buddhas is the abode of all meritorious qualities.

These are as described below:

As for this wisdom of all the buddhas,
no matter whether it be up in the heavens or in the world,
there is no wisdom anywhere that can even equal it,
how much the less might there be any superior to it?

It is because of this very wisdom that all buddhas
receive deep respect and reverential obeisance
from the *deva*s, from the *asura*s,
and from all the world's humans.

The buddhas use this wisdom to liberate themselves
and also use it to liberate other people.
If one acquires this wisdom of the buddhas,
this is someone who is a treasury of meritorious qualities.

Regarding "delight in those who completely and thoroughly practice the buddhas' powers and the sovereign masteries,"[216] "thorough practice" refers to long-enduring practice of all the practices. "The powers" refers to the ten wisdom powers. "Sovereign masteries" refers to the ability to do precisely as one wishes in whatever one does. If one feels profound delight in the complete and thorough practice of the dharmas of the buddhas' ten powers and sovereign masteries, such a person will be able before long to swiftly attain *anuttarāsamyaksaṃbodhi*.

There are five reasons for delighting in the complete and thorough practice [of the powers and sovereign masteries], namely:

First, due to reverential esteem for the teachings and directives of all buddhas;

Second, due to the fact that all buddhas have such great disciples;
Third, due to their personal realization of all dharmas;
Fourth, due to their ability to draw in those who have fallen away;
Fifth, due to their ability to then rescue those who have fallen away.

These are as described below:

[They delight] due to revering the buddhas' incomparable teachings,
due to the existence of the fourfold and eightfold classes
of the Buddha's sons of six and threefold types,
due to their capacity to become the teachers even of the *deva*s,
due to the buddhas' wisdom eye
with which they see all dharmas manifest directly before them,

and due to their ability to draw in and rescue, bringing to liberation
even those people who have fallen away such as
those who, by heinous evil deeds, have severed roots of goodness,
those who have broken the moral precepts, and other such beings.

If there be a person who [delights] in those who thoroughly practice
the buddhas' powers and sovereign masteries,
then nirvana as well as the merit of the heavens
will always be as if resting in the palm of his hand.

[Regarding the "buddhas' powers,"][217] in circumstances such as these, 105c
the buddhas are able to use a buddha's powers to accomplish five types of endeavors, namely:

First, they may induce beings to train in the *śrāvaka* disciple vehicle;
Second, they may induce beings to train in the *pratyekabuddha* vehicle;
Third, they may induce beings to train in the Dharma of the Great Vehicle;
Fourth, in the case of those whose powers have become perfectly complete, they may enable their attainment of liberation;
Fifth, in the case of those whose powers are as yet inferior, they may enable them to abide in worldly happiness.

These are as described below:

The buddhas use their spiritual powers
to influence beings who have developed renunciation,

perhaps influencing them to train either in the Small Vehicle,
or in the Intermediate Vehicle, or in the Great Vehicle.

In the case of those whose powers are completely fulfilled,
they enable them to attain liberation.
For those whose powers are still incomplete,
they assist their celestial rebirth or their happiness within the world.

As for "their sovereign masteries,"[218] there are five matters in which the buddhas possess sovereign mastery, namely:

First, sovereign mastery in the spiritual superknowledges;
Second, the attainment of sovereign mastery over their own minds;
Third, the attainment of sovereign mastery in complete cessation;
Fourth, the attainment of sovereign mastery in the psychic powers of the *āryas*;[219]
Fifth, sovereign mastery in determining their own life spans.

These are as described below:

They have sovereign mastery in flying and other [superknowledges]
and they have sovereign mastery over their own minds
as well as in the *dhyāna* absorption of complete cessation
that for them is [as easy] as entering and exiting their own abodes.

They can transform all things, whether pure or impure,
in accordance with their own minds.[220]
Their life spans cannot be diminished by others,
for, so long as they sustain the conditions, their lives will be endless.

Just as it is for such sovereign masteries as these,
so too it is with respect to all dharmas.
It is for these reasons that [the buddhas], the lions among men,
are known as those who possess the sovereign masteries.

Regarding being "able to refute all ideas involving wrong views,"[221] this is a reference to whatever strays far from the right path such as the ninety-six kinds of non-Buddhist paths favored by common people, and other such wrong views. A general characterization of such wrong ideas would include the claim that the five aggregates constitute a self, that there is a self that possesses the five aggregates, that there is a self contained within the five aggregates, that the five aggregates are contained within a self, or that there exists a self apart from the five aggregates. These ideas are as described below:

> If [one posits that] the five aggregates constitute a self,
> thereby falling into the annihilationist [fallacy],
> one thus dispenses with the efficacy of karmic causes and conditions
> and posits liberation in the absence of the requisite efforts.
>
> As for the rest [of the wrong views], they are of four types.
> As for those positing a signless self distinct from the aggregates,
> whatsoever is signless is necessarily a nonexistent dharma.
> All [of the other fallacies] should be refuted in this same way.

Then again, it is the five erroneous views that constitute wrong ideas, namely: wrong views, the view of [the five-aggregate] "person" as constituting a self, extreme views, seizing upon views, and views that seize on precept observance [alone as constituting the path]. These are as described below:

> One demolishes the wrong views about cause and effect,
> the twenty kinds of views referencing a "person,"
> views positing the ultimacy of existence or nonexistence,
> [views esteeming] inferior endeavors as supreme,
> and [the view that] it is solely by the power of precept observance 106a
> that one succeeds in achieving liberation.
>
> As with the earlier refutation [of a self] identical to or distinct
> [from the five aggregates], these views are refuted in just such a way.
> Using right thought and the eightfold path to refute them,
> one explains that these are the bases for attaining liberation.

Regarding "preserving and protecting the buddhas' right Dharma,"[222] this refers to someone who is able to preserve and protect the Dharma as taught by all buddhas, namely the twelve categories of scriptural text. Because his mind is able to believe and accept them, the ten courses of good karmic action can cause this person to succeed in reaching *anuttarāsamyaksaṃbodhi.*

There are five reasons why one should accept and protect the right Dharma, namely:

First, because one realizes the obligation to repay the kindness of all buddhas;
Second, in order to cause the Dharma to abide for a long time;
Third, in order to perform the most supreme form of offering, thus making an offering to the buddhas themselves;
Fourth, in order to be of benefit to an incalculable number of beings;
Fifth, because right Dharma is the rarest of all things.

These are as described below:

> If a person wishes to devote himself
> to those endeavors bequeathed by all buddhas
> and also wishes to cause the Dharma to remain for a long time
> by presenting the most supreme offering to the buddhas,
>
> then, because he wishes to heal
> the serious diseases that afflict beings,
> because he has realized that all the bhagavats
> obtained this Dharma through having to undergo suffering,
>
> and because, understanding these conditions of its origination,
> he realizes that the Dharma is a rarity difficult to come by—
> [for all these reasons], he who is wise
> should therefore cherish and protect the Dharma.

In this connection, there are five bases by which one's actions might qualify as "cherishing and protecting right Dharma," namely:

First, one cultivates [the path] according to the way it was taught;
Second, one influences others to practice in accordance with the Dharma;
Third, one extricates any thorns that might destroy the Buddha's Dharma;
Fourth, one abandons the four seals of darkness;
Fifth, one practices [in accordance with] the four seals of greatness.[223]

These are as described below:

In one's own relationship with the Dharma of the buddhas,
one abides in accordance with how the Buddha taught it.
One retains a mind of compassion, is not miserly with Dharma,
and also influences others to abide within it.

Moreover, one crushes the armies of Māra
and also refutes the claims of the non-Buddhist treatise masters.
On encountering those who detest the Dharma of the buddhas,
with a mind free of hatred, one refutes their claims.

One departs from the four seals of blackness
while taking on the practice of the four seals of greatness.
One who is able to act in such a way is deemed to be
someone who cherishes and protects right Dharma.

As for their being "valiant,"[224] there are five bases because of which the bodhisattva is deemed to be valiant, namely:

First, because he crushes Māra's thieves;
Second, because he crushes the non-Buddhist partisan thieves;
Third, because he crushes the thieves of the afflictions;
Fourth, because he crushes the thieves of the sense faculties;
Fifth, because he crushes the thieves of the five aggregates.

These are as described below:

Māra the Evil One marshaled his armies
and, at the *bodhi* tree, sought to harm the Buddha,
always seeking opportunities to take advantage of the Buddha 106b
and disturb the minds of his audience.
Once the Buddha sun had arisen and shone upon the world,
Māra made the request intended to cause him to enter nirvana.

He is forever confusing those who take on the training,
attempting to destroy their paths to liberation,
even to the point that, to this very day,
his determination to accomplish this still never ceases.

These who detest nirvana
are the great thieves of good people.
One must use moral virtue, *dhyāna* concentration, and wisdom
to crush adversaries possessed of Māra's powers.

There are those who, of the opinion that they are wise,
always slight the buddhas out of arrogance
and use all different sorts of tactics
to destroy the Buddha's Dharma, manifesting for that very reason.

They always detest the Buddha's disciples
and, having become failures themselves, they teach others to fail.
These various classes of non-Buddhists
are the great thieves in the world.

One ought to use a mind free of hatred
and one should use the wisdom based on extensive learning.
Then, availing oneself of the power of the great resolve,
one should utterly demolish these non-Buddhist adversaries.

The power of the afflictions brings forth karmic actions,
cyclic existence, and descent into the wretched destinies.
It is because of obstacles caused by the power of the afflictions
that one remains unable to practice the great path.

It is because of the power of the afflictions
that one falls into all sorts of wrong views.
It is because of the power of the afflictions
that one does not practice the path to the elixir of immortality.

It is because of all these reasons
that the afflictions are the worst of all the great thieves.
Through right mindfulness, concentration, and wisdom,
one becomes able to crush the thieves of the afflictions.

If one is dragged along by the thieves of the sense faculties,
they cause a person to descend into the wretched destinies

and also cause one to fall into celestial and human realms
wherein one does not succeed in reaching nirvana.

Now, given [the plight caused by] these sense faculty thieves,
how could one fail to use a sense of shame, dread of blame,
and right mindfulness as well as wisdom
to utterly crush the thieves of the sense faculties?

These are analogous to [the stratagems of] people of the world
who may resort to gently persuasive words, or to deception,
or to wealth and valuables, or even to swords and lances,
using these four means to drive away the thieves.

It is because of these five aggregates
that one undergoes birth, aging, sickness, and death,
also falls into the realms of immense terror,
and becomes subject to undergoing intense suffering and anguish.

It because of the five aggregates
that one is plunged into grief and then sobs and weeps.
It is also because of the five aggregates
that one undergoes all the different sorts of sufferings.

Therefore you should realize
the need to use the dharmas of knowledge and vision
to utterly crush [the ruinous power of] the five aggregates 106c
just as one would defeat adversaries or thieves.

As for [the bodhisattva's] being "able to endure,"[225] he is one whose resolve is strong, who is possessed of the marks of a great man, and who is possessed of a profound and distant vision. There are five grounds for his being deemed "able to endure," namely:

First, when he succeeds in the endeavors he has vowed to achieve, his mind does not become elated;

Second, when he does not succeed in the endeavors he has vowed to achieve, his mind does not become dejected;

Third, when pain and anguish cut close, his mind remains unmoved;

Fourth, when his body is beset by pleasurable experiences, his mind still remains unchanged;
Fifth, his state of mind runs deep and sees far. Thus whether he has been given cause for anger or cause for joy, his mind remains inscrutable.

These are as described below:

When his body or mind experience some new suffering,
his mind still remains unmoved.
No matter what sort of pleasurable experience comes,
his greatly wise mind does not change.

Even where he is given cause for anger, joy, or fear,
no one else can fathom [his state of mind].
Wherever one possesses marks of resolute intentions such as these,
this person is said to be one who is "able to endure."

Regarding [the bodhisattva's] diligent "vigor,"[226] there are five circumstances in which he is diligent in his practice of vigor, namely:
First, he is diligently vigorous in preventing the arising of bad dharmas that have not yet arisen;
Second, he is diligently vigorous in cutting off and destroying bad dharmas that may already have arisen;
Third, he is diligently vigorous in causing the arising of good dharmas that have not yet arisen;
Fourth, he is diligently vigorous in increasing any good dharmas that have already arisen;
Fifth, he is diligently vigorous in ensuring that nothing can obstruct whatever endeavors he has taken up in the world.

These are as described below:

He cuts off evil dharmas that have already arisen
just as one might get rid of a venomous snake.
He cuts off any evil dharmas that have not yet arisen
just as one might block off the waters of a flood.

He brings about the growth of [already arisen] good dharmas
just as one might water a sweet fruit's seedling.
He strives to bring forth goodness that has not yet arisen
just as one might use a wooden friction drill to light a fire.

In pursuing his good endeavors in the world,
he acts with such diligent vigor as permits no obstruction.
All buddhas say of a person such as this
that he is to be known as one who is diligently vigorous.

As for "solid resolve in the teaching of beings,"[227] if, during all that time in which he teaches beings in the five vehicles, the bodhisattva's mind remains unturned even as he experiences at the hands of others the giving of offerings, slighting, arrogance, detestation, love, terror, suffering, bliss, extreme exhaustion, and other such situations, he thereby qualifies as one who "proceeds with solid resolve in the teaching of beings."

As for the five vehicles, they are:
First, the buddha vehicle;
Second, the *pratyekabuddha* vehicle;
Third, the *śrāvaka* disciple vehicle;
Fourth, the *deva* vehicle;
Fifth, the human vehicle.

These are as described below:

You should use singleminded focus[228]
and all your powers,
while relying on many different sorts of skillful means
and abandoning any thoughts of hate or love

as you proceed to teach every sort of being, 107a
doing so with a pure mind that has abandoned defilement,
thereby influencing them to gain what in countless lifetimes
is a rarity: the unsurpassable [buddha] vehicle.

If one enters among those who have no such strength
and thus have no capacity to abide in the Great Vehicle,

> one may in sequence teach either the *pratyekabuddha* vehicle,
> the *śrāvaka* disciple vehicle, or the vehicles of *deva*s or humans.

As for "not coveting their own happiness,"[229] this refers to not being attached to any sort of bliss. There are five reasons why the bodhisattva does covet his own happiness, namely:

First, all pleasures are just as ephemeral as a bubble on the water;
Second, worldly pleasures transform into suffering;
Third, they are a product of the conjunction of many conditions;
Fourth, they are a product of cravings;
Fifth, they are but a minor bliss like that of a mere drop of honey.

These are as described below:

> Pleasures abide for but a short time, like a bubble
> and they transform into suffering like food laced with poison.
> Relying on a three-part conjunction, they exist through contact
> and arise because of the ulcerous boil of desire.
>
> If one abandons desire and craving,
> then there is no pleasure that exists apart from them.
> [Pleasures] are like a dry well or a drop of honey,
> for there is but little bliss and an abundance of suffering.
>
> Whosoever aims to be of benefit to beings
> should not have any sort of covetous attachment.

Regarding [their refraining from covetous attachment] "to living a measurelessly long life,"[230] there are five reasons why the bodhisattva does not covet or selfishly cherish his own body, namely:

First, the body did not come forth from previous lives;
Second, it shall not go on to future lives;
Third, it is not a durable entity;
Fourth, it is devoid of any self;
Fifth, there is nothing in it qualifying as the property of a self.

These are as described below:

Your body is but a collection of many sorts of filth
entirely filled up with impurities.
It did not come forth to the present from previous lives,
and it will not be taken forth to one's future lives.

Even though one might provide for and serve it well for a long time,
it will still break its obligation to repay great kindness.
This body is not a durable entity,
for, like a foam bubble, it will be destroyed before long.

Whatsoever is the product of conditions has no fixed nature.
Having no fixed nature, it is therefore not a self-existent entity.
Therefore, one should realize that [the body]
is not a self and is not the possession of a self.

This body is possessed of countless faults.
Thus one should not selfishly cherish it.

There are five reasons why the bodhisattva does not selfishly cherish a long life span, namely:

First, because he delights in the life of wisdom;
Second, because he is frightened at the prospect of committing any karmic transgression [in order to preserve it];
Third, because he is mindful of the countless deaths one has undergone throughout the course of beginningless samsara;
Fourth, because [death] is an experience jointly shared by all beings;
Fifth, because [death] is unavoidable.

These are as described below:

Because, through abundant learning and right discourse about it,
one comes to prize one's life of wisdom,
because one fears that, when [trying to avoid] losing one's life,
one might produce the evil of karmic transgressions,

and also, because one observes that no one 107b
can escape [the clutches of] the king of death

and hence it cannot be avoided through the power
of expedients dependent on wealth or knowledge—

How then could anyone devoted to cultivating good dharmas
still continue to cherish this life?

As for "They are supreme in all their endeavors,"[231] if one absolutely must be able to complete whatever endeavor he begins, this is the mark of a superior person. There are five endeavors that, once the bodhisattva has begun them, he absolutely must bring to completion, namely:

First, [the accumulation of] wealth;
Second, giving;
Third, the observance of the moral precepts;
Fourth, the cultivation of meditative concentration;
Fifth, [the cultivation of] the virtues associated with the path.

These are as described below:

One strives diligently to accumulate wealth
and, with utmost sincerity, [uses it] to engage in giving.
In their sequence, he purifies his observance of the moral precepts
and then vigorously strives to acquire the *dhyāna* absorptions.

He implements many different skillful means
for bringing forth liberation through the eightfold path.
This is how, in all the endeavors that one takes up,
one comes to be known as a superior person.

Regarding being "free of fault in all the works they do,"[232] whatever endeavors this bodhisattva engages in is of the sort that is not criticized by the wise. There are five reasons that whatever he does is free of fault and is not criticized by the wise, namely:

First, he engages in works that he is capable of accomplishing;
Second, they produce a greatly beneficial result;
Third, they do no damage to the Dharma;
Fourth, they are free of any subsequently resulting faults;
Fifth, they result in an immensely fine reputation.

These are as described below:

He first makes all different sorts of assessments
regarding matters of his own ability and the ease of accomplishment,
ensuring that what is gained by this endeavor
will constitute an immeasurably great resulting benefit,

that it will not interfere with the good Dharma,
that, once it has been accomplished, nothing bad will follow from it,
that it will be of a sort that is praised by good people,
and that it will cause a fine reputation to spread widely.

Whichever works are initiated by the wise
are of a sort that they are free of any fault.
Issues of feasibility and ease of accomplishment
are matters for which one is individually responsible.
Those possessed of measureless great qualities,
will swiftly bring about a resulting benefit.

It is in this manner that the wise come to know
that there will be no subsequent fault arising from this,
and that they should devote diligent vigor to this task,
whereupon they then engage in endeavors such as these.

Regarding "They abide in purity of every kind and come forth through the practice of all the supreme bases [of meritorious qualities],"[233] there are five causal bases for [the bodhisattva's coming forth through] all the supreme bases and for his possessing every kind of purity, namely:

First, he has resolute intentions that are pure;

Second, his dedications of merit are pure;

Third, his own practice of the supreme bases [of meritorious qualities] accords with the way he explains them to others;

Fourth, he influences others to practice them;

Fifth, he abandons all dharmas contrary to the supreme bases [of meritorious qualities], namely false speech, miserliness, covetousness, frivolous restlessness, and delusion.

These are as described below:

The bodhisattva possesses profound and pure intentions,
abandons flattery and deviousness,
107c always relies upon the four supreme bases,
and dedicates his merit to the realization of buddhahood.

He first cultivates good dharmas himself
and thereafter influences others to practice them.
The bodhisattva who proceeds in this manner
is one for whom the four supreme bases are pure.

As for "The ten courses of good karmic action enable these persons to reach the station of the bhagavats who possess the ten powers,"[234] if one cultivates the ten courses of good karmic action in this manner, they enable a person to reach that state wherein he is possessed of the ten powers. "The ten powers" refers to the possession of right and universal knowledge. One who acquires right and universal knowledge is then himself a buddha. There are five causal bases for one's being referred to as a "bhagavat,"[235] namely:

First, [through his right and universal knowledge,] he has severed all doubts with respect to the past;
Second, he has severed all doubts with respect to the future;
Third, he has severed all doubts with respect to the present;
Fourth, he has severed all doubts with respect to dharmas that transcend the three periods of time;
Fifth, he has severed all doubts regarding the ineffable dharmas.

These are as described below:

With regard to the beginningless past,
they have an utterly penetrating comprehension free of doubts.
With regard to the boundless future,
they know it with a penetrating comprehension free of doubts.

All of the boundless worlds
throughout the ten directions of the present
as well as what transcends the three periods of time,
including the sublime dharmas of the unconditioned

and also the fourteen ineffable dharmas[236]—
they know those too with a comprehension free of doubts.
They are therefore treasuries of meritorious qualities,
the buddhas, those renowned as the World-honored Ones.

The ten courses of good karmic action are able to cause bodhisattvas who perfect such meritorious qualities as these to reach *anuttarāsamyaksaṃbodhi*. Therefore whoever seeks to attain buddhahood should cultivate the ten courses of good karmic action in this manner.

Chapter 31[237]

Guarding the Moral Precepts

It is in this way that this bodhisattva practices the courses of good karmic action.

> In both good and bad courses of karmic action,
> there are general characteristics as well as specific characteristics.
> Each of these are to be clearly distinguished and known
> as possessing two corresponding types of karmic results.

As for the general characteristics of the resulting retributions of the ten courses of good karmic action, these may consist of either rebirth in the heavens or rebirth among humans.

As for the specific characteristics of the resulting retributions, they are 108a
as follows:

In the case of the good karmic action of abandoning the killing of beings, there are two resultant karmic retributions: First, long life span. Second, having but little illness.

From the good karmic action of abandoning stealing, there are two resultant karmic retributions: First, one obtains great wealth. Second, one becomes independently wealthy.

From the good karmic action of abandoning sexual misconduct, there are two resultant karmic retributions: First, one's wife will be chaste and good. Second, she cannot be "ruined" by others.[238]

From the good karmic action of abandoning false speech, there are two resultant karmic retributions: First, one will not be slandered by anyone. Second, one will not be cheated or deceived by others.

From the good karmic action of abandoning divisive speech, there are two resultant karmic retributions: First, one will gain a fine following. Second, one's [reputation] will not be ruined by others.

From the good karmic action of abandoning harsh speech, there are two resultant karmic retributions: First, one will hear whichever sounds one delights in hearing. Second, one will not become embroiled in disputes.

From the good karmic action of abandoning scattered or inappropriate speech, there are two resultant karmic retributions: First, people will trust and accept whatever one says. Second, whatever one says will be definitely decisive.

From the good karmic action of abandoning covetousness, there are two resultant karmic retributions: First, one will be easily contented. Second, one will have but few wants.

From the good karmic action of abandoning ill will, there are two resultant karmic retributions: First, wherever one is reborn, one will always seek to bring about fine circumstances for others. Second, one will not delight in tormenting or harming other beings.

From the good karmic action of maintaining right views, there are two resultant karmic retributions: First, one will abandon flattery and deviousness. Second, whatever one sees will be pure in character.

The same principles apply in the matter of the ten courses of bad karmic action. As for the general characteristics of their resulting karmic retributions, if one has engaged in them to a high degree, one falls into the hell realms. If one has engaged in them to a middling degree, one will fall into the animal realms. If one has engaged in them to a lesser[239] degree, then one will to fall into the realms of the hungry ghosts.

As for the specific karmic retributions [associated with the ten courses of bad karmic action], they are as follows:

From the bad karmic action of killing beings, there are two resultant retributions: First, a short life span. Second, much illness.

From the bad karmic action of stealing, there are two resultant karmic retributions: First, poverty. Second, loss of wealth.

From the bad karmic action of sexual misconduct, there are two resultant karmic retributions: First, one will have an ugly and evil wife who is also unchaste. Second, one will be ruined by her.

From the bad karmic action of false speech, there are two resultant karmic retributions: First, one will be slandered by others. Second, one will be cheated and deceived by others.
From the bad karmic action of divisive speech, there are two resultant karmic retributions: First, one will gain a bad following. Second, one will have a following vulnerable to destruction.
From the bad karmic action of harsh speech, there are two resultant karmic retributions: First, one will have to listen to sounds that one loathes. Second, one will be forever embroiled in disputes.
From the bad karmic action of scattered or inappropriate speech, there are two resultant karmic retributions: First, one's words will not be trusted and accepted. Second, one's speech will have neither beginning nor end.
From the bad karmic action of covetousness, there are two resultant karmic retributions: First, one's mind will never know contentment. Second, one will have an abundance of insatiable desires.
From the bad karmic action of ill will, there are two resultant karmic retributions: First, one will be bad-natured. Second, one will delight in tormenting other beings.
From the bad karmic action of maintaining wrong views, there are two 108b
resultant karmic retributions: First, one's mind will tend toward flattery and deviousness. Second, one will tend to fall into wrong views.

Having known the Dharma, one cherishes and delights in it
and one's mind becomes unshakable in the Dharma.
When in the midst of beings,
one's mind of kindness and compassion becomes ever greater.

As for "cherishing the Dharma," one cherishes only the Dharma and sees nothing superior to the Dharma. In this context, "Dharma" refers to the ten courses of good karmic action discussed earlier.

As for "delighting in the Dharma," one delights only in the Dharma and in nothing else.

As for "one's mind remains unshakable in the Dharma," the bodhisattva never abandons the Dharma even when threatened with the loss of his life.

As the bodhisattva practices dharmas such as these, when he is in the midst of other beings, his kindness and compassion toward them become ever greater. Although kindness and compassion do exist on the first ground, their quality therein cannot match their quality as they exist on this ground. This is because he now has a penetrating comprehension of the causes and conditions for karmic offenses and karmic merit.

Beings are pitiable, for they are all under the influence of their own karma and are unable to gain independence from it. This being the case, one's mind then remains free of any thoughts affected by hatred or anger. For one who practices in this way, kindness and compassion do indeed become ever greater. He reflects in this manner:

> Alas! These beings!
> They have fallen so very deeply into wrong views.
> I must explain right views for them
> and thus cause them to gain entry into the path of what is right.

Having gained this penetrating comprehension of the causes and conditions for karmic offenses and karmic merit, the bodhisattva engages in the deep practice of kindness and compassion for all beings, thinking thus:

> Beings are so pitiable. Because they do not know the true character of dharmas, for the most part they engage in false thinking and thus develop all manner of wrong views. It is because of their wrong views that they produce all manner of afflictions, and it is because of their afflictions that then create all sorts of karma. And it is because they produce these karmic causes and conditions that they then turn about in samsara's cycle of births and deaths.
>
> I previously brought forth the resolve to seek *anuttarāsamyaksaṃbodhi*. In order to bring about the liberation of beings, I should explain right views for them. I should liberate all of these beings and influence them to enter the true path so that are then caused to attain liberation.

Having reflected thus, one comes to realize that all beings are beset by all manner of afflictions, as described below:

> One contemplates the afflictions they have brought forth
> as well as the defilement associated with those afflictions,

all of the different sorts of black and evil karmic actions they do,
and all the diverse sorts of suffering and anguish they undergo.

One bears in mind all of these beings, feeling pity for their plight
and for the many ways in which they have become so deficient.
Having taken up all of these different contemplations,
one realizes, "They are all just as I myself have been."

One then immediately brings forth the mind of compassion
and uses the skillful means of bringing forth a great aspiration:
"Oh, how might I be able to influence these beings
to succeed in extinguishing all their many sufferings?"

Regarding "afflictions" and "defilement associated with those afflictions," "afflictions" refers to any of the dharmas subsumed by the fetters whereas "defilement" refers to [whatever arises from] being "obsessed"[240] [by the afflictions].

[More specifically,] those afflictions subsumed by the fetters include greed, hatred, conceit, ignorance, the view of a real self in association with the body [or any of the other four aggregates],[241] extreme views, seizing on 108c
views, seizing on unprincipled precepts, wrong views, and doubt. These ten [consisting of three] root and [seven] subsidiary afflictions are distinguished according to their relationship to the three realms of existence and according to whether they are to be severed by directly seeing the [four] truths or whether they are to be severed by meditative cultivation.[242] As a consequence [of these distinctions], there are ninety-eight latent tendencies.[243]

Those not subsumed by the fetters include non-faith, absence of a sense of shame, absence of a dread of blame, flattery, deviousness, restlessness, regretfulness,[244] rigid attachment, indolence, neglectfulness, drowsiness, malice, miserliness, jealousy, arrogance, impatience, and gluttony. These too are distinguished according to their relationship to the three realms of existence and according to whether they are to be severed by directly seeing the [four] truths or whether they are to be severed by meditative cultivation. As a consequence [of these distinctions], there are one hundred and ninety-six obsessive defilements.

There are others who explain "afflictions" as phenomena residing in deep mental dispositions and explain "defilements" as phenomena abiding at a more superficial level of mind.

There are yet others who explain that it is all of the hindrances that constitute "obsessive defilements" whereas all else falls within the sphere of "afflictions."

Regarding "black and evil karmic actions," this refers to those seven courses of karmic action [among the ten courses of bad karmic action] that actually do constitute [physical or verbal] karmic actions together with thought that has come under the influence of covetousness, ill will, or wrong views. These are able to engender painful karmic retributions.

As for "all the different sorts of suffering and anguish," whatsoever bad experiences are undergone by the body correlate with "suffering" whereas whatsoever bad experiences are undergone by the mind correlate with "anguish." Alternatively, one may explain that present-life sufferings are what correlate with "suffering" whereas "anguish" corresponds to later experiences occurring through descent into the wretched destinies.

Regarding "the many ways in which they have become so deficient," "deficiencies" refers here to inadequacies in sense faculties, limbs, or physical bodies, in what is essential to sustain life, or in faith, observance of the moral precepts, or other such meritorious qualities.

Because the remaining lines are easy to interpret in accordance with the verse statements, no further explanation is necessary.

Once one has contemplated in this manner, one realizes:

> Beings are ever so pitiable.
> For those who have fallen into the two vehicles,
> I shall make a vow for their sakes
> to cause them to dwell in the Great Vehicle.[245]

This circumstance accords with this *Ten Grounds Sutra* wherein Vajragarbha Bodhisattva himself said:[246]

> This bodhisattva abandons the ten courses of bad karmic action while also influencing beings to abide in the ten courses of good karmic action. For the sake of these beings, he strives profoundly to gain the supreme

mind, the fine mind, the delighting mind, the pitying mind, the kind and compassionate mind, the beneficial mind, the protective mind, the mind that sees other beings as one's own, the mind that acts as a great teacher, the mind that draws in others, and the mind that accepts others. He thinks, "All of these beings are so very pitiable. They have fallen into all different sorts of wrong thought and wrong views, and thus travel along in wrong and hazardous paths. I should now influence them to abide in the true path of right views.

"All these different groups of beings engage in mutual disputation and fighting. They always feel anger toward one another as mutual hatred and torment blaze up between them. This being the case, I should influence them to instead abide in the unsurpassably great kindness.

"These beings are insatiable, so much so that they covet any advantages enjoyed by others and pursue wrong livelihoods as their means of survival. I should influence them to instead abide in the pure actions of body, speech, and mind.

"Abiding among causes and conditions associated with greed, hatred, and delusion, these beings are forever generating all the different sorts of afflictions and fetters while never availing themselves of the means whereby they might seek to escape their plight. I should extinguish their sufferings and anguish and influence them to instead abide in the state that is free of sufferings and anguish.

"These beings have had their vision obscured by ignorance and thus have wandered into a dense forest of darkness so deeply that they are unable to escape from it by themselves. Having abandoned the light of wisdom, they have strayed into the hazardous and evil path of the various
[wrong] views. I should rescue them and cause them then to acquire the 109a
eye of unimpeded wisdom. Using this wisdom eye, they will not follow other people, but rather will know all dharmas in accordance with their true character.

"These beings have fallen into the long river of births and deaths and are about to descend into the pit of the hell realms, animal realms, hungry ghost realms, and *asura* realms. They are on the verge of falling into the net trap of perversity and deviousness hidden from their view by the weeds of the many different afflictions.

"Having no guide, they are not even motivated to escape from their predicament. They claim that the path is not the path and that what is not the path is indeed the path. The minions of Māra, their adversaries, always pursue them. Having no good guide, they obey the ideas of Māra and stray far from the Dharma of the Buddha.

"I should cause beings such as these to pass beyond these hazardous and evil roads in the cycle of births and deaths so that they may be able to dwell in the city of all-knowledge that is free of fear and free of decay.

"All these beings have become caught and carried along, drifting, in the current of the flood of desire, the flood of existence, the flood of [wrong] views, and the flood of ignorance in which they are pulled under by the great waves of the many different karmic offenses and are submerged in the river of craving. They are swept along by the waves of the cycle of births and deaths, caught in a swirling whirlpool that pulls them around and around in a current from which they cannot escape.

"They are drowned and rotted by the salty waves of desirous ideation, hateful ideation, and tormenting ideation.[247] They are seized and held by that *rākṣasa* of the view of a real self in association with the body. They enter into the deep woods of the five desires, are seized by the defilements of sensual enjoyments, and are blown about on the high plateau of conceit.

"[Beings] are so extremely pitiable. There is no island [of respite] for them, nor do they have any means of rescue. They are stuck in the empty village of the six sense bases from which they are unable to move. There is no one with the skill to take them on beyond. I should now transport all such beings in the sturdy and durable ship of the great compassion and wisdom, taking them to the continent of all-knowledge where they shall become safe, secure, and free of fear.

"These beings produce such an abundance of suffering that they are indeed pitiable. They are confined within the prison of birth, death, sorrow, lamentation, suffering, and anguish wherein they are much inclined toward greed, anger, craving, and hatred. They fall into the four inverted views, are harmed by the venomous snakes of the four great elements, are tortured by their five aggregate enemies, are ensnared by the deceptive thief of sensual enjoyments' defilements, and undergo measureless suffering and anguish in the empty village of the six sense bases.

"I should demolish their prison of samsara and cause them to attain unimpeded sovereign mastery in the security and bliss of nirvana.

"These beings are so extremely pitiable. With such narrow, inferior, and petty minds, they have come to delight in paltry sorts of benefit. They have shrunken back from, fallen away from, and become bereft of the resolve to attain all-knowledge. Even when they do seek a means of escape, they then only delight in the vehicles of *śrāvaka* disciples or *pratyekabuddha*s. I should cause them to gain the truly great resolve by influencing them to delight in the vast and magnificent dharmas of a buddha."

[Next, we have:]

> If the bodhisattva carries forth his practice in this manner,
> he will gain the power arising from upholding the moral precepts.
> Having thoroughly known how to bring forth good karmic actions,
> he strives to cause them to increase.
> If one proceeds thus, he will thereby become a son of the Buddha
> and will deeply enter the Ground of Stainlessness.

Regarding "the power arising from upholding the moral precepts," if one is singleminded in purely fulfilling the moral precepts associated with the ten courses of good karmic action, then he will acquire the power derived from cultivating and accumulating merit.

As for the ability "to bring forth good karmic actions," one knows well
how to personally bring forth and increase the courses of good karmic action 109b
and also knows how to cause other beings to do so as well.

As for his "deeply entering" [the Ground of Stainlessness], his practices become ever more far-reaching to the point that they exhaust its very limits and depths.

As for the term "son of the Buddha," whosoever is able to carry on his practice in accordance with the Dharma is one who is known as "a son of the Buddha."

From the point of its initial arising on the first ground on through to the second ground in which it increases, this bodhisattva should diligently practice vigor in this manner.

When the bodhisattva succeeds in reaching
the boundaries of the Ground of Stainlessness,
he will then be able to see
a hundred or a thousand buddhas.

In discussing the first ground, we already explained the *pratyutpanna samādhi* and the dharmas assisting acquisition of the *samādhi* in which one sees the buddhas of the present era. Specifically, these included using the thirty-two major marks, eighty secondary characteristics, and forty dharmas exclusive to the buddhas in practicing mindfulness of the Buddha without having any attachment to any dharma. We also discussed the means to enhance the *samādhi* and enable the complete development of the powers arising from its fruition.

Question: If, by virtue of having already reached the limits of the first ground, a bodhisattva is able to see the buddhas, then, on entering the second ground, he should then be able to see the buddhas. Why then do you now state that, only upon reaching the limits of the second ground, does one, then and only then, see the buddhas? If that is truly the case, then it must be that one loses this *samādhi* on first entering the second ground and only then regains it later on.

Response: When first entering the second ground, one still sees the buddhas and still does not fall back from this *samādhi*. It is only because you have not well understood the intended meaning of the verse that you have posed this challenge.

In the beginning and middle phases of the second ground, one still only sees a hundred buddhas. It is only when one reaches its very limits that one is then able to see from a hundred up to a thousand buddhas. Once one has seen the buddhas, one's mind is filled with immense joy. It is because of one's zeal to achieve success in the Buddha's Dharma that one then becomes diligent in practicing vigor.

One immediately becomes able to use the four requisites
to make offerings to the buddhas.
He is then able to receive again the ten courses of karmic action
in the abodes of the buddhas.

"The four requisites" refers to robes, food and drink, bedding, and medicines. One may deduce for himself the meaning of the rest of the verse.

> Having performed acts such as these,
> one receives the courses of good karmic action from the buddhas
> and, even throughout a hundred thousand myriads of *kalpa*s,
> one never allows his practice to become damaged or lost.

"Never allowing this practice to become damaged" means that one does not allow one's practice of the moral precepts to become scant or weak. One may also say that it is purity in one's endeavors that defines non-damage. "Loss" refers to complete discontinuance of one's practice.

It is in this manner that this bodhisattva has passed through the first ground and entered the second ground. This matter is as described below:

> One thoroughly abandons the defilement of miserliness
> and delights in the practice of pure giving.
> By thoroughly abandoning the defilement of miserliness,
> one gains a deep love of purity in upholding the moral precepts.

"Purity" refers to practicing giving with a mind devoted exclusively to goodness, one that is not mixed with any of the afflictions. "Deep love" [of purity in the moral precepts] refers to abiding so solidly in it that one never 109c
relinquishes that practice.

On this ground, there are no further residual traces of the defilement associated with miserliness or the defilement associated with breaking precepts. It is because of this that this ground is referred to as "stainless."

The bodhisattva who in this manner remains free of thoughts inclined toward miserliness or the breaking of moral precepts is especially proficient in the practice within the four means of attraction known as "pleasing words" and is also especially proficient in the practice within the six *pāramitā*s referred to as "the perfection of moral virtue."

"Proficient" refers here to having engaged in extensive practice whereby one's power in that practice has becomes ever more deeply developed.

Question: If on the second ground one has already acquired strength in one's practice of *śīla-pāramitā,* the perfection of moral virtue, now, as one discusses this ground, one should explain the aspects, the arising, the powers, the purification, and the distinctions associated with *śīla-pāramitā.*

Response:

> In a general discussion of the perfection of *śīla,*
> there are sixty-five aspects.
> As for its arising, powers, purification, and distinctions,
> these are discussed in place after place elsewhere in this treatise.

Śīla-pāramitā, as a topic of discussion, is measureless and boundless. To speak of it only in general terms, there are sixty-five aspects. As for the other subtopics, in particular the arising of moral virtue, the powers of moral virtue, the purification of moral virtue, and distinctions to be made with regard to moral virtue, these factors are discussed in detail both earlier and later on in this treatise.

[This interpretive approach] is in accordance with the "The Harmonious Dharma of the Buddha" chapter of the *Jeweled Summit Sutra,* wherein, in the presence of the Buddha, Akṣayamati Bodhisattva spoke of the sixty-five aspects of *śīla-pāramitā,* stating that *śīla* refers to the following: [248]

> It is not [physically] tormenting any being;[249]
> It is not having any thought of stealing the possessions of others;
> It is not being attached to any outward visual forms;
> It is not deceiving beings;
> Through ensuring the complete unity of retinues, it is not engaging in divisive speech;
> Through being well able to patiently endure harsh words [from others], it is being free of harsh speech;
> Through always contemplating and evaluating whether one's speech is beneficial, it is being free of scattered or inappropriate speech;
> Through delighting in the continued happiness of others, it is being free of covetousness;
> Through patiently enduring every sort of suffering, it is being free of ill will;
> Through not praising teachers of other paths, it is right view;
> Through faith in purification of the mind, it is faith in the Buddha;[250]
> Through knowing that the Dharma is genuine, it is faith in the Dharma;

Through delighting in venerating and revering the assemblies of worthies and *ārya*s, it is faith in the Sangha;

Through full prostrations, the making of offerings, and other expressions of reverential respect, it is mindfulness of the Buddha;

Through having mental dispositions by which one is fearful of transgressing against even the most minor moral precept, it is moral virtue that does not become diminished or weak;

Through not relying on any of the other vehicles, it is moral virtue that is undamaged;

Through abandoning erroneous practice, it is moral virtue that does not become deficient;

Through the nonarising of evil afflictions, it is moral virtue that does not become admixed [with impure aspects];

Through the most ultimate and constant delight in increasing and strengthening good dharmas, it is moral virtue that remains unsullied;

Through practicing in accordance with one's wishes, it is moral virtue characterized by sovereign mastery;

Through not doing anything criticized by the wise, it is moral virtue that is praised by the *ārya*s;

Through always abiding in mindfulness guided by stable wisdom, it is easily practiced moral virtue;

Through the complete absence of karmic transgressions in all that one does, it is irreproachable moral virtue;

Through guarding the sense faculties, it is skillfully guarded moral virtue;

Through being one of whom all buddhas are mindful, it is illustrious moral virtue;

Through receiving in proper measure things obtained in accordance with the Dharma,[251] it is moral virtue characterized by but few wants;

Through the severance of covetousness, it is moral virtue that knows contentment;

Through renunciation in both body and mind, it is moral virtue 110a
characterized by renunciation;

Through abandoning the many sorts of boisterous speech, it is moral virtue appropriate to a forest hermitage;
Through having no need to look to anyone else in the hope of obtaining anything, it is moral virtue perfectly complete in the lineage bases of the *ārya*s;
Through being one who possesses roots of goodness, it is moral virtue characterized by refined practice of the *dhūta* austerities;
Through [its efficacy in bringing about] rebirth among humans and *deva*s, it is moral virtue characterized by practice consistent with the manner in which it has been taught;
Through devotion to rescuing all beings, it is moral virtue characterized by kindness;[252]
Through enduring every sort of suffering, it is moral virtue characterized by compassion;
Through resolve that does not retreat and sink away, it is moral virtue characterized by joy;
Through abandoning both hatred and affection, it is moral virtue characterized by equanimity;
Through subduing the mind, it is moral virtue marked by seeing one's own faults;
Through protecting the minds of others, it is unerring moral virtue;
Through skillfully guarding the precepts, it is moral virtue that is well restrained.;[253]
Through devotion to the ripening of beings, it is moral virtue characterized by giving;
Through having nothing for which one wishes, it is moral virtue characterized by patience;
Through not desisting and withdrawing from endeavors, it is moral virtue characterized by vigor;
Through accumulating the dharmas assisting *dhyāna,* it is moral virtue characterized by *dhyāna;*
Through insatiable pursuit of abundant learning and roots of goodness, it is moral virtue characterized by wisdom;
Through gaining wisdom from abundant learning, it is moral virtue that seeks abundant learning;

Through accumulating the dharmas that assist the seven limbs of enlightenment, it is moral virtue that draws close to good spiritual guides;
Through relinquishing erroneous paths, it is moral virtue characterized by the abandonment of bad spiritual guides;
Through contemplating impermanence, it is moral virtue characterized by nonattachment to the body;
Through diligently accumulating roots of goodness, it is moral virtue characterized by not trusting [in the durability of] one's life;
Through purity in one's resolute intentions, it is moral virtue characterized by freedom from regrets;
Through purity in one's actions, it is moral virtue that is not false;
Through resolute intentions that are free of defilement, it is moral virtue that is free of heat;
Through skillfulness in initiating karmic actions, it is moral virtue that is free of sorrow;
Through not elevating oneself [above others], it is moral virtue that is free of conceit;
Through abandoning defiled desires, it is moral virtue that does not indulge frivolous restlessness;
Through maintaining a straightforward mind, it is moral virtue that does not elevate oneself [above others];
Through maintaining a well-regulated mind, it is moral virtue possessed of a sense of shame;
Through not bringing forth evil thoughts, it is moral virtue trained in goodness;
Through extinguishing all afflictions, it is moral virtue characterized by quiescence;
Through practicing in accordance with [the original] explanations, it is moral virtue that follows what has been taught;
Through practicing the dharmas constituting the four means of attraction, it is moral virtue characterized by the transformative teaching of beings;
Through not erring in [the practice of] one's own dharma, it is moral virtue that protects the Dharma;

> Through [maintaining one's] fundamental purity, it is moral virtue in which all vows are fulfilled;
> Through dedicating [one's merit] to realization of the unsurpassed path, it is moral virtue that leads to acquiring the dharmas of the Buddha;
> Through maintaining a mind of uniformly equal regard for all beings, it is moral virtue that leads to acquiring the Buddha's *samādhi*s.

Venerable Śāriputra, as for these sixty-five aspects [of the perfection of *śīla*], [were one to exhaustively list them,] the aspects of all bodhisattva's pure moral virtue would be endlessly numerous.

Now, as for the arising of the moral precepts, this is a matter discussed in place after place [elsewhere in this treatise].

Briefly stated, there are eight categories involved in the arising of the moral precepts, four arising from association with the body and four arising from association with speech. Those arising from association with the body are the abandonment of taking life, the abandonment of inflicting torment and suffering on beings, the abandonment of stealing, and the abandonment of sexual misconduct. Those associated with the mouth are the abandonment of lying, divisive speech, harsh speech, and scattered or inappropriate speech. These are the eight.

These eight categories of moral precepts arise by taking them on [as
110b ongoing obligations]. These dharmas associated with taking them on, when separately distinguished in terms of taking them on physically, taking them on verbally, and taking them on mentally result in a combined total of twenty-four subcategories. When further considered in terms of the twenty-four associated with [the injunction against] instructing others [to commit any of these transgressions], the twenty-four associated with [the injunction against] rejoicing in [transgressions directly committed by others], and the twenty-four associated with [the injunction against] carrying them out oneself, this results in a total of ninety-six, all of which occur in connection with the desire realm.

These [moral precepts] arise commencing with this very day and night. How is this the case? After the initial mental moment of taking on [the obligation imposed by the moral precept] has expired, throughout the entire day and night, during the second [and all subsequent] mental moments thereafter [the force of that moral precept] constantly arises.

One's use of the associated merit is also just the same. How is this the case? After the initial mind-moment associated with an act of giving expires, beginning with the second mind-moment, as one uses [this merit], it is constantly produced.[254] This is the nature of the process as it occurs in association with good physical karmic actions.

There are those [instances of the arising of the moral precepts] that are subsumed within the ten courses of good karmic action and those that are not subsumed therein. This is the situation as it occurs in connection with the desire realm.

As for those [instances of the arising of moral precepts] that occur in connection with the form realm, there are two kinds: first, those [moral precepts] arising from association with the body, and second, those [moral precepts] arising from association with speech. As for those arising from association with the body, this refers to the abandonment of karmic offenses not subsumed among the ten courses of bad karmic action.[255]

In the case of those [moral precepts] arising from association with speech, this refers to the abandonment of scattered or inappropriate speech.[256] Taking on this moral precept involves taking it on physically, taking it on verbally, and taking it on mentally. Taking all of these categories into account, this amounts to two times three, a subtotal of six.

Similarly, there are thus also another six associated with the injunction against instructing others [to carry out any given karmic transgression], another six associated with [the injunction against] rejoicing [in transgressions committed by others], and another six associated with [the injunction against] carrying out [any given transgression] oneself. This yields in total four times six, for a net total of twenty-four. When these are added to the previously cited ninety-six, this brings the grand total to one hundred and twenty.

In much the same fashion, moral precepts also arise in association with the character of one's actions. Thus there is also an arising of moral precepts at the time one attains the realization of the path and there is also an arising of moral precepts at the time one retreats from the path. So too, there may also be an arising of moral precepts in association with one's first taking on birth.

Because this subject [of the arising of moral precepts] is so very expansive in its scope, we now only present this condensed explanation.

As for the powers associated with the moral precepts, as growth occurs in the corresponding *pāramitā,* one's practice of moral virtue becomes ever stronger. Also, in direct correlation with whichever of the grounds one has entered, there will also be a corresponding enhancement in the solidity of one's practice of moral virtue and hence also in the powers associated with it.

As for the purification of the moral precepts, not damaging or destroying moral precepts, not allowing deficiencies or diminishment in their practice, and so forth—these are all just as previously explained.

Additionally, the characteristic features of purity or impurity in one's practice of moral virtue correspond to their treatment in the dharma of the seven types of *brahmacarya.*[257] As related in the sutras, it is by virtue of seven manifestations of sexual desire[258] that the moral virtue [of one who practices *brahmacarya*] is impure, namely:

First, although one may indeed have cut off sexual relations, with a defiled mind, one might nonetheless still accept either bathing or massage performed by a woman;

Second, with a defiled mind, one might smell the perfume of a woman, engage in conversation with her, or participate in mutual joking with her;

Third, with a defiled mind, one might engage in mutual gazing with her;

Fourth, even though there might be a physical barrier separating one from a woman, with a defiled mind, he might still listen to her voice;

Fifth, one might have earlier talked and joked with a woman and later, even though separate from her, he might still recall that experience, being unable to let it go;

Sixth, one has restricted oneself from sexual relations [only] for a particular period of time, after which one will indulge in it again later on;[259]

Seventh, someone might temporarily cut off all sexual relations, doing so hoping that he will thereby be reborn in the heavens and enjoy sexual pleasures there together with celestial maidens while also gaining wealth and pleasure in future lives.

Therefore, [in cases such as these, even though] one has cut off sexual relations, these are still instances of impurity [in moral virtue]. Apart from these seven types of situations, [the practice of *brahmacarya*] does constitute purity in the practice of moral virtue.

Regarding distinctions in moral virtue, a twofold distinction consists of, first, that characterized by the presence of the contaminants, and second, that characterized by the absence of the contaminants.

A threefold distinction consists of that connected with the desire realm, that connected with the form realm, and that with no connections [anywhere in the three realms].

A fourfold distinction consists of two types of right speech and right karmic action subsumed within right livelihood together with a different two types of right speech and right karmic action not subsumed within right livelihood.

A fivefold distinction consists of the common person's moral virtue, a bodhisattva's moral virtue, a *śrāvaka* disciple's moral virtue, a *pratyeka-buddha*'s moral virtue, and the unsurpassable moral virtue of a buddha.

A sixfold distinction consists of:

First, desire realm [moral virtue] of body and speech subsumed within right livelihood;

Second, [desire realm moral virtue of body and speech] not subsumable within right livelihood; 110c

Third, form realm [moral virtue] of body and speech subsumed within right livelihood;

Fourth, [form realm moral virtue of body and speech] not subsumable within right livelihood;

Fifth, [moral virtue] of body and speech that is free of the contaminants and which is subsumed within right livelihood;

Sixth, [moral virtue of body and speech that is free of the contaminants] but not subsumed within right livelihood.

A sevenfold distinction consists of the seven [physical and verbal] courses of good karmic action.

An eightfold distinction consists of the previously mentioned eight [types of arising of moral virtue] consisting of those four associated with the body and those four associated with speech.

A ninefold distinction consists of the seven [physical and verbal] courses of good karmic action in addition to the twofold distinction [according to presence or absence of the contaminants] cited earlier.

A tenfold distinction consists of three types of moral virtue associated with the path, three types of antidotal moral virtue, and three types of simple moral virtue. These nine types are all free of the contaminants. With the addition of moral virtue involving the contaminants, the total number of types comes to ten.

So it is that we have all these many different categories of moral virtue.

Question: The *śrāvaka* disciple vehicle claims that karmic actions of body and speech are the bases of *śīla,* moral virtue. Where these two consist of good karmic actions, they are deemed to be good. Where these two consist of bad karmic actions, they are deemed to be bad. Thus they hold that good karmic actions of body and speech constitute [the practice of] *śīla*. Does this treatise take these to constitute *śīla* or does it instead take *śīla* to involve some other additional factor?

Response:

It is not merely karmic actions of body and speech
that constitute *śīla*.
Cultivation, close personal engagement, and delight in practice
also constitute what is meant by *śīla*.

These three factors each contribute to the meaning of this single concept: cultivation, close personal engagement, and delight in practice.

Question: If one takes cultivation, close personal engagement, and delight in practice as [also] determining what is meant by *śīla,* then all dharmas could be considered as associated with *śīla*. How so? Because they may all be associated with constant cultivation, close personal engagement, and delight in practice. Therefore, you should explain what constitutes the supreme cultivation of *śīla*.

Response:

If it is based on the nonexistence of "I" and "mine,"
the renunciation of conceptual elaboration,

> and realizes nothing at all is apprehensible as [inherently existent], then this is what is meant by *śīla*.

If one does not know the true character of all inward and outward dharmas, then, because one may generate arrogance and clinging attachment due to one's attachment to *śīla,* one may thereby open the door to all sorts of karmic offenses.

Therefore, if one does not perceive any self among the inward dharmas, does not perceive anything belonging to a self among the outward dharmas, if one realizes that all these inward and outward dharmas are ultimately empty and devoid of anything that is apprehensible, and if one also refrains from conceptual elaboration seizing on any characteristics in what is ultimately empty, then this is what constitutes the supreme [practice of] *śīla.*

And why is this so? In *śīla* such as this, there is not even the slightest mental error, how much the less could there be any [error in the actions] of either body or speech? Therefore, the buddhas and the bodhisattvas are those who are foremost in their ability to practice *śīla,* for they do not apprehend any [inherent existence] in any dharma. This is what constitutes the supreme practice of *śīla*. As related in the *Kāśyapa Sutra,* the Buddha told Kāśyapa:[260]

> *Śīla* refers to the nonexistence of self, to the nonexistence of nonself, to the nonexistence of doing, to the nonexistence of anything that is done, to the nonexistence of a doer, to the nonexistence of practice, to the nonexistence of non-practice, to the nonexistence of name, to the nonexistence of form, to the nonexistence of characteristics, and to the nonexistence of the absence of characteristics. There is neither goodness nor nongoodness. There is neither quiescent cessation nor nonexistence of quiescent cessation. There is no grasping and no relinquishing. There are no beings and no causes and conditions for the existence of any being. There is no body, no speech, and 111a
> no mind, no world, no worldly dharmas, no reliance on the world. There is no elevation of oneself by virtue of one's *śīla,* no belittling of others because of [their absence of] *śīla,* no development of overweening pride because of one's *śīla,* and no distinguishing between this one and that one because of *śīla*.
>
> Kāśyapa, this is what constitutes the *śīla* of all worthies and *ārya*s, the *śīla* that has gone beyond the three realms, that is free of all contaminants, and that retains no connections [anywhere within the three realms].

This also accords with Akṣayamati Bodhisattva's statement to Śāriputra in the chapter on *śīla*:[261]

> *Śīla* refers to not making any discriminating assertion claiming the existence of any being. One does not claim that any self exists, does not claim that anyone possessed of a soul or anyone possessed of a life exists. One does not claim that there is any person, does not claim that there is anyone who has been raised up, does not claim that there is any form aggregate or any feeling, perception, formative factor, or consciousness aggregate. One does not claim that there exists any earth element or any water, fire, or wind element;
>
> *Śīla* refers to not discriminating the existence of any eye characteristic, to not discriminating the existence of any visual form characteristic, to not discriminating the existence of any ear characteristic, any sound characteristic, any nose characteristic, any smell characteristic, any tongue characteristic, any flavor characteristic, any body characteristic, any characteristic of tangible objects, any mind characteristic, or any characteristic of dharmas as objects of mind;
>
> *Śīla* refers to not discriminating the existence of body, speech, or mind;
>
> Because *śīla* involves maintaining a focused mind, it is therefore characterized by singlemindedness;
>
> Because it involves skillful selection among dharmas, it is therefore characterized by wisdom;
>
> *Śīla* refers to arriving at emptiness, to reaching the ultimate limit of signlessness that does not involve any admixture with the three realms of existence, and to wishlessness, nonarising, and the unproduced-dharmas patience;
>
> *Śīla* refers to not coming forth from the past, not going forth to the future, and not abiding between them, either;
>
> *Śīla* refers to not dwelling in the conjunction of mind faculty, mind consciousness, and thoughts [as objects of mind];
>
> *Śīla* refers to not relying on the desire realm, to not relying on the form realm, and to not relying on the formless realm;
>
> *Śīla* refers to abandoning the dust of greed, to ridding oneself of the defilement of hatred, to extinguishing the darkness of ignorance, to not

falling into either eternalism or annihilationism, and to not contradicting production as characterized by [the conjunction of] multiple conditions;

Śīla refers to abandoning the conception of a self, to relinquishing the conception of anything belonging to a self, and to not dwelling in the view of a real self in association with the body;

Śīla refers to not being attached to designations and characteristics being incompatible with name and form;[262]

Śīla refers to not being under the direction of any of the fetters;

[*Śīla* refers to] not being overpowered by any of the obsessions;

[*Śīla* refers to] not abiding in any of the hindering doubts or regrets;

Śīla refers to not abiding in roots of bad action associated with greed, to transcending roots of bad action associated with hatred, and to severing roots of bad action associated with delusion;

Śīla refers to the happiness of the delighted mind free of anxiety and free of mental fever;

Śīla refers to not destroying the Dharma body, this through not severing the lineage of the buddhas, to not severing the lineage of the Dharma, this through not making discriminations regarding the nature of dharmas, and to not severing the lineage of the Sangha, this through being characterized by [cultivation of] the unconditioned.[263]

Śāriputra, this is what is meant by the supreme and unsurpassed *śīla* of bodhisattvas. *Śīla* of this sort is inexhaustible. With the sole additional exception of the buddhas, *śīla* [as practiced by all others] is in every case exhaustible.

This is as stated herein:

> Beginning with the *śīla* of the common person
> and ending with that practiced by a *pratyekabuddha,*
> all of these are characterized by exhaustibility.
> It is only that of bodhisattvas that is inexhaustible.

Even though all of the *śīla* practice coming forth from the common per- 111b
son results in their long-enduring enjoyment of its karmic fruits, it is all finally completely exhausted. Even all *śīla* ever practiced by all arhats and *pratyekabuddha*s is finally exhausted as well.

However, because the bodhisattva's practice of *śīla* is based on the realization of the nonexistence of a self or anything belonging to a self, on the abandonment of the idea that any dharma can be apprehended at all, and on the extinguishing of all conceptual elaboration, it is therefore utterly inexhaustible. This is as described by Akṣayamati Bodhisattva in the chapter on *śīla:*[264]

> Because [the karmic fruits of] the *śīla* practiced by common people come to an end in accordance with the stations of rebirth into which they are reborn, [the karmic fruits of] their *śīla* become exhausted. Because the five spiritual powers acquired by non-Buddhist practitioners come to an end when they regress, [the karmic fruits of] their *śīla* become exhausted. Because [the karmic fruits of] the ten courses of good karmic action as practiced by humans are exhaustible, [the karmic fruits of] their *śīla* become exhausted.
>
> Because the merit of the *deva*s in the desire realm is exhaustible, [the karmic fruits of] their *śīla* become exhausted. Because the four *dhyāna*s and the four immeasurable minds as practiced by *deva*s in the form realm are exhaustible, [the karmic fruits of] their *śīla* become exhausted. Because the stations into which the *deva*s of the formless realm may be reborn in accordance with their meditative absorptions are exhaustible, [the karmic fruits of] their *śīla* become exhausted.
>
> Because learners and those beyond learning [in the *śrāvaka* disciple vehicle] come to an end with their entry into nirvana, [the karmic fruits of] their *śīla* are exhaustible. Because the *pratyekabuddha*s do not possess the great compassion, [the karmic fruits of] their *śīla* are exhaustible.
>
> Venerable Śāriputra, only the *śīla* of bodhisattvas is inexhaustible. Why? It is from the bodhisattva's practice of *śīla* that there emerge all the different manifestations of *śīla*. Because those karmic causes are inexhaustible, the associated karmic fruits are also inexhaustible. Because the *śīla* of bodhisattvas is inexhaustible, the *śīla* of the tathāgatas is also inexhaustible. As a consequence, the *śīla* as practiced by all these great men is inexhaustible.

Question: When you explained the more general aspects of *śīla,* you spoke of sixty-five different aspects of *śīla*[-*pāramitā*] and stated that, among *śrāvaka* disciples, there are eight kinds of *śīla,* four arising in association with the body and four arising in association with speech. How is there no contradiction between these [two different ways of enumerating the types of *śīla*]?

Response: They are not mutually contradictory. How is this so?

> Although [those aspects] are not the very essence of *śīla,*
> because they are beneficial, they are referred to as its aspects.
> As for those eight kinds of physical and verbal karmic actions,
> those do constitute the essence of *śīla.*

Although those sixty-five aspects do not constitute the very essence of *śīla,* because they are nonetheless beneficial to those eight relatively coarse categories of physical and verbal *śīla,* they are therefore referred to as aspects of *śīla*. In general, whatever is able to be of benefit [to this practice] is regarded as an aspect [of *śīla*]. This is analogous to the custom of referring to all the [monarch's] elephants, horses, feather fans, and canopies as aspects of kingship. Consequently, although the *dhyāna* absorptions, wisdom, and so forth are not themselves the very essence of *śīla,* because they are beneficial to the practice of *śīla,* they too are regarded as aspects of *śīla.*

Chapter 32[265]

An Explanation of the *Dhūta* Austerities

The bodhisattva practices the dharma of *śīla* in this way:[266]

> Having observed its ten benefits, one should wear
> the two and six types of robes in accordance with that dharma.
> Additionally, due to having observed its ten benefits,
> one should obtain food on the almsround for one's entire life.

Wishing to completely fulfill the practice of upholding the various cate- 111c
gories of moral precepts and having observed that there are ten associated benefits from doing so, one should take up the practice of wearing the two types and the six types of robes. What are those ten benefits? They are:

First, because this assists a sense of shame and a dread of blame;

Second, because this allows one to protect oneself from cold, heat, mosquitoes, horseflies, and poisonous insects;

Third, because this displays the proper deportment of a *śramaṇa;*

Fourth, because, whenever *deva*s or humans lay eyes on the Dharma robes, they are moved to respect and veneration comparable to what they would feel when coming upon a stupa or temple;

Fifth, because one wears the dyed robes with the mind of renunciation and not out of some desire to wear what is considered fine;

Sixth, because one wears the robes to accord with the ideal of quiescence and not to be ablaze with the fire of afflictions.

Seventh, because when one wears the Dharma robes, if there is something bad in one's character, this is easy for others to observe.

Eighth, because when one wears the Dharma robes, one requires no additional adornments;

Ninth, because in wearing the Dharma robes, one acts in accordance with the eightfold path of the *ārya*s;

Tenth, because I should be vigorous in practice of the path, I should not wear the *kāṣāya* robes for even a moment during which I am beset with defiled thoughts.

Having observed these ten benefits, one should wear the two types of robes: First, robes contributed by a householder. Second, cast-off robes.

As for the six types of robes, they are: First, *kārpāsa* (cotton) cloth robes. Second, *kṣaumā* (linen) cloth robes. Third, *kauśeya* (silk) cloth robes. Fourth, animal hair robes. Fifth, red hemp robes. Sixth, white hemp robes.

As for, "having observed its ten benefits, one should obtain food on the almsround for one's entire life," [those ten benefits are:]

First, what I obtain [on the almsround] is able to sustain my life is my own responsibility and no one else's;[267]

Second, [having reflected,] "May those beings who provide me with food be caused to find refuge in the Three Jewels," one may then go ahead and eat;

Third, [one reflects,] "Whenever someone provides me with food, I should bring forth a thought of compassion for them and resolve to be diligent in practicing vigor so they may abide well in their practice of giving." Having reflected thus, one may then eat;

Fourth, this is a practice that accords with the instructions of the Buddha;

Fifth, one is easily satisfied and easily nourished through this practice.

Sixth, one practices a dharma that crushes potential arrogance;

Seventh, this practice plants roots of goodness for gaining the invisible summit mark [of a buddha's body];

Eighth, by observing the practice of obtaining food on the almsround, others engaged in the cultivation of good dharmas will emulate my practice;

Ninth, through this practice one refrains from forming close ties with particular men or women, whether old or young;

Tenth, by practicing the strictly sequential method of obtaining food on the almsround, one develops a mind of uniformly equal regard for all beings that assists the acquisition of the knowledge of all modes.

Although the Buddha did permit accepting invitations for meals,
if one wishes to provide for one's own benefit

while also benefiting other people,
one should not accept invitations for meals.

"One's own benefit" refers here to the ability to perfect [the cultivation of] all the *pāramitās*. "Benefiting others" refers here to teaching beings in such a way that one induces them to abide in [accordance with] the Three Jewels. A practitioner who acts accordingly will benefit himself while also benefiting others.

Because one has observed its ten benefits,
one never abandons residing in a solitary wilderness dwelling.
In order to visit and console the sick, to listen to Dharma,
or to provide teachings, one may then go to a temple.

For the *bhikṣu* who has taken up the practice of dwelling in a forest hermitage, although it may increase many different sorts of meritorious qualities, generally speaking, it is due to seeing ten benefits from this that, for the rest of his life, he should never abandon this practice. What are the ten benefits? They are as follows:

First, one retains complete freedom to come and go at will;
Second, one thus easily does away with conceptions of "I" and "mine"; 112a
Third, there is nothing to impede one's dwelling wherever one wishes;
Fourth, one's mind increasingly delights in forest hermitage practice;
Fifth, one's dwelling place conduces to but few wants and few responsibilities;
Sixth, for the sake of perfecting the meritorious qualities, one should give up any selfish cherishing for his own body or life;[268]
Seventh, one departs far from the boisterous chatter of the crowds;
Eighth, even though one's practice is [devoted to perfecting] the meritorious qualities, one seeks no kindness in return;
Ninth, it becomes easy to achieve singlemindedness in accordance with one's cultivation of *dhyāna* concentration;
Tenth, through abiding in a solitary wilderness location, one easily develops unimpeded reflections.[269]

As for coming to the temple to visit and console the sick or for the other abovementioned reasons:

If there are situations where, for particular reasons,
one comes and abides at the stupa or temple,
Still, in every such situation,
one never abandons one's perception of emptiness and serenity.

Although a *bhikṣu* may have taken on the dharma of lifetime forest hermitage dwelling, if situations emerge involving particular causes and conditions, he may then go and enter the stupa or temple, for the Dharma of the Buddha has both exceptions and restrictions in such cases. In this respect, it is not like the non-Buddhist approaches to forest hermitage dwelling. [This practice] is defined by always delighting in abiding in an empty and serenely quiet place. Hence one never relinquishes the perception of all dharmas as empty. This is because the very essence of all dharmas is that they are all ultimately empty [of any inherent existence of their own].

Question: What are the reasons for which one might come to the stupa or temple?

Response:

First, to provide for the care of the sick;
Second, to seek medical supplies to treat one's own sickness;
Third, for one who is sick to search for a physician to treat his illness;
Fourth, to teach the Dharma to the sick;
Fifth, to teach the Dharma to the other *bhikṣus*;
Sixth, to listen to teachings on Dharma;
Seventh, in order to pay respects and make offerings to greatly virtuous monastics;
Eighth, in order to provide for the needs of the *ārya* Sangha;
Ninth, to study and recite profound scriptures;
Tenth, to instruct others in the study of profound scriptures.

There are reasons such as these that justify coming to the stupa or temple.

One is vigorous in cultivating the various types of thought
as one accords with the dharma of the forest hermitage.
The *bhikṣu* who has been residing
in a forest hermitage abode

> should always be vigorous and diligent in bringing forth
> the many different good dharmas,
> in great courageousness in one's resolve to realize nonself,
> and in extinguishing every sort of fear.

Regarding the application of vigor in a forest hermitage, this is exemplified by the *bhikṣu* who, because he has cut off covetousness and does not cherish his body, life, or offerings, always strives with diligence and vigor both day and night as, for his entire life,[270] he accords with forest hermitage practice, doing so with the same urgency one would feel in putting out a fire in one's own turban.

As for "[cultivating the various types of] thought," this refers to the thought of renunciation, the thought of non-ill will, and the thought of non-harming as well as to the other types of wholesome thought.[271]

Then again, this also refers to:

Cultivating mindfulness of the Buddha as the possessor of right and universal knowledge and as the most revered among all beings;
Cultivating mindfulness of the Buddha's Dharma as well spoken;
Cultivating mindfulness of his Sangha of disciples as according with right practice [of the path].

Furthermore, cultivating thought appropriate to dwelling in a forest hermitage refers as well to cultivating all of the various contemplative ideation that accords with emptiness, that accords with signlessness, and that accords with wishlessness.

Additionally, this refers to contemplative thought accordant with the four supreme bases [for the development of meritorious qualities] and concordant with the six *pāramitā*s.

These are the various sorts of thought that are accordant with the dharma 112b
for abiding in a forest hermitage.

Then again, this is similar to what the Buddha told Ugra the Elder, when explaining the bodhisattva path practices of both laity and monastics:[272]

> If a monastic bodhisattva takes on the dharma of forest hermitage practice, he should reflect in this manner:

"Why am I choosing to abide in a forest hermitage setting? It is not solely because I abide in a forest hermitage setting that I qualify as a *śramaṇa,* for there are many sorts of beings who abide in a forest hermitage setting. Mostly inclined toward evil and not toward goodness, they do not guard the sense faculties, do not cultivate with vigor, and do not cultivate the good dharmas. Take for example the musk deer, monkeys, the many sorts of birds, evil bandits, *caṇḍāla*s, and other such people, none of whom are *bhikṣu*s. So, for what purpose am I choosing to abide in a forest hermitage setting?"

One must indeed accomplish one's purpose. Elder, what sorts of things constitute one's purpose? [They include the following:]

1. So that one's thoughts will not be scattered;
2. To acquire [consummate practice of] the *dhāraṇī*s;
3. To cultivate the mind of kindness;
4. To cultivate the mind of compassion;
5. To abide with sovereign mastery in the five types of spiritual superknowledges;
6. To completely fulfill the practice of the six *pāramitā*s;
7. To avoid abandoning the resolve to realize all-knowledge;
8. To cultivate the knowledge of skillful means;
9. To attract beings [into the Dharma];
10. To facilitate beings' success [in cultivating the path];
11. To avoid abandoning the four means of attraction;
12. To become ever mindful of the six objects of mindfulness;[273]
13. To avoid abandoning vigor in the acquisition of extensive learning;
14. To engage in correct contemplative analysis of dharmas;
15. To practice in accordance with right liberation;
16. To achieve the realization of the fruits [of the path];
17. To abide in the right and definite position (*samyaktva-niyāma*);
18. To preserve and protect the Buddha's Dharma;
19. To abide in right views through faith in karmic retributions;
20. To abide in right intentional thought through abandoning all recollective and discriminating thought;
21. To abide in right speech through teaching Dharma for beings in accordance with their own resolute beliefs;

22. To abide in right action through acting in ways that extinguish [bad] karma;
23. To abide in right livelihood through extinguishing affliction driven habitual karmic propensities;
24. To abide in right effort through striving for the attainment of the unsurpassed path;
25. To abide in right mindfulness through contemplation of dharmas that are not false;
26. To abide in right meditative concentration through the attainment of comprehensive wisdom;
27. To not be frightened by emptiness;
28. To not be made fearful by signlessness;
29. To not be overwhelmed by wishlessness;
30. To be guided by wisdom in taking on one's bodies;
31. To rely on the meaning, not merely on the words;
32. To rely on wisdom, not merely on consciousness;
33. To rely on sutras of ultimate meaning, not on sutras whose meaning is nonultimate;
34. To rely on Dharma, not on persons.

Elder, it is [purposes] such as these that constitute the beneficial endeavors that the renunciant bodhisattva *bhikṣu* should bring forth.

As for "according with the dharma of the forest hermitage," this refers to cultivation of the four *dhyāna*s, the four immeasurable minds, the heavenly ear, the heavenly eye, cognition of others' thoughts, cognition of past lives, the spiritual superknowledges, and so forth.

As for "extinguishing every sort of fear," there are three reasons for this practitioner's ability to extinguish fear: 112c

First, because he sees that dharmas are characterized by nonexistence of self and the nonexistence of anything belonging to a self, he is therefore able to dispel fear;

Second, because he has the power of skillful means;

Third, because he has the power of mental courage, he is able to dispel fear.

Regarding this matter of "seeing the nonexistence of self and the nonexistence of anything belonging to a self," this is just as presented earlier, in the [third chapter's] treatment of the first ground, where ridding oneself of five kinds of fear was discussed.[274]

As for "the power of skillful means," in this treatise, it is mindfulness that rightly reflects upon karma and its retributions that constitutes the power of skillful means. One should reflect in this way, "All of the great kings may be deep in their palaces where their security is ensured by the fourfold elephant, cavalry, chariot, and infantry battalions that surround and serve them. Even so, once the karmic causes and conditions sustaining their rule finally come to an end, even they are compelled to undergo all of the different events that eventually bring about their ruin and anguish.

"Also, in the case of those who are protected by the causes and conditions of their karmic actions, even though they might travel a hazardous road, sail far out onto the waters of the great sea, or walk amid the ranks of battling armies, they will still remain entirely safe and free of any personal calamities.

"Given the karmic causes and conditions established in my previous lives, no matter whether I reside in the village or in a forest hermitage, I will still definitely be compelled to undergo its karmic retribution."

Having contemplated matters in this way, one thereby succeeds in extinguishing fear. Furthermore, one thinks, "If, to protect myself, I choose to go forth into the city or village, thus abandoning this living in a forest hermitage, there will be nothing there that is able to exceed the protection afforded me by good physical karmic actions, good verbal karmic actions, and good mental karmic actions."

This is just as told to King Prasenajit by the Buddha himself when he said:[275]

> If a person practices good physical karmic actions, practices good verbal karmic actions, and practices good mental karmic actions, this is what affords a person the best personal protection. Were this person to claim of himself, "I am hereby well protected," this would indeed be a proclamation of the truth.
>
> Great King, even though this man would not be surrounded and guarded by the fourfold battalions of the army, he can still be regarded

as being well protected. And why is this so? It is because this form of protection is inward protection, not mere outward protection.

[Thus one may be moved to reflect,] "Therefore I do in fact qualify as personally well protected by virtue of my practice of good physical karmic actions, good verbal karmic actions, and good mental karmic actions."

One may additionally reflect thus, "All of these birds, beasts, snakes, and such that abide in the vicinity of this forest hermitage—even without practicing good physical karmic actions, good verbal karmic actions, or good mental karmic actions, they are free of fear due to dwelling far from the village. How could one as knowledgeable as I fail to even match [the fearlessness of] these birds, beasts, and other creatures?"

Through reflecting in these various ways, one does away with all of one's fears.

Additionally, by resorting to mindfulness of the Buddha, one can dispel all fear-inducing circumstances that may arise in a forest hermitage. As is stated in a sutra:[276]

> When any of you *bhikṣu*s are dwelling in a forest hermitage setting, whether beneath a tree, or in some empty building, it could happen that you might be overcome with fear, even to the point that your heart sinks and your hair stands on end. At just that very point, you should become mindful of me [by my ten names]: Thus Come One (Tathāgata), Worthy of Offerings (Arhat), Of Right and Universal Enlightenment (*samyak-saṃbuddha*), Perfect in the Clear Knowledges and Conduct (*vidyā-caraṇa-sampanna*), Well-Gone One (*sugata*), Knower of the Worlds (*lokavid*), Unsurpassed Tamer of Those to Be Tamed (*anuttarā-puruṣa-damya-sārathi*), Teacher of *Deva*s and Humans (*śāstā-deva-manuṣyāṇām*), Enlightened One (Buddha), World-honored One (Bhagavat). When you become mindful in this way, your fear will immediately disappear.

As for "great courageousness," this refers to possessing resolve that is not timid or weak and which is decisive in seeking the path. This is as described here:

> The *bhikṣu* who abides in the wilderness 113a
> should draw upon the power of courageous resolve

to extinguish all fears,
being mindful of the Buddha as the one who is fearless.

In a case where someone has created karma
and fears that he will be unable to escape [its retribution],
even if he is not fearful, he will still not escape it.
Hence, if one is fearful, then one loses his rightful benefit.

Thus, if one realizes that he cannot avoid it,
and yet allows this to destroy other benefits one might achieve,
then one thereby involves himself in the affairs of petty men
and engages in behavior a *bhikṣu* should never adopt.

If one is to have something that one fears,
then one should instead fear samsara.
All the various forms of fear
have this cycle of births and deaths as their cause.

Therefore, one who practices the path
wishing to gain liberation from samsara
while also rescuing others
should not give rise to fear.

As stated by the Buddha in the *Sutra on Abandoning Fear* when discussing the dharma of fearfulness:[277]

In an instance where a *śramaṇa* or brahman is abiding in a forest hermitage, he should reflect as follows, "It is because of impure physical karma, because of impure verbal karma, because of impure mental karma, because of thoughts devoted to what is impure, because of elevating self and diminishing others, because of an indolent mind, because of false recollective thinking, because of an unconcentrated mind, and because of one's delusions that one is overcome by fear. And it is because of the very opposite qualities consisting of purity of physical karma and so forth that one then becomes free of fear."

Additionally, for the sake of the Elder Ugra, the Buddha said:[278]

The monastic bodhisattva who resides in a forest hermitage should reflect thus, "For what purpose am I here?"

He should then immediately realize, "It is because of a desire to abandon fear that I have come here. Fear of what? It is fear of the many sorts of befuddling disturbances, fear of the chattering of crowds, fear of greed, hatred, and delusion, fear of arrogance, fear of anger and hostility, fear of jealousy over offerings received by others, fear of visual forms, sounds, smells, tastes, touchables, fear of the *māra* of the five aggregates, fear of all circumstances involving delusion-induced obstacles, fear of untimely speech, fear of claiming to have seen what one has not seen, fear of claiming to have heard what one has not heard, fear of claiming to have awakened when one has not yet awakened, fear of claiming to know what one does not know, fear of the *śramaṇa*'s defilements, fear of mutual detestation, fear of all the places of rebirth throughout the desire realm, the form realm, and the formless realm, and fear of falling into the hell realms, the animal realms, the hungry ghost realms, or any of the other difficulties.[279] To state it briefly, it is because of fear of all evil and unwholesome dharmas that I have come to abide here.

"If one lives as a householder, delights in its many sorts of commotion, does not cultivate the path, and abides in wrong thought, he will not be able to achieve emancipation from such points of fear as these.

"There were the bodhisattvas of the past, all of whom resided in a forest hermitage, abandoned all fears, reached the state of fearlessness, and gained all-knowledge. So too, all bodhisattvas of the future shall also
dwell in a forest hermitage, abandon all fears, and gain all-knowledge. All 113b
of the bodhisattvas of the present also undertake the practice of residing in a forest hermitage and thereby abandon all fears, reach the station of fearlessness, and gain all-knowledge.

"Therefore, given that I fear all of these sorts of bad circumstances, in order to transcend all fears, I too should take up the practice of abiding in a forest hermitage dwelling.

"Furthermore, all fears arise due to attachment to a self, due to affection for and acceptance of a self, due to the conception of a self, due to the perception of a self, due to esteeming a self, due to discriminations conceiving of a self, and due to protection of a self.

"Were I to take up the practice of abiding in a forest hermitage dwelling but still fail to abandon this attachment to a self, then this would amount to abiding in a forest hermitage in vain."

Furthermore, Elder, whosoever perceives that there is anything at all that is apprehensible [as inherently existent] does not truly reside in a forest hermitage. Whosoever abides in the conception of a self or anything belonging to a self does not truly reside in a forest hermitage. Whosoever abides in thoughts affected by the inverted views does not truly abide in a forest hermitage.

Elder, so it goes even up to the point that, not even one who conceives of nirvana [as inherently existent] truly abides in a forest hermitage, how much the less could it be that someone who conceives of afflictions [as inherently existent] truly abides in a forest hermitage.

Elder, just as the grass and trees in the vicinity of a forest hermitage are entirely free of fear, so too is the bodhisattva. When abiding in a forest hermitage, one should envision oneself as like the grass and trees, envision oneself as like stones or tiles, envision oneself as like a reflection in a pool of water, and envision oneself as like a mere image in a mirror. One should imagine speech to be merely echoes and should imagine one's thoughts to be like magical illusions. In any of this, who is it that could possibly be frightened? And who is it that could be struck with fear?

The bodhisattva then undertakes right contemplation of the body, observing the nonexistence of self and the nonexistence of anything belonging to a self. He observes that there is no being, no one possessed of a soul, no one possessed of a life, no one who has been raised up, no one identifiable as male, no one identifiable as female, no knower, and no perceiver.

Fear itself is but a product of false discriminations. Thus one reflects, "Then I should not simply follow along with false discriminations."

In just this way, the bodhisattva should be just like the grass or trees as he abides in a forest hermitage. He should also be aware that all dharmas are also just like this.

It is the cutting off of all forms of struggle and disputation that truly qualifies as abiding within a forest hermitage. It is the nonexistence of self, the nonexistence of anything belonging to a self, and the not belonging to anything at all that truly qualify as the bases of abiding in a forest hermitage.

One should not delight in the many sorts of noisy dwelling places of either householders or monastics. The buddhas do not permit a *bhikṣu* dwelling in a forest hermitage to abide together with either a householder or a monastic.

Question: Did the Buddha forbid one to gather together with anyone else in the community?

Response: No. He did not.

> The Buddha permitted meeting with others in four circumstances
> but did not permit it otherwise.
> Therefore one should draw close [to others] in those situations,
> while still abiding well apart in other circumstances.

Thus the bodhisattva who abides in a forest hermitage is permitted to join in four types of assemblies. Specifically, he may enter assemblies gathered to hear the teaching of Dharma, may enter assemblies to teach beings, may enter assemblies to make offerings to the Buddha, and may enter assemblies gathered to prevent abandoning the resolve to gain all-knowledge.

Therefore one is only permitted to gather together with others in these 113c
four circumstances. [The *bhikṣu* dwelling in a forest hermitage] should not draw close to others in other circumstances.

Additionally, the bodhisattva should reflect in this manner, "How should I establishing a forest hermitage dwelling that is closely adherent to those permitted by all buddhas? Could it perhaps be that this is not actually a forest hermitage dwelling and that I merely suppose it to be a forest hermitage dwelling? Could I perhaps be mistaken about the meaning of this?"

Question: What then are the aspects of a forest hermitage dwelling that a bodhisattva should know?[280]

Response: In the sutras, the Buddha himself declared:

> Abiding in a forest hermitage refers to not abiding in any dharma, to not taking refuge in any of the sense objects, to not seizing on any mark of any dharma, and to not coveting any visual forms, sounds, smells, tastes, or tangible objects;

Abiding in a forest hermitage refers to dwelling in a manner wherein one has nothing upon which one relies, this because [one realizes that] all dharmas are uniformly equal;

Dwelling in a forest hermitage refers to abiding in a manner free of contradictions because of the goodness of one's own mind;

Dwelling in a forest hermitage refers to dwelling in a manner whereby one relinquishes all the burdens and abides in delighted happiness;

Dwelling in a forest hermitage refers to abiding in a manner whereby one becomes liberated from all afflictions and one becomes free of all fears;

Dwelling in a forest hermitage refers to dwelling in a manner whereby one crosses beyond the floods;[281]

Dwelling in a forest hermitage refers to abiding in the lineage bases of the *āryas*;[282]

Dwelling in a forest hermitage refers to being satisfied with what one obtains in the course of things;

Dwelling in a forest hermitage refers to dwelling in a way that one is easily satisfied, easily supported, and inclined to but few wants;

Dwelling in a forest hermitage refers to abiding in a manner whereby one achieves the fulfillment of wisdom;

Dwelling in a forest hermitage refers to abiding in a manner whereby one rightly practices [what one has acquired through] extensive learning;

Dwelling in a forest hermitage refers to directly manifesting the realization of the emptiness, signlessness, and wishlessness gates to liberation;

Dwelling in a forest hermitage refers to abiding in a manner wherein one severs all the bonds and gains liberation;

Dwelling in a forest hermitage refers to abiding in a manner that accords with the twelvefold chain of causation;

Dwelling in a forest hermitage refers to abiding in a manner whereby one reaches the state of ultimate quiescence in which one has already done what is to be done;

Dwelling in a forest hermitage refers to abiding in a manner compliant with all classes of moral precepts, compliant with all types of practice assisting acquisition of the meditative absorptions, compliant with all types of practice beneficial to wisdom, compliant with all types of practice that facilitate easy achievement of liberation, compliant with all classes of practice facilitating easy acquisition of the knowledge and vision of liberation, compliant with whatever practices facilitate easy practice of the dharmas conducive to realization of *bodhi,* and compliant with whatever is able to conduce to accumulating all meritorious qualities associated with the *dhūta* austerities;

Dwelling in a forest hermitage refers to achieving a penetrating comprehension of the truths;

Dwelling in a forest hermitage refers to seeing and knowing the aggregates;

Dwelling in a forest hermitage refers to [realizing that] the nature of all things is identical to the nature of dharmas;[283]

Dwelling in a forest hermitage refers to abandoning the twelve sense bases;

Dwelling in a forest hermitage refers to never forgetting one's resolve to attain *bodhi;*

Dwelling in a forest hermitage refers to contemplating emptiness without being frightened by it;

Dwelling in a forest hermitage refers to being able to protect and preserve the Buddha's Dharma;

Dwelling in a forest hermitage refers to [practicing in a manner whereby] one who seeks liberation does not err with regard to the meritorious qualities;

Dwelling in a forest hermitage refers to [practicing in a manner whereby], if one is a person capable of gaining all-knowledge, he will thus achieve increased benefit.

If a bodhisattva dwelling in a forest hermitage is able to practice in this way, he will swiftly achieve complete fulfillment of the six perfections. How might this be so?

If a bodhisattva abiding in a forest hermitage does not have a selfish cherishing even for his own body or life, this is the practice of 114a
dāna-pāramitā, the perfection of giving;

If he maintains purity in the three kinds of good karmic actions and enters the refined practice of the *dhūta* austerities, this is the practice of *śīla-pāramitā,* the perfection of moral virtue;

If he does not generate any hatred toward any other beings but rather extends a mind of universally inclusive kindness to all of them, and if he only accepts and delights in the vehicle of all-knowledge and no other vehicle, this is the practice of *kṣānti-pāramitā,* the perfection of patience;

If he makes the solemn personal vow to abide in a forest hermitage and never leave this place so long as he has not yet rightly realized the [unproduced-]dharmas patience, this is the practice of *vīrya-pāramitā,* the perfection of vigor;

If, having gained the *dhyāna* absorptions, his cultivation of roots of goodness is not done with an eye toward taking rebirth in the stations of rebirth to which they correspond,[284] this is the practice of *dhyāna-pāramitā,* the perfection of *dhyāna* meditation;

If one's person and the forest hermitage have become of the same suchness, if one's person and *bodhi* have become of the same suchness, and if these are all indistinguishable from ultimate reality, this is the practice of *prajñā-pāramitā*, the perfection of wisdom.

The Buddha permitted those possessed of four dharmas to abide in a forest hermitage.

What then are those four dharmas? As the Buddha told the Elder [Ugra], they are:

First, extensive learning;

Second, thorough knowledge of the definitive meaning;

Third, delight in the cultivation of right mindfulness;

Fourth, practice accordant with the manner in which [the Dharma] was taught.

People of this sort should take up the practice of dwelling in a forest hermitage.

Additionally, there are bodhisattvas whose afflictions are deep and dense. If such a person abides in the midst of noisy crowds, he will bring forth yet more afflictions. Therefore he should dwell in a forest hermitage in order to subdue afflictions.

Then again, there are bodhisattvas who have acquired the five spiritual superknowledges. Because these practitioners may wish to teach *deva*s, dragons, *yakṣa*s, or *gandharva*s and assist their success [on the path], they should dwell in a forest hermitage.

Yet again, there are bodhisattvas who think thus, "Dwelling in a forest hermitage is the circumstance praised and permitted by all buddhas."

Moreover, dwelling in a forest hermitage assists the fulfillment of all good dharmas and increases roots of goodness. Afterward, one may then enter the village and teach Dharma for the welfare of beings. If one's intention is to develop such meritorious qualities, one may then dwell in a forest hermitage.

Also:

> In the *Sutra of the Resolute King,*
> The Buddha told Ānanda:
> "The *bhikṣu* who dwells in a forest hermitage
> should dwell in four fourfold dharmas."

A bodhisattva who wishes to abide in a forest hermitage [may do so for these purposes]:

First, to depart far from both laypeople and monastics;
Second, out of a wish to study and recite profound scriptures;
Third, as a means of leading forth other beings, thereby influencing them to develop the meritorious qualities arising from dwelling in a forest hermitage;
Fourth, to engage in uninterrupted day and night practice of mindfulness of the Buddha.

There are another four dharmas:
First, one does not generate a thought of hatred toward other beings even for the duration of a finger snap;
Second, one should not allow drowsiness to blanket one's mind even for the briefest moment;
Third, one should not conceive of [an inherently existent] being even for the briefest moment;
Fourth, one should not forget one's resolve to attain *bodhi* even for the briefest moment.

There are yet four more dharmas:

114b First, one should always engage in quiet sitting [meditation] and refrain from joining together with groups;

Second, one should always delight in meditative walking;

Third, one always contemplates all dharmas without any conception of their being either new or old;

Fourth, one should never depart from the profound dharmas of emptiness, signlessness, and wishlessness.

Again, there are four additional dharmas:

First, one cultivates the four *dhyāna*s but does not cultivate worldly *dhyāna* meditation. Thus, in one's cultivation of the four immeasurable minds, one brings forth thoughts of compassion focusing on beings as the objective condition, but without seizing on any mark [of the existence] of any being;

Second, although one cultivates the [immeasurable] mind of kindness, one does not perceive any [inherently existent] being as the object. Although one cultivates the [immeasurable] mind of sympathetic joy, one does not crave happiness [for oneself]. And, although one cultivates the [immeasurable] mind of equanimity, one never forsakes any being;

Third, although one may perceive oneself as compliant with the four lineage bases of the *ārya*s, one does not take that as a basis for elevating oneself and looking down on others;

Fourth, one personally engages in the accumulation of extensive learning while also practicing in accordance with what one has learned.

These are the [four sets of] four dharmas [as presented in that scripture]. There is an additional related topic, as below:

One who has no wisdom and has no vigor
and yet dwells alone in an isolated place
then acquires four dharmas
and also acquires yet another four dharmas.
He also encounters three additional situations.
Circumstances such as these are as described by the Buddha.

Of all the meritorious qualities, the *bhikṣu* who dwells in a forest hermitage should diligently cultivate these, [namely wisdom and vigor]. Why? Because, of all the meritorious qualities associated with a forest hermitage, it is these two factors that are able to generate all of the [other] meritorious qualities.

If a *bhikṣu* were instead to give into delusion and indolence while abiding in a forest hermitage, he will acquire four wrong dharmas:

First, he will spend much of his time sleeping;
Second, he will become much inclined to want offerings;
Third, he will take advantage of these [special] circumstances[285] to pretend to be extraordinary;
Fourth, he will become unhappy with dwelling in a forest hermitage.

He will also acquire four additional dharmas:
First, he will develop overweening pride due to which he will think he has already attained what he has not yet attained;
Second, he will come to abhor profound scriptures;
Third, he will ruin [his ability to realize] the dharmas of emptiness, signlessness, and wishlessness;
Fourth, his mind will generate hatred for those who uphold the profound scriptures.

There are three additional circumstances that might occur. If he abides in a forest hermitage while failing in vigor and having no wisdom, he may meet some woman and fall into behavior contrary to the Dharma due to which he either commits a *saṃghāvaśeṣa* offense, commits a grave offense, or transgresses against the moral precepts and returns to lay life.[286] These are the three.

There are additional related topics, as below:

> Extensive discussion of dharmas practiced in solitary wilderness life
> as well as the dharmas associated with the almsround
> and the virtues of practicing the other ten *dhūta* austerities—
> all of these should also be extensively explained.

In the course of the preceding discussion, we have presented an extensive explanation of two of the twelve *dhūta* austerities.[287] The meritorious qualities of the other ten *dhūta* austerities should be similarly understood. How so? This is because these two practices have served to open the door into the other ten *dhūta* austerities. Thus the others may now be easily understood. As for those other ten *dhūta* austerities, they are:

First, wearing robes made [only] of cast-off rags;
Second, [taking one's daily meal in but] a single sitting;
Third, always sitting, [even when sleeping];
Fourth, having taken the meal, not accepting food or drink at the wrong times;
Fifth, possessing only a single three-part set of robes;
Sixth, wearing an animal hair robe;
Seventh, laying out one's sitting mat wherever one happens to be;
Eighth, dwelling at the foot of a tree;
114c Ninth, dwelling out in the open;
Tenth, dwelling in a charnel field.

"Cast-off rag robes" refers to those that have been thrown away by others. After having accepted them, one then wears them. "Accepting" refers here to either mental or verbal assent.

"In but a single sitting" refers to taking one's meal at the first place one accepted it and then refraining from taking any further food [for that entire day].

"Always sitting" means one never lies down, even at night.

"After the meal, refraining from any beverages" refers to not accepting any beverage at the wrong time,[288] not even those made merely with crystalized sugar or other nutritional substances.

"Possessing only the single set of three robes" means one only accepts that single set of three robes and does not collect any other clothing whatsoever.

"Wearing an animal hair robe" refers to wearing a robe made of cloth woven from coarse animal hairs such as felt cloth or *kambala* (wool) cloth.

"Laying out one's sitting mat wherever one happens to be" refers to simply going along with whatever sitting spot is available that does not involve causing someone else to get up and move.

"Dwelling at the foot of a tree" refers to delighting in dwelling out beneath the trees, never going into a sheltered location.

"Dwelling out in the open" simply refers to living out on the open ground.

"Dwelling in a charnel field" refers to always spending the night in the area where the dead bodies are cast off in order to accord with the mind of renunciation.

This is what is meant by the twelve *dhūta* austerities that facilitate purity in the observance of the moral precepts.

There are ten benefits from wearing cast-off rag robes, namely:

First, one does not have to mix with the laity simply to acquire robes;

Second, one need not appear to solicit robes simply to acquire clothing;

Third, nor is one compelled to present the appearance of finding some expedient to discuss obtaining robes;

Fourth, one is not compelled to go off and search in the four directions in order to obtain robes;

Fifth, even if one does not obtain a robe, one is still free of distress;

Sixth, even if one does obtain a robe, one is not elated;

Seventh, worthless material is easily come by in a way that does not risk committing transgressions;

Eighth, this practice accords with the initially received explanation of the methods for obtaining the four requisites;[289]

Ninth, one thereby becomes just another one of those who wear coarse [and common] clothing;

Tenth, one thereby avoids becoming the object of others' covetousness.

[Taking one's meal in but] a single sitting also has ten benefits, as follows:

First, one does not experience the weariness and inconvenience of going off in search of a second meal;

Second, as a consequence, one accepts but little [food];

Third, there is none of the weariness and inconvenience entailed by what one would consume [by compelling others to provide additional meals];

Fourth, one is spared the weariness and inconvenience of readying oneself [for an additional meal];

Fifth, one adopts an approach to eating that is consistent with more refined practice;

Sixth, one eats only after one's previous meal has been entirely digested;

Seventh, one devotes less effort to fending off difficulties [associated with obtaining food];
Eighth, one has fewer illnesses;
Ninth, one's body feels lighter and more at ease;
Tenth, one's experience of the body is pleasant.

Always sitting [and never lying down to sleep] also has ten benefits, as follows:[290]

First, one does not seek physical pleasure;
Second, one does not seek pleasure from sleeping;
Third, one does seek pleasure from [good] bedding;
Fourth, one is spared the aches associated with lying down on a sleeping mat;
Fifth, one does not pursue physical desires;
Sixth, it becomes easy to achieve success in sitting in *dhyāna* meditation;
Seventh, it becomes easy to study and recite scriptures;
Eighth, one spends less time sleeping;
Ninth, one's body feels light and rises easily;
Tenth, one devotes but little mental effort to seeking sitting cushions, bedding, and clothing;

There are also ten benefits of refraining from accepting food or drink at the wrong time,[291] after one has already eaten, as follows:

First, one thereby avoids excessive eating;
Second, one does not become full when eating;
Third, one avoids desire for fine flavors;
Fourth, one has fewer things one otherwise desires;
Fifth, one has fewer interfering difficulties;
Sixth, one has fewer illnesses;
Seventh, one easily feels full;
Eighth, one is easily supported;
Ninth, one is easily satisfied;
Tenth, one's body remains free of weariness when sitting in *dhyāna* meditation or studying scriptures.

Possessing only the single three-part set of robes also has ten benefits, as follows:

First, one is spared the weariness and inconvenience associated with seeking robes beyond the single three-part set of robes;
Second, one is spared the weariness and inconvenience of storing and protecting [additional clothing];
Third, one collects fewer things;
Fourth, one is satisfied with whatever one is wearing; 115a
Fifth, this refines one's practice of the moral precepts;
Sixth, one remains free of encumbrances when traveling;
Seventh, one's body feels lighter and more at ease;
Eighth, this practice accords with standards of practice for dwelling in a forest hermitage;
Ninth, no matter where one goes, one has nothing that one treasures;
Tenth, one's practice accords with the path.

Accepting robes made of animal hair also has ten benefits, as follows:
First, one is a wearer of coarse clothes;
Second, one seeks but little;
Third, one can sit down anywhere;
Fourth, one can lie down anywhere;
Fifth, it is easy to wash;
Sixth, it is easy to dye;
Seventh, it is seldom ruined by insects;
Eighth, it is difficult to ruin;
Ninth, one has no need of any additional clothing;
Tenth, one does not neglect one's pursuit of the path.

Laying out one's sitting mat wherever one happens to be also has ten benefits, as follows:
First, one is spared the weariness and difficulty of seeking out a good monastic dwelling in which to live;
Second, one is spared the weariness and difficulty of seeking out a good seat and bed;
Third, one avoids aggravating those of senior monastic rank;
Fourth, one gives no cause for distress to those of junior monastic rank;
Fifth, one has few wants;
Sixth, one has few tasks;

Seventh, one uses whatever is available in the course of things;
Eighth, since one uses but little, one has but few responsibilities;
Ninth, one avoids the creation of causes or conditions for disputes;
Tenth, one avoids appropriating a spot used by someone else.

Dwelling beneath a tree also has ten benefits, as follows:
First, one is spared the weariness and inconvenience of seeking out a sheltered dwelling;
Second, one is spared the weariness and inconvenience of seeking lodging;[292]
Third, one is spared the weariness and inconvenience of indulging one's own preferences;
Fourth, one is spared the weariness and inconvenience of appropriating things for one's own use;
Fifth, one does not even have an address;
Sixth, one has no disputes;
Seventh, one complies with the dharma regulating the four necessities;
Eighth, one uses but little, uses only what is easily obtained, and avoids transgressions;
Ninth, one accords with correct cultivation of the path;
Tenth, one need not practice amid the noisiness of groups.

Dwelling in a charnel field also has ten benefits, as follows:
First, one is always acquiring the perception of impermanence;
Second, one is always acquiring the perception of death;
Third, one is always acquiring the perception of the unloveliness [of the body];
Fourth, one is always acquiring the perception of the unenjoyability of all worldly existence;
Fifth, one is always developing renunciation of all who are dear to oneself;
Sixth, one is always attaining the mind of compassion;
Seventh, one abandons all frivolous restlessness;
Eighth, one's mind always abides in renunciation;
Ninth, one remains diligent in the cultivation of vigor;
Tenth, one is able to dispel all fears.

Dwelling out in the open also has ten benefits, as follows:
First, one does not have to find a tree to dwell beneath;
Second, one abandons everything one owns;
Third, one remains free of disputes;
Fourth, when going elsewhere, one has nothing one treasures;
Fifth, one seldom indulges frivolous restlessness;
Sixth, one is able to endure wind, rain, cold, heat, mosquitoes, horseflies, poisonous insects, and such;
Seventh, one remains unpierced by the thorn of noise;[293]
Eighth, one avoids arousing the hatred of other beings;
Ninth, one is himself also able to enjoy freedom from sorrow and hostility;
Tenth, one is able to avoid places frequented by noisy crowds;

> As explained for the five types of solitary wilderness dweller, 115b
> just so understand correctness in the other meritorious qualities.
> In instances where one is to study, recite, or teach others,
> one may leave one's solitary wilderness dwelling.

There are five distinct categories of *bhikṣu*s who dwell in a forest hermitage, namely:

First, there are those who, with evil intentions, seek gain and offerings;
Second, there are those who practice in a forest hermitage because of their own stupidity and dull faculties;
Third, there are those who establish a forest hermitage because they are insane, deluded, or deranged;
Fourth, there are those who establish a forest hermitage in order to practice the *dhūta* austerities;
Fifth, there are those who establish a forest hermitage because it is a practice praised by all buddhas, bodhisattvas, worthies, and *ārya*s.

Of these five categories of forest hermitage dwellers, those taking up the practice in order to cultivate the *dhūta* austerities and those taking up the practice because it has been praised by all buddhas, bodhisattvas, worthies, and *ārya*s are both good, whereas the other three may be reprimanded.

Just as with this fivefold distinction among those dwelling in a forest hermitage, so too should one distinguish and know [the differences among] the practitioners of the other eleven *dhūta* austerities.

Question: The Buddha said that whosoever has taken up the practice of dwelling in a forest hermitage should never abandon it. If there are extenuating circumstances, is it or is it not permissible to abandon it?

Response:

> One may leave one's forest hermitage
> in order to study or recite scriptures.

If a *bhikṣu* wishes to receive others' teachings on the study or recitation of the Dharma of the scriptures, or, alternatively, if he wishes to instruct others in such study or recitation, he may leave his forest hermitage and come into the stupa or temple. It is permissible to leave for these purposes.

> When teaching others in study and recitation,
> one should not do so wishing to attract offerings or support.
> Rather, one should immediately bring to mind the Buddha, [thinking],
> "Even[294] the Buddha had endeavors he was intent on accomplishing."

When one emerges from his isolated forest hermitage to teach others in study and recitation, one should not do so seeking to attract respect or offerings of support. Rather, one should bring to mind the Buddha, thinking, "If even the Buddha[295] had endeavors he was intent on accomplishing, how much the more should this be so for someone like me?"

"Bringing to mind the Buddha" in this context refers to recalling that
the Buddha is the Tathāgata, the One of Right and Universal Enlighten-
ment, one to whom even the *deva*s, dragons, spirits, *gandharva*s, *asura*s,
*garuḍa*s, *kiṃnara*s, *mahoraga*s, Śakra, ruler of the *deva*s, the Four Heavenly
115c Kings, humans, and nonhumans all make offerings, one who serves as the
unsurpassable field of merit for all beings. [One recalls that] not even he
seeks offerings or support from anyone. He just continues on in pursuing
the endeavors he has taken up. [Thus one reflects:] "Now I am one who still
does not know anything, one who is just a beginner in the training. How then
could I be worthy to receive anyone's offerings?"

Additionally, one should reflect as follows:

> I am the one who should be devoted
> to making offerings to all beings,
> for, rather than expecting them to make offerings,
> I should be benefiting myself while also benefiting others.

What then is meant by "benefiting oneself"? If one esteems the receiving of offerings [from others], then he loses the merit that would otherwise arise through giving the gift of Dharma. If, on the other hand, one refrains from esteeming the receiving of offerings, then one may acquire the meritorious qualities arising from giving the Dharma to others.

What then is meant by "benefiting others"? If one esteems others' offerings and then teaches them to study and recite scriptures, they will then think, "The teacher instructs us only in order to gain worldly benefit for himself and not for the sake of the Dharma." If someone makes offerings to his spiritual teacher when under the influence of these sorts of thoughts, he will not reap a great amount of merit. If, on the other hand, he were to feel profound esteem for the teacher solely out of reverence for the Dharma, he would acquire an immense amount of merit. This is what constitutes "benefiting others."

> In one's striving to acquire wisdom from others,
> one should not cherish even one's own body or life.

If the practitioner wishes to seek wisdom from others, he should then be willing even to sacrifice his own body and life in this quest. "Sacrifice" means that for the sake of acquiring wisdom one is so diligent, vigorous, and reverently respectful of his spiritual teacher that he does not even cherish his own body and life.

Question: Why should one, in striving for wisdom, revere the spiritual teacher even to the point that one does not even cherish one's own body and life?

Response:

> If every one of his words and every one of his thoughts
> were to be accorded that very number of *kalpa*s
> during which one might bow in reverence to the spiritual teacher
> able to teach this treatise,

> as one also took care to avoid any flattering or devious thought,
> and, suffused with deep affection, [bowed in] reverence to him
> day and night without cease, [one should indeed wish to do so,]
> continuing on even to the end of just such a number of *kalpa*s.

[If one allotted a number of *kalpa*s of devotion] corresponding to however many words are in the treatises taught by one's spiritual teacher in addition to however many thoughts he used in providing that instruction, and if the mind of the beneficiary of the teachings remained entirely free of any flattery and deviousness in his demonstrations of reverence performed without cherishing his own body and life, and if he carried on with that reverence day and night with earnestness that remained undiminished from beginning to end—although one might indeed carry through with just such devotion, one still would be unable to adequately repay the kindness of the spiritual teacher's benefiting one with the wisdom of this treatise.

The disciple should therefore abandon any thoughts of flattery or deviousness, should not selfishly cherish his own body and life, and should crush any arrogance. Even were the teacher to slight him, his thoughts of reverence and affectionate regard should remain undiminished. Rather, he should bring forth thoughts of deep affection for him, should bring forth the most profoundly sincere reverence for him, should think of the spiritual teacher as he would his own parents, should think of him as a great teaching master, should think of him as his good spiritual guide, should think of him as someone able to do what is most difficult, and should realize that [the teacher's kindness] is something difficult to ever adequately repay.

If one's spiritual teacher has already permitted them, then one should take
116a up the tasks one usually does, for one does not need the teacher's [additional] permission to do so. If there are other tasks that arise, then one is to consult the teacher for his opinion, whereupon one performs the tasks accordingly. Thus one should also cherish and esteem whatever one's teacher cherishes and esteems.

One must not seek to reap any worldly advantage from one's relationship with one's spiritual teacher. One must not seek the teacher's praise and must also not seek name and fame [on account of that relationship]. Rather, one should seek only to obtain the Dharma jewel of wisdom.

In the event the teacher makes some mistake, one should allow it to always remain a private matter. If the teacher has committed some infraction and it has come to light, one should use some expedient to conceal it.

One should proclaim and make widely known the meritorious qualities possessed by one's teacher while also sincerely delighting in listening to, accepting, upholding, comprehending, contemplating, and practicing in accord with the import of his teachings.

As for striving to "benefit oneself and also benefit others," one must not become a mere straw disciple, must not become a disastrous disciple,[296] must not become a defiled disciple, must not become a disciple who allows [the lineage to go to] ruin, and must not become a useless disciple. One must not allow oneself to fall into any such transgressions as these.

One must abide solely within the dharma appropriate to a good disciple. One should make offerings to one's spiritual teacher. This is as described in the *Pratyutpanna*[*-samādhi*]*-sūtra* in which the Buddha told Bhadrapāla:

> If a bodhisattva wishes to acquire this *samādhi,* he should be diligent and vigorous in bringing forth thoughts of reverential esteem toward all his teachers, thoughts recognizing the rare good fortune to encounter them. In the case of those from whom one has received teachings personally spoken by them or those from whom one has obtained volumes of scriptural texts, one should express deeply sincere reverence for these teachers, regarding them as one would one's own parents, regarding them as one's good spiritual guides, and regarding them as great teaching masters. This is because they are able to teach Dharma such as this which is able to assist one's realization of *bodhi.*
>
> Bhadrapāla, whether one strives to follow in the bodhisattva path or one seeks the way of a *śrāvaka* disciple, if one were to fail to bring forth thoughts of deep reverence for the teacher as the source of one's becoming able to study and recite this Dharma, if one were to fail to think of one's teacher as one would one's own parents, regarding him as one's good spiritual guide, and regarding him as a great teaching master, it would then be impossible for one to correctly understand[297] this Dharma in such a way that it would not perish but rather would abide for a long time without disappearing.

Why is this? Bhadrapāla, it is because of just such failure to accord reverence that the Buddha's Dharma disappears.

Therefore, Bhadrapāla, whether one strives to follow in the bodhisattva path or one seeks the way of a *śrāvaka* disciple, were one to bring forth thoughts of reverential respect for whoever one heard this Dharma from and whoever was the source of one's being able to study, recite, or write out this Dharma, bringing forth thoughts regarding him as one would one's own parents, regarding him as one's good spiritual guide, and regarding him as a great master of the teachings—if one were able to do that, then it is indeed possible that whatsoever one has studied, recited, and written out, and whatsoever one had not obtained but has now obtained might now be able to remain [in this world] for a long time.

And why is this? Because it is due to having a mind of reverential respect that the Buddha's Dharma does not disappear. Therefore, Bhadrapāla, I am now telling you: One must bring forth thoughts of profound reverential respect toward teachers such as this, bringing forth thoughts regarding them as one would one's own parents, regarding them as good spiritual guides, and regarding them as great masters of the teachings. This being so, one is to comply with what I have herein instructed.

Chapter 33[298]

Aids to Gaining the Fruits of *Śīla*

In order to pursue extensive learning and then practice in accord with the way it was taught after understanding the meaning of that extensive learning, a bodhisattva such as this becomes able to purify his practice of *śīla*. Thus one should cultivate the dharmas used to purify one's practice of *śīla* (moral virtue).

Question: Which dharmas are able to purify one's practice of *śīla*? 116b

Response:

> Guard the actions of body, speech, and mind
> while also not apprehending any dharma by which one guards it.
> Never permit any admixture of the view of a self
> or any of the other views.
> Dedicate the merit from this to the attainment of all-knowledge.
> These four methods purify one's practice of *śīla*.

If the practitioner cultivates these four dharmas, his observance of *śīla* will naturally become pure. "Guarding the actions of body, speech, and mind" refers to always using right mindfulness in one's physical, verbal, and mental actions even to the point that one does not allow oneself to err through committing even the most minor transgressions, acting in this like the tortoise who always takes such care in guarding his head and feet.

Because this practitioner deeply delights in emptiness, in his comprehension of the supreme meaning, he does not even apprehend [the existence of] any dharma by which one guards the three types of actions. There are others who, although they do indeed perceive the emptiness of dharmas, they are still of the opinion that the knower of emptiness remains [as an existent entity]. It is for this reason that [the verse] says, "Never permit any admixture of the view imputing a self," the view of a being, the view of a person, the view of a soul, the view of a life,[299] or the view of a knower.

"Dedicating [merit to the realization of] all-knowledge" means one does not dedicate the merit arising from upholding the moral precepts to any other sort of fortunate result, but rather only dedicates it to the liberation of all beings through one's quest to attain buddhahood. These are the four [dharmas that enable the purification of moral virtue].

There are yet another four dharmas by which one is able to bring about the purification of one's practice of *śīla*, namely:

> If one has no conceptions of a self or anything belonging to a self,
> if one also has no annihilationist or eternalist views,
> and if one penetrates the dharma explaining multiple conditions,
> one will then be able to purify one's practice of *śīla*.

"Freedom from conceptions of a self or anything belonging to a self" refers to not being attached to thoughts imputing the existence of a self or anything belonging to a self. One need only realize that these ideas are empty, false, and inverted and hence there is no dharma of [the existence of] a self.

One "has no annihilationist or eternalist views" because annihilationist and eternalist views are possessed of numerous faults.

As for "penetrating the dharma that explains multiple conditions," by knowing that all dharmas are products of many conditions and hence are devoid of any fixed nature of their own, one practices the Middle Way.

[By availing oneself of] four such dharmas such as these, one is able to purify one's practice of *śīla*.

There are four additional dharmas through which one is able to purify one's practice of *śīla*, namely:

> One practices the four lineage bases of the *ārya*s,
> adopts the twelve *dhūta* austerities,
> also does not delight in the noise of crowds,
> and bears in mind why one left home [to become a monastic].

"The four lineage bases of the *ārya*s" refers to being satisfied with whatever robes one has already obtained, to being satisfied with whatever food and drink one has already obtained, to being satisfied with whatever dwelling place[300] one has already obtained, and to delighting in severance and delighting in cultivation.

"The twelve *dhūta* austerities" are:
Adopting the dharma of dwelling in a forest hermitage;
Obtaining one's food through the almsround;
Wearing robes made of cast-off rags;
[Taking one's daily meal in but] a single sitting;
Always sitting [to sleep, never lying down];
Having taken the meal, not accepting food or drink at the wrong times;
Possessing only a single three-part set of robes;
Wearing only an animal hair robe;
Laying out one's sitting mat wherever one happens to be;
Dwelling at the foot of a tree;
Dwelling out in the open (lit. "on empty ground");
Dwelling in a charnel field.

"Not delighting in the noise of crowds" refers to avoiding meeting together with either laypeople or monastics. There are those who, although they have taken up the dharma of dwelling in a forest hermitage, because they have many acquaintances and friends, often have many people coming 116c
and going. Therefore, it refers here to "not delighting in the noise of crowds," whether through not going off to other places or through being disinclined to gather together with others.

As for "bearing in mind why one left home [to become a monastic]," one who is focused on *śīla* practice reflects thus, "Why did I leave the home life to become a monastic?" Having pondered this, because one accords with the endeavors appropriate to the monastic's life and wishes to succeed in these, he practices in a manner that accords with the way [monastic cultivation] was taught. These are the four.

There are another four dharmas by which one can purify one's practice of *śīla,* namely:

> [One sees that] the five aggregates have no arising or destruction,
> [sees] the six elements[301] as like the nature of dharmas,
> sees that the six sense faculties are empty [of inherent existence],

and does not become attached to worldly expressions.
[Practice] that accords with these four dharmas
also enables one to purify one's practice of *śīla*.

As for "[seeing that] the five aggregates have no arising or destruction," this means that, by contemplating the five aggregates from root to branch, one perceives their absence of arising and destruction.

As for "[seeing that] the six elements" consisting of earth and so forth "are like the nature of dharmas,"[302] this means that, just as the nature of dharmas cannot be apprehended, so too, the six elements cannot be apprehended, either.

One realizes that, although the six sense faculties involve pain, pleasure, and such, they do so through causes and conditions linked to the mind and mental dharmas. Thus, by resorting to investigative applications of right wisdom, one realizes that they are empty [of any inherent existence].

One then utterly comprehends the nature of all three of these associated categories, realizing that in every case they are entirely empty [of inherent existence].

There are practitioners who develop an attachment to emptiness that then also hinders cultivation of the path. Hence it states here that one must not develop an attachment to emptiness that simply conforms to worldly uses of the word "emptiness."

Dharmas such as these enable one to purify one's practice of *śīla*.

Question: If this is truly so, why do you speak here of the dharmas of the five aggregates?

Response: It is because they are empty. All dharmas of the five aggregates are empty. As for the very last part where it states that one must not become attached to emptiness, this means that even "emptiness" should be relinquished. If one accords with this, then there will be no dharma of erroneous doubtfulness impeding one's practice of *śīla*.

Question: Because the dharmas of the five aggregates are possessed of characteristic marks and that which can be marked, they do therefore definitely exist. Take for instance the [canonical] declarations that "the form aggregate is characterized by being assailed by what is painful"[303] and "awareness of pain and pleasure is the characteristic of the feeling aggregate." Given that they obviously possess such characteristics, how can one claim that [the aggregates] are neither empty nor non-empty?

Response:

Affliction and destruction are marks of the form aggregate.
What all goes into making this form?
If affliction is indeed a characteristic mark of form,
apart from its marks, there is nothing amenable to being marked.

And where then do these characteristic marks abide?
There is no mark nor anything that can be marked.
The entire world is finally nonexistent.
There is neither any mark nor anything that can be marked.

Characteristic marks and that which can be marked
are neither conjoined nor not conjoined.
In their coming forth, they have no place from which they come.
In going away, they also have no place to which they go.

If one posits either a conjoining or a nonconjoining
through which one establishes either marks or what is markable,
then to proceed in this way is mistaken
with regard to both marks and what is markable.

This would be to use marks to establish what is markable. 117a
[However,] marks themselves are not self-established.
Since even marks themselves cannot be established,
how then could they [be used to] establish what is markable?

The beings of the world are so extremely pitiable,
for they distinguish marks and what is markable,
become deluded in pursuing all manner of deviant paths,
and are cheated and deceived by deviant teachers.

Marks and what is markable then are just
devoid of marks and devoid of anything that can be marked.

Given such a visibly apparent situation as this,
how could one fail to realize [what is so obvious]?

Pursuant to imputations of the existence of marks and the markable,
there exist such [merely] conceptual elaborations as these.
And whenever such conceptual elaborations as these arise,
one then falls into a position associated with afflictions.[304]

Moreover, the practitioner employs the gateway of [understanding that all phenomena] neither come into existence nor pass away to facilitate the contemplation of the aggregates, sense realms, and sense bases as empty [of inherent existence]. This is as described here:

The dharmas of birth, aging, sickness, and death,
when arising, have no place from which they come.
The dharmas of birth, aging, sickness, and death,
when extinguished, have no place to which they go.

It is the nature of the aggregates, sense realms, and sense bases that,
when arising, they have no place from which they come,
and, when extinguished, they have no place to which they go.
Just so is the meaning of the Buddha's Dharma.

So too with fire, which is not in the human effort used to make it,
is also not present in the friction drill or wood,
and is not in their coming together, either,
even as it still does exist due to their all having come together.

If the fuel is entirely consumed, the fire will then die out.
Yet, when it does die out, there is no place to which it goes.
It exists due to the coming together of conditions,
yet, if those conditions scatter, it becomes entirely nonexistent.

So too is this the case with the eye consciousness
that does not abide in the eye,
also does not abide in visual forms,
also does not abide between them,

also does not abide in their combination,
also is not found apart from them,
also does not come thither from elsewhere,
yet does exist due to such a combination,

and which, when the combining scatters, then becomes nonexistent.
So too it also is with all dharmas.
When arising, there is no place from which they come,
and when extinguished, there is no place to which they go.

This is analogous to a dragon's mental powers
through which the dark clouds appear.
They do not emerge from the body of the dragon,
nor do they arrive from some other place,

and yet the rain from these great dark clouds
pours down throughout the entire world,
after which it then evaporates,
yet has no place to which it goes.

Just as such clouds neither come nor go,
so too it is with all dharmas.
When they arise, there is no place from which they come, 117b
and, when destroyed, there is no place to which they go.

They are also like a man who has been painted on a wall
that does not reside in any or all of the colors,
also does not reside in their combination,
and also does not abide in the wall.

It does not abide in the painter,
nor does it abide in the paintbrush.
It does not come forth from elsewhere,
yet it exists because of all of these coming together.

When that combination scatters, it then no longer exists.
So too it is with all dharmas.

When they exist, there is no place from which they come.
When they cease to exist, there is no place to which they go.

The lamp flame does not abide in its oil,
also does not emerge from its wick,
and also does not arrive from some other place,
and yet, because of the oil and the wick, it exists.

If its causes and conditions end, it is extinguished.
When it is extinguished, there is no place to which it goes.
All dharmas' characteristics of coming forth and departing
are in every case also just like this.

There are another four dharmas by which one can purify one's practice of *śīla,* namely:

One is able to contemplate the nature of one's own body
and refrains from elevating oneself or diminishing others.
Since these two cannot be apprehended,
one abides in mental pliancy, free of any conceit.
One contemplates all dharmas as uniformly equal.
These four serve to purify one's *śīla*.

As for being "able to contemplate the nature of one's own body," the practitioner has this thought: "This body of mine is characterized by impurity, impermanence, and mortality. What true worth[305] does it possess?"

Having reflected in this manner, one does not elevate oneself and look down on others.

Because one has a resolute belief that both self and others are devoid of "I" and "mine," one realizes that they cannot be apprehended at all.

As for "mental pliancy," having acquired these dharmas, one's mind then abides in lightness, suppleness, and the capacity to endure and acquiesce in dharmas. It is due to this mental pliancy and delight that one does not elevate himself above others.

As for "contemplating all dharmas as uniformly equal," this means that, because [one realizes] they are empty, one contemplates all conditioned and unconditioned dharmas as equal and devoid of any distinctions as to those which are superior, those which are middling, and those which are inferior. This is as described here:

> If one would posit that, because of the inferior,
> there thereby exist the middling and the superior,
> since the inferior does not itself create the middling or the superior,
> how then could they exist because of the inferior?
> And for the inferior itself to have become "inferior,"
> middling and superior would definitely have existed beforehand.
>
> If one would posit that, because of the middling,
> there thereby exist the inferior and the superior,
> since the middling does not itself create the inferior or the superior,
> how could they exist because of the middling?
> And for the middling itself to have become "middling,"
> inferior and the superior would definitely have existed beforehand.
>
> If one would posit that, because of the superior,
> there thereby exist the middling and the inferior,
> since the superior does not itself create the middling or the inferior,
> how could they exist because of the superior?
> And for the superior itself to have become "superior," 117c
> middling and inferior would definitely have existed beforehand.
>
> It cannot be that, due to the inferior, [middling and superior exist].
> Nor can it be that it is *not* because of it [that they exist].
> If [the middling and superior] already existed previously,
> they could not exist because of the inferior.
> And if [the middling and superior] were previously nonexistent,
> how could they succeed in becoming the middling and superior?
>
> It cannot be that, due to the middling, [inferior and superior exist].
> Nor can it be that it is *not* because of it [that they exist].
>
> If [the inferior and the superior] already existed previously,
> they could not exist because of the middling.
> And if [the inferior and the superior] were previously nonexistent,
> how could they succeed in becoming the inferior and the superior?

It cannot be that, due to the superior, [inferior and middling exist].
Nor can it be that it is *not* because of it [that they exist].
If [the middling and the inferior] definitely already existed,
they could not exist because of the superior.
And if [middling and inferior] were certainly previously nonexistent,
how could they succeed in becoming middling and inferior?

Additionally, because their emptiness is of a singular character, one contemplates all dharmas as uniformly equal. So too it is with beings. This is as described here:

In the midst of what is empty, the wise
do not speak of any distinguishable characteristic signs.
In the singularity of emptiness, there are no differentiations.
If one is able to perceive emptiness in this manner
this then is to see the Buddha,
for the Buddha is no different from emptiness.

It is said that all buddhas are one,
all beings are one,
all dharmas are but a single dharma,
and no distinctions exist between superior, middling, or inferior.

All of the buddhas, the bhagavats,
transcend both inherently existent and externally created nature.
So too do all beings
transcend both inherently existent and externally created nature.

All dharmas are also just so
in transcending inherently existent and externally created natures.
It is because of just such causes and conditions
that they are said to be of a singular character.

If one claims that buddhas exist, this is wrong.
If one claims no buddhas exist, this is also wrong.
If one claims that beings exist, this is wrong.
If one claims that no beings exist, this is also wrong.

If one claims dharmas exist, that is wrong.
If one claims that no dharmas exist, that is also wrong.
It is because they transcend both "existence" and "nonexistence"
that they are said to be uniformly equal.

All the buddhas, the bhagavats,
all beings, and also all dharmas
are in every case ungraspable.
This is what is meant by the uniform equality of all dharmas.

All buddhas, beings,
and dharmas have no differences.
Because one cannot make any distinctions among them,
they are said to be of a single uniform equality.

All buddhas, all beings, 118a
and all dharmas,
even as they enter into arising, enduring, and destruction,
abide in quiescent cessation and do not exist at all.

Nor do they have any place from which they have come,
nor do they have any place to which they go.
It is because of their neither coming nor going
that they are said to be of a single uniform equality.

All buddhas, all beings,
and all dharmas
are, in every case, entirely nonexistent
and utterly beyond all of the paths of existence.

These three are not equal,
are not unequal,
are not both equal and unequal,
and are neither equal nor unequal.
It is in this way that one explains all dharmas
as being in every case equal and devoid of distinctions.

There are another four dharmas by which one can purify one's practice of *śīla*. They are as described below:

> Being well able to maintain a resolute belief in emptiness,
> not being frightened by the dharma of signlessness,
> maintaining the great compassion toward beings,
> and being able to acquiesce in the nonexistence of self—
> It is through four dharmas such as these
> that one is also able to purify one's practice of *śīla*.

It is because of a practitioner's complete comprehension of all dharmas as devoid of any self-existent nature or any externally created nature that he is referred to as having "a resolute belief in emptiness." This is as described here:

> All dharmas whatsoever
> never arise on the basis of any inherently existent nature.
> If they arise from multiple conditions,
> they should then exist through that which is other.
>
> Given they do not arise through any inherently existent nature,
> how then could they arise through that which is other?
> If an inherently existent nature is not established,
> then any nature existing through some "other" is also nonexistent.
>
> If they transcend any arising from an inherently existent nature,
> then they are devoid of any inherently existent nature.
> If they have transcended any inherently existent nature,
> then they are [also] devoid of any mark of inherent existence.
>
> An inherently existent nature and marks of inherent existence
> do not exist on the basis of conjoining
> and do not become nonexistent through separation.
> Hence they are both devoid of any fixed existence.
>
> Dharmas cannot be produced from that which is other,
> nor can they be produced from themselves,
> nor can they be produced by both self and other,
> and yet, apart from those two, they cannot be produced, either.

If no inherent existence can be established for itself,
how then could it possibly be produced from what is other?
If one departs from dharmas that are mere worldly conventions,
then "self" and "other" are entirely nonexistent.

If that which is other were produced from that which is other,
then that "other" would have no substance of its own.
If it had no substance, then it could not even exist.
From what thing then can there be the arising of what is other?

Because it has no substance of its own, 118b
production from some other is also a nonexistent [possibility].
Since all four [tetralemma ideas] are empty [of inherent existence],
no dharma whatsoever has any fixed arising or destruction.

As for "not being frightened by signlessness," it is because of one's resolute belief [in signlessness] and one's utter transcendence of all signs that one is not frightened. This is as described here:[306]

If everything is signless,
then everything is identical with whatever possesses signs.
Quiescent cessation is signless
and is identical with whatever is an existent dharma.[307]

If one contemplates the dharma of signlessness,
whatever is signless is [seen as] the same as what possesses signs.
If one says that one is cultivating signlessness,
that is just a noncultivation of signlessness.

Were one to relinquish all strategizing and attachments[308]
and designate that as constituting signlessness,
such seizing on this sign of having relinquished attachments
then becomes the very absence of liberation.

In general, it is because of the existence of grasping,
that then, because of that grasping, there then is relinquishing.
It is the abandonment of grasping and whatever thing is grasped[309]—
It is on this basis that one then refers to "relinquishing."

As for the one who grasps, the grasping to which he resorts,
as well as that dharma that is subject to being grasped,
whether as conjoined or separate, they are all entirely nonexistent,[310]
for these are all synonymous with quiescent cessation.

If any dharma's signs are established on the basis of causes,
this is just something devoid of any [inherently existent] nature.
Whatever is devoid of any [inherently existent] nature—
this is just something that is devoid of any [inherently existent] signs.

If a dharma has no [inherently existent] nature—
this is just something that is signless.
How can one assert that it has no [inherently existent] nature?
It is precisely because it is synonymous with signlessness.[311]

If one uses [such terms as] "existence" and "nonexistence,"
"both" and "neither" should be permissible as well,[312] for,
although one may speak thus, so long as one's mind is not attached,
one thereby remains free of any fault in doing so.

Where has there ever first existed some dharma
that, afterward, was not destroyed?
Wherever there was first some fire
that, afterward, was then extinguished,
the quiescent cessation of these existent signs
is identical to the quiescent cessation of whatsoever is signless.

Therefore, as for these words about quiescent cessation
as well as the one who speaks about quiescent cessation,
from the beginning onward, they have not been quiescent[313]
nor have they been nonquiescent,
nor have they been both quiescent and nonquiescent,
nor have they been neither quiescent nor nonquiescent.

Regarding "maintaining compassion toward beings," because beings are countless and boundless, one's mind of compassion is also expansive in that very same way. Also, the Dharma of all buddhas is measureless, boundless, and endless, like empty space. The mind of compassion is the very foundation

of the Dharma of all buddhas. It is because it is able to bring about the realization of the great Dharma that it is referred to as the "great" compassion. Among all beings, the one who is the greatest is the Buddha. It is because it 118c
is practiced by the Buddha that it is referred to as the "great" compassion.

As for "acquiescence in the dharma of nonself," one accomplishes this because one has a resolute faith in the true Dharma. It is because it is the one path to nirvana taken by all buddhas that it is known as "the dharma of nonself."

If one enters into this dharma and one's mind is unable to endure it, this is like putting a small plant into a fire, whereupon it is entirely burned up. However, if one puts real gold into a fire, it is able to endure it and it remains entirely undiminished.

In the same way, if a common person, one who has not cultivated roots of goodness, attempts to enter [the dharma of] nonself, he will be unable to bear it and will immediately bring forth erroneous doubts about it. This bodhisattva, however, has cultivated roots of goodness for countless lifetimes. His wisdom has become fiercely sharp and he is sustained by the protective mindfulness of all buddhas. Although he may not yet have cut off the fetters, when he enters into the dharma of nonself, his mind is able to endure and accept it.

"The dharma of nonself" is a reference to all such dharmas as the aggregates, the sense realms, the sense bases, and the twelvefold chain of causation. The causes and conditions through which one demolishes [the view of] self are as discussed earlier.

Therefore, if one wishes to purify one's practice of *śīla,* one should practice these four dharmas.

Furthermore:

> There are four individuals who destroy *śīla*
> even when seeming to uphold *śīla.*
> The practitioner should be vigorous
> in exerting self-control and taking care not to act [as they do].

In the "Kāśyapa" chapter of the *Jeweled Summit Sutra,* the Buddha told Kāśyapa:[314]

There are four kinds of *bhikṣu*s who break the moral precepts while seeming as if they are *bhikṣu*s who uphold the moral precepts. What are those four? Kāśyapa, there are *bhikṣu*s who are completely able to perfectly practice the moral precepts of the scriptures and yet claim that a self exists. Kāśyapa, this is what is meant by breaking the moral precepts while seeming as if one is upholding the moral precepts.

Then again, Kāśyapa, there are *bhikṣu*s who recite and retain the moral precept scriptures and guard their practice of the moral precepts, but who do not move from and never abandon their view of a real self in association with the body. This is what is meant by breaking the moral precepts while seeming as if one is upholding the moral precepts.

Yet again, Kāśyapa, there are *bhikṣu*s who are perfect in their practice of the twelve *dhūta* austerities while nonetheless maintaining the view that dharmas have a fixed existence. This is what is meant by breaking the moral precepts while seeming as if one is upholding the moral precepts.

Then again, Kāśyapa, there are *bhikṣu*s who focus on beings as the objective condition in their cultivation of the mind of kindness but who, on hearing that all conditioned things[315] are characterized by nonproduction, their minds are filled with terror. This is what is meant by breaking the moral precepts while seeming as if one is upholding the moral precepts.

Kāśyapa, these are the four kinds of persons who break the moral precepts even while seeming as if they are upholding the moral precepts.

Furthermore:

According to what the Bhagavat has taught,
there are four types of *śramaṇa*s
of which one should become the fourth
while distancing oneself from the first three kinds.[316]

As for these four kinds of *bhikṣu*s referred to here that are found in the "Kāśyapa" chapter, one should learn to become the fourth kind of *śramaṇa* while avoiding becoming any of the other three kinds. What then are those four? The Buddha told Kāśyapa:

There are four kinds of *śramaṇa*s, namely:

First, those who, merely in form and appearance, seem to be *śramaṇas*;

Second, those *śramaṇa*s who merely feign extraordinary deportment;
Third, those who are *śramaṇa*s simply because they covet fame and self-benefit;
Fourth, *śramaṇa*s who genuinely carry on right practice.

What is meant by one who is a *śramaṇa* merely in form and appearance? He adopts the form of the *śramaṇa* and adopts the appearance of a *śramaṇa,*
doing so specifically through wearing a *saṃghāṭī* robe, shaving off his hair 119a
and beard, and carrying a blackened bowl, while nonetheless still engaging in impure physical actions, impure verbal actions, and impure mental actions. He does not seek to reach nirvana and does not seek to become good. He is miserly and indolent and practices evil dharmas. He breaks the moral precepts and does not delight in cultivation of the path. This is what is meant by one who is a *śramaṇa* merely in form and appearance.

What is meant by the *śramaṇa* who merely feigns extraordinary deportment? He is perfect in the four kinds of deportment. He investigates the truths, is comfortable and serene in getting by on whatever robes and food he has already acquired, is devoted to the practice of the four lineage bases of the *ārya*s, avoids gathering together with either laypeople or monastics, and speaks but little, but he does all these things in order to seize the attentions of others with a mind that is not pure.

Deportment of this sort is not done for the sake of goodness, is not done for the sake of reaching nirvana, and is done with an implicit view that seizes on all dharmas as having a fixed and definite existence. [Such a practitioner] fears the dharmas of emptiness and nonexistence in just the same way as one might fear falling into a pit. Whenever he sees anyone who speaks of emptiness, he thinks of him as an enemy. This is what is meant by the *śramaṇa* who merely feigns extraordinary deportment.

What is meant by one who is a *śramaṇa* simply because he covets fame and self-benefit? There are those *śramaṇa*s who, although they are able to force themselves to uphold the moral precepts, as they do so, they think, "How can I cause other people to know me as one who upholds the moral precepts?"

Although they are able to force themselves to strive after extensive learning, [as they do so, they think,] "How can I cause other people to know me as someone possessed of extensive learning?"

Although they are able to force themselves to take up the dharma of abiding in a forest hermitage, [as they do so, they think,] "How can I cause other people to know that I am a forest hermitage dweller?"

Although they are able to force themselves to have but few wants, to be easily satisfied, and to practice the dharmas of one who dwells in solitude, [as they do so, they think,] "How can I cause other people to know that I have but few wants, am easily satisfied, and practice the dharmas of one who dwells in solitude?"

They do not do these things in order to develop a mind of renunciation, do not do them in order to destroy the afflictions, do not do them in order to strive in the eightfold right path of the *ārya*s, do not do them in order to reach nirvana, and do not do them in order to bring about the liberation of all beings. This is what is meant by the *śramaṇa* who covets fame and self-benefit.

What is meant by the *śramaṇa* who genuinely carries on right practice? There is a type of *śramaṇa* who does not retain any selfish cherishing even of his own body, how much the less might he cherish fame or self-benefit? On being taught that all dharmas are empty and that nothing whatsoever exists, his mind is filled with great joy and he proceeds to practice in accordance with that teaching.

He does not have any selfish cherishing even of nirvana as he carries on his practice of *brahmacarya,* how much the less might he have any selfish cherishing of [any station of rebirth within] the three realms?

He is not even attached to the view that sees the emptiness [of all dharmas], how much the less might he become attached to the existence of a self, a person, a being, a soul, a life, a knower, or a seer?

He seeks liberation even in the midst of the afflictions and does not seek it anywhere outside. He contemplates all dharmas as fundamentally pure and undefiled. This person relies only on himself and does not rely on anyone else. Through [his direct knowing of] the true character of all dharmas, he does not even covet the Dharma body, how much the less the form body. He sees dharmas as transcending marks and as inexpressible in words. He does not even make any discriminating distinctions among those in the community of *ārya*s who course in the unconditioned, how much the less might he do so among those in the common multitude of people? He does not for the sake of severance or for the sake of cultivation abhor samsara on the one hand and delight in nirvana on the other. For him, there is neither bondage nor liberation. He realizes that the Dharma of the buddhas has no fixed aspects and, having realized this, he neither comes and goes in samsara, nor opts to enter nirvana, either.

Kāśyapa, this is what is meant by the *śramaṇa* who accords with genuine practice. Kāśyapa, you should all be diligent in the practice of the genuine practice *śramaṇa*. Do not allow yourselves to be harmed for 119b
the sake of a reputation.

Moreover:

Do not uphold the practice of *śīla*
merely for the sake of kingship or other such things.
Also, do not uphold the practice of *śīla*
to obtain a particular rebirth or other such aims.

The practitioner who wishes to purify his practice of *śīla* should not practice it for the sake of such things as kingship. With regard to such things as becoming a king, when speaking for the benefit of the stalwart Pure Virtue, the Buddha said, "Son of good family, as for the bodhisattva who practices *śīla:*

He will never break a moral precept even at the cost of his own life;
He does not uphold the moral precepts hoping to become a king;
He does not uphold the moral precepts hoping to achieve celestial rebirth;
He does not uphold the moral precepts hoping to become Śakra, ruler of the *deva*s, hoping to become the Brahma Heaven King, or hoping to gain wealth, happiness, or unconstrained and independent power;
He does not uphold the moral precepts for the sake of fame or praise, for the sake of offerings, for the sake of a long life span, or for the sake of drink, food, robes, bedding, medicines, or other life-sustaining things;
He does not uphold the moral precepts in reliance on dharmas concerned with rebirths and such. Hence he does not do so for the sake of being reborn among *deva*s or humans;
He does not uphold the moral precepts because of concerns having to do with himself;

He does not uphold the moral precepts because of concerns having to do with others;
He does not uphold the moral precepts because of present-life concerns;
He does not uphold the moral precepts because of future-life concerns;
He does not uphold the moral precepts out of concerns associated with his physical form, out of concerns associated with feelings, perceptions, formative factors, or consciousnesses, out of concerns associated with the eyes, out of concerns associated with the sense bases, or out of concerns associated with the ears, nose, tongue, body, or mind faculty;
He does not uphold the moral precepts out of concerns associated with the desire realm, form realm, or formless realm;
He does not uphold the moral precepts to be liberated from the wretched destinies of the hell realm, the animal realm, the hungry ghost realm, or the *asura* realm;
He does not uphold the moral precepts out of fear of being poverty-stricken when reborn among the *deva*s;
He does not uphold the moral precepts out of fear of being poverty-stricken when reborn among humans;
He does not uphold the moral precepts out of fear of being poverty-stricken when reborn among the *yakṣa*s."

Question: If [this bodhisattva] does not [uphold the moral precepts] out of concern for these sorts of things, then for the sake of which sorts of things does he uphold the moral precepts?

Response:

It is because he wishes to cause the Three Jewels
to abide for a long time that he upholds the moral precepts.
It is because he wishes to obtain the many different sorts
of benefits that he upholds the moral precepts.

As for "causing the Three Jewels to abide for a long time":
It is in order to prevent the cutting off of the lineage of the buddhas that he upholds the moral precepts;

It is in order to turn the wheel of Dharma that he upholds the moral precepts;
It is in order to attract a community of *ārya*s that he upholds the moral precepts;
It is in order to gain liberation from birth, aging, sickness, death, lamentation, grief, pain, and melancholy that he upholds the moral precepts;
It is in order to facilitate the liberation of all beings that he upholds the moral precepts;
It is in order to cause all beings to gain peace and happiness that he upholds the moral precepts;
It is in order to cause beings to reach a peaceful and secure[317] place that he upholds the moral precepts;
It is in order to cultivate the *dhyāna* absorptions that he upholds the moral precepts;
It is in order to gain wisdom, liberation, and the knowledge and vision of liberation that he upholds the moral precepts.

These matters are just as extensively discussed in the *Pure Virtue Sutra*.

> The bodhisattva who is able in this fashion
> to perfect the practice of *śīla*
> will not lose the ten benefits 119c
> or the many other different types of benefits.
>
> Additionally, he will not fall down into
> erroneous paths associated with the four difficulties.
> He will not encounter the four dharmas associated with loss and
> he will not encounter the four dharmas associated with destruction,
>
> He will also gain the four dharmas
> by which one does not deceive the buddhas or others.
> He is able to pass beyond susceptibility to falling into the hells
> and the rest of the ten terror-inducing circumstances.

"Will not lose the ten benefits" refers to:
Not losing the ability to always become a wheel-turning king;
Not losing the non-neglectful mind when acting in that capacity;

Not losing the ability to always become Śakra, ruler of the *deva*s;
Not losing the non-neglectful mind when acting in that capacity;
Never losing one's quest to seek the path of all buddhas;
Never losing those things that all bodhisattvas are taught;
Never losing the unimpeded knowledge of eloquence;
Never losing [the pursuit of] the planting of roots of goodness and merit and the fulfillment of whatsoever one has vowed to accomplish;
Never losing that due to which one is praised by all buddhas, bodhisattvas, worthies and *ārya*s;
Never losing the ability to swiftly perfect the attainment of all-knowledge.

These are the ten [benefits of perfecting the practice of *śīla*].

"The many other different types of benefits" refers to never retreating from or losing one's many different sorts of meritorious qualities. This is as described in the sutras:

The bodhisattva who skillfully guards his ability to uphold the moral precepts:
Is always praised by the *deva*s;
Is well protected by the dragon kings;
Is the beneficiary of people's offerings;
Is always borne in mind by all buddhas;
Always serves as a great teacher of those in the world;
And is sympathetically mindful of beings

As for "not falling down into erroneous paths associated with the four difficulties," the bodhisattva who is able to perfect the practice of *śīla* in this manner will not fall into places [of rebirth] beset with the four difficulties, namely:

First, he will not be born into a place in which the Buddha is not present;
Second, he will not be born into a household in which wrong views hold sway;
Third, he will not take rebirth among the long-lived *deva*s;
Fourth, he will not be reborn into any of the wretched destinies.

"The four dharmas associated with loss" are:

First, he never loses the resolve to attain *bodhi;*

Second, he never loses his mindfulness of the Buddha;
Third, he never loses his constant quest for extensive learning;
Fourth, he never loses his ability to call to mind the events experienced across the course of countless lifetimes.

Regarding "not encountering the four dharmas associated with destruction" this refers to:
First, never encountering the destruction of the Dharma;
Second, never encountering weapons or war;
Third, never encountering noxious poisons;
Fourth, never encountering hunger.

As for "gaining the four dharmas of nondeception," they are:
First, one does not deceive the buddhas of the ten directions;
Second, one does not deceive *deva*s, spirits, or other such beings;
Third, one does not deceive beings;
Fourth, one does not deceive oneself.

Also, regarding "passing beyond the ten terror-inducing circumstances," the bodhisattva who purifies the moral precepts in this way thereby becomes able to pass beyond any vulnerability to falling down into the hells or into any of the other situations contained in the ten terror-inducing circumstances. What then are those ten? They are:
First, one is able to pass beyond the fear of falling into the hell realms;
Second, one is able to pass beyond the fear of falling into the animal realms;
Third, one is able to pass beyond the fear of falling into the hungry ghost realms;
Fourth, one is able to pass beyond the fear of becoming poverty-stricken;
Fifth, one is able to pass beyond the fear of slander, rebuke, and bad reputation;
Sixth, one is able to pass beyond the fear of being overcome by the various sorts of afflictions;
Seventh, one is able to pass beyond the fear of reaching the [irreversible] 120a
"right and definite position" (*samyaktva-niyāma*) [in the paths] of the *śrāvaka* disciples and the *pratyekabuddha*s;

Eighth, one is able to pass beyond the fear of [falling into the destinies of] *deva*s, humans, dragons, spirits, *yakṣa*s, *gandharva*s, *asura*s, *garuḍa*s, *kiṃnara*s, *mahoraga*s, and others;
Ninth, one is able to pass beyond the fear of weapons or war, noxious poisons, water, fire, lions, tigers, wolves, and injury by other men;
Tenth, one is able to pass beyond the fear of adopting wrong views.

If the bodhisattva is able in this manner to purify his observance of the moral precepts, then he will be able to abide within the Dharma of all buddhas, namely the forty exclusive dharmas, and he will also be able to become a Dharma vessel.

Chapter 34[318]

In Praise of the Moral Precepts

The bodhisattva who purifies his observance of the moral precepts in this manner is able to gather together all sorts of meritorious qualities and derive all manner of benefits. This is as stated by Akṣayamati Bodhisattva when he said:

Then again, to offer but a brief praise of a few aspects of *śīla:*

Śīla is the basis for the monastic's experiencing the foremost joyous delight that is comparable to the most supreme delight enjoyed by a youth who has both wealth and noble birth;

[*Śīla*] brings about the proliferation and growth of good dharmas, just as when a kind mother raises her child;

[*Śīla*] is able to protect one from ruinous calamity, just as when a father protects his child;

Śīla is able to bring about for monastics complete accomplishment in all forms of great benefit, just as great wealth is able to bring about great benefit for a householder;

Śīla is as able to rescue one from all forms of suffering torment, just as when right action accords with what is principled;

Śīla is as revered by good people as the dharma of repaying others' kindnesses;

Śīla is just as cherished and esteemed by people as a long life span;

Śīla is as esteemed by the wise as wisdom itself;

Those who strive to gain liberation thoroughly guard their practice of *śīla* just as carefully as high officials guard the secrets of the king;

Those who delight in the benefits of the path cherish and value *śīla* just as deeply as those who delight in nirvana cherish and value the Dharma of the Buddha;

The wise thoroughly guard their practice of *śīla* with the same urgency as those who cherish their own lives guard their physical safety and urgently seek rescue when death threatens;

The supreme [good fortune] of encountering *śīla* is comparable to that of meeting a good guide in the midst of grave danger;

Śīla adorns the worthy ones with purity and, in this, it is analogous to the daughter of nobility who, possessed of a sense of shame and dread of blame, remains undefiled;

Śīla is the initial entryway into meritorious qualities, just as not engaging in flattery and deviousness opens the way to acquiring fine benefits;

Śīla is the most important foundation of *brahmacarya,* just as the straight mind is the foundation of right views;

Śīla is the origin of all dharmas of great people, just as the straight mind is the origin of success in seeking an important position;

Śīla is a treasure trove of meritorious qualities comparable to non-negligence and right mindfulness in their ability to bring forth every sort of benefit;

[*Śīla*] is also comparable to a worthy friend who is good in the beginning, good in the middle, and good to the end;

[*Śīla*] is something beyond which one who trains in right Dharma must never go and, in this, he is like the ocean which always remains within its boundaries;[319]

Śīla is the dwelling place of meritorious qualities and, in this, it is also like the great earth upon which the myriad things depend;

Śīla serves to moisten all of the meritorious qualities of goodness and, in this, it is analogous to the rain falling down from the sky that moistens and benefits the seeds and enables the growth of the five kinds of roots;

[*Śīla*] is like fire in its ability to cook things and provide all sorts of benefits and, in this, it is like the [energetic] winds that sustain the body;

120b *Śīla* is able to accommodate all fruits of the path and, in this, it is also like empty space that contains and takes in the myriad things.

[*Śīla*] is also like the magically auspicious vase that is able to bring forth anything that one might wish for, and it is also like fine cuisine in its ability to benefit all of one's faculties;

Śīla is well able to open all paths and it is able to cause all one's faculties to become purified and unimpeded;

One's wisdom life relies upon *śīla* as its foundation, just as the life of the body depends upon the breath as its very foundation;

Śīla is the most superior of all points of reliance, just as it is the king upon whom all his subjects rely;

Śīla serves as the lord of all the meritorious qualities, just as the chief general commands the entire army;

Śīla is the source of the many varieties of happiness and, in this, it is like the compliant wife who is well able to satisfy all the wishes of her husband;

Whether it be in striving to reach nirvana or in gaining rebirth in the heavens, *śīla* constitutes the provisions sustaining those training on the path and, in this, it is like the essential clothing and provisions that one traveling afar must take along on his travels;

Śīla leads people along in such a way that they are caused to reach a good place and, in this, it is like finding a good guide who escorts one along a hazardous road;

Śīla delivers people from the faults of samsara and, in this, it is like a sturdy ship by which one is able to cross a great ocean;

Śīla is well able to put an end to all calamities wrought by the afflictions and, in this, it is like a good medicine that is able to eliminate the many sorts of diseases;

Śīla's weapons are able to defend one against Māra's thieves and, in this, they are like the weapons of a good army that are able to counter an enemy's troops;

Just as a beloved relative leads one through hardships and does not desert one, so too, *śīla* leads people through all manner of ruinous torment, continues to protect them, and never abandons them;

Śīla is able to illuminate even the darkness of delusion in one's future lives and, in this, it is like the light of a great lamp that is able to dispel the darkness;

Śīla is able even to deliver one out of the wretched destinies and, in this, it is like finding a good bridge when crossing deep waters;
Śīla is able to dispel the extreme fever of the afflictions and, in this, it is like a cool room that is able to get rid of scorching heat;
Even when on the verge of falling into the wretched destinies, *śīla* is able to come to the rescue and, in this, it is like a fierce sword-brandishing warrior rescuing someone in terror;
Every common person should feel a deeply cherishing fondness for *śīla* like that of the bodhisattvas training in the supreme basis of truthfulness;[320]
The practitioner's skillful practice of *śīla* is just like all bodhisattvas' practice of the supreme basis of relinquishment;
The skillful cultivation of *śīla* on the part of the practitioner who has gained the fruits [of the path] is just like all bodhisattvas' cultivation of the supreme basis of quiescence;
Guarding and upholding the practice of *śīla* causes one to attain the fruits [of the path], just like a bodhisattva who cultivates the wisdom supreme basis;
One who refrains from damaging the Dharma is able to purify his practice of *śīla* in a manner comparable to the purity and stainlessness of the bodhisattvas;
Bad people abandon *śīla,* just as flattering and devious people abandon the straight mind;
Neglectful people do not practice *śīla* and, in this, they are like miserly people who do not practice kindly giving;
Neglectful people abandon *śīla* and, in this, they are like those prone to inappropriate and frivolous speech who abandon the dharma of quiescence;
Stupid people are bereft of *śīla* just as a blind man does not see the five colors;
An unreflective person is as far from *śīla* as one who has abandoned the eightfold right path is far from nirvana;
Those who truly love themselves deeply delight in *śīla* just as an arhat deeply loves the Dharma;

Śīla is able to ensure that the good dharmas by which one remains free of afflictions continue on uninterruptedly just as the Buddha's emergence in the world ensures that goodness will continue 120c
without cease;

Śīla is able to cause the fruits of the path to abide [in the world], just as the Buddha's spiritual power causes the Dharma to remain for a long time;

Śīla is just like the Buddha in that it benefits both oneself and others;

Śīla thoroughly protects all good meritorious qualities, just as a king who understands right timing is able to defend the country's borders;

Śīla quiets the mind of the practitioner, just as when a stream-enterer,[321] by revealing in timely fashion [moral code infractions], remains free of subsequent regrets;

Śīla ensures that one shall ultimately and definitely reach nirvana, just as the bodhisattva vow ensures that one will ultimately become a buddha;

Śīla is also like a good plot of farmland that is well irrigated which, when sown with seeds, produces a rapidly growing crop;

Śīla is the cause of right conduct just as knowing the right time, knowing the right place, and so forth are the causes of success in all endeavors;

Just as a handsome man possessed of merit and wisdom is revered and esteemed by others, so too is *śīla* respected by both self and others;

Just as when one's merit has become ripe one's mind is peaceful and secure, so too is *śīla* able to cause one's mind to become peaceful and secure and to enjoy all its beneficial rewards;

Śīla is able to cause the practitioner to be delighted, just as a fine son is able to inspire delight in his father's mind;

Śīla is a dharma that causes fearlessness in one who is free of faults, just as when a person becomes free of faults his mind then becomes free of fear;

Śīla causes one to become free of all fear and free of the evil of moral transgressions in both the present life and future lives;

Others are inspired to make offerings and give praise to whoever upholds the practice of *śīla*, for others are moved by him to feel joy and realize that they too have some part in it;
Śīla causes one to feel affection for other beings, just as when one cultivates the meditation on [measureless] kindness;
Śīla motivates one to do away with the sufferings of others, just as when one cultivates the meditation on [measureless] compassion;
Śīla bestows joyfulness, just as when one cultivates the meditation on [measureless] sympathetic joy;
Śīla causes one to become free of both hatred and desire, just as when one cultivates the meditation on [measureless] equanimity;
Śīla inspires faith on the part of others, just as the four kinds of good speech are able to win the trust of others;
Śīla brings delight in its practice, just as dharmas of the world always bring delight to the mind [of a worldly person];
Just as extensive learning is the cause of delight in speech, *śīla* is the cause of consistency between one's words and one's actions;
Śīla is the cause of fearlessness, just as eloquence also brings about fearlessness;
Śīla is the cause of renown, just as complete comprehension of all scriptures brings a fine reputation;
Śīla is a dharma capable of bringing about one's rescue, just as being one who is easy to converse with ensures one will be rescued by them;
Śīla is a dharma that is able to bring about successful attainment of the clear knowledges and liberation and, in this, it is comparable to practicing in accordance with the teachings;
Śīla is the characteristic feature of all buddhas and, in this, it is comparable to *anuttarāsamyaksaṃbodhi*;
Śīla is a dharma that aids cultivation of the path and, in this, it is like *samādhi*'s role in assisting the attainment of wisdom;
Śīla causes a person to have no difficulties that he fears, just as someone possessed of great courage has nothing that he fears;
Śīla is the gathering place of every form of meritorious quality, for just as the Himalayas are the repository of precious things, faith,

the other meritorious qualities, and all marvelous phenomena[322] rely on *śīla* for their very existence;

Śīla is like the great sea in that it contains the many sorts of extraordinary things;

Also, just as to obtain fine fruit one relies on a tree, so too *śīla* is what provides people with whichever fruit they find pleasing. This is just as when one who pursues right wisdom then acquires [its fruits] in accordance with his practice;

Śīla is that by which one is cleansed even without the aid of water; 121a

Śīla is the most superior of sublime incenses, one that does not come forth from some root, trunk, branch, leaf, blossom, or fruit;

Śīla is an adornment that surpasses that of any jewelry, for it always remains with one's person and cannot be stolen by anyone;

Śīla provides a great bliss not born of any of the five desires and it bestows the reward of sublime bliss in future lives as well;

Śīla is that which is praised by all worlds' *deva*s, humans, *māra*s, Brahmās, *śramaṇa*s, and brahmans;

The happiness produced by *śīla* abides independently in one's own person for it is not obtained from anyone else and it is also the excellent means for gaining celestial rebirth or nirvana;

Śīla is the right ford for crossing the river of faith, one that is free of quicksand, tiles, stones, thorns, or brambles, and one that may be entered at will so as to skillfully cross without being impeded by anything;

Śīla is a form of precious wealth free of ruin or anguish;

Śīla is the indestructible path of purity that is comparable to a level road that can be traveled without difficulty;

Śīla is a fine farm field that, even without having to plant it or harvest it, one naturally obtains its fruits;

Śīla is the fruit tasting of the elixir of immortality that, even though not obtained from a tree or produced from a plant, is incomparably delicious;

Śīla is a *mañjūṣaka* flower that does not grow forth from either water or land and never wilts;

Śīla dispels the fever of the afflictions and, in this, it is like bathing in cool waters;

Śīla provides complete protection superior to that of even swords or staves, hence the practitioner of *śīla* is respected, but not because others fear him;

Śīla is a station of sovereign mastery that is free of any disputation or struggle;

Śīla is a fine jewel not extracted from the mountains or drawn forth from the great sea, one whose value is incalculable;

Śīla is able to take one beyond the fear of not surviving, beyond the fear of entering the assembly, beyond the fear of interrogation and beating, and beyond the fear of falling into the hells;[323]

Śīla always follows along with a person in present and future lives, just as a shadow follows its form.

Chapter 35[324]

The Karmic Rewards of the Moral Precepts

The comprehensive explanation of purification related to the bodhisattva's Ground of Stainlessness is hereby concluded. The bodhisattva dwelling on this ground always becomes a wheel-turning king. This second of the ten grounds is referred to as the Ground of Stainlessness. It is because covetousness and the rest of the ten bad karmic actions are all cut off at the very root that it is referred to as "stainless." A bodhisattva on this ground engages in the deep practice of *śīla-pāramitā*. In the event that this bodhisattva has not yet abandoned the desires, the causes and conditions associated with this ground's karmic rewards result in his becoming a wheel-turning king ruling over the four continents who obtains a thousand-spoked gold wheel.

Its rim is adorned with many different sorts of precious jewels and its hub is made of real beryl. It has a circumference of fifteen *li*.[325] It is protected by a hundred kinds of *yakṣa*s. It is able to fly through the air leading a fourfold army with agility, strength, and speed like that of the king of the golden-winged [*garuḍa*] birds, like that of the wind, or like that of a single thought, so that it is then able, wherever it goes, to put an end to all calamities and conquer any enemies.

All of the lesser kings come and declare their allegiance and submission. Of all of his relatives, clans, and subject peoples, there are none who do not both love and revere him. He is able to emanate radiance that illuminates
everywhere. The sage king's clan members wear many different kinds of 121b
floral chaplets with interspersed adornments of pearls. The five kinds of music follow him wherever he goes. An extraordinarily marvelous jeweled canopy hangs down over and around him. As he walks along, many different sorts of flower blossoms, incenses, and powdered sandalwood rain down as offerings as there also burn genuine black aloe wood incense and ox-head sandalwood incense. His body is scented with yellow sandalwood fragrance. On both sides of that wheel, heavenly maidens stand in attendance, holding

white whisks. The canopy above him is composed of all sorts of precious jewels. The wheel itself has all sorts of different rare things adorning it. This is what is meant by his "gold wheel treasure."

[As for his elephant treasure,] it possesses all the characteristics of an elephant and its body is huge and white like a king of mountains made of real silver. It comes from a herd of great elephants in the magic mountains. It is able to fly through the air, decisively defeat, and drive away in retreat all of the other great elephant kings, including Airāvaṇa, Ajñāna, Vāmana, and the rest. This is what is meant by his "white elephant treasure."

[As for his horse treasure,] it possesses all the characteristics of horses and is the color of a peacock's neck. Its body has agility and speed like that of the king of the golden-winged [*garuḍa*] birds and it can fly unimpeded through the air. This is what is meant by his "horse treasure."

[As for his prime minister of military affairs treasure,] he is one who has been born into a noble clan with a body that is free of illness, possessed of great strength, and a physical form of pristine appearance. His memory and thought are deep and far-reaching and he is possessed of a straight and resilient mind. He is solid in his observance of the precepts and he has deep reverence and affection for the king. He is able to penetrate the meaning of the many different classic scriptures as well as the technical skills and arts. This is what is meant by his "prime minister of military affairs treasure."

As for his treasury minister treasure, like the heavenly king of great wealth, he is characterized by such repletion in wealth that a thousand myriads of *koṭi*s of kinds of precious jewels form a treasury that always follows along with him wherever he goes, attended by retinue of a thousand myriads of *koṭi*s of *yakṣa*s. All of this is the karmic reward for his karmic actions in previous lives. [All of the precious jewels in the treasury] are well known and distinguished, including the gold, silver, *indranīla* sapphires, *mahānīla* sapphires, diamonds, malachite, *musāra-galva,* carnelian, coral, *sphaṭika, maṇi* jewels, real pearls, beryl, and all of the other different kinds of precious things. Precisely how much goes out and how much comes in is also well known. In accordance with whatever is fitting, he is able to use these so that he is able to fulfill the wishes of the king. This is what is meant by his "treasury minister treasure."[326]

[As for his jewel treasure, it emanates] light like the sun or moon that produces illumination that extends for sixteen *yojana*s. It is shaped like a huge drum and it is able to extinguish many different kinds of insect venom, noxious energies, pestilences, and pain. Of all the humans and *deva*s who see it, none fail to cherish it. It is adorned with fine flowers and necklaces, and, wherever it is placed, a banner is flown on high. It radiates an awe-inspiring and extraordinary radiance that is able to cause beings to bring forth thoughts of wonder and immense joy. This is what is meant by his "jewel treasure."

[Regarding a wheel-turning king's "jade maiden" treasure,] her fingernails are vermillion-colored and thin. Her physical form is straight, tall, and imposing. Her complexion is smooth, soft, and neither plump nor thin. Variations in the contours of her flesh are gradual in the transitions of her muscles and skin from dense and full to fine and delicate. Her tender skin would be ill-suited for coarse tasks. Her body is as stable and firm in its stance as the trunk of a *tāla* tree. In place after place on her body, auspicious characters are clearly visible. The silhouette outline of the auspicious tree adorns her body as well. The insignias of the king of elephants, king of bulls, and king of horses, as well as other such emblems as the imperial canopy emblem, the fish emblem, and the parks and forests emblems grace her body as adornments.

Her anklebones appear flat and not prominent. Her feet have a profile like
the shell of a tortoise. The sides of her feet are entirely red. Her heels are 121c
round and broad. Her calves are soft and smooth. Her knees are rounded and not prominent. Her thighs are shaped like golden pillars, like a plantain tree's trunk, or like an elephant's trunk while also being soft, smooth, radiantly lustrous, even, round, straight, and graced by three horizontal creases. Her belly is even and not prominent. Her umbilicus is round and deep. Her back is flat and straight. Her breasts are like *bimba* fruit or like [the breasts of] a pair of mandarin ducks. They are rounded and prominent but not sagging, while also being soft, smooth, and fresh and pristine in appearance.

Also, her arms are slender, even, round, and long, with joints that are hidden and hence not apparent. The profile of her nose is straight and not jutting prominently outward. It is neither large nor small, and its nostrils are hidden and hence not visible.

Her two cheeks are not sunken, but rather are even and full. They are not high, but rather are full on both sides.

Her forehead is flat, broad, and graced with an auspicious emblem. Her ears are soft, hang downward, and wear priceless earrings.

Her teeth appear like a strand of real pearls or like a new crescent moon and are the color of snow or alabaster. Her lips, a rosy cinnabar-red, appear like *bimba* fruits, are well matched above and below, and are neither coarse nor fine. They resemble strands of red pearls.

Her eyes are white with dark blue[327] [irises] and the margin between the two colorations is clearly defined. [Her eyes] are graceful, long and wide. They glisten with brightness and clarity. The lashes are bluish, with close-grown hairs that are long, but not disarrayed.

Her eyebrows are neither too thick nor too thin, neither too high nor too low, and they form the shape of new crescent moons. They are prominent and long with their two sides symmetrical.

Her hair is soft while also being fine, smooth, glossy, and not disarrayed.

Her body always emanates an incense-like scent similar to the fragrance rising forth from newly opened containers of various fine perfumes. All of the pores of her body always emit a truly sublime *candana* sandalwood's famous scent that is well able to please anyone's mind.

Her mouth always has the fragrance of a blue lotus.

Her body is as soft as a *kalaviṅka* bird and she is perfectly adorned with the sublimely smooth raiment of the *deva*s.

Her mind is free of any tendency toward flattery or deviousness. She is straightforward, trustworthy, and endowed with a sense of shame and dread of blame. She deeply loves and reveres the king. She knows the right time, knows the right place, and is well equipped with means for drawing the king's attentions. Whether sitting or standing, her words are well able to match the king's intentions and accord with the course of the king's thoughts. She always speaks pleasing words and, like a virtuous maiden among humans, she is replete in the many sorts of fine qualities. Her appearance is comparable to that of the heavenly maiden Tiluduoma,[328] for it has a purity and clarity that shines like the moon on the fifteenth night of the month. Her appearance is also comparable to that of Indra's consort, Śācī. She wears heavenly raiment, a floral chaplet of the *deva*s, celestial scents, and has many [strands of] radiant heavenly gold, *maṇi* jewels, and pearls adorning her body. She is well versed in singing, dancing, music, and all of the other arts of pleasurable entertainment and humor while also being well possessed of all the ways to be freely able to cause the king to be delighted.

Among all women, this woman is the very best. Such is the description of the king's "jade maiden treasure."

The wheel-turning king also has four spontaneously manifesting qualities:

First, his physical appearance is handsome and dignified and, in this, he is foremost, unmatched by anyone living on any of the four continents;
Second, he remains free of sickness and pain;
Third, he is deeply loved by his people;
Fourth, he has a very long life span.

He teaches beings that, through abiding by the ten courses of good karmic action, they are able to keep the heavenly palaces full, are able to diminish the *asura* hordes, are able to diminish the number of beings in the wretched destinies, and are able to increase their numbers in the good stations of rebirth.

In whatever endeavors he undertakes, he primarily seeks what is most 122a
beneficial to beings. Thus, without using armies and weapons, he institutes order in accordance with the Dharma and ensures peace and happiness among all the feudal princes.

Outwardly, he has no fear of hostile countries on his borders. Inwardly, he has no fear of secret plots against his reign. Additionally, his country remains free of plague, famine, or any of the disasters, locusts, or other ruinous and anguishing circumstances.

All the kings in the border regions pledge their allegiance and submit to him. He is attended by a large retinue and is able to swiftly gather people [to become loyal followers]. Thus there are none able to attack and damage his domain. His fourfold army is possessed of abundant might. He is loved and respected by all brahmans, merchants, and common people.

Sweet, fragrant, and delectable food comes to him spontaneously. The boundaries of his domain increase by the day and never shrink. He is well able to reach a penetrating comprehension of all the classic scriptures, arts, mathematics, and spiritual incantations, all of which he can retain and invoke. He is skilled in his ability to debate, discuss, and clearly distinguish their meaning and import. Those in his assembly of officials are all well possessed of awe-inspiring virtue. He is always devoted to philanthropic giving that no one can match.

His thousand sons are all as handsome as the sons of the *deva*s and they are possessed of awe-inspiring virtue, courage, strength, and the ability to crush even the strongest of enemies.

The palace in which he dwells is replete with halls, towers, and pavilions like those supreme palaces enjoyed by the Four Heavenly Kings and Indra.

Whatsoever the king instructs is unable to be subverted by anyone anywhere on the four continents. It is only this one king whose marks of awe-inspiring power are so complete that none are able to match him.

His voice is deep, carries far, is easily heard, easily understood, and is never scattered or disordered. And, like the sound of the *kalaviṅka* bird, it is beautiful, soft, harmonious, refined, and pleasing to the ear of the hearer.

His retinue is of like mind and incapable of obstructiveness. Wherever he abides, whether on the land, the water, or moving through the air, there is no one able to impede his travel. He has awesome power that is courageous and abundant with which he can undertake and succeed in great endeavors.

He thinks of and asks after the welfare of the aged. He never deceives anyone. His mind has no jealousy. He does not tolerate anything contrary to Dharma and he has no hatred.

His personal deportment is serene and dignified and it is neither restless nor impetuous. Whatever he says is sincere and true and he never utters divisive speech. In whatever he does, he upholds the moral precepts and cultivates a mind imbued with goodness. In initiating or halting endeavors, he knows the right time and never fails to employ appropriate methods.

His facial expression is amiable and, in speaking, he is always inclined to a subtle smile. He never scowls or glowers at anyone. For those who have encountered misfortune, he does whatever is beneficial for them. Those who have already been benefited thereby come to feel deep gratitude and to feel disposed toward a sense of shame and dread of blame.

He is possessed of great wisdom, awe-inspiring virtue, and a dignified manner while also being able to abide in patience. He has the marks of the great man and his nature is such that he may manifest fierce severity. He is able to swiftly complete every endeavor he takes up. He first assesses circumstances correctly and then acts accordingly. Because the king has the Dharma eye, whatever he does is exceptional.

Where he has those who are possessed of good judgment, he delegates tasks to them. If they are incapable of fulfilling their duties, he then seeks further for other surrogates who are worthy and wise.

He is skillful in accumulating karmic merit and wealth. By virtue of his own purity, he is able to guard his own actions and defend against breaking any of the moral precepts.

He bestows much wealth and treasure and, in this, he is comparable to King Vaiśravaṇa. He possesses great strength like Śakra, ruler of the *deva*s.

He is as majestic and entrancing as the full moon and as radiant as the sun. He has the capacity to endure of the earth and his mind is as deep as
the ocean. He is not shaken in the least by either pain or pleasure, and, like 122b
Sumeru, king of the mountains, none of the winds can make him quaver and he is the repository of all jewels and marvelous things.

He is one in whom all the excellent meritorious qualities reside. He acts as the close friend and relative of everyone in the entire world and he is a place of refuge for all who are beset by suffering or affliction. He is a refuge for those who have no refuge and a shelter for those who have no shelter. He can dispel the fear of those beset by fear.

Such are the characteristics of the wheel-turning sage king.

> He is able to reverse the path of those who break moral precepts
> and then influence them to abide in good dharmas.
> All the other endeavors to which he is devoted
> are as previously explained in the discussion of the first ground.

As for "reversing the path of those who break moral precepts," he is able to influence beings to relinquish evil actions and take up those endeavors that are conducive to peace and happiness.

As for "influencing them to abide in good dharmas," he is able to turn beings away from evil actions of body, speech, and mind and influence them to take up the good karmic actions of body, speech, and mind.

As for these endeavors being "as previously explained in the discussion of the first ground," this refers to being able to see the buddhas and acquire the *samādhi*s. The only difference is that, on that ground, hundreds of buddhas are seen, whereas on this ground, thousands of buddhas are seen.

Notes

1 Although it is common to see the Sanskrit title of this work reconstructed in English academic articles as *Daśabhūmika-vibhāṣā-śāstra,* this based on its Chinese title, *Shizhu piposha lun* (十住毘婆沙論), "Ten Grounds *Vibhāṣā* Treatise." Akira Hirakawa, in *Buddhist Chinese-Sanskrit Dictionary* (Tokyo: Reiyūkai Hatsubaimoto Innātorippusha, 1997) reconstructs this title as simply *Daśabhūmika-vibhāṣā,* probably because he recognized that the *lun* (論) or "treatise" in the Chinese title was only ever intended by Kumārajīva and other translators to notify the Chinese reader that a *vibhāṣā* is a kind of treatise. That is to say, he most likely did *not* intend it as a translation of the Sanskrit word *śāstra.*

2 Joseph Walser writes in his article "Nāgārjuna," in John Powers, ed., *The Buddhist World* (London; New York: Routledge, Taylor & Francis Group, 2016), p. 498: "Of two things we can be fairly certain. First, according to two sixth-century catalogues of Buddhist texts translated into Chinese, Dharmarakṣa translated a work called the *Treatise Commentary on the Sutra of Ten Stages* (*Daśabhūmika-vibhāṣa-śāstra*) in 265 C.E. that he ascribes to Nāgārjuna."

3 Although the Taishō edition of this text restarts the chapter numbering after Chapter 27 by designating Chapter 28 as "Chapter 1," I instead follow the chapter numbering of the Song, Yuan, Ming, and Gong editions of the Chinese Buddhist canon, all of which number this treatise as consisting of a series of thirty-five continuously numbered chapters. The apparent rationale for the Taishō edition's restarting the numbering at Chapter 28 is to call the reader's attention to the fact that the first twenty-seven chapters are at least nominally devoted to explaining the first ground whereas the final eight chapters constitute a new section consisting of Nāgārjuna's explanation of the second ground. In any case, the reader should be aware that headings of these sorts for the most part originate with the Chinese translation team, not with the Indian text.

4 This condensed description of each chapter borrows from and expands upon a very similar Chinese-language narration found in "A Simplified Introduction to the Daśabhūmika *Vibhāṣā*" (十住毘婆沙論簡介) by the Chinese Buddhist monk Hou Guan of the Fuyan Buddhist Studies Institute (福嚴佛學院, 釋厚觀, 09/18/2001), http://www.fuyan.org.tw/main_edu/1521-00c.doc, accessed July 2018.

5 These "four bases of meritorious qualities" are truth, relinquishing, quiescence, and wisdom.

6 The four lineage bases of the *āryas* (*catur-āryavaṃśa*) are delighting in mere sufficiency in clothing, delighting in mere sufficiency of food and drink, delighting in

mere sufficiency of bedding, and delighting in the severance [of evil] and the cultivation [of goodness].

7 I translate here as "monastic preceptor" and "monastic Dharma teacher" what the Kumārajīva text retains in transliteration as *upādhyāya* and *ācārya* respectively.

8 In this translation, "good spiritual friend" and "good spiritual guide" are alternative renderings for the same Chinese terms (善知識) and Sanskrit (*kalyāṇamitra*). "Good spiritual friend" is used to refer to those companions on the spiritual path who support one's adherence to the teachings. "Good spiritual guide" is used to refer to spiritual friends who also serve as mentors upon whom one relies for spiritual guidance as one cultivates the path.

9 The Lokāyata school of ancient Indian philosophy is a materialist doctrine the founding of which is often attributed to Bṛhaspati who is thought to have lived around 1000 B.C.E.

10 Given the readings in the immediately preceding passage and in the verse which follows below, for consistency's sake, I emend the Taishō reading of *da zang* (大藏), "great treasuries," here in favor of the Song, Yuan, Ming, and Gong editions reading of *guangda zang* (廣大藏), "vast treasuries."

11 I emend the reading of the Taishō text here by preferring on sensibility grounds the Song, Yuan, and Ming editions' *guang shuo* (廣說), "extensive explanation," to the Taishō edition's *guang* (廣), "extensive."

12 I translate here as "benefactors" what the Kumārajīva text retains in transliteration as "*dānapati*."

13 To correct an apparent graphic-similarity scribal error, I emend the reading of the Taishō text here by preferring the Song, Yuan, Ming, and Gong editions' *zengshang man* (增上慢), "overweening pride," to the Taishō edition's untranslatable *zengshang man* (憎上慢).

14 Although the arrangement of the Taishō text does not make this clear, it is obvious that these first four five-character phrases form a quatrain upon which the following paragraph comments. Hence I have formatted the text accordingly.

15 This most likely refers to the *Pratyutpanna-samādhi-sūtra* preserved in the Taishō canon as the *Banzhou sanmei jing* (般舟三昧經; T.418:902c23–919c5). Paul Harrison has produced a translation of this text for the BDK English Tripiṭaka Series, in the volume entitled *The Pratyutpanna Samādhi Sutra/The Śūraṅgama Samādhi Sutra* (Moraga, CA: BDK America, Inc., 1998), pp. 1–107.

16 I emend the reading of the text here (but still keep the emendation in brackets since there are no supporting variants in any of the other editions), this to correct an obvious scribal error wherein the name of the third of these "four bases of meritorious qualities" is missing from this sentence. The missing "basis" here is *mie* (滅), "quiescence" (*upaśamādhiṣṭhāna*).

17 These four bases of meritorious qualities (四功德處: 諦, 捨, 滅, 慧; *satyādhiṣṭhāna, tyāgādhiṣṭhāna, upaśamādhiṣṭhāna, prajñādhiṣṭhāna;* truth, relinquishment [generosity], quiescence, and wisdom) are brought up repeatedly in this and other Nāgārjunian treatises, sometimes in slightly varying order and sometimes, as in the present case, with the Chinese translation using slightly variant terminological choices for one of the four list components.

18 "Arms appearing like golden gate bars" is a rather obscure simile that I have never encountered. The Song, Yuan, Ming, Gong editions have *chan* (鋋), which would be the equally obscure "like golden spears."

19 To correct an apparent graphic-similarity scribal error, I emend the reading of the Taishō text here by preferring the Song, Yuan, Ming, and Gong editions' *sheng* (生), "growth," to the Taishō edition's *zhu* (主), "ruler."

20 The "reply that sets aside the question" is one of polite refusal to provide an answer, not because the answer is not known, but because the question involves a false premise making the query absurd on the face of it, because providing the answer would only promote endless frivolous and fruitless speculation on the part of the questioner (as with the fourteen imponderables), or because providing an answer would in no way serve the goal of spiritual liberation.

21 More specifically, the component lists comprising the thirty-seven wings of enlightenment are: the five faculties, the five powers, the seven limbs of *bodhi,* the eightfold path, the four stations of mindfulness, the four right efforts, and the four foundations of psychic power.

22 "Foes" refers here to the three poisons, i.e., the afflictions. An arhat has completely destroyed them. Venerable Bhikkhu Bodhi points out that this pronouncement references the word play in the word *arahant,* where it is explained that they are those who are enemy (*ari*) destroyers (*hanta*).

23 Perhaps due to corruption of the manuscript at some point in its long history, the following list contains only seventy-four of the eighty secondary characteristics.

24 The *saṃkakṣikā* is the monastic's robe that is worn over the left shoulder and under the right arm.

25 The *nivāsana* is the monastic's skirt-like inner robe.

26 The *saṃghāṭī* is the monastic's outer robe.

27 "Eight kinds of *ārya*s" usually refers to those eminences who reside at the four candidate stages and the four realization stages on the *śrāvaka* vehicle path. The first is candidate for stream-entry and the eighth is the fully realized arhat.

28 *Garuḍa* birds prey on young dragons, hence the mention that, at least when attending Dharma teachings by buddhas, they manage to remain uncharacteristically free of any mutual hostility.

29 Although the Taishō text has *xiang* (相), "appearance," here it is as an often encountered and more or less standard short-form abbreviation for *xiang* (想), "thought."

30 Venerable Bhikkhu Bodhi notes that this is a stock description of the Buddha's teaching of the Dharma as found in the *sutta*s of the Nikāyas, as for example: *ādikalyāṇaṃ majjhe kalyāṇaṃ pariyosāne kalyāṇaṃ sātthaṃ sabyañjanaṃ,* etc., and *sandiṭṭhiko akālika ehipassiko opanayako paccattaṃ veditabbo viññūhi.*

31 Kumārajīva transliterated rather than translated these fruits of the path (*srota-āpanna, sakṛdāgāmin, anāgāmin*) that, with the exception of arhat, I have elected to translate.

32 The emendation proposed by the 2009 edition of CBETA (和>知) involving a supposed graphic-similarity scribal error is itself erroneous and irrelevant. This verse simply restates an idea clearly articulated late in Chapter 18 (*Nāgārjuna's Treatise on the Ten Grounds, Volume I,* p. 303): "Through not allowing estrangement to occur among other beings or among one's relatives, and through being able to cause those who have become estranged to be reunited, one acquires the mark of male genital ensheathment. Due to having [planted the karmic causes that result in] this mark, one acquires many disciples." See 65b18–20: 能善調人不令眾生親里遠離.若有乖離還令和合故得陰藏相.有是相故多得弟子.

33 "Genital ensheathment" of course also associates with transcendence of sensual desire and, as an incidental implication, that there may therefore be no biological sons via which the patrilineal lineage might continue.

Here, the metaphoric interpretation points out that it is the pure wisdom eye (pure by virtue of an absence of attachments) that leads to the continuance of the lineage of the buddhas, this because it is a buddha's wise teachings flowing from his possession of the wisdom eye that beget "the sons of the Buddha," i.e., the bodhisattvas who will themselves become the buddhas of the future who carry on his Dharma lineage.

34 These are eight voice qualities possessed only by the buddhas: (1) extremely fine, (2) gentle, (3) appropriate, (4) possessed of venerable wisdom, (5) non-feminine, (6) unmistaken, (7) deep and far-reaching, and (8) inexhaustible. These are discussed at length in Section 59 of *A Sequential Explanation of the Initial Gateway into the Dharma Realm* (法界次第初門, T.1925:697a15–b20) composed by the famous meditation master and immensely prolific Tiantai hermeneutic school exegete Zhiyi (沙門釋智顗, a.k.a. 陳隋國師智者大師).

35 Because the received text's listing of these forty exclusive dharmas presents them in a somewhat different order than occurs as they are actually presented and discussed in the text, I reorder and renumber them here to follow the actual order of their presentation. I do so based on the usually factual assumption that the section titles and preliminary lists in translations of Sanskrit texts are for the most part *not* part of the original text, but rather are added by the Sanskrit-to-Chinese translator to assist the reader, or, in this case, perhaps by the editors and scribes in Kumārajīva's translation bureau. For those interested in the erroneously ordered and numbered list found here in the received text, it is as follows:

1. Sovereign mastery of the ability to fly;
2. [The ability to manifest] countless transformations;
3. Boundless psychic powers of the sort possessed by *ārya*s;
4. Sovereign mastery of the ability to hear sounds;
5. Immeasurable power of knowledge to know others' thoughts;
6. Sovereign mastery in [training and subduing] the mind;
7. Constant abiding in stable wisdom;
8. Never forgetting;
9. Possession of the powers of the *vajra samādhi;*
10. Thorough knowing of matters that are unfixed;
11. Thorough knowing of matters pertaining to the formless realm's meditative absorptions;
12. The completely penetrating knowledge of all matters associated with eternal cessation;
13. Thorough knowing of the nonform dharmas unassociated with the mind;
14. The great powers *pāramitā;*
15. The [four] unimpeded [knowledges] *pāramitā;*
16. The *pāramitā* of perfectly complete replies and predictions in response to questions;
17. Perfectly complete implementation of the three turnings in speaking Dharma;
18. Their words are never spoken without a purpose;
19. Their speech is free of error;
20. Invulnerability to harm by anyone;
21. They are the great generals among all *ārya*s;

22–25. They are able to remain unguarded in four ways;

26–29. They possess the four fearlessnesses;

30–39. They possess the ten powers;

40. They possess the unimpeded liberations.

36 Venerable Bhikkhu Bodhi notes: "This is a category in Sarvāstivāda Abhidharma (not in the Theravāda Abhidhamma), which indicates the author is familiar with the Sarvāstivāda system."

37 "Without a purpose" here is literally "empty" (in the sense of "in vain" or "fruitlessly").

38 Venerable Bhikkhu Bodhi notes: "See *Aṅguttara Nikāya* 7:58. The four are: conduct of body, speech, and mind, and livelihood."

39 To correct an apparent graphic-similarity scribal error, I emend the reading of the Taishō text here by preferring the Song, Yuan, Ming, and Gong editions' *neng* (能), "able to," to the Taishō edition's *suo* (所), "that which."

40 Venerable Bhikkhu Bodhi notes: "See *Aṅguttara Nikāya*, Sevens, no. 40 (see also Sixes, no. 24):

> Bhikkhus, possessing seven qualities, a bhikkhu exercises mastery over his mind and is not a servant of his mind. What seven? Here, (1. a bhikkhu is skilled in

concentration; (2. skilled in the attainment of concentration; (3. skilled in the duration of concentration; (4. skilled in emergence from concentration; (5. skilled in fitness for concentration; (6. skilled in the range of concentration; and (7. skilled in resolution regarding concentration. Possessing these seven qualities, a bhikkhu exercises mastery over his mind, and is not a servant of his mind.

41 This appears to be yet another instance of Kumārajīva's use of *xing* (性), usually translated as "nature," as a translation for *dhātu,* which is more ordinarily translated into Sino-Buddhist Classical Chinese as *jie* (界), "realm."

42 Venerable Bhikkhu Bodhi notes: "In the above [passage: 諸相諸觸諸覺諸念亦知起知住知生知滅], 相 is clearly another instance of the confusion between 相 and 想 so common in Chinese texts. The Pāli part parallel has *saññā.* See the end of *Majjhima Nikāya* 123, where the Buddha says he knows "the arising, persistence, and passing away of *vedanā, saññā,* and *vitakka.*"

43 In response to my earlier draft translation of *emo* (惡魔) here as "evil demon," Venerable Bhikkhu Bodhi notes:

Here there is no doubt that 惡魔 is none other than the infamous Māra, a particular individual, not just any "evil demon." See *Samyutta Nikāya* 4:24, "Seven Years of Pursuit":

On one occasion the Blessed One was dwelling at Uruvelā on the bank of the river Nerañjarā at the foot of the Goatherd's Banyan Tree. Now on that occasion Māra the Evil One had been following the Blessed One for seven years, seeking to gain access to him but without success….

Then Māra the Evil One, in the presence of the Blessed One, recited these verses of disappointment:

There was a crow that walked around
A stone that looked like a lump of fat.
"Let's find something tender here," [he thought,]
"Perhaps there's something nice and tasty."
But because he found nothing tasty there,
The crow departed from that spot.
Just like the crow that attacked the stone,
We leave Gotama disappointed.

44 These five are past dharmas, present dharmas, future dharmas, unconditioned dharmas (referred to below as "those that transcend the three periods of time"), and ineffable dharmas.

45 I emend the text here to correct an apparent graphic-similarity scribal error, preferring the Song, Yuan, Ming, and Gong editions' *san* (三), "three," to the Taishō text's *er* (二), "two." The rationale for the emendation is evident in the paragraph's discussion of "three" dharmas that are "strung together," not merely "two."

46 I have made the same emendation here as in the previous note.

47 Venerable Bhikkhu Bodhi notes that this incident involving the elephant named Nālagiri is described in the Vinaya, *Cullavagga* II 194 foll. of the Pali Text Society's Pāli edition.

48 As described later in the text, "The twelve *dhūta* austerities" are:

Adopting the dharma of dwelling in a forest hermitage;
Obtaining one's food through the almsround;
Wearing robes made of cast-off rags;
[Taking one's daily meal in but] a single sitting;
Always sitting to sleep, [never lying down];
Having taken the meal, not accepting food or drink at the wrong times;
Possessing only a single set of three robes;
Wearing only an animal hair robe;
Laying out one's sitting mat wherever one happens to be;
Dwelling at the foot of a tree;
Dwelling out in the open (lit., "on empty ground");
Dwelling in a charnel field.

49 Venerable Bhikkhu Bodhi notes: "In the Pāli these are laid out as parallel descriptive terms. The Pāli actually has nine synonymous terms. See *Aṅguttara Nikāya* 1:174."

50 Based on Venerable Bhikkhu Bodhi's very sensible suggestion that "quiescent cessation" (寂滅) is probably here as elsewhere simply a somewhat opaque sounding Sino-Buddhist translation of "nirvana," I have rendered it as such throughout this entire passage as well as in other places throughout the text where the context demands it.

51 I have been unable to find a Sanskrit antecedent for this Chinese transliteration of a type of *ṛṣi,* a *pisuo* (脾娑) *ṛṣi*. Venerable Bhikkhu Bodhi suggests that this may be a transliteration of *viśvarśi* (*viś ṛṣi*).

52 Venerable Bhikkhu Bodhi notes that one can find approximate Pāli canon parallels at *Majjhima Nikāya* 110.4, *Middle Length Discourses of the Buddha,* p. 892, and *Aṅguttara Nikāya* 3:3.

53 Venerable Bhikkhu Bodhi notes: "The story of Ciñcā the brahmin girl occurs in the *Dhammapada* Commentary, commenting on verse 176. See Burlingame, *Buddhist Legends* III 19 foll."

54 Venerable Bhikkhu Bodhi notes: "In the Pāli Canon, this incident is referred to in Udāna Section 38."

55 Venerable Bhikkhu Bodhi notes: "The incident is at *Saṃyutta Nikāya* 4:18 (Pali Text Society ed. I 113–14)."

56 Venerable Bhikkhu Bodhi notes: "The story is in the Pāli Vinaya in *Cullavagga,* chapter 7; Pali Text Society ed II 194–96."

57 Venerable Bhikkhu Bodhi notes: "This [story] is at the beginning of the Pārājika chapter of the Vinaya."

[58] Venerable Bhikkhu Bodhi notes: "His departure from the Sangha and denunciation of the Buddha are mentioned at the beginning of *Majjhima Nikāya* 12. *Majjhima Nikāya* 105 is spoken to him, and his arguments with the Buddha about arahants are at *Dīgha Nikāya* 23."

[59] Venerable Bhikkhu Bodhi notes: "See *Aṅguttara Nikāya* 7:58: Four things that the Tathāgata does not have to guard: conduct of body, speech, and mind, and livelihood."

[60] "The *upoṣadha* dharma" is a reference to spiritual purification, in particular the two days of the month when monastics recite the precepts and the days of the month in which pious laypeople voluntarily take on a semi-monastic level of moral precept observance.

[61] This is verse 183 of the *Dhammapada.*

[62] The first four lines here correspond to *Dhammapada* 361.

[63] This corresponds to verse 362 of the *Dhammapada.*

[64] Venerable Bhikkhu Bodhi notes: "See *Aṅguttara Nikāya* 5:181 foll.: 'Bhikkhus, there are these five kinds of forest dwellers. What five? (1) One who becomes a forest dweller because of his dullness and stupidity; (2) one who becomes a forest dweller because he has evil desires, because he is driven by desire; (3) one who becomes a forest dweller because he is mad and mentally deranged; (4) one who becomes a forest dweller, [thinking]: "It is praised by the buddhas and the buddhas' disciples"; (5) and one who becomes a forest dweller for the sake of fewness of desires, for the sake of contentment, for the sake of eliminating [defilements], for the sake of solitude, for the sake of simplicity. The fifth is pronounced the best.'"

[65] Venerable Bhikkhu Bodhi notes: "I think the author here is referring to the Buddha's hesitation, immediately after his enlightenment, about going out and teaching the Dharma. See *Majjhima Nikāya* 26.19, *Saṃyutta Nikāya* 6:1, etc."

[66] Venerable Bhikkhu Bodhi notes: "This is at *Majjhima Nikāya* 26.22–23. Interestingly the author here takes a similar perspective on *sarvajñatā* as the Theravāda commentaries, that knowledge arises when the Buddha directs his attention to some issue (*āvajjanapaṭibaddhaṃ buddhassa bhagavato ñāṇaṃ*), in contrast to the later Mahāyāna view that the Buddha perpetually knows everything simultaneously."

[67] The second part of the Chinese text's title, "Forty Dharmas Exclusive to Buddhas: The Exclusive Dharma of Thoroughly Knowing What Is Unfixed," is misleading because "the exclusive dharma of thoroughly knowing what is unfixed" only describes the first few pages of this long chapter that in fact discusses all of the remaining exclusive dharmas (nos. 10–40). I have therefore dropped this misleading phrase from the chapter title. One should be aware that these chapter titles almost certainly do not originate with Nāgārjuna but rather with Kumārajīva's translation team.

[68] Venerable Bhikkhu Bodhi notes: "The above corresponds to *Majjhima Nikāya* no. 136."

69 Commenting on the corresponding passages as preserved in the Pāli canon, Venerable Bhikkhu Bodhi notes: "The Pāli *sutta* with the simile of the raft mentions all four fruits (*Majjhima Nikāya* 22; see the end). But the proposition about one of two fruits occurs in a number of other suttas, such as the *Satipaṭṭhāna Sutta* (see end of *Majjhima Nikāya* 10)."

70 Regarding this *Ekottara Āgama*'s *Shejiali Sutra* (舍迦梨經), I have so far been unable to locate the Sanskrit for its title.

71 Venerable Bhikkhu Bodhi comments:

The above corresponds to *Aṅguttara Nikāya* 10:217 (also 10:218). Note that there are three modes in which the karmic results may be received, in both the Pāli and Chinese versions: in the present life (現受報), upon rebirth (that is, the next life, 生受), or in a subsequent life (after the next one, 後受).

Here is the Pāli followed by my English rendering:

217. *Nāhaṃ, bhikkhave, sañcetanikānaṃ kammānaṃ katānaṃ upacitānaṃ appaṭisaṃviditvā byantībhāvaṃ vadāmi. Tañca kho diṭṭheva dhamme upapajje vā apare vā pariyāye. Na tvevāhaṃ, bhikkhave, sañcetanikānaṃ kammānaṃ katānaṃ upacitānaṃ appaṭisaṃveditvā dukkhass'antakiriyaṃ vadāmi.*

"Bhikkhus, I do not say that there is a termination of volitional kamma that has been done and accumulated so long as one has not experienced [its results], and that may be in this very life, or in the [next] rebirth, or on some subsequent occasion. But I do not say that there is making an end of suffering so long as one has not experienced [the results of] volitional kamma that has been done and accumulated."

72 Again, I have so far been unable to find the Sanskrit name for this transliterated title, *Ekottara Āgama*'s *Afuluo Sutra*.

73 Venerable Bhikkhu Bodhi notes: "The Pāli parallel is *Majjhima* 58: *Abhayarāja-kumāra Sutta*."

74 These "three groups" refers to the *tri-skandha* (三聚) as that term is used to categorize the karmic destinies of beings. Those who are "definitely deviant" or "erroneous" are definitely bound to be unsuccessful in reaching enlightenment whereas those who are "definitely righteous" or "correct" are definitely bound to succeed in becoming enlightened. In his *Mahāprajñāpāramitā-upadeśa,* in commenting on a passage in the *Great Perfection of Wisdom Sutra* that brings up the topic of these three groups, Nāgārjuna points out that it is the ability or inability to destroy the inverted views that is pivotal in determining one's position in this threefold categorization. It is those who may or may not encounter the karmic conditions enabling the destruction of these inverted views who are categorized as "indefinite." (See T.1509:647c27–648a1.)

75 These four "repositories of Dharma" (Dharma-*piṭaka*) are identified by Nāgārjuna in his *Mahāprajñāpāramitā-upadeśa* as (1) the Sutra-*piṭaka,* (2) the Vinaya-*piṭaka,* (3) the Abhidharma-*piṭaka,* and (4) the Kṣudraka-*piṭaka* (T.1509:143c23–25).

76 These are "delectable absorptions" (*āsvādana-samādhi*), which are characterized by the arising of extremely pleasurable meditation states to which the unskilled or unwise meditator is vulnerable to becoming attached.

77 Venerable Bhikkhu Bodhi notes: "The Pāli parallel is the opening passage of *Dīgha Nikāya* no. 14, almost verbatim the same."

78 I emend the reading of the Taishō text here by preferring on sensibility grounds the Song, Yuan, Ming, and Gong editions' *ci jing* (此經), "this sutra," to the Taishō edition's *jing ci* (經此), "sutra this."

The sutra to which this text refers is obviously the *Ten Grounds Sutra* on which Nāgārjuna's *Shizhu piposha lun* comments. This topic of the expansiveness of the Buddha's knowledge and vision is treated at great length in the sutra itself.

79 Venerable Bhikkhu Bodhi notes: "The names of *pratyekabuddhas* are mentioned in *Majjhima Nikāya* 116. I would posit the following equivalents" [for a few of the *pratyekabuddhas* mentioned here]:

無垢 = Ariṭṭha
華相 = Tagarasikhī
喜見 = Piyadassī.

80 Venerable Bhikkhu Bodhi notes: "Parallel to the above is *Aṅguttara Nikāya* 6:62 Section 6: (6) "Then, Ānanda, having encompassed his mind with my own mind, I understand some person thus: 'Wholesome qualities and unwholesome qualities are found in this person.' On a later occasion, having encompassed his mind with my own mind, I understand him thus: 'This person does not have even a mere fraction of a hair's tip of an unwholesome quality. This person possesses exclusively bright, blameless qualities. He will attain *nibbāna* in this very life.'"

81 Venerable Bhikkhu Bodhi notes: "[This passage is found] in *Majjhima Nikāya* 12."

82 Venerable Bhikkhu Bodhi notes: "The following passage comes toward the end of *Majjhima Nikāya* 12."

83 This long paragraph beginning with "Supposing…" has the appearance of language quoted from a sutra. However, having failed to locate it, I frame it here as simply Nāgārjuna's amplification of the meaning of the immediately preceding passage, which Venerable Bhikkhu Bodhi recognized as having a Pāli analogue in *Majjhima Nikāya* 12.

84 Potaliputta is the name as recorded in the Pāli canon. I'm not sure about the Sanskrit for this name.

85 The name Samiddhi is as recorded in the Pāli canon; Sanskrit uncertain.

86 Venerable Bhikkhu Bodhi notes that the following passage is found in the beginning of *Majjhima Nikāya* 136.

87 Rāhula was the Buddha's son; Devadatta was someone intent on killing the Buddha.

88 Venerable Bhikkhu Bodhi suggest that this passage may be alluding to *Aṅguttara Nikāya* 4:111, "Kesi the Horse Trainer."

89 This refers to *satkāyadṛṣṭi*.

90 Again, although in these last two cases, the Chinese is literally "gain the path" (得道), per Hirakawa, *Buddhist Chinese-Sanskrit Dictionary,* p. 451, column 2, this corresponds to: "*bodhi, abhisaṃbuddha, saṃbodhi-prāpta*." Franklin Edgerton, *Buddhist Hybrid Sanskrit Grammar and Dictionary* (New Haven, CT: Yale University Press, 1953), in turn suggests "becoming perfectly enlightened" for *abhisambuddhana* (p. 58, column 2).

91 Although *brahmacarya* (梵行) generally refers to celibate spiritual practice, it may just as well be thought of as "the holy life" or "the spiritual life." Venerable Bhikkhu Bodhi notes that this scriptural quote "is found in many places in the Nikāyas: e.g., beginning of *Majjhima Nikāya* 148: *Bhagavā etadavoca—'dhammaṃ vo, bhikkhave, desessāmi ādikalyāṇaṃ majjhe kalyāṇaṃ pariyosānakalyāṇaṃ sātthaṃ sabyañjanaṃ, kevalaparipuṇṇaṃ parisuddhaṃ brahmacariyaṃ pakāsessāmi*."

92 Venerable Bhikkhu Bodhi notes: "In the Pāli *sutta*s, the second wonder is being able to declare another person's thoughts." For the three wonders, see *Aṅguttara Nikāya* 3:60: "There are, brahmin, these three kinds of wonders. What three? The wonder of psychic potency, the wonder of mind-reading, and the wonder of instruction (*iddhipāṭihāriyaṃ ādesanāpāṭihāriyaṃ anusāsanī-pāṭihāriyaṃ*; also at *Dīgha Nikāya* 11.3–8, I 212–14). The second is explained thus: There is one who…declares: 'Your thought is thus, such is what you are thinking, your mind is in such and such a state.' And even if he makes many declarations, they are exactly so and not otherwise."

93 I have been unable to locate either the Sanskrit or Pāli antecedents for the titles of these scriptures, *Poheti* and *Uttara.* Venerable Bhikkhu Bodhi also notes: "I'm not sure of the references here. Perhaps the former is the *Potaliya Sutta, Majjhima Nikāya* 54, but I'm not sure."

94 Venerable Bhikkhu Bodhi notes: "[The Pāli canon analogue for] the following is at *Majjhima Nikāya* 12 and *Aṅguttara Nikāya* 4:8."

95 I emend the reading of the Taishō text here by preferring on sensibility grounds the Song, Yuan, Ming, and Gong editions' *wei wei* (微畏), "slightest fear," to the Taishō edition's *shi* (是), "this."

96 Venerable Bhikkhu Bodhi notes that the analogue passage in the Pāli canon is found at *Dīgha Nikāya* no. 20.

97 Venerable Bhikkhu Bodhi notes: "See *Majjhima Nikāya* 115 and *Aṅguttara Nikāya* 1:277."

98 Venerable Bhikkhu Bodhi notes: "The above, too, is in *Majjhima Nikāya* 115 and *Aṅguttara Nikāya* 1:284 foll."

99 Venerable Bhikkhu Bodhi notes: "On this, see *Majjhima Nikāya* 45, 46."

100 Venerable Bhikkhu Bodhi notes: "This may be an allusion to *Aṅguttara Nikāya* 5:28."

101 Venerable Bhikkhu Bodhi notes: "This may be an allusion to *Aṅguttara Nikāya* 5:27."

102 This is a concept with numerous similar alternative explanations, most of which refer to the immense amount of merit and time required to acquire the thirty-two marks and eighty minor characteristics of a buddha's body and finally achieve buddhahood. This is discussed in greater detail in Nāgārjuna's commentary on the *Great Perfection of Wisdom Sutra,* T.25:57b5–27.

103 Nārāyaṇa is a powerful celestial eminence regarded as a Dharma protector in Buddhism.

104 As is quite common with the syntax of multi-line Classical Chinese verses, this quatrain requires the rearrangement of its lines to produce a sensible and naturally flowing statement in English.

105 "Eight classes in four pairs" (四雙八輩) refers to the four preliminary phases and four fruition stages on the individual liberation path of the *śrāvaka* disciples.

106 Venerable Bhikkhu Bodhi notes: "見聞覺知 = Pāli *diṭṭhaṃ, sutaṃ, mutaṃ, viññātaṃ,* where *mutaṃ* is explained as things sensed through the other three sense faculties: smell, taste, and touch."

Hence, in "seen, heard, sensed, and known" (per Hirakawa's *Buddhist Chinese-Sanskrit Dictionary: dṛṣṭa-śruta-mata-jñāta* or *dṛṣṭa-śruta-mata-vijñāta*), "sensed" (*mata*) refers to the sensory function of the olfactory, gustatory, and tactile sense faculties. Therefore this series is intended to refer to the functions of all six sense faculties and their corresponding consciousnesses.

107 To correct an apparent scribal error very likely originating in homophony, I emend the reading of the text here, preferring on sensibility grounds the homophonous *de* (得), "achieved," of the Song, Yuan, Ming, and Gong editions to the Taishō text's *de* (德), "qualities."

108 "Five characteristics" here is slightly ambiguous. It could refer particularly to the five types of desire which together constitute the first of the five hindrances (visible forms, sounds, smells, tastes, and touchables; or wealth, sex, fame, food, and leisure). Alternatively, it may be intended to refer to all five of the "five hindrances" that must be eliminated to access deep states of meditation (desire, ill will, lethargy and sleepiness, excitedness and regretfulness, and afflicted doubtfulness).

109 To correct an apparent graphic-similarity scribal error, I emend the reading of the Taishō text here by preferring the Song, Yuan, Ming, and Gong editions' *li* (力), "power," to the Taishō edition's *fen* (分), "portion."

110 I am not sure precisely what Nāgārjuna intended by "the six categories of meanings associated with the forty exclusive dharmas," set forth in his preceding praise verses.

111 The Sanskrit antecedent of *shixiang* (實相) in Kumārajīva translations is usually *dharmatā,* i.e., the true nature of all dharmas; i.e., *śūnyatā;* i.e., the utter absence of inherent existence in any and all phenomena.

112 To correct an apparent graphic-similarity scribal error, I emend the reading of the Taishō text here by preferring the Song, Yuan, Ming, and Gong editions' *shen* (深), "deep" or "profound," to the Taishō edition's *ran* (染), "defiled." Nāgārjuna's discussion of this line corroborates the correctness of the emendation.

113 When translated into Chinese, "Tathāgata" means "Thus Come One."

114 Again, this most likely refers to the *Pratyutpanna-samādhi-sūtra* preserved in the Taishō canon as the *Banzhou sanmei jing* (般舟三昧經, T.418:902c23–919c5).

115 "Overweening pride," *zeng shang man* (增上慢), corresponds to the Sanskrit *adhimāna.*

116 To correct an obvious graphic-similarity scribal error, I emend the reading of the Taishō text here by preferring the Song, Yuan, Ming, and Gong editions' *zeng* (增), "increase," to the Taishō edition's *zeng* (憎), "detest."

117 "Characteristic sign" refers here to any of the signs associated with three sequential levels of practice described at the very beginning of this chapter:

1. The thirty-two marks and eighty secondary characteristics of a buddha's form body;

2. The Dharma body of the buddhas;

3. The true character [of all dharmas], i.e., "emptiness of inherent existence" (*śūnyatā*). This "emptiness of inherent existence" is evidenced by: (A) their being merely composite constructs of subsidiary conditions; (B) their being merely evanescently transient states in a chain of serial causality; and (C) their being mere names attached to (A) and (B) to which one falsely imputes individual reality.

118 To correct an obvious graphic-similarity scribal error, I emend the reading of the Taishō text here by preferring the Song, Yuan, Ming, and Gong editions' *zhai* (齋), "ritual purification," to the Taishō edition's *qi* (齊), "uniform."

Also, "precepts of abstinence" refers here to *aṣṭāṅgasamanvāgataṃ upavāsaṃ,* the laity's formal acceptance and observance of the practice of upholding the eight precepts that include celibacy and not eating after midday. One observes this enhanced level of lay precept practice either continuously or on the eighth, fourteenth, fifteenth, twenty-third, twenty-ninth, and thirtieth days of each lunar month.

119 This reference to laypeople staying in a monastery probably refers to the not uncommon practice of allowing laypeople to live in separate quarters on monastery grounds when they are continuously training in these eight lay precepts for a predetermined period of time.

120 I translate here as "monastic preceptor" and "monastic Dharma teacher" what the Kumārajīva text retains in transliteration as *upādhyāya* and *ācārya* respectively.

121 Kumārajīva retained the Sanskrit term for "benefactor" (*dānapati*), which I have opted to translate here.

122 Venerable Bhikkhu Bodhi notes: "This is the practice of seeking alms at every door, without skipping over houses where the people do not give or give poor quality food."

The rationale for observing this "proper sequence" is that, since providing alms to monks and nuns produces karmic merit, one would not want to deny that opportunity to anyone.

[123] If "unwholesome remorsefulness" seems somewhat opaque, this would refer first and foremost to regretting having done something good or regretting not having done something bad.

[124] "Demolishing through separation" most likely refers to the "deconstructive analysis" involved in such contemplations as the contemplation of the thirty-two (or thirty-six) parts of the body, the nine stages of the decomposition of a rotting corpse, the white-boned skeleton contemplation, etc. All of these contemplations serve as powerful antidotes to sensual desire.

[125] This attainment of the sign of unloveliness refers to directly perceiving the unloveliness of sensually attractive physical forms so completely that the image of their unloveliness is retained even in the absence of the initially contemplated meditation object. This is often accomplished by deeply practicing the contemplations of the parts of the body, the stages of decomposition of a rotting corpse, or the white-boned skeleton.

[126] Hirakawa, *Buddhist Chinese-Sanskrit Dictionary,* gives the Sanskrit as *saṃrañjanīyaṃ dharmam*. These six dharmas refer to mutual harmoniousness, respect, equality, and fairness in matters pertaining to body, speech, mind, precepts, views, and benefits received (food, robes, shelter, etc.).

[127] These five bases of liberation (Skt. *vimukty-āyatanāni*) are five different circumstances under which, with or without the advantage of correct teaching from a qualified Dharma teacher or fellow practitioner, a practitioner may come to engage with and find success in cultivation, establish his mind in concentration, and then finally achieve liberation. Venerable Bhikkhu Bodhi refers us to *Aṅguttara Nikāya* 5:26 for the precise canonical explanation.

[128] Venerable Bhikkhu Bodhi refers us to *Aṅguttara Nikāya* 9:29.

[129] Venerable Bhikkhu Bodhi refers us to *Aṅguttara Nikāya* 8:80.

[130] Venerable Bhikkhu Bodhi refers us to *Aṅguttara Nikāya* 8:80, noting that this is found in the second part of that sutta.

[131] The "nine signs [of the deterioration of the corpse]" are the *navasaṃjñā,* for which Venerable Bhikkhu Bodhi refers us to *Aṅguttara Nikāya* 9:16.

[132] Venerable Bhikkhu Bodhi refers us to *Aṅguttara Nikāya* 8:30.

[133] "No apprehensible reality" (無所得) refers to emptiness of inherent existence, i.e., there is nothing in or about these *dhyāna* absorptions that can be gotten at as ultimately real.

[134] Venerable Bhikkhu Bodhi notes: "Items 43–45 are at *Saṃyutta Nikāya* 35:238, 'The Simile of the Vipers.'"

135 Venerable Bhikkhu Bodhi notes: "This may also be in *Saṃyutta Nikāya* 35:238: 'The further shore, which is safe and free from danger': this is a designation for Nibbāna."

136 This appears to be a quotation from the *Pratyutpanna-samādhi-sūtra.*

137 "Compulsory karmic retributions" most likely refers here to heinous karmic offenses that entail immediate retribution during or at the end of this very life, such as patricide, matricide, killing an arhat, drawing the blood of a buddha, or causing a schism in the monastic sangha.

138 This statement seems contradictory. As such, I am not particularly confident that this sentence is not corrupted or that I have interpreted its intent correctly.

139 The immediately preceding Abhidharmic analytic categories are in some cases phrased so tersely in the Chinese as to be mildly obscure. Hence I may not have rendered all of them with definitively precise accuracy.

140 These eight verse lines are a verbatim quote from the very beginning of Chapter 3 (*Nāgārjuna's Treatise on the Ten Grounds, Volume I*) on the characteristic features of the first bodhisattva ground (26a19–22).

141 Again, the first two of these five verses roughly correspond to the Kumārajīva and Buddhayaśas translation of the *Ten Grounds Sutra* (T.286:500b8–11).

142 As noted in Chapter 2 (*Nāgārjuna's Treatise on the Ten Grounds, Volume I*), again, *biding* (必定), "stage of certainty," is a translation of the Sanskrit *avaivartika*, the stage of irreversibility from which one can never again fall back in one's progress on the path.

143 These twenty verse lines are a verbatim quote from the very beginning of Chapter 2 (*Nāgārjuna's Treatise on the Ten Grounds, Volume I*) on entry into the first of the ten bodhisattva grounds (23a23–b3).

144 Kumārajīva retained the Sanskrit *sarvajña,* which I have chosen here to translate as "all-knowledge."

145 With the exception of a minor phrase variation in the second of these twenty-eight lines, this is a verbatim quote from the opening lines of Chapter 4 (*Nāgārjuna's Treatise on the Ten Grounds, Volume I*), "On the Purification of the Ground" (28c24–29a8).

146 Each of these seven are clearly explained at the very beginning of Chapter 3 (*Nāgārjuna's Treatise on the Ten Grounds, Volume I*).

147 Again, these were "disbelief, breaking of precepts, having but little learning, covetousness, indolence, chaotic thoughts, and absence of wisdom."

148 The Chinese text here simply transliterates a Sanskrit term for "passport" as *weipotuo* (韋婆陀), which I prefer to translate.

149 At this point in Nāgārjuna's text, there is an interpolated note, most likely inserted by the Kumārajīva translation team: "The Chinese translation of the Sanskrit *weituo* (韋陀) is 'unopposed' and it means 'passport.'"

[150] Again, "the five hindrances" is a reference to desire, ill will, lethargy and sleepiness, excitedness and regretfulness, and afflicted doubtfulness, hindrances that must be overcome in order to successfully enter deep states of meditation.

[151] "[T]he other [forms of wisdom]" most likely refers to "wisdom that arises from contemplation" and "great wisdom," both of which were mentioned just above in discussing the metaphoric significance of firewood in this extended analogy that forms the basis of two-thirds of this chapter.

[152] *Zhengwei* (正位), "right and fixed position," seems to usually correspond to the Sanskrit *samyaktva-niyāma,* for which Edward Conze and Gakujutsu Zaidan Suzuki, *Materials for a Dictionary of the Prajñāpāramitā Literature* (Tokyo: Suzuki Research Foundation, 1967), give "certainty to have got safely out of this world," or, in the case of *samyaktva-niyata*, "destined for salvation."

[153] "Faculties" here is a reference to "the five root faculties" that once developed become "the five powers": faith, vigor, mindfulness, concentration, and wisdom.

[154] I emend the reading per the Song, Yuan, Ming, and Gong editions to correct the Taishō edition's mistaken inclusion here of *bu* (不), "not." Absent this correction, the statement would result in the exact opposite of the obviously intended meaning.

[155] This line could also be plausibly rendered as "the hazardous and bad road of samsara."

[156] In other words, "This is tantamount to committing suicide [on the path to spiritual liberation]."

[157] In this particular passage, especially following on the heels of his warning about "neglectfulness," Nāgārjuna is presenting a very close paraphrase of five verses from his own *Bodhisaṃbhāra-śāstra,* verses 24–28. I quote them here from my own complete translation of that treatise along with its early Indian commentary, *Nāgārjuna's Guide to the Bodhisattva Path: Treatise on the Provisions for Enlightenment. The Bodhisaṃbhāra Śāstra by Ārya Nāgārjuna* (Seattle: Kalavinka Press, 2009):

024
Until one develops the great compassion and the patiences,
Even though he may have gained irreversibility,
The bodhisattva is still subject to a form of "dying"
Occurring through the arising of negligence.

025
The grounds of the Śrāvakas or the Pratyekabuddhas,
If entered, constitute "death" for him
Because he would thereby sever the roots
Of the bodhisattva's understanding and awareness.

026
At the prospect of falling into the hell-realms,
The bodhisattva would not be struck with fright.

The grounds of the Śrāvakas and the Pratyekabuddhas
Do provoke great terror in him.

027
It is not the case that falling into the hell realms
Would create an ultimate obstacle to *bodhi.*
If one fell onto the grounds of the Śrāvakas or Pratyekabuddhas,
That would create an ultimate obstacle.

028
Just as is said of one who loves long life
That he is frightened at the prospect of being beheaded,
So too the grounds of the Śrāvakas and Pratyekabuddhas
Should provoke in one this very sort of fear.

158 The Chinese translation preserved a shorthand rendering of the third hindrance (as "drowsiness") and fourth hindrance (as "excitedness"), for which I have supplied the standard complete rendering of these classic Indian Buddhist technical terms, the third and fourth of which are dual-component hindrances.

159 This is most likely referring to the fact that his adherence to moral virtue is not pursued in order to achieve rebirth in the heavens.

160 This most likely refers to preventing oneself from taking rebirth in the form realm heavens because they constitute an obstacle to cultivation of the bodhisattva path.

161 "Four means of attraction" refers to giving, pleasing words, beneficial actions, and joint endeavors.

162 The four immeasurable minds are kindness, compassion, sympathetic joy, and equanimity.

163 See note 3 regarding the chapter numbering. (The Taishō edition calls this "Chapter One.")

164 As revealed by the discussion in the Digital Sanskrit Buddhist Canon's digitized edition of the of the *Ten Grounds Sutra* (P. L. Vaidya, ed., *Daśabhūmikasūtram;* hereafter DSBC) of the second bodhisattva ground, *shi zhong xin* (十種心) "ten types of *resolute intentions*" here and in the ensuing *Shizhu piposha lun* discussion correspond to the Sanskrit *cittāśaya.*

165 The DSBC *Ten Grounds Sutra* accords fairly closely with the *Shizhu piposha lun* order of this list of ten "resolute intentions" (*cittāśaya*) as it is presented in the following explanation. It records the Sanskrit antecedents as *ṛjvāśaya* (= *ārjava*?), *mṛdvāśaya, karmaṇyāśaya, damāśaya, śamāśaya, kalyāṇāśaya, asaṃsṛṣṭāśaya, anapekṣāśaya, udārāśaya, māhātmyāśaya.*

166 These six verses correspond to verses 12–17 of Nāgārjuna's *Bodhisaṃbhāraśāstra*. I quote them here from my own complete translation of that treatise along with

its early Indian commentary, *Nāgārjuna's Guide to the Bodhisattva Path: Treatise on the Provisions for Enlightenment:*

012
From the very beginning, the bodhisattva
Should accord with the power of his abilities
And use skillful means to instruct beings,
Causing them to enter the Great Vehicle.

013
Even if one taught beings as numerous as the Ganges' sands
So that they were caused to gain the fruit of arhatship,
Still, by instructing but a single person to enter the Great Vehicle,
One would generate merit superior to that.

014
Instructing through resort to the Śrāvaka Vehicle
Or through resort to the Pratyekabuddha Vehicle
Is undertaken where, on account of lesser abilities,
Beings are unable to accept instruction in the Great Vehicle.

015
Where even when relying on Śrāvaka or Pratyekabuddha Vehicles
In addition to the Great Vehicle teachings,
There are those who still cannot accept any such instruction,
One should strive to establish them in merit-creating situations.

016
If there be persons unable to accept
Instruction conducing either to the heavens or to liberation,
Favor them through bestowing present-life benefits.
Then, as befits one's powers, one should draw them in.

017
Where, with regard to particular beings, a bodhisattva
Has no conditions through which to instruct them,
He should draw forth the great kindness and compassion
And should refrain from abandoning them.

[167] To correct an apparent graphic-similarity scribal error, I emend the reading of the Taishō text here by preferring the Song, Yuan, Ming, and Gong editions' *guo* (果), "resultant," to the Taishō edition's *yi* (異), "different." (The immediately following question in the ensuing text echoes this word choice and corroborates the validity of the emendation.)

[168] Although this teaching seems to be addressed exclusively to men regarding their behavior vis-à-vis women, that is only because most women were illiterate at the time and never would have encountered this treatise outside of a lecture format where its universal applicability would have been made clear.

169 In Buddhist texts, "restricted orifice" refers to oral sex, anal sex, etc.

170 This "scattered or inappropriate speech" usually translates *saṃbhinnapralāpa,* which, in addition to the definitions mentioned here, is usually also interpreted to include "lewd, dirty, or off-color speech." This traditional subdefinition is implicitly and euphemistically referenced here a few lines below as one of the traditional meanings of "speech contrary to Dharma."

171 "Volition" (思) could be referring here to premeditation, i.e., deliberate intentionality.

172 Venerable Bhikkhu Bodhi notes: "Items sixteen and seventeen here correspond to functions relating to the four noble truths: the truth of the path is *bhāvetabba*, 'to be cultivated.' The truth of suffering is *pariññeyya,* 'to be well understood.'"

173 Venerable Bhikkhu Bodhi notes: "[This refers to] *pahātabba*: the function pertaining to the second noble truth."

174 I am not entirely sure about the accuracy of my translation of the following fourfold list. I may have misunderstood it or it may be slightly corrupted.

175 Because some of these listed distinctions seem contradictory, I am not confident that I have correctly rendered the intended meaning of the Abhidharmic technical terms here. It may also be the case that the text has become somewhat corrupted.

176 Because this would seem to be a contradiction, I am not sure I have translated this correctly. There are five instances of this same statement (with minor variations) in this chapter.

177 Venerable Bhikkhu Bodhi notes: "The above [two cases] refer to two stages or degrees of an affliction: the stage of *anuśaya,* where it remains as a latent tendency; and the stage of obsession, where it arises and dominates the mind."

178 Venerable Bhikkhu Bodhi notes: "This latter alternative presumably refers to abandoning the taking of life in world-transcendent (*lokottara*) states of mind."

179 This twelvefold list has become slightly corrupted at some point, but not irretrievably so. (As noted below, I correct the corruption by emendation.) As received, it duplicates the sixth member of the list, "For what is it a condition?" (與誰作緣?), and leaves out another member of the list that we encounter in the ensuing discussion, "What is the benefit?" (何利益?).

180 The received editions of this text mistakenly duplicate list item number 6 here as "8. For what is it a condition?" I have emended the text to correct this obvious scribal error by inserting the missing list item, "What is the benefit?" (何利益?), which is found in the ensuing discussion at 97a27–8.

181 Venerable Bhikkhu Bodhi notes: "This may be alluding to a passage in the early sutras, see *Aṅguttara Nikāya* 6.63: 'It is volition, O monks, that I call karma. For having willed, one acts by body, speech, or mind.' Thus covetousness, etc., are here considered not to be karma (in the sense of actual action) because they are mental

states associated with or corresponding to volition rather than actions in their own right. The Theravāda Abhidhamma differs, considering covetousness, etc., both karma and paths of karma. They are mental karma (*manokamma*)."

182 The phrase "there is no fixed subjective agent [involved in its creation]" (無有定主) can refer to one or both of two ideas: (1) the absence of any sort of creator god involved in the creation of the world; or (2) the absence of any inherently existent "self" in oneself or in any of the other beings who collectively create all the causes and conditions for the creation, abiding, and destruction of the world, this through the causal power of their good and bad karmic deeds.

183 In referring to it as the "Nonextensive Heaven" (不廣天), Nāgārjuna uses an extremely rare name for this Avṛha Heaven. (There is only one other use of this name in the entire Taishō canon.) The more common Chinese name is "No Affliction Heaven" (無煩天).

184 See note 3 regarding chapter numbering. (The Taishō edition calls this "Chapter Two.")

185 In commenting on this line that I might otherwise translate as "and who always disbelieve that the world/is possessed of *the dharma of* stability and security—," Venerable Bhikkhu Bodhi notes: "In Sanskrit and Pāli, *-dharma*/*-dhamma* is often used as a suffix to indicate 'having the nature of' or 'subject to.' Thus (P) *sabbe sattā maraṇadhammā*, 'all beings are subject to death/have the nature of dying.' I suspect that the Sanskrit original of this line used '*dharma*' [法] in that function, thus [the sense of this may be] 'The world does not have a stable and secure nature.'"

186 "*Śrāvaka*" means, in essence, "auditor," i.e., "those who learn by listening."

187 Venerable Bhikkhu Bodhi notes: The Pāli version, *Aṅguttara Nikāya* 1:328, *Numerical Discourses of the Buddha,* p. 121: "Bhikkhus, just as even a trifling amount of feces is foul smelling, so too I do not praise even a trifling amount of existence, even for a mere finger snap."

188 Nāgārjuna seems to be referring here to the pivotal importance of one's last thoughts at the moment of death that may so strongly influence whether or not one then enters good or bad rebirth circumstances.

189 To clarify, "what is unlovely, stinking, defiled, and ungrateful for kindnesses" is intended to refer to the human body.

190 Venerable Bhikkhu Bodhi notes: "See *Saṃyutta Nikāya* 35:28, *Connected Discourses of the Buddha,* p. 1143."

191 Venerable Bhikkhu Bodhi notes: "This sequence is found in several places in the Nikāyas, especially in the *Aṅguttara*. See *Aṅguttara Nikāya* 10:1–4 and 11:1–4. Here, 厭 = *nibbidā*, which I render 'disenchantment,' while 離 is *virāga*, 'dispassion' or 'detachment.'"

192 Regarding Sīvalī, Venerable Bhikkhu Bodhi notes: "尊者施曰羅. This is probably Ven. Sivali. Since 捨 can mean either 'generosity' or 'relinquishment,' the two connect Sivali's past-life merits with his special facility as a monk."

From G. P. Malasekhara, *Dictionary of Pali Proper Names* (London: J. Murray, 1937): "In Padumuttara Buddha's time he made the resolve to be pre-eminent among recipients of gifts, like Sudassana, disciple of Padumuttara. To this end he gave alms for seven days to the Buddha and his monks. In the time of Vipassī Buddha he was a householder near Bandhumatī. The people gave alms to the Buddha and the Order in competition with the king, and when they were in need of honey, curds and sugar, Sīvalī gave enough of these for sixty-eight thousand monks.... Sīvalī was declared by the Buddha (A.i.24). pre-eminent among recipients of gifts.... Sīvalī went to the Himālaya with five hundred others, to test his good luck. The gods provided them with everything. On Gandhamādana a *deva,* named Nāgadatta, entertained them for seven days on milk rice." Accessed online: http://www.palikanon.com/english/pali_names/s/siivalii.htm.

193 Venerable Bhikkhu Bodhi notes: "*Aṅguttara* 4: 143: 'Bhikkhus, there are these four lights. What four? The light of the moon, the light of the sun, the light of fire, and the light of wisdom. These are the four lights. Of these four lights, the light of wisdom is foremost.'"

194 See note 3 regarding chapter numbering. (The Taishō edition calls this "Chapter Three.")

195 Although slightly ambiguous, their "twofold vows" most likely refers to their vows to accomplish both self-benefit and other-benefit, i.e., to become buddhas themselves while also facilitating the awakening of all other beings.

196 See the chapter-commencing verse, lines 1–2.

197 See the chapter-commencing verse, line 4.

198 As noted by Venerable Bhikkhu Bodhi, here *shan* (善) does not have its somewhat more usual meaning of "goodness" (*kuśala*). Rather, as in many places in Kumārajīva translations, it serves here as an intensifying modifier. When modifying "purity," as in the "*su*" of *suviśuddha*, it would instead mean "thorough," "thoroughgoing," or "complete" purity.

199 See note 198 above for an explanation of this somewhat less usual use of the *shan* (善) in *shan qingjing* (善清淨).

200 Although not explicitly stated here, the "three types of purity" may refer to either (or both) of two explanations offered earlier in the sutra. Here are the two previous explanations:

1. In Chapter 5 (*Nāgārjuna's Treatise on the Ten Grounds, Volume I*), we had: "As for 'purity,' this means that one has completely developed the three types of purity, namely purity in physical actions, purity in verbal actions, and purity in mental actions."

2. In Chapter 28 specifically referring to the bodhisattva's practice of these ten courses of good karmic action on this second bodhisattva ground, the verse and the prose explanation immediately following read:

If a bodhisattva still at the border with the first ground
employs three kinds of purity
to abide securely in the ten courses of good karmic action,
he will then be able to bring forth decisive resolve.

Once this bodhisattva comes to dwell on the second ground, he then distinguishes with utter clarity these ten good and bad courses of karmic action. Having come to know these matters, he applies three kinds of purity to his abiding in the ten courses of good karmic action, namely:

He does not personally kill any being;
He does not instruct others to kill any being;
And he does not delight in the karmic offense of killing.

201 See the chapter-commencing verse, line 3.

202 See Chapter 5, "The Explanation of the Vows" (*Nāgārjuna's Treatise on the Ten Grounds, Volume I*), wherein these ten "ultimate ends" that define the infinity of the bodhisattva vows are listed as follows:

[Hence these vows are made:]
First, until the end of the realms of beings;
Second, until the end of the realms of worlds;
Third, until the end of the realms of empty space;
Fourth, until the end of the Dharma realm;
Fifth, until the end of the realm of nirvana;
Sixth, until the end of the realms in which buddhas are born;
Seventh, until the end of the realms of all buddhas' knowledge;
Eighth, until the end of everything that can be taken as an object of mind;
Ninth, until the end of the knowledge associated with the range of all buddhas' actions;
And tenth, until the end of the permutations of the knowledge of worldly dharmas.
These are the ten [ways in which vows are] ultimately enduring.

203 See chapter-commencing verse, line 3.

204 See chapter-commencing verse, line 5.

205 This is clearly a reference to "the right and fixed position" (*samyaktva-niyāma*) wherein the bodhisattva becomes immune to the temptations of opting for the nirvana prized by adherents of the *śrāvaka* disciple vehicle and the *pratyekabuddha* vehicle.

206 See chapter-commencing verse, line 5.

207 See chapter-commencing verse, line 6.

208 See chapter-commencing verse, line 6.

209 See chapter-commencing verse, line 7.

210 Venerable Bhikkhu Bodhi points out that this "*maintaining vigilance* at all times throughout the first watch and the last watch of the night" is stock material in the early *sutta*s that should not be misunderstood as referencing "achieving awakening" (覺悟) as such. See *Numerical Discourses of the Buddha*, pp. 212, 427, etc.

211 I prefer here to translate what the Kumārajīva text preserves as the transliterations of the Sanskrit for the perfections: "One first speaks of *dāna-pāramitā,* then *śīla-pāramitā,* then *kṣānti-pāramitā,* then *vīrya-pāramitā,* then *dhyāna-pāramitā,* and then *prajñā-pāramitā.*"

212 See chapter-commencing verse, line 8.

213 See chapter-commencing verse, line 9.

214 Having already made it clear in the above fivefold list that it is a good thing to disdain the dharmas of petty people and esteem the dharmas of great men, here one is reminded to still retain completely equal compassionate regard for the people themselves.

215 See chapter-commencing verse, line 10. ("[They] deeply cherish the wisdom of the buddhas….")

216 See chapter-commencing verse, lines 11–12.

217 See chapter-commencing verse, line 12.

218 See chapter-commencing verse, line 12.

219 Venerable Bhikkhu Bodhi notes: "For these, see *Aṅguttara Nikāya* 5:144, *Numerical Discourses of the Buddha,* pp. 761–762 along with note 1144. *Paṭisambhidāmagga* calls them 'powers of the noble ones' (*ariy'iddhi*)."

220 This is a reference to number four, "the psychic powers of the *ārya*s."

221 See chapter-commencing verse, line 13.

222 See chapter-commencing verse, line 14.

223 A search of the Taishō canon indicates that in both cases (whether "dark" or "great"), these "four seals" refer to four levels of trustworthiness in determining whether or not any given teaching that one has received is to be trusted as truly originating with the Buddha.

224 See chapter-commencing verse, line 15.

225 See chapter-commencing verse, line 15.

226 See chapter-commencing verse, line 15.

227 See chapter-commencing verse, line 16.

228 I emend the text here to accord with four other editions by substituting 汝 for 如 to correct an apparent homophonic scribal error, this because the resulting reading is much more plausible than the extremely forced reading that retaining 如 would yield.

229 See chapter-commencing verse, line 17.

230 See chapter-commencing verse, line 18.

231 See chapter-commencing verse, line 19.

232 See chapter-commencing verse, line 20.

233 See chapter-commencing verse, lines 21–22.

234 See chapter-commencing verse, lines 23–24.

235 Although, per Monier Williams' *Sanskrit-English Dictionary,* the meaning of the Sanskrit word *bhagavat* is "possessing fortune, fortunate, prosperous, happy" or "glorious, illustrious, divine, adorable, venerable," in Buddhism it is one of the ten primary names of any and all buddhas that are intended to call to mind all of the Buddha's qualities including his perfect wisdom and virtue. The Chinese translation is "World-honored One" (世尊). Other common English translations (per the *Princeton Dictionary of Buddhism*) are "Blessed One," "Exalted One," or "Lord." It is because of the wide range of connotations of the name that rather than translate the Chinese honorific, I usually prefer to simply use the now fairly common Sanskrit term "Bhagavat." (I *do* translate it in the following verse, however.) "Bhagavan" is essentially the same word that one encounters in other translations and other traditions as (again, per the *Princeton Dictionary of Buddhism*) *bhagavān, bhagavad, bhagawan,* and *bhagwan.*

236 "The fourteen ineffable dharmas" is a reference to the fourteen "unanswered" or "undeclared" (*avyākṛta*) dharmas.

237 See note 3 regarding the chapter numbering. (The Taishō edition calls this "Chapter Four.")

238 Although the language itself is not specific, the implicit reference is to extramarital relationships, perhaps voluntary, perhaps not.

239 I emend the text here (at 108a17, second character) by replacing the clearly erroneous *bu* (不), "not," with the doubtlessly intended *xia* (下), "lesser," to correct an obvious graphic-similarity scribal error not noticed in either Taishō or in any of its recorded alternate editions.

240 "Obsessed" (纏) corresponds to the Sanskrit *paryavasthāna* and refers to the active phase of entanglement by the afflictions.

241 "[T]he view of a real self in association with the body [or any of the other four aggregates]" (身見) corresponds to the Sanskrit *satkāyadṛṣṭi.*

242 Venerable Bhikkhu Bodhi notes that, on the *śrāvaka* vehicle path, this severance via seeing the four truths occurs upon realizing stream-entry, whereas severance through meditative cultivation occurs on the three higher stages of the path to arhatship.

243 What is referred to here as "the ninety-eight fetters" (九十八使) is elsewhere rendered somewhat more precisely as "the ninety-eight latent tendencies" (九十八隨眠, Skt. *anuśaya*), hence I translate accordingly.

244 I emend the reading here to correct a fairly obvious graphic-similarity scribal error by preferring on doctrinal sensibility grounds Song, Yuan, Ming, and Gong editions' *hui* (悔), "regret," to the Taishō edition's *wu* (侮), "to insult."

245 I have followed four other editions (Song, Yuan, Ming, and Gong) in placing these four lines into verse format. The correctness of this couldn't be clearer, especially given the combination of even line length, context, and unavoidably obvious Chinese rhyming of the quatrain's third line with the first line and fourth line with the second line.

246 This very long quotation (two and a half pages, ending at the next set of stanza lines) corresponds fairly closely to a second ground passage in the Kumārajīva and Buddhayaśas *Ten Grounds Sutra* translation (T.286:505b5–c20) and also to the corresponding second ground passage in the Śikṣānanda translation of the *Avataṃsaka-sūtra*'s "Ten Grounds" chapter (T.279:186a10–b22).

247 Venerable Bhikkhu Bodhi notes: "This is a reference to the three wrong thoughts (*vitarka*): sensual thought, thought of ill will, and thought of harming."

248 The following passage corresponds quite closely with a long passage in the "Akṣayamati" chapter of the *Mahāsaṃnipāta-sūtra* (in the Taishō canon's Chinese translation by Dharmakṣema in 413 C.E.: 大方等大集經卷第二十七 –無盡意菩薩品第十二之一; T.397:189c27–190b10). However, that translation lists "sixty-seven" rather than the "sixty-five" to which Nāgārjuna refers in this treatise that was probably composed two centuries before Dharmakṣema's translation.

249 This aspect of moral virtue together with the next nine correspond to the ten courses of good karmic action.

250 This aspect of moral virtue together with the next two correspond to the Three Refuges.

251 Venerable Bhikkhu Bodhi points out that "things that accord with Dharma" (如法物) is probably best construed as "things *obtained* in accordance with the Dharma," because it directly corresponds to "*yathādhammaṃ lābha*" in the Pāli scriptures.

252 This aspect of moral virtue and the next three correspond to the four immeasurable minds.

253 This aspect of moral virtue together with the next five correspond to the six perfections. Here the first two perfections are listed in reverse order.

254 I emend the reading here to correct a fairly obvious graphic-similarity scribal error by preferring (due to issues of doctrinal sensibility and explicitly stated parallelism) the Song, Yuan, Ming, and Gong editions' *chang* (常), "constantly," to the Taishō edition's *dang* (當), "should."

255 Venerable Bhikkhu Bodhi notes: "This is referring to the abandoning of physical bad karma not included in the ten karmic paths, for, in the form realm, there is no killing, stealing, and sexual misconduct—indeed, there is no sexuality there, no private property, and the beings have fixed life spans. Since the three transgressions

are impossible there, there is no abandoning them; but minor types of unwholesome physical conduct might exist there, and one must abstain from these."

256 Venerable Bhikkhu Bodhi offers a clarifying note here with respect to bad karmic actions associated with speech in the form realm: "This [mention of scattered or inappropriate speech] is not just an example; apparently there is no lying, divisive speech, or harsh speech in the form realm, but there is scattered speech."

257 *Brahmacarya,* lit., "brahman conduct," refers to the celibate spiritual life.

258 Venerable Bhikkhu Bodhi notes: "See *Aṅguttara Nikāya* 7:50, *Numerical Discourses of the Buddha,* pp. 1038–1039. The sixth is different from the Pāli version."

259 As mentioned in the above note, the Pāli version of number six is different, as follows: "(6)…he does not recollect laughing, talking, and playing with women in the past…but he looks at a householder or a householder's son enjoying himself furnished and endowed with the five objects of sensual pleasure…."

260 Venerable Bhikkhu Bodhi located what appears to be very nearly this same passage in the *Mahāratnakūṭa* collection (大寶積經), T.310:636c28.

261 Venerable Bhikkhu Bodhi located this passage in the *Mahāvaipulya-mahāsaṃnipāta-sūtra* (大方等大集經), T.397:190b11.

262 "Name and form" (名色 = *nāmarūpa*) is a reference to the five aggregates.

263 The *Mahāvaipulya-mahāsaṃnipāta-sūtra* translation's version of this passage clarifies this sangha-related clause with "by *cultivation* of the unconditioned" (T.397:190b28: 不斷僧種, [17] 修無為故). Note 17 in that edition tells us that the Song, Yuan, Ming, and Gong editions reading has 以修 instead of just 修.

264 The *Mahāvaipulya-mahāsaṃnipāta-sūtra* translation's version of this passage is found at T.397:190c1.

265 See note 3 regarding the chapter numbering. (The Taishō edition calls this "Chapter Five.")

266 Venerable Bhikkhu Bodhi offers the following supplementary note on the austerities:

> Ten ascetic practices are mentioned in the *Aṅguttara Nikāya* at 5:181–90, each distinguished as fivefold in accordance with the reasons they are undertaken. In the Theravāda tradition, the standard list of ascetic practices is expanded to thirteen, described and analyzed in *Visuddhimagga*, Chapter 2. Ten agree with those in this chapter. They differ in that the *Daśabhūmika-vibhāṣā-śāstra* includes two not in the *Visuddhimagga* system: wearing robes made of animal hairs, and not accepting drinks other than water after mid-day. The *Visuddhimagga* list includes three not in this *Daśabhūmika-vibhāṣā-śāstra:* walking on alms round by going to every house, without skipping any (a narrowing of the ascetic practice of eating only food collected on alms round); eating only from the alms bowl (refusing the use of other plates and saucers); and refusing food brought after one has started

one's meal (but still within the time limits). The latter seems to be a different interpretation of the ascetic practice the *Daśabhūmika-vibhāṣā-śāstra* system interprets as refusing drinks after mid-day.

267 The Chinese text for this first reflection is ambiguous. It seems to allude to the idea that whatever one receives (or doesn't receive) on the almsround is a direct reflection of whether or not one has created enough merit, hence being able to continue in this is one's own responsibility and no one else's.

268 The implication here is that one should be willing to abandon any concerns for personal comfort as one vigorously pursues very rigorous bodhisattva path practices.

269 "Unimpeded reflections" here likely refers to such reflections as those devoted to deep understanding and realization of the three gates to liberation, the four immeasurables, the four bases of meritorious qualities, and the six perfections (as implied just below at 112a27–29).

270 Due to the requirements of sensibility, I emend the reading of the text here in accordance with the Song, Yuan, Ming, and Gong editions by adding a missing character, *ji* (及), before Taishō's *shen* (身) to produce *jishen* (及身), which I take here to mean "for one's entire life."

271 Venerable Bhikkhu Bodhi notes: "What is mentioned here are the three kinds of wholesome thought, namely, thought of renunciation, thought of non-ill will, and thought of non-harming. Note that *chujue* (出覺) is *nekkhamma-vitakka,* 'thought of renunciation.' See for example *Majjhima Nikāya* 19, on the three kinds of wholesome thought:

"*Tassa mayhaṃ, bhikkhave, evaṃ appamattassa ātāpino pahitattassa viharato uppajjati nekkhammavitakko...abyāpādavitakko...pe...avihiṃsāvitakko.*"

272 Venerable Bhikkhu Bodhi notes that this is Ugra, the subject of the *Ugraparipṛcchā-sūtra,* and that this passage can be found in the *Mahāratnakūṭa-sūtra* (大寶積經卷第八十二，郁伽長者會第十九), beginning at T.310:477c24.

273 "Six objects" likely refers to the "six recollections" (*anusmṛti*) of the Buddha, Dharma, and Sangha, moral virtue, generosity, and the *deva*s.

274 The relevant verse from Chapter 3 (*Nāgārjuna's Treatise on the Ten Grounds, Volume I,* p. 48; 27a15–18) is:

He is free of the fear of not surviving,
the fear of death, the fear of the wretched destinies,
the fear of the Great Assembly's awesome virtue,
the fear of ill repute, and the fear of being disparaged.
As for fear of imprisonment, shackles, and manacles,
and the fear of beatings or capital punishment,
given that he is free of a self or any possessions of self,
how then could he have any such fears as these?

275 Venerable Bhikkhu Bodhi notes that the Pāli parallel is *Saṃyutta Nikāya* 3:5.

276 Venerable Bhikkhu Bodhi notes: "The Pāli parallel is *Saṃyutta Nikāya* 11:3. The author of this work is evidently very familiar with the Nikāyas/Āgama collections."

277 Venerable Bhikkhu Bodhi notes: "The Pāli parallel for this passage is the first part of *Majjhima Nikāya Sutta* 4"; see *The Middle Length Discourses of the Buddha,* pp. 102–103.

278 As noted earlier by Venerable Bhikkhu Bodhi, again, this is Ugra, the subject of the *Ugraparipṛcchā-sūtra*. This particular passage can be found in the *Mahāratnakūṭa-sūtra* (大寶積經卷第八十二，郁伽長者會第十九), beginning at T.310:478a20.

279 "Difficulties" here is probably a reference to the eight difficulties of which the hells, animals, and hungry ghosts are the first three items in the list.

280 I emend the reading of the Taishō text here by preferring on sensibility grounds the Song, Yuan, Ming, and Gong editions' *zhi* (知), "to know," to the Taishō edition's *hehe* (和合), "to harmonize."

281 This is probably meant to refer to the four floods (Skt. *catvāra oghāḥ*, *catur-ogha*): sensual desire (*kāmarāga*), [craving for] continuing existence (*bhava*), ignorance (*avidyā*), and views (*dṛṣṭi*). These are identical to the "contaminants" (*āsrava*).

282 Again, the four lineage bases of the *ārya*s (*catur-āryavaṃśa*) are (1) delighting in mere sufficiency in clothing, (2) delighting in mere sufficiency of food and drink, (3) delighting in mere sufficiency of bedding, and (4) delighting in the severance [of evil] and the cultivation [of goodness].

283 "Nature of dharmas" usually corresponds to the Sanskrit *dharmatā*. Still, although somewhat less likely, given that Kumārajīva very regularly uses *xing* (性) to translate *dhātu,* this might also be construed to mean "Dwelling in a forest hermitage refers to [realizing that] all realms together constitute the Dharma realm."

284 "The stations of rebirth to which they correspond" refers to rebirth in the heavens of the form realm.

285 I emend the reading of the Taishō text here by preferring on sensibility grounds the Song, Yuan, Ming, and Gong editions' *ci yinyuan* (此因緣), "these [special] circumstances," to the Taishō edition's *yinyuan* (因緣), "[special] circumstances."

286 A *saṃghāvaśeṣa* offense is a serious offense, such as touching a woman motivated by a thought of desire, that requires a meeting of the *bhikṣu* sangha to determine the disciplinary penalty. "Grave offense" here is a euphemism for sexual intercourse, a *pārājika* offense that entails expulsion from the monastic community. The third case, "transgressing against the precept and returning to lay life," refers to committing either of the above sorts of offenses and then voluntarily setting aside the robes, rather than waiting for the *bhikṣu* sangha's formal judgment on the matter.

287 These first two *dhūta* austerities just discussed at length were always (1) gaining one's sustenance from the almsround and (2) dwelling in a forest hermitage.

[288] "Not accepting any beverage at the wrong time" means that that one does not accept any beverage but water outside of that very mealtime. "Wrong time" has the additional meaning of "not after midday."

[289] Venerable Bhikkhu Bodhi notes: "When one first receives full ordination, the teacher explains the ideal form of the four requisites: using cast-off robes, food obtained on alms round, dwelling at the foot of a tree, and using cow's urine for medicine. Then he explains the more lenient alternatives. Thus *chushou* (初受), ['the initially received explanation'], refers to what was first explained at one's ordination."

[290] To clarify, this in no way restricts standing or walking. It is entirely a matter of never lying down, not even during sleep.

[291] Again, although it is not mentioned here, in addition to its otherwise referenced meanings, "at the wrong time" also means "not after midday."

[292] Venerable Bhikkhu Bodhi notes that this *zuo wo ju* (坐臥具), *senāsana*, lit., "seats and beds," is a term of convenience for "a dwelling place."

[293] Venerable Bhikkhu Bodhi notes: "This is an allusion to a sutra in which the Buddha says that "noise is a thorn for one attaining the first *dhyāna*." See *Aṅguttara Nikāya* 10:72: "Thorns":…(5) Noise is a thorn to the first *jhāna*. (6) Thought and examination are a thorn to the second *jhāna*. (7) Rapture is a thorn to the third *jhāna*. (8) In-and-out breathing is a thorn to the fourth *jhāna*."

[294] To correct an apparent graphic-similarity and/or homophonic scribal error, I emend the reading of the Taishō text here by preferring the Song, Yuan, Ming, and Gong editions' *shang* (尚), "even," to the Taishō edition's *chang* (常), "always." The correctness of the emendation is corroborated by the commentary in the next paragraph.

[295] To correct an apparent omission, I emend the reading of the Taishō text here by preferring on sensibility grounds the Song, Yuan, Ming, and Gong editions' insertion of an additional character, *fo* (佛), "Buddha," to begin this sentence. The emended reading then exactly echoes the text of the verse upon which this sentence comments.

[296] I emend the reading of the Taishō text here by preferring on sensibility grounds the Song, Yuan, Ming, and Gong editions' *yang* (殃), "disastrous," to the Taishō edition's *da* (大), "great."

[297] I emend the reading of the text here in accordance with the Song, Yuan, and Ming (but not Gong) editions by preferring on sensibility grounds *tong* (通), "understand," to the Taishō edition's *song* (誦), "recite."

[298] See note 3 regarding the chapter numbering. (The Taishō edition calls this "Chapter Six.")

[299] I emend the reading of the text here in accordance with the Song, Yuan, Ming, and Gong editions by preferring on sensibility grounds the inclusion of an apparently lost item of the often encountered rather standard list found later on in this same chapter that includes *mingzhe jian* (命者見), "the view of a life."

[300] Again, even though this *zuo wo ju* (坐臥具) would seem to refer to "seats and beds," it is a hyperliteral translation of the Sanskrit *senāsana,* a term of convenience for "lodging" or "dwelling place."

[301] Yet again, both here and directly below, Kumārajīva is translating *xing* (性), more usually "nature," as *dhatu,* usually "realms" or "elements." We know this both from context and from comparisons of his *Ten Grounds Sutra* translation with a much later Sanskrit edition of that sutra. This rendering of *xing* is somewhat inconsistently applied by the Kumārajīva translation team, hence we must rely on context sensibility to determine which Sanskrit antecedent is being referenced in any given passage. This line presents a perfect example of that inconsistency of usage, for it is used in *both* senses here, first as "elements," then as "nature."

[302] "The six elements" (*ṣaḍ-dhātu*) are earth, water, fire, wind/air, space, and consciousness.

[303] Regarding this statement that "the form aggregate is characterized by being assailed by what is painful," Venerable Bhikkhu Bodhi notes:

> 如說色是苦惱相": There is a word play in the Pāli (and, presumably its Sanskrit counterpart) that [although successfully captured in this passage translated by Kumārajīva], wasn't reflected in the Chinese translation [of the *Saṃyukta Āgama*]. A Pāli *sutta* (*Saṃyutta Nikāya* 22:79) playfully tried to derive *rūpa* = material form from the verb *ruppati,* meaning something like "to be molested, to be assailed"—"assailed by cold, by heat, by hunger and thirst, etc." There is no real etymological connection between *rūpa* and *ruppati,* but the pun works. Here is the Pāli:
>
> *Kiñca, bhikkhave, rūpaṃ vadetha? Ruppatī ti kho, bhikkhave, tasmā "rūpan" ti vuccati. Kena ruppati? Sītenapi ruppati, uṇhenapi ruppati, jighacchāyapi ruppati, pipāsāyapi ruppati, ḍaṃsamakasavātātapasiriṃsapasamphassenapi ruppati.*
>
> The Chinese parallel is *Saṃyukta Āgama* 46 (雜阿含經, T.99:11b26–29; 若可閡可分, 是名色受陰. 指所閡, 若手, 若石, 若杖, 若刀, 若冷, 若暖, 若渴, 若飢, 若蚊, 虻, 諸毒虫, 風, 雨觸, 是名觸閡, 是故閡是色受陰).

[304] To correct an apparent graphic-similarity scribal error, I emend the reading of the Taishō text here by preferring the Song, Yuan, Ming, and Gong editions' *duo* (墮), "to fall," to the Taishō edition's *sui* (隨), "to follow."

[305] In Classical Chinese literature, *zhi* (直), "straight, direct, etc.," is interchangeable with *zhi* (值), "worth, value, etc.," and I have translated it accordingly here as this is clearly the meaning intended by the Kumārajīva translation team.

[306] This very long verse is a nearly verbatim repetition of the verse found earlier in the treatise in Chapter 8 (*Nāgārjuna's Treatise on the Ten Grounds, Volume I,* 39c21–40a13). There are eight variant characters as noted in the following notes 307–308 and 310–311 (underlined characters).

307 The Chapter 8 (*Nāgārjuna's Treatise on the Ten Grounds, Volume I*) version of this verse has "and is identical with whatever is possessed of signs" instead of "and is identical with whatever is an existent dharma" (即為是有相 instead of 即為是有法).

308 The Chapter 8 (*Nāgārjuna's Treatise on the Ten Grounds, Volume I*) version of this verse has "Were one to relinquish all covetousness" instead of "Were one to relinquish all strategizing and attachments" (若捨諸貪著 instead of 若捨諸計著).

309 The Chapter 8 (*Nāgārjuna's Treatise on the Ten Grounds, Volume I*) version of this verse has "There is someone who grasps and something that is grasped" instead of "It is the abandonment of grasping and whatever thing is grasped" (誰取取何事 instead of 離取取何事).

310 The Chapter 8 (*Nāgārjuna's Treatise on the Ten Grounds, Volume I*) version of this verse has "whether as conjoined or separate, they are all entirely nonexistent" instead of "whether as conjoined or separate, they are all devoid of existence" (共離俱不有 instead of 共離俱無有).

311 The Chapter 8 (*Nāgārjuna's Treatise on the Ten Grounds, Volume I*) version of this verse has "It is precisely because it is signless" instead of "It is precisely because it is synonymous with signlessness" (即為是無相 instead of 即名為無相).

312 These first two verse lines are referring to the four alternative propositions of the tetralemma: (1) it exists, (2) it does not exist, (3) it both exists and does not exist, and (4) it neither exists nor does not exist.

313 The Chapter 8 (*Nāgārjuna's Treatise on the Ten Grounds, Volume I*) version of this verse has a fairly nonconsequential variant for one of the characters in this line (先亦非寂滅 instead of 先來非寂滅).

314 The following passage corresponds to a section of the *Great Jeweled Summit Sutra* (大寶積經, T.310:636c17–29).

315 *Xing* (行), more usually "action(s)," refers here instead to *saṃskāra*s, hence here the translation as "all conditioned things."

316 This verse and the very long passage that follow are also found in the *Great Jeweled Summit Sutra* (大寶積經, T.310:636a29–b29).

317 I emend the reading of the text here in accordance with the Song, Yuan, Ming, and Gong editions by preferring on sensibility grounds *anwen* (安隱), "peaceful and secure," to the Taishō edition's *anle* (安樂), "peaceful and happy"; the latter appears to be a result of scribal absentmindedness in reflexively repeating the immediately preceding concept, which would produce an unlikely redundancy.

318 See note 3 regarding the chapter numbering. (The Taishō edition calls this "Chapter Seven.")

319 Venerable Bhikkhu Bodhi notes: "See *Aṅguttara Nikāya* 8:19, [where this is listed as] one of the qualities of the ocean."

[320] Here and in the following three paragraphs, the text is referring to the four supreme bases for the generation of meritorious qualities, namely truth, relinquishment, quiescence, and wisdom.

[321] "Stream-enterer" here is literally "one who has acquired the fruit of the path of a *srota-āpanna*."

[322] "Marvelous phenomena" (希有事) is generally intended to refer to miraculous occurrences brought about by spiritual powers (希有= *adbhuta*, "supernatural").

[323] Venerable Bhikkhu Bodhi notes: "*Aṅguttara Nikāya* 9:5 mentions these four fears. See *Numerical Discourses of the Buddha,* p. 1255." This topic of the fears to which a bodhisattva is invulnerable is also extensively treated in Chapter 3 of this treatise (*Nāgārjuna's Treatise on the Ten Grounds, Volume I*) in the discussion of the characteristics of the bodhisattva who has reached the second bodhisattva ground.

[324] See note 3 regarding the chapter numbering. (The Taishō edition calls this "Chapter Eight.")

[325] As of the Tang dynasty, a couple hundred years after Kumārajīva made this translation, a Chinese "mile" (*li* = 里) was roughly 1,060 feet, i.e., a fifth of a U.S. mile or a third of a kilometer. As of the end of the Han dynasty, a couple hundred years before this translation was made, it was roughly 1,365 feet, i.e., a quarter of a U.S. mile or four-tenths of a kilometer. Using these measures as a basis, the circumference of this wheel would be between 3 and 3.9 U.S. miles, or between 5 and 6 kilometers.

[326] Although this is literally "householder treasure" (居士寶, Skt. *gṛhapati ratna*), the literature makes it clear that this is a minister of the treasury.

[327] To correct an apparent graphic-similarity scribal error, I emend the reading of the Taishō text here by preferring the Song, Yuan, Ming, and Gong editions' *qing* (青), "blue," to the Taishō edition's *jing* (睛), "eye."

[328] A search of CBETA suggests that this is the only place in the entire Chinese Buddhist canon that this transliteration appears, hence any Sanskrit reconstructions I might suggest for this celestial maiden's name would be mere conjecture.

Glossary

Abhidharma: A category of Buddhist texts devoted to detailed scholastic analyses of the teachings contained in the sutras.

afflictions: Otherwise known as "the three poisons" (*triviṣa*), these are (1) greed, including lust and desire in general; (2) hatred, including all of the permutations of aversion such as irritation, anger, and rage; and (3) delusion or ignorance. There are many subcategories of afflictions (*kleśa*s) listed in the various dharma schemas. For example, in the Sarvāstivāda school, there are six root afflictions and ten subsidiary afflictions.

aggregates: *See* five aggregates.

anāgāmin: A "nonreturner," one who has gained the third of the four fruits of the individual liberation path of the *śrāvaka* disciple.

anuttarasamyaksaṃbodhi: The "utmost, right, and perfect enlightenment" of a buddha.

arhat: One who, having put an end to all of the afflictions, fetters, and contaminants; and, having put an end to rebirth, has gained the fourth and final fruit on the individual liberation path of the *śrāvaka* disciple.

ārya: One who has realized one of the fruits of the path from which they can never fall away. This includes any of the eight fruits of the arhat path, or any of the irreversible stations on the bodhisattva path to buddhahood.

asaṃkhya/asaṃkhyeya: In Sanskrit, an incalculably and infinitely large number.

asura: As one of the paths of rebirth, this refers to a demigod or titan. More generally, beings characterized by much anger, hatred, jealousy, and contentiousness who may also appear as humans, animals, hungry ghosts (*preta*s), or hell-dwellers.

avadāna stories: Stories of the previous lives of a buddha.

avaivartika: One who has become irreversible on either the individual liberation path of the arhats or on the universal liberation path of the bodhisattvas and buddhas. Throughout this text, "stage of certainty" (必定, 必定地) is most likely a translation of *avaivartika.*

bases of psychic powers: The four bases of psychic power (*catvāra ṛddhi-pāda*) are zeal (*chanda*), vigor (*vīrya*), [concentration of] mind/thought (*citta*), and reflective or investigative consideration, examination, or imagination (*mīmāṃsā*).

Bhagavat: One of the titles of a buddha, variously translated as "Blessed One," "Lord," or in Chinese Buddhist texts, "World-honored One" (*shizun* 世尊).

bhikṣu: A fully ordained celibate Buddhist monk within one of the traditional schools of Buddhism.

bhikṣuṇī: A fully ordained celibate Buddhist nun within one of the traditional schools of Buddhism.

bhūta ghost: According to Monier Williams' *A Sanksrit-English Dictionary,* one of the many meanings of *bhūta* is "a spirit (good or evil), the ghost of a deceased person, a demon, imp, goblin." The *Princeton Dictionary of Buddhism* has "A class of harm-inflicting and formless obstructing spirits (i.e., 'elemental spirits')"; "sometimes equivalent to preta (hungry ghosts)"; "Because they obstruct rainfall, the bhūta are propitiated by rituals to cause precipitation."

bodhi: "Enlightenment" or "awakening." In its most exalted form this refers exclusively to the utmost, right, and perfect enlightenment (*anuttarasamyaksaṃbodhi*) of a buddha.

bodhimaṇḍa: The "site of enlightenment" where enlightenment is cultivated and fully realized. It may be used as a general reference to Buddhist temples, though it often refers specifically to the site beneath the *bodhi* tree where a buddha gains complete realization of utmost, right, and perfect enlightenment.

bodhisattva: Beings who, in their pursuit of the utmost, right, and perfect enlightenment of buddhahood, is equally dedicated to achieving buddhahood for themselves while also facilitating all other beings' achievement of buddhahood. Their primary practice is classically described as focusing on the six (or ten) "perfections" (*pāramitās*): giving, moral virtue, patience, vigor, meditative skill (*dhyāna*), and world-transcending wisdom (*prajñā*). *See also pāramitās*.

bodhi tree: The tree in Bodhgaya in the Indian state of Bihar under which the Buddha reached enlightenment approximately two thousand six hundred years ago.

Brahmā: Per *The Princeton Dictionary of Buddhism:* "An Indian divinity who was adopted into the Buddhist pantheon as a protector of the teachings…and king of the Brahmaloka ["Brahma world"] (in the narrow sense of that term)." "*Brahmaloka*" here refers to the first three heavens of the form realm.

brahmacārin: Per Monier Williams, *A Sanskrit-English Dictionary:* "A young brahman who is a student of the Vedas (under a preceptor) or who practices chastity, a young brahman before marriage (in the first period of his life)."

brahmacarya: Celibacy.

brahman: Someone who belongs to the highest caste in Hinduism; a member of the Hindu priestly caste.

buddha: Anyone who has achieved utmost, right, and perfect enlightenment (*anuttarasamyaksaṃbodhi*), whether referring to the Buddha of the present era in this world, Śākyamuni Buddha, any of the seven buddhas of antiquity, or, in Mahayana cosmology, any of the countless buddhas of the ten directions and three periods of time.

clear knowledges: Refers to the "three knowledges" (*trividyā*): (1) remembrance of previous lives (*pūrvanivāsānusmṛti*), (2) knowledge of beings' rebirth destinies (*cyutyupapādajñāna*), and (3) knowledge of the destruction of the defiling contaminants or "taints" (*āsravakṣaya*).

contaminants (Skt. *āsrava*): These are usually defined as either threefold or fourfold: (1) sensual desire (*kāma*); 2) [craving for] becoming (*bhāva*), i.e., the craving for continued existence; (3) ignorance (*avidyā*), i.e., delusion; (4) views (*dṛṣṭi*). This fourth type is not included in some listings. Common alternate translations include "taints" and "outflows" and, less commonly, "influxes" and "fluxes."

dāna-pāramitā: The perfection of giving.

desire, form, and formless realms. *See* three realms of existence.

*deva*s: Divinities residing in the heavens that collectively constitute the highest of the six rebirth destinies within the realm of samsara. There are twenty-seven categories of *deva*s and their heavens in the desire realm, form realm, and formless realm. Although the lifespans of the *deva*s in these various heavens may be immensely long, when their karmic merit runs out they are all still destined to eventually fall back into the other five paths of rebirth, where they are reborn in accordance with their residual karma from previous lifetimes.

dhāraṇī: There are many types, but the two main types are (1) mantra-like spells that serve the purpose of protection from negative spiritual forces such as ghosts and demons, and (2) formulae that aid the retention even for countless lifetimes of the Dharma teachings one has acquired in this and previous lives.

Dharma: The teachings of the Buddha.

Dharma realm: As a Buddhist technical term, "Dharma realm" or "dharma realm" (Skt. *dharmadhātu*) has at least several levels of meaning. (1) At the most granular level, "dharma realm" refers to one of the eighteen sense realms, dharmas as "objects of mind" (*dharma-āyatana*). (2) In the most cosmically and metaphysically vast sense, "Dharma realm" refers in aggregate to all conventionally existent phenomena and the universally pervasive noumenal "true suchness" (*tathatā*) that underlies and characterizes all of those phenomena. In this sense, it is identical with the "Dharma body" (Skt. *dharmakāya*). (3) As a classifying term, "dharma realm" is used to distinguish realms of existence, as in the ten dharma realms consisting of the realms of buddhas, bodhisattvas, *śrāvaka* disciples, *pratyekabuddha*s, devas, *asura*s, humans, animals, hungry ghosts, and hell-dwellers; or metaphysical modes of existence, as in the "four dharma realms" of the Huayan hermeneutic tradition that speaks of the dharma realm of the "noumenal" (synonymous with emptiness or *śūnyatā*); the dharma realm of the "phenomenal"; the dharma realm of the unimpeded interpenetration of the phenomenal and the noumenal; and the dharma realm of the unimpeded interpenetration of all phenomena with all other phenomena (in a manner that resonates somewhat with quantum entanglement and nonlocality).

dharmas: (1) Fundamental constituent aspects, elements, or factors of mental and physical existence, as for instance, "the one hundred dharmas" in which Vasubandhu analytically catalogued all that exists. In this sense, dharmas are somewhat analogous to the elements of the periodic table in chemistry. (2) Any individual teaching, as for instance in "the dharma of conditioned origination."

Dharma wheel (Skt. *dharmacakra*): Refers to the eight-spoked wheel emblematic of the Buddha's teaching of the eightfold path of the *ārya*s or "noble ones," consisting of right views, right volition or intentional thought, right speech, right physical action, right livelihood, right effort, right mindfulness, and right meditative concentration. This term is also synonymous with the three turnings of the four truths as initially taught by the Buddha to his original five disciples.

dhūta, dhūtaṅga, or *dhūtaguṇa* austerities: In contrast to the nonbeneficial ascetic practices of non-Buddhists (lying on a bed of nails, etc.), these are practices that are beneficial to progress on the path, such as wearing only patchwork robes sewn from discarded cloth, eating only food obtained on almsrounds, eating only a single meal each day, always sitting and never lying down, dwelling at the base of a tree, and residing in a charnel field where one observes the stages of the body's decomposition.

dhyāna: A general term broadly corresponding to all forms of Buddhist meditative skill. The Chinese *chan* (禪) and the Japanese term *zen* are transliterations of the same Sanskrit word *dhyāna.* All forms of Buddhist "calming" and "insight" meditation are subcategories of *dhyāna.*

dhyāna-pāramitā: The perfection of meditative skill.

eight difficulties: Birth in the realms of hells, as a hungry ghost, as an animal, as a long-lived *deva;* birth in a border region (where there is no Buddha Dharma); birth as someone who is blind, deaf, mute, or otherwise has impaired physical or mental faculties; birth as someone who possesses merely worldly knowledge and intelligence (and hence who uses their cleverness to deny the truth of the Dharma); and birth at a time before or long after a buddha appears in the world.

eighteen sense realms: The six sense faculties of the eyes, ears, nose, tongue, body, and mind; their corresponding six sense objects (visual forms, sounds, smells, tastes, touchables, and ideas, etc. as objects of mind); and the six sense consciousnesses (visual, auditory, olfactory, gustatory, tactile, and mental).

eight precepts: Eight vows involving abstaining from (1) killing; (2) taking what is not given; (3) sexual misconduct; (4) false speech; (5) ingesting intoxicants; (6) using perfumes, wearing jewelry or other personal adornments, and dancing, singing, or watching such performances; (7) sleeping on a high or wide bed; and (8) eating after midday.

fetters: (Skt. *saṃyojana*): Ten mental characteristics of unenlightened existence that bind beings to uncontrolled rebirths in the six destinies of rebirth: (1) "truly existent self view," the wrong view that believes in the existence of an eternally existent self in association with the five aggregates; (2) "skeptical doubt" about the truth of the Dharma and the path to enlightenment; (3) "clinging to [the observance of] rules and rituals" in and of themselves as constituting the path to spiritual liberation; (4) sensual desire; (5) ill will; (6) desire for rebirth in the heavens of the form realm; (7) desire for rebirth in the heavens of the formless realm; (8) "conceit," i.e., the belief that "I" exist; (9) "agitation" or "restlessness" that prevents deep concentration; and (10) "ignorance."

five aggregates: (1) form; (2) feelings (i.e., sensations as received through the eyes, ears, nose, tongue, body, or mind); (3) perceptions; (4) karmic formative factors (such as volitions); and (5) consciousness (visual, auditory, olfactory, gustatory, tactile, and mental).

five desires: Desire for wealth, sex, fame, flavors, and leisure; or, alternatively, the objects of the five basic sense faculties (i.e., visual forms, sounds, smells, tastes, and touchables).

five faculties: Faith, vigor, mindfulness, concentration, and wisdom.

five powers: When the five faculties of faith, vigor, mindfulness, concentration, and wisdom are fully developed, they bceome the five powers.

five precepts: Five vows involving abstaining from killing, stealing, sexual misconduct, false speech, and ingesting intoxicants.

four bases of meritorious qualities: Truth, relinquishment, quiescence, and wisdom. Per Ven. Bhikkhu Bodhi, the Sanskrit correlates of the Pāli terms *saccādhitthāna, cāgādhitthāna, upasamādhitthāna* (= base of peace), and *paññādhitthāna* are *satyādhiṣṭhāna, tyāgādhiṣṭhāna, upaśamādhiṣṭhāna,* and *prajñādhiṣṭhāna.*

four bases of supernatural power: Zeal, vigor, mind, and investigation.

four great elements: Earth, water, fire, and wind.

four requisites: Food obtained on almsrounds, robes, residences, and medicines, which are necessary for monastic life.

four right efforts: Causing already arisen evil to cease; causing not yet arisen evil to not arise; causing already arisen goodness to increase; causing not yet arisen goodness to arise.

four stations of mindfulness: Mindfulness of the body; mindfulness of feelings or sensations (experienced via the eyes, ears, nose, tongue, body, and mind consciousnesses); mindfulness of thoughts or mind states; mindfulness of dharmas.

four truths/four truths of the *ārya*s: The fundamental Buddhist teaching of suffering, the origination of suffering, the possibility of the cessation of suffering; and the path to its cessation.

gandharva: A type of celestial music spirit that is said to rely on fragrances as its means of survival.

garuḍa: A type of spirit that manifests as an immense golden-winged bird that feeds on young dragons.

ground/grounds: Levels or planes of spiritual development through which a practitioner proceeds on the way to complete enlightenment.

hindrances: Usually refers to "the five hindrances" of desire, ill will, lethargy and sleepiness, excitedness and regretfulness, and afflicted doubtfulness. These five hindrances must be overcome in order to successfully enter deep states of meditation.

individual enlightenment path: This refers to the paths to transcendence of samsara and realization of nirvana taken by those who choose to cultivate either the path to arhatship or the path to pratyekabuddhahood. An alternate designation for these two types of individuals is the two vehicles. *See also* two vehicles.

inverted views: The four inverted views (Skt. *viparyāsa-catuṣka*) consist of imputing permanence to the impermanent, pleasure to what cannot deliver it, self to what is devoid of any inherently existent self, and purity to what does not actually possess that quality. Standard objects of such upside-down perceptions are thought or mind states, the six categories of "feeling" manifesting in association with the six sense faculties, dharmas (as components of the falsely imputed "self"), and the body.

kalaviṅka bird: The Himalayan cuckoo bird that sings with an incomparably beautiful sound even before it breaks out of its shell.

kalpa: A Sanskrit term that roughly corresponds to the English term "eon," with the primary distinction that in Buddhist and Hindu cosmology *kalpa*s occur in various relatively precisely designated immensely long durations.

kāṣāya robe: The robes of a fully ordained *bhikṣu* or *bhikṣuṇī.*

kiṃnara (Pāli *kinnara*):A type of celestial music spirit with the body of a human and the head of a horse.

kumbhāṇḍa: According to Monier Williams' *A Sanskrit-English Dictionary:* "Having testicles shaped like a kumbha [a winter melon]," a class of demons (at whose head stands Rudra). *The Princeton Dictionary of Buddhism* has: "In Sanskrit, a type of evil spirit, and typically listed along with especially *rākṣasa,* but also *piśāca, yakṣa,* and *bhūta* spirits. Virūḍhaka, one of the four world-guardians, who protects the southern cardinal direction, is usually said to be their overlord, although some texts give Rudra this role instead. The *kumbhāṇḍa* are also sometimes listed among the minions of Māra, evil personified."

koṭī: A number defined in chapter 30 of the *Flower Adornment Sutra* as the product of multiplying a *lakṣa* (100,000) by a *lakṣa*, equaling 10,000,000, i.e., ten million.

kṣaṇa: A micro-moment, variously defined; one traditional definition is "a ninetieth of a finger-snap." Elsewhere in the text, it may appear as "a single thought," "mind-moment," or "thought-moment" as approximate translations of the term.

kṣānti-pāramitā: The perfection of patience.

kṣatriya: The second of the four castes of traditional Indian society consisting primarily of the warrior and royalty class.

kṣetra: Refers to a land or realm or field; in Buddhist texts it may refer specifically to a "buddha land."

mahāsattva: A great bodhisattva, one who has cultivated the bodhisattva path for countless *kalpa*s.

mahoraga: A type of serpent spirit often portrayed as having the upper body of a human and the lower body of a snake.

Māra/*māra*(s): In Buddhism, Māra is generally regarded as the personification of evil and death, a particular deity dwelling in one of the heavens of the desire realm who delights in interfering with spiritual liberation from perpetual rebirths in samsara. More specifically, there are said to be four kinds of *māra*s: (1) the *māra* of the five mental and physical aggregates in association with which all beings wander endlessly in samsara; (2) the *māra* of the afflictions consisting of the three poisons of greed, hatred, and delusion and all of their subcategories; (3) the *māra* of death; and, as mentioned above, (4) the deity known as Māra as well as all of his *devaputra* minions. Additionally, there are also "ghost and spirit" *māra*s who may manifest in countless ways to interfere with a practitioner's cultivation of the path.

mātṛkā: "Matrices" consisting of lists of dharmas, technical terms, and concepts discussed in the sutras. They served as the basis for the Abhidharma.

mind-moment: *See kṣaṇa.*

nayuta: A very large number, usually defined as one hundred billion.

nirvana: The ultimate goal of the path of Buddhist spiritual cultivation that corresponds to the elimination of the three poisons (greed, hatred, and delusion) and the end of compulsory and random rebirth in samsara, the cycle of existences in the six realms of rebirth, those of *devas*, *asura*s (demigods), humans, animals, hungry ghosts, and the hells. In the case of the individual liberation path practitioner exemplified by arhats and *pratyekabuddha*s, all future existence ends for them with the acquisition of nirvana. In the case of the universal liberation practitioners exemplified by bodhisattvas and buddhas, they achieve the direct cognition of the emptiness of all beings and phenomena and realize an ongoing realization of a nirvana-like state even though they have vowed to take on intentional rebirths within samsara in order to facilitate the spiritual liberation of all beings.

nirvana without residue: The final nirvana realized at death by fully awakened beings whether they are arhats, *pratyekabuddhas*, or buddhas.

nivāsana robe: The monastic's skirt-like inner robe.

once-returner. *See sākṛdāgāmin.*

pāramitās: The six (or ten) "perfections" cultivated and perfected by the bodhisattva on the path to buddhahood.

Paranirmitavaśavartin Heaven: The Paranirmitavaśavartin Heaven is the sixth of the six desire realm heavens. *The Princeton Dictonary of Buddhism* has: "The heaven of the gods who have power over the creations of others, or the gods who partake of the pleasures created in other heavens."

piśāca: As per *The Princeton Dictonary of Buddhism:* "In Sanskrit, 'flesh-eater,' a class of ogres or goblins, similar to *rākṣasa* and *yakṣa,* who eat human flesh." The female is called *piśācī.*

prajñā: World-transcending wisdom that cognizes and understands all phenomena associated with "self," others, and the world as they truly are and in accordance with ultimate reality.

prajñā-pāramitā: The perfection of wisdom.

pratyekabuddha: One who, on his own and in the absence of a buddha or the teaching of Dharma, achieves a level of enlightenment comparable to that of an arhat through the contemplation of the cycle of dependent origination (*pratītyasamutpāda*). Mahayana literature attributes this ability to awaken in the absence of a buddha or the Dharma to direct exposure to the Dharma in previous lives, the seeds of which enable enlightenment in the present life. *See also* two vehicles.

pratyutpanna samādhi: A *samādhi* in which one becomes able to see the buddhas of the present and listen to them teach the Dharma.

provisions (for enlightenment) (Skt. *bodhisaṃbhāra*): The spiritual prerequisites for enlightenment that must be accumulated in order to fully realize the path to buddhahood, usually considered to be merit (*puṇya*) and knowledge (*jñāna*).

pūtana: As per *The Princeton Dictonary of Buddhism:* "Stinking hungry demons."

rākṣasa: A swift-flying malignant flesh-eating demon that changes its form to seduce humans and eat them.

sakṛdāgāmin: "Once-returner," one who has gained the third of the four fruits of the individual liberation path of the *śrāvaka* disciple.

samādhi: This refers both to any single instance of one-pointed concentration and also, more usually, to enduring states of persistently maintained one-pointed concentration.

saṃghāṭī robe: The monastic's outer robe.

saṃkakṣikā robe: The monastic's robe that is worn over the left shoulder and under the right arm.

samsara: Usually rendered in Sino-Buddhist translation as "birth and death" (*shengsi* 生死), this refers to the endless cycle of rebirths in the six realms of rebirth,. those of *deva*s (gods), *asura*s (demigods or titans), humans, animals, hungry ghosts (*preta*s), and hell-dwellers.

sangha/Sangha: A community of at least ten fully ordained *bhikṣu*s in Buddhist countries or at least five fully ordained *bhikṣu*s in countries where Buddhism is being established for the first time. As the third object of refuge in the Three Refuges or the Three Jewels, it refers exclusively to those who have already acquired one of the fruits of the path from which they can never fall away, whether on the individual liberation paths of arhats or *pratyekabuddha*s or the bodhisattva path.

śarīra: The remains or "relics" of eminent monks, bodhisattvas, or buddhas that are contained in their cremation ashes.

seven enlightenment factors: Assessment or skillful selection of dharmas, vigor, joy, mental pliancy, mindfulness (the Pāli tradition often places "mindfulness" first in this list of seven), concentration, and equanimity with respect to the *saṃskāra* (karmic formative factors) aggregate.

śīla-pāramitā: The perfection of moral virtue.

six rebirth destinies: The realms of rebirth as gods (*deva*s), *asuras* (demigods or titans), humans, hungry ghosts (*preta*s), animals, and hell-dwellers.

skandha. See five aggregates.

skillful means (Skt. *upāya*): Individually tailored skillful techniques adopted by the bodhisattva in teaching various kinds of beings. A variety of techniques are adopted precisely because all beings possess different capacities, karmic obstacles, and predilections, due to which they respond best to teachings that are directed specifically to them.

spiritual superknowledges: The usual Sanskrit antecedent for "spiritual superknowledges" is *abhijñā* ("superknowledges") or *ṛddhi* ("supernatural powers"). This includes such abilities as the six superknowledges of spiritual powers, the heavenly eye, the heavenly ear, cognition of others' thoughts, past life recall for both self and others, and complete elimination of all "defiling contaminants" or "taints" (*āsrava*s).

śramaṇa: Generally, a mendicant, one who has left the home life and relies on alms for sustenance. In the Buddhist context, this refers specifically to a *bhikṣu,* i.e., a Buddhist monk.

śrāvaka/śrāvaka disciple: A follower of the individual liberation path to arhatship. *See also* two vehicles.

stream-enterer (Skt. *srota-āpanna*) One who has gained the first of the four fruits of the path to arhatship.

śūdra: A member of the fourth and lowest caste of traditional Indian Hindu society, consisting primarily of servants and menials. The Buddha and Buddhism do not recognize any of the castes as valid distinctions among human beings.

sutra: A scripture attributed to the Buddha.

Tathāgata ("Thus Come One"): One of the ten primary titles by which all buddhas are known.

tathatā: "Suchness," i.e., the true nature of the ultimate reality of any and all things as they really are.

ten directions: North, south, east, west, the four midpoints, zenith, and nadir.

thirty-seven wings of enlightenment/thirty-seven enlightenment factors: These consist of the four stations of mindfulness, the four right efforts, the four bases of supernatural powers, the five faculties, the five powers, the seven enlightenment factors, and the eightfold path of *ārya*s.

Three Jewels: Buddha, Dharma, and Sangha. *See also* Three Refuges.

three periods of time: Past, present, and future.

three realms of existence: The desire realm ((*kāma-loka*), the (subtle) form realm (*rūpa-loka*), and the formless realm (*ārūpya-loka*) constitute the three spheres of existence in which all of the many different classes of beings endlessly take rebirth unless and until they transcend samsara and realize nirvana.

Three Refuges: Buddha, Dharma, and Sangha, the Three Jewels in which one "takes refuge" to become a Buddhist disciple and upon which one must rely to advance on the Buddhist path.

three vehicles: The *śrāvaka* disciple vehicle, the *pratyekabuddha* vehicle, and the great vehicle (Mahayana), which culminate in arhatship, pratyekabuddhahood, and buddhahood, respectively.

three wretched destinies: The three lowest realms of rebirth as either an animal, hungry ghost (*preta*), or hell-dweller.

trichiliocosm: A world system consisting of countless worlds.

Tripiṭaka: The three divisions of the threefold Buddhist canon: sutras (scriptures attributed to the Buddha or disciples authorized by the Buddha), commentarial treatises (*śāstras*), and moral codes (Vinaya).

Tripiṭaka master: One who has completely mastered the three divisions of the threefold Buddhist canon.

twelve sense bases: The six sense faculties of the eyes, ears, nose, tongue, body, and mind and their respective sense objects (visual forms, sounds, smells, tastes, touchables, and ideas, etc. as objects of mind).

two vehicles: The two individual liberation paths taught by the Buddha, those of the *śrāvaka* disciple that leads to arhatship and of the *pratyekabuddha* that leads to pratyekabuddhahood.

vaiśya: A member of the third caste in traditional Indian society, comprised primarily of the merchant and agricultural classes.

vajra: An indestructible substance equated with the substance of diamond; a symbol of indestructibility. Also, a pestle-shaped scepter or "thunderbolt" weapon held by Dharma protectors and deities.

vibhāṣā: An extensively detailed explanatory treatise.

vinaya(s)/Vinaya: The Buddhist moral codes. Capitalized, the third part of the Tripiṭaka.

vīryapāramitā: The perfection of vigor.

wheel-turning king (Skt. *cakravartin*): In Buddhism, a universal monarch.

worthy (Skt. *bhadra*): In Mahayana literature, a "worthy" is a bodhisattva practitioner who has brought forth the bodhisattva vow but who is still cultivating the preparatory stages and thus has not yet reached the ten bodhisattva grounds and has not yet become an *ārya.*

yakṣa: A kind of either good or evil spirit that possesses supernatural powers and may either serve as a guardian or a demon.

yojana: A measure of distance in ancient India usually defined as being the distance an ox cart could travel in one day without unharnessing (somewhat less than ten miles).

Bibliography

Bodhi, Bhikkhu, trans. *The Connected Discourses of the Buddha: A New Translation of the Saṃyutta Nikāya translated from the Pāli;* original translation by Bhikkhu Bodhi, *Teachings of the Buddha.* Somerville, MA: Wisdom Publications, 2000.

—. *The Numerical Discourses of the Buddha: A Translation of the Aṅguttara Nikāya (Teachings of the Buddha).* Boston: Wisdom Publications, 2012.

Buddharakkhita, Acharya, trans. *The Dhammapada: The Buddha's Path of Wisdom.* Introduction by Bhikkhu Bodhi. Kandy, Sri Lanka: Buddhist Publication Society, 1990; Onalaska, WA: Pariyatti Editions reprint 2019.

Burlingame, Eugene, Buddhaghosa, and Charles Rockwell Lanman. *Buddhist Legends.* Harvard Oriental Series vols. 28–30. Cambridge, MA: Harvard University Press, 1921.

Buswell, Jr., Robert E., and Donald S. Lopez, Jr., eds. *The Princeton Dictionary of Buddhism.* Princeton, NJ: Princeton University Press, 2014.

Conze, Edward, and Gakujutsu Zaidan Suzuki. *Materials for a Dictionary of the Prajñā-pāramitā Literature.* Tokyo: Suzuki Research Foundation, 1967.

Dharmamitra, trans. *Nāgārjuna on the Six Perfections: An Ārya Bodhisattva Explains the Heart of the Bodhisattva Path. Exegesis on the Great Perfection of Wisdom Sutra Chapters 17–30 by the Great Indian Buddhist Patriarch Ārya Nāgārjuna.* Seattle: Kalavinka Press, 2009.

—. *Nāgārjuna's Guide to the Bodhisattva Path: Treatise on the Provisions for Enlightenment. The Bodhisaṃbhāra Śāstra by Ārya Nāgārjuna.* Seattle: Kalavinka Press, 2009.

—. *The Bodhisaṃbhāra Treatise Commentary: The Early Indian Exegesis on Ārya Nāgārjuna's Treatise on the Provisions for Enlightenment (The Bodhisaṃbhāra Śāstra).* Seattle: Kalavinka Press, 2009

—. *The Flower Adornment Sutra: An Annotated Translation of the Avataṃsaka Sutra Including a Commentarial Synopsis of the Flower Adornment Sutra,* Vol. 2, Chapter 26, "The Ten Grounds," pp. 871–1056. Seattle: Kalavinka Press, 2023.

—. *The Ten Grounds Sutra: The Daśabhūmika Sūtra. The Ten Highest Levels of Practice on the Bodhisattva's Path to Buddhahood.* Seattle: Kalavinka Press, 2020.

Edgerton, Franklin. *Buddhist Hybrid Sanskrit Grammar and Dictionary.* William Dwight Whitney Linguistic Series. New Haven, CT: Yale University Press, 1953.

Harrison, Paul, trans. *The Pratyutpanna Samādhi Sutra,* in *The Pratyutpanna Samādhi Sutra/The Śūraṅgama Samādhi Sutra,* pp. 1–107. Moraga, CA: BDK America, Inc., 1998.

Hirakawa, Akira. *Buddhist Chinese-Sanskrit Dictionary (Bukkyō Kan-Bon daijiten).* Tokyo: Reiyūkai: Hatsubaimoto Innātorippusha (霊友会：発売元いんなあとりっぷ社), 1997.

Lamotte, Étienne. *Le Traité de La Grande Vertu de Sagesse de Nagarjuna (Mahāprajñāpāramitā-śāstra),* 3 vols. Louvain-la-Neuve: Institut Orientaliste de Louvin, 1944–1980.

Malalasekera, G. P. *Dictionary of Pāli Proper Names*. Indian Texts Series. London: J. Murray, 1937.

Ñāṇamoli, Bhikkhu, and Bhikkhu Bodhi, trans. *The Middle Length Discourses of the Buddha: A New Translation of the Majjhima Nikāya (Teachings of the Buddha).* Boston: Wisdom Publications in association with the Barre Center for Buddhist Studies, 1995.

Nattier, Jan. *A Few Good Men: The Bodhisattva Path According to the Inquiry of Ugra (Ugraparipṛcchā).* Studies in the Buddhist Traditions. Honolulu: University of Hawai'i Press, 2003.

Pruden, Leo, trans. *Abhidharmakośabhāṣyam of Vasubandhu,* 4 vols. Translated into French by Louis de Vallée Poussin. Fremont, CA: Asian Humanities Press, Jain Publishing Co., 1990.

Rahder, J., trans. *Daśabhumikasutra.* Leuven, Belgium: J. B. Istas, 1926.

—, comp. *Glossary of the Sanskrit, Tibetan, Mongolian, and Chinese Versions of the Daśabhūmika-Sūtra.* Buddhica, Documents et Travaux pour l'Étude du Bouddhisme publiés sous la direction de J. Przyluski, Deuxième Série; Documents—Tome I. Paris: Librarie Orientaliste Paul Geuthner, 1928.

Ruegg, David. *The Literature of the Madhyamaka School of Philosophy in India.* History of Indian Literature, vol. 7, fasc. 1. Wiesbaden: Harrassowitz, 1981.

Takakusu, Junjiro, and Kaigyoku Watanabe, eds. *Taishō shinshū daizōkyō,* 85 vols. Tokyo: Taishō Issaikyō Kankōkai (大正一切經刊行會), 1924–1934.

Travagnin, Stefania. "Yinshun's Recovery of *Shizhu Piposha Lun* 十住毗婆沙論: A Madhyamaka-based Pure Land Practice in Twentieth-Century Taiwan," *Contemporary Buddhism* 14/2 (2013): 320–343. https://doi.org/10.1080/14639947.2013.832497.

Vaidya, P. L., ed. *Daśabhūmikasūtram.* Darbhanga: The Mithila Institute of Post-Graduate Studies and Research in Sanskrit Learning, 1969.

Walser, John. "Nāgārjuna," in John Powers, ed., *The Buddhist World,* pp. 496–511. Routledge Worlds. London; New York: Routledge, Taylor & Francis Group, 2016.

Williams, Sir Monier-Monier. *A Sanskrit-English Dictionary.* Delhi: Sri Satguru, n.d.

Zhonghua dian zi fo dian xie hui. CBETA Chinese Electronic Tripiṭaka Collection (CBETA dian zi fo dian ji cheng), Version 2004. Taipei: Zhonghua dian zi fo dian xie hui (中華電子佛典協會).

Index

A

B

D

I

J

K

L

P

Q

R

Y

BDK English Tripiṭaka
(First Series)

Abbreviations

Ch.: Chinese
Skt.: Sanskrit
Jp.: Japanese
Eng.: Published title

Title		Taishō No.
Ch.	Chang ahan jing (長阿含經)	1
Skt.	Dīrghāgama	
Eng.	*The Canonical Book of the Buddha's Lengthy Discourses, Volume I* (2015) *The Canonical Book of the Buddha's Lengthy Discourses, Volume II* (2017) *The Canonical Book of the Buddha's Lengthy Discourses, Volume III* (2018)	
Ch.	Zhong ahan jing (中阿含經)	26
Skt.	Madhyamāgama	
Eng.	*The Madhyama Āgama (Middle-length Discourses), Volume I* (2013) *The Madhyama Āgama (Middle-length Discourses), Volume I* (2020) *The Madhyama Āgama (Middle-length Discourses), Volume III* (2022) *The Madhyama Āgama (Middle-length Discourses), Volume IV* (2023)	
Ch.	Dasheng bensheng xindi guan jing (大乘本生心地觀經)	159
Eng.	*The Mahayana Sutra of Previous Lives and Contemplation of the Mind-ground* (2021)	
Ch.	Fo suoxing zan (佛所行讚)	192
Skt.	Buddhacarita	
Eng.	*Buddhacarita: In Praise of Buddha's Acts* (2009)	
Ch.	Zabao zang jing (雜寶藏經)	203
Eng.	*The Storehouse of Sundry Valuables* (1994)	

Title		Taishō No.
Ch.	Faju piyu jing (法句譬喻經)	211
Eng.	*The Scriptural Text: Verses of the Doctrine, with Parables* (1999)	
Ch.	Xiaopin banruo boluomi jing (小品般若波羅蜜經)	227
Skt.	Aṣṭasāhasrikā-prajñāpāramitā-sūtra	
Ch.	Jingang banruo boluomi jing (金剛般若波羅蜜經)	235
Skt.	Vajracchedikā-prajñāpāramitā-sūtra	
Ch.	Daluo jingang bukong zhenshi sanmoye jing (大樂金剛不空眞實三麼耶經)	243
Skt.	Adhyardhaśatikā-prajñāpāramitā-sūtra	
Eng.	*The Sutra of the Vow of Fulfilling the Great Perpetual Enjoyment and Benefiting All Sentient Beings Without Exception* (in *Esoteric Texts,* 2015)	
Ch.	Renwang banruo boluomi jing (仁王般若波羅蜜經)	245
Skt.	*Kāruṇikārājā-prajñāpāramitā-sūtra	
Ch.	Banruo boluomiduo xin jing (般若波羅蜜多心經)	251
Skt.	Prajñāpāramitāhṛdaya-sūtra	
Ch.	Miaofa lianhua jing (妙法蓮華經)	262
Skt.	Saddharmapuṇḍarīka-sūtra	
Eng.	*The Lotus Sutra* (Revised Second Edition, 2007)	
Ch.	Wuliangyi jing (無量義經)	276
Eng.	*The Infinite Meanings Sutra* (in *Tiantai Lotus Texts,* 2013)	
Ch.	Guan Puxian pusa xingfa jing (觀普賢菩薩行法經)	277
Eng.	*The Sutra Expounded by the Buddha on Practice of the Way through Contemplation of the Bodhisattva All-embracing Goodness* (in *Tiantai Lotus Texts,* 2013)	
Ch.	Dafangguang fo huayan jing (大方廣佛華嚴經)	279
Skt.	Avataṃsaka-sūtra	
Ch.	Shengman shizihou yisheng defang bianfang guang jing (勝鬘師子吼一乘大方便方廣經)	353
Skt.	Śrīmālādevīsiṃhanāda-sūtra	
Eng.	*The Sutra of Queen Śrīmālā of the Lion's Roar* (2004)	
Ch.	Wuliangshou jing (無量壽經)	360
Skt.	Sukhāvatīvyūha	
Eng.	*The Larger Sutra on Amitāyus* (in *The Three Pure Land Sutras,* Revised Second Edition, 2003)	

Title		Taishō No.
Ch.	Guan wuliangshou fo jing (觀無量壽佛經)	365
Skt.	*Amitāyurdhyāna-sūtra	
Eng.	*The Sutra on Contemplation of Amitāyus* (in *The Three Pure Land Sutras,* Revised Second Edition, 2003)	
Ch.	Amituo jing (阿彌陀經)	366
Skt.	Sukhāvatīvyūha	
Eng.	*The Smaller Sutra on Amitāyus* (in *The Three Pure Land Sutras,* Revised Second Edition, 2003)	
Ch.	Da banniepan jing (大般涅槃經)	374
Skt.	Mahāparinirvāṇa-sūtra	
Eng.	*The Nirvana Sutra* (Volume I, 2013)	
Ch.	Fochuibo niepan lüeshuo jiaojie jing (佛垂般涅槃略説教誡經)	389
Eng.	*The Bequeathed Teaching Sutra* (in *Apocryphal Scriptures,* 2005)	
Ch.	Dizang pusa benyuan jing (地藏菩薩本願經)	412
Skt.	*Kṣitigarbhapraṇidhāna-sūtra	
Ch.	Banzhou sanmei jing (般舟三昧經)	418
Skt.	Pratyutpanna-buddhasammukhāvasthita-samādhi-sūtra	
Eng.	*The Pratyutpanna Samādhi Sutra* (1998)	
Ch.	Yaoshi liuli guang rulai benyuan gongde jing (藥師琉璃光如來本願功德經)	450
Skt.	Bhaiṣajyaguru-vaiḍūrya-prabhāsa-pūrvapraṇidhāna-viśeṣavistara	
Eng.	*The Scripture of Master of Medicine, Beryl Radiance Tathāgata* (2018)	
Ch.	Mile xiasheng chengfo jing (彌勒下生成佛經)	454
Skt.	*Maitreyavyākaraṇa	
Eng.	*The Sutra That Expounds the Descent of Maitreya Buddha and His Enlightenment* (2016)	
Ch.	Wenshushili wen jing (文殊師利問經)	468
Skt.	*Mañjuśrīparipṛcchā	
Eng.	*The Sutra of Mañjuśrī's Questions* (2016)	
Ch.	Weimojie suoshuo jing (維摩詰所説經)	475
Skt.	Vimalakīrtinirdeśa-sūtra	
Eng.	*The Vimalakīrti Sutra* (2004)	
Ch.	Yueshangnü jing (月上女經)	480
Skt.	Candrottarādārikā-paripṛcchā	
Eng.	*The Sutra of the Girl Candrottarā* (2018)	

Title	Taishō No.
Ch. Zuochan sanmei jing (坐禪三昧經) Eng. *The Sutra on the Concentration of Sitting Meditation* (2009)	614
Ch. Damoduoluo chan jing (達磨多羅禪經)	618
Ch. Yuedeng sanmei jing (月燈三昧經) Skt. Samādhirāja-candrapradīpa-sūtra	639
Ch. Shoulengyan sanmei jing (首楞嚴三昧經) Skt. Śūraṅgamasamādhi-sūtra Eng. *The Śūraṅgama Samādhi Sutra* (1998)	642
Ch. Jinguang ming zuishengwang jing (金光明最勝王經) Skt. Suvarṇaprabhāsa-sūtra	665
Ch. Dasheng rulengqie jing (大乘入楞伽經) Skt. Laṅkāvatāra-sūtra	672
Ch. Jie shenmi jing (解深密經) Skt. Saṃdhinirmocana-sūtra Eng. *The Scripture on the Explication of Underlying Meaning* (2000)	676
Ch. Yulanpen jing (盂蘭盆經) Skt. *Ullambana-sūtra Eng. *The Ullambana Sutra* (in *Apocryphal Scriptures,* 2005)	685
Ch. Sishierzhang jing (四十二章經) Eng. *The Sutra of Forty-two Sections* (in *Apocryphal Scriptures,* 2005)	784
Ch. Dafangguang yuanjue xiuduoluo liaoyi jing (大方廣圓覺修多羅了義經) Eng. *The Sutra of Perfect Enlightenment* (in *Apocryphal Scriptures,* 2005)	842
Ch. Da Biluzhena chengfo shenbian jiachi jing (大毘盧遮那成佛神變加持經) Skt. Mahāvairocanābhisambodhi-vikurvitādhiṣṭhāna-vaipulyasūtrendrarājanāma-dharmaparyāya Eng. *The Vairocanābhisaṃbodhi Sutra* (2005)	848
Ch. Jinggangding yiqie rulai zhenshi she dasheng xianzheng dajiao wang jing (金剛頂一切如來眞實攝大乘現證大教王經) Skt. Sarvatathāgata-tattvasaṃgraha-mahāyānābhisamaya-mahākalparāja Eng. *The Adamantine Pinnacle Sutra* (in *Two Esoteric Sutras,* 2001)	865

	Title	Taishō No.
Ch.	Suxidi jieluo jing (蘇悉地羯囉經)	893
Skt.	Susiddhikara-mahātantra-sādhanopāyika-paṭala	
Eng.	*The Susiddhikara Sutra* (in *Two Esoteric Sutras,* 2001)	
Ch.	Modengqie jing (摩登伽經)	1300
Skt.	*Mātaṅgī-sūtra	
Eng.	*The Mātaṅga Sutra* (in Esoteric Texts, 2015)	
Ch.	Mohe sengqi lü (摩訶僧祇律)	1425
Skt.	*Mahāsāṃghika-vinaya	
Ch.	Sifen lü (四分律)	1428
Skt.	*Dharmaguptaka-vinaya	
Ch.	Shanjianlü piposha (善見律毘婆沙)	1462
Pāli	Samantapāsādikā	
Ch.	Fanwang jing (梵網經)	1484
Skt.	*Brahmajāla-sūtra	
	The Brahmā's Net Sutra (2017)	
Ch.	Youposaijie jing (優婆塞戒經)	1488
Skt.	Upāsakaśīla-sūtra	
Eng.	*The Sutra on Upāsaka Precepts* (1994)	
Ch.	Miaofa lianhua jing youbotishe (妙法蓮華經憂波提舍)	1519
Skt.	Saddharmapuṇḍarīka-upadeśa	
Eng.	*The Commentary on the Lotus Sutra* (in *Tiantai Lotus Texts,* 2013)	
Ch.	Shizha biposha lun (十住毘婆沙論)	1521
Skt.	*Daśabhūmika-vibhāṣā	
Eng.	*Nāgārjuna's Treatise on the Ten Grounds, Volume I* (2024)	
	Nāgārjuna's Treatise on the Ten Grounds, Volume II (2025)	
Ch.	Fodijing lun (佛地經論)	1530
Skt.	*Buddhabhūmisūtra-śāstra	
Eng.	*The Interpretation of the Buddha Land* (2002)	
Ch.	Apidamojushe lun (阿毘達磨俱舍論)	1558
Skt.	Abhidharmakośa-bhāṣya	
Ch.	Zhonglun (中論)	1564
Skt.	Madhyamaka-śāstra	

Title		Taishō No.
Ch.	Yüqie shidilun (瑜伽師地論)	1579
Skt.	Yogācārabhūmi-śāstra	
Ch.	Cheng weishi lun (成唯識論)	1585
Eng.	*Demonstration of Consciousness Only* (in *Three Texts on Consciousness Only,* 1999)	
Ch.	Weishi sanshilun song (唯識三十論頌)	1586
Skt.	Triṃśikā	
Eng.	*The Thirty Verses on Consciousness Only* (in *Three Texts on Consciousness Only,* 1999)	
Ch.	Weishi ershi lun (唯識二十論)	1590
Skt.	Viṃśatikā	
Eng.	*The Treatise in Twenty Verses on Consciousness Only* (in *Three Texts on Consciousness Only,* 1999)	
Ch.	She dasheng lun (攝大乘論)	1593
Skt.	Mahāyānasaṃgraha	
Eng.	*The Summary of the Great Vehicle* (Revised Second Edition, 2003)	
Ch.	Bian zhongbian lun (辯中邊論)	1600
Skt.	Madhyāntavibhāga	
Eng.	*Analysis of the Middle and Extremes* (2021)	
Ch.	Dasheng zhuangyanjing lun (大乘莊嚴經論)	1604
Skt.	Mahāyānasūtrālaṃkāra	
Ch.	Dasheng chengye lun (大乘成業論)	1609
Skt.	Karmasiddhiprakaraṇa	
Eng.	*A Mahayana Demonstration on the Theme of Action* (in *Three Short Treatises by Vasubandhu, Sengzhao, and Zongmi*, 2017)	
Ch.	Jiujing yisheng baoxing lun (究竟一乘寶性論)	1611
Skt.	Ratnagotravibhāga-mahāyānottaratantra-śāstra	
Ch.	Yinming ruzheng li lun (因明入正理論)	1630
Skt.	Nyāyapraveśa	
Ch.	Dasheng ji pusa xue lun (大乘集菩薩學論)	1636
Skt.	Śikṣāsamuccaya	
Ch.	Jingangzhen lun (金剛針論)	1642
Skt.	Vajrasūcī	
Eng.	*The Diamond Needle* (2023)	

Title		Taishō No.
Ch.	Zhang suozhi lun (彰所知論)	1645
Eng.	*The Treatise on the Elucidation of the Knowable* (2004)	
Ch.	Putixing jing (菩提行經)	1662
Skt.	Bodhicaryāvatāra	
Ch.	Jingangding yuqie zhongfa anouduoluo sanmiao sanputi xin lun (金剛頂瑜伽中發阿耨多羅三藐三菩提心論)	1665
Eng.	*The Bodhicitta Śāstra* (in *Esoteric Texts,* 2015)	
Ch.	Dasheng qixin lun (大乘起信論)	1666
Skt.	*Mahāyānaśraddhotpāda-śāstra	
Eng.	*The Awakening of Faith* (2005)	
Ch.	Shimoheyan lun (釋摩訶衍論)	1668
Ch.	Naxian biqiu jing (那先比丘經)	1670B
Pāli	Milindapañhā	
Eng.	*The Scripture on the Monk Nāgasena* (2021)	
Ch.	Banruo boluomiduo xin jing yuzan (般若波羅蜜多心經幽贊)	1710
Eng.	*A Comprehensive Commentary on the Heart Sutra (Prajñāpāramitā-hṛdaya-sūtra)* (2001)	
Ch.	Miaofalianhua jing xuanyi (妙法蓮華經玄義)	1716
Ch.	Guan wuliangshou fo jing shu (觀無量壽佛經疏)	1753
Ch.	Sanlun xuanyi (三論玄義)	1852
Ch.	Dasheng xuan lun (大乘玄論)	1853
Ch.	Zhao lun (肇論)	1858
Eng.	*Essays of Sengzhao* (in *Three Short Treatises by Vasubandhu, Sengzhao, and Zongmi,* 2017)	
Ch.	Huayan yisheng jiaoyi fenqi zhang (華嚴一乘教義分齊章)	1866
Eng.	*Treatise on Doctrinal Distinctions of the Huayan One Vehicle* (2023)	
Ch.	Yuanren lun (原人論)	1886
Eng.	*Treatise on the Origin of Humanity* (in *Three Short Treatises by Vasubandhu, Sengzhao, and Zongmi,* 2017)	
Ch.	Mohe zhiguan (摩訶止觀)	1911
Eng.	*Great Cessation-and-Contemplation, Volume I* (2024)	

Title		Taishō No.
Ch.	Xiuxi zhiguan zuochan fayao (修習止觀坐禪法要)	1915
Ch.	Tiantai sijiao yi (天台四教儀)	1931
Eng.	*A Guide to the Tiantai Fourfold Teachings* (in *Tiantai Lotus Texts,* 2013)	
Ch.	Guoqing bai lu (國清百録)	1934
Eng.	*The Hundred Records of the Temple of National Purity* (2022)	
Ch.	Zhenzhou Linji Huizhao chanshi wulu (鎮州臨濟慧照禪師語録)	1985
Eng.	*The Recorded Sayings of Linji* (in *Three Chan Classics,* 1999)	
Ch.	Foguo Yuanwu chanshi biyan lu (佛果圜悟禪師碧巖録)	2003
Eng.	*The Blue Cliff Record* (1998)	
Ch.	Wumen guan (無門關)	2005
Eng.	*Wumen's Gate* (in *Three Chan Classics,* 1999)	
Ch.	Liuzu dashi fabao tan jing (六祖大師法寶壇經)	2008
Eng.	*The Platform Sutra of the Sixth Patriarch* (2000)	
Ch.	Xinxin ming (信心銘)	2010
Eng.	*The Faith-Mind Maxim* (in *Three Chan Classics,* 1999)	
Ch.	Huangboshan Duanji chanshi chuanxin fayao (黄檗山斷際禪師傳心法要)	2012A
Eng.	*Essentials of the Transmission of Mind* (in *Zen Texts,* 2005)	
Ch.	Yongjia Zhengdao ge (永嘉證道歌)	2014
Eng.	*Yongjia's Song of Actualizing the Way* (2021)	
Ch.	Chixiu Baizhang qinggui (勅修百丈清規)	2025
Eng.	*The Baizhang Zen Monastic Regulations* (2007)	
Ch.	Yibuzonglun lun (異部宗輪論)	2031
Skt.	Samayabhedoparacanacakra	
Eng.	*The Cycle of the Formation of the Schismatic Doctrines* (2004)	
Ch.	Ayuwang jing (阿育王經)	2043
Skt.	Aśokāvadāna	
Eng.	*The Biographical Scripture of King Aśoka* (1993)	
Ch.	Maming pusa zhuan (馬鳴菩薩傳)	2046
Eng.	*The Life of Aśvaghoṣa Bodhisattva* (in *Lives of Great Monks and Nuns,* 2002)	

Title		Taishō No.
Ch.	Longshu pusa zhuan (龍樹菩薩傳)	2047
Eng.	*The Life of Nāgārjuna Bodhisattva* (in *Lives of Great Monks and Nuns,* 2002)	
Ch.	Posoupandou fashi zhuan (婆藪槃豆法師傳)	2049
Eng.	*Biography of Dharma Master Vasubandhu* (in *Lives of Great Monks and Nuns,* 2002)	
Ch.	Datang Daciensi Zanzang fashi zhuan (大唐大慈恩寺三藏法師傳)	2053
Eng.	*A Biography of the Tripiṭaka Master of the Great Ci'en Monastery of the Great Tang Dynasty* (1995)	
Ch.	Gaoseng zhuan (高僧傳)	2059
Ch.	Biqiuni zhuan (比丘尼傳)	2063
Eng.	*Biographies of Buddhist Nuns* (in *Lives of Great Monks and Nuns,* 2002)	
Ch.	Gaoseng Faxian zhuan (高僧法顯傳)	2085
Eng.	*The Journey of the Eminent Monk Faxian* (in *Lives of Great Monks and Nuns,* 2002)	
Ch.	Datang xiyu ji (大唐西域記)	2087
Eng.	*The Great Tang Dynasty Record of the Western Regions* (1996)	
Ch.	Youfangjichao: Tangdaheshangdongzheng zhuan (遊方記抄: 唐大和上東征傳)	2089-(7)
Ch.	Hongming ji (弘明集)	2102
Eng.	*The Collection for the Propagation and Clarification of Buddhism, Volume I* (2015) *The Collection for the Propagation and Clarification of Buddhism, Volume II* (2017)	
Ch.	Fayuan zhulin (法苑珠林)	2122
Eng.	*A Forest of Pearls from the Dharma Garden, Volume I* (2019)	
Eng.	*A Forest of Pearls from the Dharma Garden, Volume II* (2019)	
Eng.	*A Forest of Pearls from the Dharma Garden, Volume III* (2020)	
Eng.	*A Forest of Pearls from the Dharma Garden, Volume IV* (2020)	
Eng.	*A Forest of Pearls from the Dharma Garden, Volume V* (2022)	
Eng.	*A Forest of Pearls from the Dharma Garden, Volume VI* (2023)	

Title		Taishō No.
Ch.	Nanhai jigui neifa zhuan (南海寄歸内法傳)	2125
Eng.	*Buddhist Monastic Traditions of Southern Asia* (2000)	
Ch.	Fanyu zaming (梵語雜名)	2135
Jp.	Shōmangyō gisho (勝鬘經義疏)	2185
Eng.	*Prince Shōtoku's Commentary on the Śrīmālā Sutra* (2011)	
Jp.	Yuimakyō gisho (維摩經義疏)	2186
Eng.	*The Expository Commentary on the Vimalakīrti Sutra* (2012)	
Jp.	Hokke gisho (法華義疏)	2187
Jp.	Hannya shingyō hiken (般若心經秘鍵)	2203A
Eng.	*The Key to the Secret of the Heart Sutra* (2023)	
Jp.	Daijō hossō kenjin shō (大乘法相研神章)	2309
Jp.	Kanjin kakumu shō (觀心覺夢鈔)	2312
Eng.	*Oberving the Mind, Awakening from a Dream* (2021)	
Jp.	Risshū kōyō (律宗綱要)	2348
Eng.	*The Essentials of the Vinaya Tradition* (1995)	
Jp.	Tendai hokke shūgi shū (天台法華宗義集)	2366
Eng.	*The Collected Teachings of the Tendai Lotus School* (1995)	
Jp.	Kenkairon (顯戒論)	2376
Jp.	Sange gakushō shiki (山家學生式)	2377
Jp.	Hizōhōyaku (秘藏寶鑰)	2426
Eng.	*The Precious Key to the Secret Treasury* (in *Shingon Texts,* 2004)	
Jp.	Benkenmitsu nikyō ron (辨顯密二教論)	2427
Eng.	*On the Differences between the Exoteric and Esoteric Teachings* (in *Shingon Texts,* 2004)	
Jp.	Sokushin jōbutsu gi (即身成佛義)	2428
Eng.	*The Meaning of Becoming a Buddha in This Very Body* (in *Shingon Texts,* 2004)	
Jp.	Shōji jissōgi (聲字實相義)	2429
Eng.	*The Meanings of Sound, Sign, and Reality* (in *Shingon Texts,* 2004)	
Jp.	Unjigi (吽字義)	2430
Eng.	*The Meanings of the Word Hūṃ* (in *Shingon Texts,* 2004)	

Title		Taishō No.
Jp.	Gorin kuji myōhimitsu shaku (五輪九字明秘密釋)	2514
Eng.	*The Illuminating Secret Commentary on the Five Cakras and the Nine Syllables* (in *Shingon Texts,* 2004)	
Jp.	Mitsugonin hotsuro sange mon (密嚴院發露懺悔文)	2527
Eng.	*The Mitsugonin Confession* (in *Shingon Texts,* 2004)	
Jp.	Kōzen gokoku ron (興禪護國論)	2543
Eng.	*A Treatise on Letting Zen Flourish to Protect the State* (in *Zen Texts,* 2005)	
Jp.	Fukan zazengi (普勧坐禪儀)	2580
Eng.	*A Universal Recommendation for True Zazen* (in *Zen Texts,* 2005)	
Jp.	Shōbōgenzō (正法眼藏)	2582
Eng.	*Shōbōgenzō: The True Dharma-eye Treasury, Volume I* (2007) *Shōbōgenzō: The True Dharma-eye Treasury, Volume II* (2008) *Shōbōgenzō: The True Dharma-eye Treasury, Volume III* (2008) *Shōbōgenzō: The True Dharma-eye Treasury, Volume IV* (2008)	
Jp.	Zazen yōjin ki (坐禪用心記)	2586
Eng.	*Advice on the Practice of Zazen* (in Zen Texts, 2005)	
Jp.	Senchaku hongan nembutsu shū (選擇本願念佛集)	2608
Eng.	*Senchaku Hongan Nembutsu Shū: A Collection of Passages on the Nembutsu Chosen in the Original Vow* (1997)	
Jp.	Kenjōdo shinjitsu kyōgyō shōmon rui (顯淨土眞實教行証文類)	2646
Eng.	*Kyōgyōshinshō: On Teaching, Practice, Faith, and Enlightenment* (2003)	
Jp.	Tannishō (歎異抄)	2661
Eng.	*Tannishō: Passages Deploring Deviations of Faith* (1996)	
Jp.	Rennyo shōnin ofumi (蓮如上人御文)	2668
Eng.	*Rennyo Shōnin Ofumi: The Letters of Rennyo* (1996)	
Jp.	Ōjōyōshū (往生要集)	2682
Jp.	Risshō ankoku ron (立正安國論)	2688
Eng.	*Risshōankokuron or The Treatise on the Establishment of the Orthodox Teaching and the Peace of the Nation* (in *Two Nichiren Texts,* 2003)	

Title		Taishō No.
Jp.	Kaimokushō (開目抄)	2689
Eng.	*Kaimokushō or Liberation from Blindness* (2000)	
Jp.	Kanjin honzon shō (觀心本尊抄)	2692
Eng.	*Kanjinhonzonshō or The Most Venerable One Revealed by Introspecting Our Minds for the First Time at the Beginning of the Fifth of the Five Five Hundred-year Ages* (in *Two Nichiren Texts,* 2003)	
Ch.	Fumu enzhong jing (父母恩重經)	2887
Eng.	*The Sutra on the Profundity of Filial Love* (in *Apocryphal Scriptures,* 2005)	
Jp.	Hasshūkōyō (八宗綱要)	extracanonical
Eng.	*The Essentials of the Eight Tradition*s (1994)	
Jp.	Sangō shīki (三教指帰)	extracanonical
Jp.	Mappō tōmyō ki (末法燈明記)	extracanonical
Eng.	*The Candle of the Latter Dharma* (1994)	
Jp.	Jūshichijō kenpō (十七條憲法)	extracanonical